Preußische Gärten
Prussian Gardens

Preußische Gärten
Prussian Gardens

Photographien
Photographs
Hillert Ibbeken

Historischer Überblick
Historical overview
Katja Schoene

Edition Axel Menges

Veröffentlicht mit freundlicher Unterstützung der Stiftung Preußische Schlösser und Gärten Berlin-Brandenburg.
Published with kind support by the Stiftung Preußische Schlösser und Gärten Berlin-Brandenburg.

ISBN 978-3-936681-68-0

Druck und Bindearbeiten/Printing and binding: Graspo CZ, a.s., Zlín, Tschechische Republik/Czech Republic

Übersetzung ins Englische/Translation into English: Ilze Klavina, Minneapolis
Gestaltung/Design: Axel Menges

Grußwort

»Preußische Gärten« – dieser Begriff ist heute auch ein Synonym für Sehnsuchtsorte in einer Welt, die sich durch eine zunehmend steigende Betriebsamkeit und Hektik auszeichnet. Einen wohltuenden Gegenentwurf stellen die königlichen Parkanlagen in Berlin, Potsdam und anderen Orten Brandenburgs dar, in denen die »Entdeckung der Langsamkeit« – so der Titel einer erfolgreichen Veranstaltungsreihe der Stiftung Preußische Schlösser und Gärten Berlin-Brandenburg – zum Erlebnis wird.

In den beeindruckenden Photos des vorliegenden Bildbands spiegelt sich das Zusammenspiel von Natur und Kunst auf das schönste. Über Jahrhunderte haben Architekten, Künstler und Gartengestalter im Auftrag ihrer damaligen Bauherren, der brandenburgischen Kurfürsten, preußischen Könige und später der deutschen Kaiser, die großartige Kulturlandschaft der preußischen Gärten geschaffen.

Mögen Sie nach dem Genuß der Photographien Lust bekommen, die Originalschauplätze der Bilder aufzusuchen und so dem Charme der »Preußischen Gärten« zu erliegen. Dazu lade ich Sie herzlich ein!

Hartmut Dorgerloh
Generaldirektor der Stiftung Preußische Schlösser und Gärten Berlin-Brandenburg

Opening remarks

»Prussian gardens« – today this term is also a synonym for places of longing in a world characterized by an increasingly rising activity and hectic pace. The royal parks in Berlin, Potsdam and elsewhere in Brandenburg represent an agreeable contrast. There, visitors may come to experience the »discovery of slowness« – the title of a successful series of events organized by the Stiftung Preußische Schlösser und Gärten Berlin-Brandenburg.

The impressive photographs of this illustrated volume beautifully reflect the interplay of nature and art. Over centuries architects, artists and garden designers, commissioned by their clients, the electors of Brandenburg, the kings of Prussia and, later, the German emperors, created the magnificent cultural landscape of the Prussian gardens.

I hope that after enjoying the photographs you will want to see the original locations where they were taken, and succumb to the charm of the »Prussian gardens«. I cordially invite you to visit us!

Hartmut Dorgerloh
General director of the Stiftung Preußische Schlösser und Gärten Berlin-Brandenburg

Vorwort

Die Gärten der preußischen Herrscher sind die Zierde ihrer Residenzen in Berlin, Potsdam und anderen Orten Brandenburgs. Sieben Beschreibungen nähern sich ihnen, indem sie ein Panorama der Gartenkunstgeschichte entwerfen: Charlottenburg ist ein kostbares Beispiel barocker Gärten. Rheinsberg führt den Wandel vom Rokoko- zum frühen Landschaftsgarten vor Augen. Sanssouci unter Friedrich II. erzählt in zarten Gartenbildern von den Ambitionen seines königlichen Initiators. Den Dialog der Landschaftsparks Neuer Garten und Pfaueninsel erfaßt ein gemeinsamer Text. Das Kapitel über Friedrich Wilhelm IV. unterbricht die Reihe der Gartenporträts, um die von diesem König angeregte Vielzahl der Anlagen gemeinsam zu würdigen: Sanssouci, Bornstedt, Lindstedt, Pfingstberg und Sacrow. Babelsberg als ein Höhepunkt der preußischen Landschaftsgartenkunst verlangt eine eigene monographische Beschreibung. Ein Gartenkünstler prägte die brandenburgische Landschaft vor allem: Das Kapitel über Peter Joseph Lenné behandelt die von ihm überformten Gärten. Neben den Erweiterungen in und um Sanssouci und den Veränderungen von Neuem Garten, Pfaueninsel und Charlottenburg sind dies Glienicke und Schönhausen in Berlin, Caputh bei Potsdam, Königs Wusterhausen in Brandenburg. Trotz der chronologischen Ordnung ist jeder Aufsatz für sich allein lesbar, und er nennt wichtige Denkmäler mit Entstehungszeiten und Ausführenden.

Für kritische Lektüre und klärende Gespräche danke ich: Adrian von Buttlar (Berlin), Jörg Deuter (Öhringen), Karl Eisbein (Babelsberg), Anett Kollmann (Dresden), Martin Pozsgai (Einsiedeln), Matthew Springett (Maldon), Matthias Struch (Berlin) und nicht zuletzt Robert F. Leitch (Rom). Mein ganz besonderer Dank gilt Michael Bischoff (Berlin), der immer geholfen hat: fachlich, stilistisch, technisch.

Katja Schoene

Foreword

The gardens of the Prussian rulers are the adornment of their residences in Berlin, Potsdam and elsewhere in Brandenburg. Seven descriptions give us a more detailed view of them as they sketch a panorama of the history of garden art: Charlottenburg is a precious example of Baroque gardens. Rheinsberg represents the change from Rococo to early landscape gardens. The delicate garden scenes of Sanssouci under Frederick II speak of the ambitions of its royal initiator. The two landscape parks Neuer Garten and Pfaueninsel share the same underlying idea. The chapter about Frederick William IV interrupts the series of garden portraits, paying homage to the numerous parks initiated by this king: Sanssouci, Bornstedt, Lindstedt, Pfingstberg and Sacrow. Babelsberg, a peak achievement of Prussian landscape garden art, demands its own monograph description. One garden artist in particular left his mark on the landscape of Brandenburg: The chapter about Peter Joseph Lenné discusses the gardens shaped by him. In addition to expansions in and around Sanssouci and modifications of Neuer Garten, Pfaueninsel and Charlottenburg, these include Glienicke and Schönhausen in Berlin, Caputh near Potsdam and Königs Wusterhausen in Brandenburg. Though the chapters are in chronological order, each can be read independently of the others, and mentions important monuments, the dates when they were created and the names of those who implemented the projects.

I should like to thank the following persons for their critical reading and clarifying discussions: Adrian von Buttlar (Berlin), Jörg Deuter (Öhringen), Karl Eisbein (Babelsberg), Anett Kollmann (Dresden), Martin Pozsgai (Einsiedeln), Matthew Springett (Maldon), Matthias Struch (Berlin) and last but not least Robert F. Leitch (Rome). Special thanks go to Michael Bischoff (Berlin), who helped in every way: professionally, stylistically and technically.

Katja Schoene

Katja Schoene

Gartenkunst in Preußen

Am Anfang war der *hortus conclusus*. Das paradiesische Urbild des Gartens bot mit seiner Abgeschlossenheit Schutz vor der umgebenden Wildnis. Zugleich war er umhegte Schönheit: bunt und duftend, Wege, Beete und Wasser harmonisch gegliedert – eine Anspielung auf den Garten Eden. Aus dem biblischen Paradies war der Mensch wegen seiner Neugier vertrieben worden. John Milton ließ Adam und Eva in seinem *Paradise lost* (*Das Verlorene Paradies*, 1658–65) »mit langsam zagem Schritt / Und Hand in Hand aus Eden ihres Wegs« wandern. »Vor ihnen lag die große weite Welt.«

Die Regeln der Mathematik, mit der die Natur berechenbar geworden war, wurden in der frühen Neuzeit das Ordnungsmodell für Bildkünste, Architektur und Garten. Die brandenburgische Landschaft um die kurfürstlichen Residenzstädte Berlin und Potsdam wurde zunächst als Jagdterrain in Besitz genommen. Unter Kurfürst Friedrich Wilhelm von Brandenburg legte man »Gestelle« oder »Stellstetten« an – Schneisen, oft zu Alleen ausgebildet. Sie markieren den Umbruch von der ummauerten Geschlossenheit des Gartenareals zum Griff in die Ferne.

Das kleine Schloß Stern Friedrich Wilhelms I. bei Potsdam markiert die Schnittstelle der 16 Gestelle, die seit 1726 das für die Parforcejagd genutzte Umland in überschaubare Segmente gliederten. Die Schneisen erleichterten die Rückkehr zum Sammelpunkt am Schloß. Architektur und Garten traten sich beim Berliner Schloß seit den Umbauarbeiten durch Andreas Schlüter (1659/1664–1714), Schloßbaudirektor seit 1699, über das Gartenportal und den Gartensaal nahe. Potsdam bricht dann etwa zeitgleich endgültig mit der renaissancezeitlichen, noch in der Oranienburger Residenz von 1651 wirksamen Tradition, Garten und Schloß voneinander zu trennen (Abb. 1).

Vor dem Schloß Potsdam wurden *par terre*, das heißt auf ebener Erde, Schmuckflächen angelegt, die wie kostbare Stickerei – Broderie – anmuteten. Weder Baum noch Laubengang störten ihre Flächigkeit, die den Ausblick auf die Havel und weiter zum Brauhausberg als Teil des kurfürstlichen Großen Tiergartens erlaubte. Noch ist die perspektivische Flucht festgelegter Bezugspunkt. Jean Baptiste Broebes läßt in seiner Ansicht von Schloß Schönhausen bei Berlin die vom Zentrum ausgreifenden Perspektiven bis zum Horizont laufen, wo sie durch Lücken in einer Hecke scheinbar noch verlängert werden (Abb. 2). Schönhausen gehörte zum Reigen der Lustschlösser des Großen Kurfürsten, mit dem er die Zentren seiner Residenzen Berlin und Potsdam umgab.

Die Geometrisierung führt als offenes System schließlich zur Verknüpfung von Räumen, Bauwerken, Gärten, Stadt und Landschaft. In Charlottenburg, der Berliner Gartenanlage der zweiten Gemahlin Friedrichs III. (1657 bis 1713), Sophie Charlotte, ist der perspektivische Endpunkt ein außerhalb der Gartengrenze gelegenes, der Wahrnehmung durch das Auge weit entzogenes Ziel. Die Koordinaten, die Schloß und Garten durchziehen, visieren es an, ohne es tatsächlich zu erreichen: Ganz Garten des Absolutismus muß sich Charlottenburg optisch strecken, als gälte es, nach den Sternen zu greifen.

Ausgangspunkt der ausgedehnten Perspektive ist Frankreich. Die Zeit des Dreißigjährigen Krieges hatte Minister Kardinal Richelieu genutzt, Frankreich zur Hauptrolle innerhalb des Ringens der Länder um die Vorherrschaft in Europa zu verhelfen. König Ludwig XIV. und sein Finanzminister Nicolas Fouquet inszenierten mit Marly, Versailles und Vaux-le-Vicomte die prächtigsten Schauspiele der Schloß- und Gartenkunst, die die europäische Welt bislang erlebt hatte. Ihr Schöpfer André Le Nôtre, erster Gärtner des Königs, wurde Inbegriff einer ganzen Epoche, deren Diktat die regelmäßige Geometrie mit unendlichem Fluchtpunkt ist. Von 1709 bis 1764 erschien in mehreren Auflagen der einflußreichste Gartentraktat dieser Zeit in Europa, Dézaillier d'Argenvilles *La Théorie et la Pratique du Jardinage*.

Im 18. Jahrhundert waren es die in Politik und Religion verschieden orientierten Fürstenhäuser, die die Staatenwelt lenkten. Der Königsstatus, den Friedrich III. von Brandenburg als König I. in Preußen, der Kurfürst von Hannover als König von England und August der Starke, Kurfürst von Sachsen als König von Polen erreicht hatten, war die Meßlatte, nach der auch weniger einflußreiche Landesherren ihre Bemühungen um Magnifizenz ausrichteten. Die Residenz mit Schloß und Garten ist Kulminationsort ihres Wetteiferns. Nach dem Dreißigjährigen Krieg galt es zwar noch für die Nachfolger des Großen Kurfürsten, den Anschluß an die Kunstleistung der europäischen Nachbarstaaten zu finden. Dennoch warteten schon die Lustgärten, die Michael Hanff, beraten durch den Festungsbaumeister Johann Gregor Memhardt, ab 1645 dem Berliner Schloß und 1664–69 der Nebenresidenz Potsdam hinzufügt, mit phantastischem Spielwerk auf. Memhardts »Neues Lusthaus« war eine muschel- und korallenverzierte Gartengrotte an der Spree, deren Röhrensystem sphärenhafte Tonwellen erklingen lassen konnte. Wasserscherze umzingelten den Spaziergänger mit kleinen Spritzfontänen.

Mythologische Sequenzen und Allegorien, wie sie die 1499 gedruckte *Hypnerotomachia Poliphili*, der Traumliebeskampf Poliphils, am Beispiel der antiken Kultur beschreibt, wurden in der Zeit des Barock zum festen Vokabular der Gartensprache. Friedrich II. (1712–1786) brachte mit Park Sanssouci in Potsdam formenstreng geordnete Gartenpartien und sinnbildhafte Ausstattung zusammen. Dem lauten, die Sinne überwältigenden Gegenspieler Versailles antwortet Sanssoucis konzentrierte Rhetorik, mit der der preußische König seine Utopie des aufgeklärten Philosophenherrschers in Szene setzte.

Für das künstlerische Dekorum der Prachtentfaltung waren geeignete Vorbilder gefragt. Der Große Kurfürst und sein Sohn orientierten sich an den Niederlanden. Deren Gartenkunst hatte der über seine Publikationen einflußreiche Hans Vredemann de Vries mit strengen, architektonisch-mathematisch konstruierten Anlagen geprägt. Der Garten des Oraniers Johann Moritz von Nassau-Siegen in Kleve, 1654, bot die früheste lange Achse nördlich der Alpen, die den Blick durch das Tal des Rheins bis hin zum Eltenberg und zu der dortigen St. Vituskirche lenkte. Er imponierte dem Großen Kurfürsten so sehr, daß er sich ihn zum Modell der eigenen Anstrengungen um Landesverschönerung wählte.

Für Friedrich II. bot – neben dem modernen Frankreich – die Vergangenheit das zweite große Vorbild. Die Antike war dem König aus der Familie der Hohenzollern Referenzgröße seines dynastischen Anspruchs, und sie gab ihm konkrete Modelle für die eigene Bildsprache an die Hand. Diese läßt die antiken Helden im Garten agieren oder holt das Pantheonmotiv als eine Art Markenzeichen imperialer Größe nach Potsdam. Den Symbol-

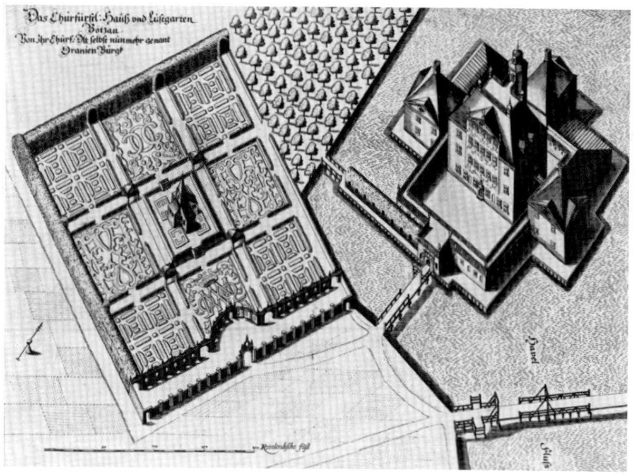

1. Caspar Merian nach Johann Gregor Memhardt, Schloß Oranienburg und Lustgarten. Radierung aus Martin Zeiler und Matthäus Merian d. Ä. Erben, *Topographia Electoratus Brandenburgici […]*, Frankfurt am Main 1652. (SPSG – Stiftung Preußische Schlösser und Gärten Berlin-Brandenburg, Potsdam.)
2. Jean Baptist Broebes, Schloß Schönhausen, nach 1733. Kolorierte Radierung. (Stiftung Stadtmuseum Berlin – Reprographie aus: Streidt, Feierabend 1999.)

1. Caspar Merian after Johann Gregor Memhardt, Schloß Oranienburg and pleasure garden. Etching from Martin Zeiler and Matthäus Merian the Elder Heirs, *Topographia Electoratus Brandenburgici […]*, Frankfurt am Main, 1652. (SPSG – Stiftung Preußische Schlösser und Gärten Berlin-Brandenburg, Potsdam.)
2. Jean Baptist Broebes, Schloß Schönhausen, after 1733. Coloured etching. (Stiftung Stadtmuseum Berlin – reproduced from: Streidt, Feierabend 1999.)

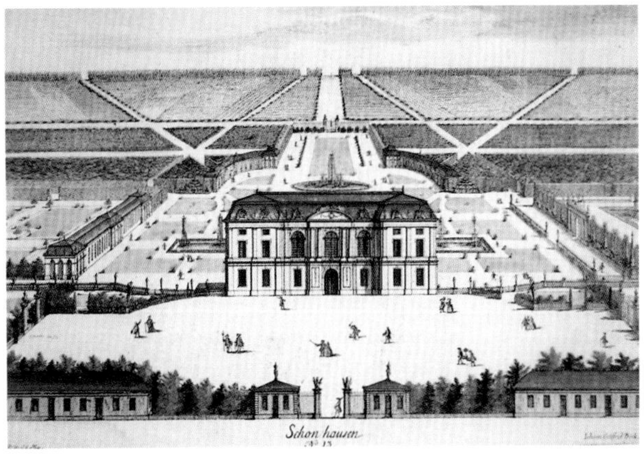

Katja Schoene

Garden art in Prussia

In the beginning there was the *hortus conclusus*. The enclosed space of the paradisiacal archetype of the garden offered protection from the surrounding wilderness. At the same time it was lovingly cared-for beauty: full of colour, fragrant, its paths, beds and bodies of water harmoniously structured – an allusion to the Garden of Eden. The first humans had been cast out of the biblical Paradise because of their curiosity. In John Milton's *Paradise Lost* (1658–65), Adam and Eve »hand in hand, with wandering steps and slow / Through Eden took their solitary way« and »the world all before them, where to choose / Their place of rest.«

The rules of mathematics thanks to which it had become possible to calculate nature became the model of order for the graphic arts, architecture and gardens in the early modern period. The Brandenburg landscape around the electoral seats of Berlin and Potsdam was first acquired as hunting grounds. Under Elector Frederick William of Brandenburg, breaks were cleared in the forests, often developed into avenues. They mark a turning point from the walled self-contained space of the garden to a design that reaches into the distance.

The small Schloß Stern of Frederick William I near Potsdam marks the intersection of the 16 breaks that subdivided the terrain used since 1726 for hunting into easily manageable segments. The breaks made it easier to return to the gathering point at the lodge. In the Berlin palace, since the renovation work by Andreas Schlüter (1659/64 to 1714), court architect since 1699, architecture and garden were brought into close proximity by way of the garden portal and the garden room. About the same time Potsdam definitively broke with the tradition of separating palace and garden that stemmed from the Renaissance and was still in evidence in the Schloß Oranienburg that dated back to 1651 (illus. 1).

In front of Schloß Potsdam, ornamental areas were laid out *par terre*, i. e., on the level ground, that looked like precious embroidery. Neither trees nor pergolas distracted from their two-dimensional quality that offered a view of the Havel River and the Brauhausberg beyond, part of the Elector's Großer Tiergarten. The perspective alignment is still a fixed reference point. In his view of Schloß Schönhausen near Berlin, Jean Baptiste Broebes has the perspectives running from the centre extending to the horizon, where they are seemingly even extended through gaps in a hedge (illus. 2). Schönhausen was one of the round of the Great Elector's summer residences with which he surrounded the centres of his Berlin and Potsdam residences.

Geometrization, being an open system, finally leads to the linking of rooms, buildings, gardens, city and landscape. In the Berlin gardens of Charlottenburg, the park of Sophia Charlotte, the second wife of Frederick III (1657 to 1713), the perspective endpoint is a point that is no longer visible, located far outside the boundaries of the garden. The coordinates that pass through palace and garden aim for this target without actually attaining it: A typical garden of absolutism, Charlottenburg must stretch optically as though it had to reach for the stars.

The point of departure of the extended perspective is France. Minister Cardinal Richelieu had used the period of the Thirty Years' War to help France attain a leading role in the struggle for predominance in Europe. With Marly, Versailles and Vaux-le-Vicomte, King Louis XIV and his minister of finance, Nicolas Fouquet, staged the most splendid spectacles of palace and garden art that the European world had experienced up to that time. Their creator, André Le Nôtre, the king's head gardener, became the epitome of an entire epoch whose dictate is regular geometry with an infinite vanishing point. From 1709 to 1764, there appeared several editions of the most influential garden treatise of the time in Europe – Dézallier d'Argenville's *La Théorie et la Pratique du Jardinage*.

In the 18th century it was the royal houses, representing different political and religious orientations, that governed the states. The royal status attained by Frederick III of Brandenburg as the first king in Prussia, the Elector of Hanover as king of England and Augustus the Strong, Elector of Saxony, as king of Poland was the measuring stick also used by less influential rulers in their efforts to achieve magnificence. A residence with a palace and garden marked the culmination of their competitive zeal. It's true that after the Thirty Years' War the successors of the Great Elector still needed to catch up with the artistic achievements of their European neighbour states. Even so the pleasure gardens that Michael Hanff, advised by fortification builder Johann Gregor Memhardt, added to the Berlin palace as of 1645 and to the secondary residence of Potsdam from 1664–69 boasted fantastic musical mechanisms. Memhardt's »Neues Lusthaus« (New Pleasance) was a garden grotto ornamented with seashells and corals by the Spree whose system of pipes could produce celestial waves of sound. Visitors strolling through the grounds were sprayed by small trick fountains.

Mythological sequences and allegories as described by the *Hypnerotomachia Poliphili*, Poliphilos' strife of love in a dream, printed in 1499, emblematic of the culture of antiquity, became the regular vocabulary of the horticultural idiom in the Baroque era. In Park Sanssouci in Potsdam, Frederick II (1712–1786) combined garden sections whose form was strictly ordered with allegorical features. Sanssouci's response to its rival Versailles, whose blatant grounds overpowered the senses, was a concentrated rhetoric with which the Prussian ruler staged his utopia of an enlightened philosopher king.

The artistic decorum involved in this display of splendour called for appropriate models. The Great Elector and his son followed models provided by the Netherlands. Hans Vredemann de Vries, influential as a result of his publications, left his mark on Dutch garden design, advocating strict, architectonically and mathematically constructed parks. The garden of the Orangeman Johann Moritz von Nassau-Siegen in Cleves, 1654, had the earliest long axis north of the Alps, focusing attention through the Rhine Valley to the Eltenberg and the St. Vituskirche (Church of St. Vitus) located there. It impressed the Great Elector so much that he chose it as the model for his own efforts to beautify his country.

Frederick II's second great model – other than modern France – was the past. For this Hohenzollern king antiquity served as the point of reference for his dynastic claim, and it provided him with concrete models for his own visual idiom. Thus the heroes of antiquity were displayed in the garden, or the Pantheon motif was brought to Potsdam as a sort of trademark of imperial greatness. Frederick had already used the symbolism of the obelisk brought from ancient Egypt to public squares in Rome, first in Rheinsberg, and later in Sanssouci, in order to speak of his own resplendent person in a subtle allusion to the French Sun King. A backdrop of ruins serves to

gehalt des vom alten Ägypten auf die Plätze in Rom ver-mittelten Obelisken nutzte Friedrich schon in Rheinsberg, später dann in Sanssouci, um in subtiler Anspielung auf den französischen Sonnenkönig Ludwig XIV. von der eigenen strahlenden Persönlichkeit zu erzählen. Eine Ruinenkulisse dient als Blickschutz für das Wasserreservoir der Parkfontänen und als ein etwa 600 m gegen Norden liegender Blickpunkt von der Ehrenhofkolonnade vor Schloß Sanssouci auf dem Hoeneberg. Sie gaukelt dem Betrachter ein Bild des Forum Romanum im antiken Rom vor, für Friedrich und seine Zeitgenossen Schauplatz eines Goldenen Zeitalters.

Den Ruinenprospekt zeigt Johann Friedrich Schleuen um 1775 aus nördlicher Sicht (Abb. 3). Vorn durchmißt ein Spaziergänger, gefolgt von seinem Hund, die Szenerie. In Johann Friedrich Nagels 1788, zwei Jahre nach Friedrichs Tod, gestochener Ansicht hat der Wanderer das künstliche Ruinenensemble um das Wasserbecken halb umrundet, um sich niederzulassen und es von Süden im Sitzen zu zeichnen (Abb. 4). Nur 13 Jahre trennen die beiden unabhängig voneinander entstandenen Veduten, die schnellen Schritts Gartengeschichte im Verlauf der Aufklärung erlebbar machen. Der Mensch, der als aktiver Protagonist an den Rand rückt, ist nicht mehr bloß Rezipient vor großer Kulisse, sondern selbst Gestalter dessen, was er sieht und nun auch sichtbar fühlen darf. Dabei hat sich die Szenerie verändert. Wilder sieht sie aus, ein bißchen zugewuchert, die Pflanzen ergreifen gar Besitz von der Architektur. An Stelle des kreisrunden Beckens mit seinem ruhigen Wasserspiegel zeigt Nagel die Naturszenerie des Wasserausflusses unterhalb der antiken Monumente. Keine geraden Linien mehr, sondern scheinbare Natürlichkeit.

Der Ruinenberg war dazu prädestiniert, seine Rokoko-Rolle des zeitversetzten Gegenspielers zu Schloß Sanssouci mit der eines Akteurs zu tauschen, der im neuen natürlichen Gartenstil sentimentale Stimmung evoziert. Theoretisch berücksichtigte erstmals Stephen Switzer in seiner *Ichnographia Rustica, or, The Nobleman, Gentleman and Gardener's Recreation* (1715–18) das Vermögen von Ruinen, den Stimmungsgehalt einer Gartenszene zu stimulieren. Nagels kleine Rückenfigur reflektiert die Wirkung der Kunst-Natur auf den Menschen. Die ersten Gartenanlagen im neuen Stil, das nach-friderizianische Rheinsberg von Friedrichs Bruder Prinz Heinrich, der Neue Garten in Potsdam und die Berliner Pfaueninsel seines Neffen und Thronfolgers Friedrich Wilhelm II. (1744–1797) sowie Friedrich Wilhelms III. (1770–1840) Paretz bei Potsdam verlassen die geometrische Ordnung, um in einer ebenso planvoll gestalteten, aber visuell natürlich-spontan daherkommenden Sprache Bild- und Raumfolgen poetisch erlebbar zu machen.

In der Frühzeit der Verlandschaftung ging es dabei oftmals zugleich auch um moralische Unterweisung oder politische Überredung. Städtisch-kultiviertes und ländliches Leben waren mittlerweile in Konflikt geraten. Jean-Jacques Rousseau forderte die Rückkehr zur Natur. Die Gartenkunst antwortete mit der *ferme ornée* – mit landwirtschaftlichen Musterhöfen, die in die gestaltete Natur integriert wurden. Die Pfaueninsel oder Paretz setzten sie um und warben mit Milchwirtschaft und Feldern für das einfache Leben. In Frankreich plante Gabriel Thouin zu Beginn des 19. Jahrhunderts in einem Akt schöpferischer Denkmalpflege einen Parkgürtel um Versailles. Für Peter Joseph Lenné (1789–1866) war der Weg geebnet, formale Gartenpartien gleichberechtigt neben das Landschaftliche zu stellen. Er erprobte es mit der Anlage Charlottenhof im Park Sanssouci oder mit der Integration des Marlystücks in den friderizianischen Garten. Zu künstlerischer Synthese formte auch Fürst Hermann Ludwig Heinrich von Pückler-Muskau (1785–1871) Geometrie und Natürlichkeit. Das zeigt Park Babelsberg seit der ersten Hälfte des 19. Jahrhunderts.

Lenné verkörpert die neuerliche Entgrenzung der gärtnerischen Anlagen in Preußen. Sein Hauptschaffen fällt in die Regierungsjahre Friedrich Wilhelms IV. (1795 bis 1861). Für den Hohenzoller erweiterte er die Berlin-Potsdamer Kulturlandschaft zu einem über lange Sichten vereinten Gartennetzwerk. Dessen harmonisierte Einzelbilder finden ihre Fluchtpunkte nicht außerhalb des Gartens wie im Barock, sondern kosten die Tiefe des Raumes in sich selbst aus: Das Sacrower Herrenhaus als Zentrum eines der vielen Lennéschen Gartenbilder an der Havel ist ferner Fokus von Pavillon und Jägerhof im Berlin-Glienicker Landschaftsgemälde aus Lennés Hand. Der im Gartenbild selbst angesiedelte Fluchtpunkt bestimmt Lennés Auffassung von Landschaft, die für ihn immer auch Ferne bedeutet – jenseits einer mathematisch erarbeiteten Perspektive.

Und wieder ist es eine Abbildung des Ruinenbergs, diesmal von Carl Daniel Freydanck aus dem Jahr 1847, die das Revolutionäre des in England hervorgebrachten Stilwandels anschaulich macht (Abb. 5). Freydanck, dessen Malerstandort sich wohl auf der Höhe des unter Friedrich Wilhelm IV. dem friderizianischen Ensemble hinzugefügten Belvederes »Normannischer Turm« befindet, rückt die antikisierenden Ruinen in den Vordergrund seiner Überschau über das von Lenné gestaltete Potsdamer Landschaftspanorama. Über Friedrichs II. Rokokoschloß Sanssouci im Mittelgrund gleitet es zu den unter Friedrich Wilhelm IV. errichteten modernen Dampfmaschinenarchitekturen, deren Erfindung auch den im Bild aufspritzenden Fontänestrahl im Sanssouci-Parterre bewirken konnte.

Mit dem Ruinenberg hatte Friedrich II. historisierend auf den Stil einer vergangenen Epoche zurückgegriffen. Der Landschaftsgarten schwelgt in der geographischen und epochalen Stilvielfalt. Vor allem England war im 18. Jahrhundert über seine Handelsbeziehungen in Kontakt mit fremden überseeischen Kulturen getreten. Die Globalisierung hinterläßt im Garten ihre Spuren in Form von vielgestaltigen Parkbauten, die von der heiteren Buntheit exotischer Welten künden. Die architektonische, bildhauerische und inschriftliche Bedeutung des Gartens akzentuieren sie zusätzlich. Gotisierende Staffagen oszillieren zwischen dem beim Betrachter hervorgerufenen Erschaudern, wie es der Philosoph Edmund Burke beschrieben hatte, und der durch Nationalstolz veranlaßten Rührung vor gotischen Bauten, die als deutsche Kulturleistung galten.

Friedrich II. hatte den Ruinenberg als antikes Gegenüber von Schloß Sanssouci inszenieren lassen, und zwar allein für das Auge. Einen Weg dorthin gab es nicht. Die spätere Gartenkunst begreift die gesamte Landschaft als Raum, über dessen Gestaltung sie verfügen kann. Dieser Raum ist gänzlich begehbar. Lenné wird später den Ruinenberg über einen Pfad mit Friedrichs Sanssouci verbinden. Zum Schlagwort für den Landschaftsgarten avanciert der Satz vom »begehbaren Landschaftsgemälde«, mit dem der Dichter Joseph Spence 1752 die Gartenkunst seiner Zeit charakterisiert. Im Auftrag des bayerischen Königs löste schließlich Friedrich Ludwig von Sckell in München den Garten als Adelsrefugium

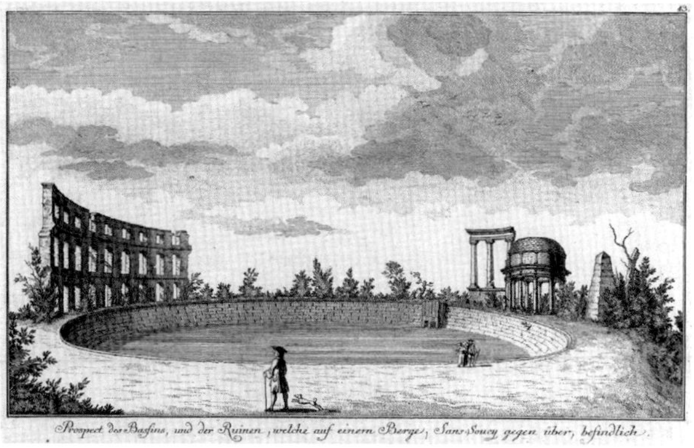

3. Johann Friedrich Schleuen, Ruinenberg mit Wasserreservoir, um 1775. Radierung. (SPSG, Potsdam.)
4. Johann Friedrich Nagel, Ruinenberg, 1788. Deckfarben. (Staatliche Museen zu Berlin, Preußischer Kulturbesitz, Kupferstichkabinett – Reprographie aus: AKat. 1999 b.)
5. Carl Daniel Freydanck, Ruinenberg mit Schloß Sanssouci, 1847. Öl auf Leinwand. (SPSG/KPM-Archiv, Potsdam.)

3. Johann Friedrich Schleuen, Ruinenberg with water reservoir, ca. 1775. Etching. (SPSG, Potsdam.)
4. Johann Friedrich Nagel, Ruinenberg, 1788. Opaque colours. (Staatliche Museen zu Berlin, Preußischer Kulturbesitz, Kupferstichkabinett – reproduced from: AKat. 1999 b.)
5. Carl Daniel Freydanck, Ruinenberg with Schloß Sanssouci, 1847. Oil on canvas. (SPSG/KPM-Archiv, Potsdam.)

conceal the water reservoir for the park's fountains, as well as a visual focus located roughly 600 m north from the colonnade of the Ehrenhof (Parade Court) in front of Schloß Sanssouci on Hoeneberg. The observer has the illusion of seeing the Forum Romanum in ancient Rome, the scene of a Golden Age for Frederick and his contemporaries.

Ca. 1775 Johann Friedrich Schleuen depicts the ruin backdrop as seen from the north (illus. 3). In the foreground a man, followed by his dog, strolls through the landscape. In Johann Friedrich Nagel's 1788 engraving, two years after Frederick's death, the wanderer has walked around half the artificial cluster of ruins surrounding the pond of water and has sat down to sketch it from the south side (illus. 4). Only 13 years separate the two views created independently from one another, which in an instant make visible horticultural history in the course of the Enlightenment. The human being who appears on the fringe as an active protagonist is no longer merely an onlooker before a magnificent backdrop, but is himself the shaper of what he sees and is now also visibly allowed to have feelings. At the same time, the scenery has changed. It looks wilder, a little overgrown, and the plants are even beginning to seize possession of the architecture. In lieu of the circular pond with its calm surface, Nagel shows the natural scene with a stream of water issuing below the ancient monuments. No more straight lines: instead, there is apparent naturalness.

The Ruinenberg – the hill with its ruins – was predestined to take on a new role; no longer the Rococo counterpart to Schloß Sanssouci, displaced in time, it is now an actor that evokes a sentimental mood in the new, natural garden style. Stephen Switzer in his *Ichnographia Rustica*, or, *The Nobleman, Gentleman and Gardener's Recreation* (1715–18) was the first to consider theoretically the ability of ruins to stimulate the atmospheric mood of a garden scene. Nagel's small figure, seen from behind, reflects the effect of man-made nature on human beings. The first gardens designed in the new style – post-Frederick Rheinsberg by Frederick's brother Prince Henry, the Neuer Garten in Potsdam and Pfaueninsel in Berlin, by his nephew and successor Frederick William II (1744–1797), and Frederick William III's (1770 to 1840) Paretz near Potsdam – abandon geometrical order, using an idiom that is just as systematically planned while appearing visually natural and spontaneous, and that makes it possible to experience spatial and visual sequences of images poetically.

In the early period of *Verlandschaftung* (return to the natural landscape) moral instruction or political persuasion was often also involved. Urban cultivated and rural life had in the meantime come into conflict. Jean-Jacques Rousseau called for a return to nature. Horticulture's response was the *ferme ornée* – agricultural model farms that were integrated in a nature shaped by human hands. Pfaueninsel or Paretz implemented this idea and promoted the simple life with dairy farming and fields. In France, at the beginning of the 19th century, Gabriel Thouin planned a green belt around Versailles in an act of creative conservation of historical monuments. For Peter Joseph Lenné (1789–1866) the way had been smoothed: formal garden areas could be placed on an equal footing with rural landscape. He put this to the test with the Charlottenhof complex in Park Sanssouci or by integrating the Marly piece in the garden of Frederick the Great. Prince Hermann Ludwig Heinrich von Pückler-Muskau (1785–1871), too, formed geometry and naturalness into an artistic synthesis, as evidenced by Park Babelsberg since the first half of the 19th century.

Lenné exemplifies the recent blurring of the borders of gardens and grounds in Prussia. His peak creative period falls within the reign of Frederick William IV (1795 to 1861). For the Hohenzollern king he expanded the Berlin-Potsdam cultural landscape into a network of gardens that was unified for long stretches. The vanishing points of its harmonized individual views are not located outside the garden, as they were in the Baroque; rather, they savor the depth of the space within themselves: The Sacrow manor house as the center of one of Lenné's many gardens on the Havel River is moreover the focus of the pavilion and hunting lodge in Lenné's landscape painting of Berlin-Glienicke. The vanishing point, which is located in the garden itself, determines Lenné's perception of landscape, which for him also always implies distance – beyond a mathematically worked-out perspective.

And again it is a depiction of the Ruinenberg, this time by Carl Daniel Freydanck from the year 1847, that illustrates the revolutionary nature of the stylistic change that originated in England (illus. 5). Freydanck, who while painting no doubt stood at the level of the belvedere known as the Normannischer Turm added to Frederick the Great's group of buildings under Frederick William IV, moves the faux ancient ruins into the foreground of his overview of the Potsdam landscape panorama created by Lenné. Over Frederick II's Rococo palace of Sanssouci in the middle ground the eye glides to the modern engine houses erected under Frederick William IV, whose invention was also able to produce the jet of water shown in the picture of the fountain on the *parterre* of Sanssouci.

With the Ruinenberg Frederick II had drawn upon the pseudo-historical style of a past era. The garden revels in a plethora of geographic and epochal styles. Especially England had come into contact with overseas cultures in the 18th century through its trade relations. Globalization has left traces in the garden in the form of a multitude of different types of park buildings that bear witness to serene and colourful exotic worlds. Globalization is also accentuated by the architectonic, sculptural and inscriptional significance of the garden. Faux gothic decorative elements either evoke shudders of awe in the viewer, as described by the philosopher Edmund Burke, or deep emotion of national pride at the sight of Gothic buildings considered to be a German cultural achievement.

Frederick II had had the Ruinenberg staged as a classical counterpart of Schloß Sanssouci, created for the eyes only. No path led to it. Later garden design understands the entire landscape as space whose configuration it can control. This space can be totally accessed on foot. Lenné will later put in a path to connect the Ruinenberg with Frederick's Sanssouci. The new catchword for the landscape garden is now the phrase »a picture to walk into«, used by the poet Joseph Spence in 1752 to characterize the garden design of his time. By order of the king of Bavaria, in Munich, Friedrich Ludwig von Sckell finally did away with the idea of the park as the refuge of the nobility: The earliest public park was open to all walks of life as of 1792.

The first flight that was made possible in 1783 by the hot-air balloon of the Montgolfier brothers broke fresh

6. Karl Friedrich Schinkel, Zweite Dekoration zur Oper *Nurmahal, Tal von Kaschmir*, 1822. Gouache, Feder. (Berlin, Kupferstichkabinett – Reprographie aus: *Karl Friedrich Schinkel. Geschichte und Poesie*, AKat. Berlin und München, München 2012.)

6. Karl Friedrich Schinkel, second decoration for the opera *Nurmahal, Tal von Kaschmir*, 1822. Gouache, pen. (Berlin, Kupferstichkabinett – reproduced from: *Karl Friedrich Schinkel. Geschichte und Poesie*, AKat. Berlin and Munich, Munich, 2012.)

auf: Der früheste Volkspark steht seit 1792 allen Ständen offen.

Der erste Flug, den 1783 der Heißluftballon der Montgolfier-Brüder möglich gemacht hatte, brach einem neuen Seherlebnis Bahn. Francesco Petrarca hatte im 14. Jahrhundert noch mühsam den Mont Ventoux in der französischen Provence erklimmen müssen, um seine Perspektive auf die Welt verändern zu können. Dagegen erlaubt die visuelle Inbesitznahme, wie Freydanck sie vorführt, über die Gärten der preußischen Könige zu fliegen. Panoramen wurden zu beliebten Spektakeln illusionistischer 360-Grad-Blicke. Die Rundumschau von oben macht Weltlandschaft erfahrbar.

Seine Absichten landschaftlicher Verschönerung leitet Friedrich Wilhelm IV. mit dem Gedanken ein, das herrscherliche Territorium zum Garten werden zu lassen. So einfach seine Worte klingen, schwingt in ihnen das Großartig-Visionäre, das Traumhafte mit, das seit den ersten Unternehmungen durch Kurfürst Friedrich Wilhelm von Brandenburg die Erschließung von Berlin und Potsdam als Raum der Gartenkunst begleitet.

Mit einer Ausgabe von *Tausendundeiner Nacht* im Gepäck unternahm Friedrich Wilhelm IV. seinen ersten Feldzug. Von der Märchenwelt inspiriert, erzählt er der Schwester Charlotte in Briefen 1816/17 die selbst erfundene orientalisierende Novelle *Die Königin von Borneo* des Ich-Erzählers, den die Flügel des Vogels Rock zum indischen Archipel nach Borneo entführen, inmitten einer phantastischen Landschaft und ebenso phantastischer Architekturen.

Der Theaterdekorateur Innocente Bellavita hatte Friedrichs Ruinenberg nach den Vorschlägen von Georg Wenzeslaus von Knobelsdorff (1699–1753) entworfen. Karl Friedrich Schinkel (1781–1841), mit dem zusammen Lenné um Berlin und Potsdam die arkadischen Gartenvisionen Friedrich Wilhelms IV. gestaltete, ist zugleich auch Szenograph. Sein zweiter Dekorationsentwurf für das Bühnenbild zur Oper *Nurmahal, Tal von Kaschmir*, 1822 (Abb. 6), kann der preußischen Gartenkunst als Schlußakkord dienen: Eine Art Weltlandschaft erträumen sich alle preußischen Herrscher, die sich am Gartenkunstwerk Berlin-Potsdam beteiligen. Doch erst die Zeit und das schöpferische Zusammenspiel von Friedrich Wilhelm IV., Schinkel und Lenné führen die Utopie an ihre Grenze. Deren Überschreitung ist der Dekorationskunst vorbehalten.

Von der Gartenterrasse, wie er sie ähnlich viele Male etwa in Potsdam bei den Römischen Bädern, dem Charlottenhof und dem Glienicker Stibadium erprobt hatte, verläßt der Bühnenbildner Schinkel die subtropische Pflanzenfülle des Vordergrunds, um über eine Ansammlung sagenhafter Bauwerke, über baumbestandene Hügel, Gewässer und Wasserspiele hinweg zu den schneeigen Höhen des sich aufgipfelnden Gebirges im Hintergrund zu führen. So ephemer wie die Kulisse eines Bühnenbilds ist der Garten ein nur allzu vergängliches Kunstwerk, dem beständigen Wandel der Tages- und Jahreszeiten, dem Wachsen und Vergehen, den Launen der Moden sowie den von Verwüstungen und Machtkämpfen geprägten Zeitläuften stets unterworfen.

Die textliche und photographische Beschreibung im vorliegenden Band sind eine Momentaufnahme. Sie unternimmt eine Annäherung an das »Geistreiche der Idee«, mit dem man bei den preußischen Gärten in Berlin und Potsdam rechnen muß. Diesen hohen Anspruch fürstlicher Landschaftskunst formulierte Lenné in einem Anflug von Ungeduld mit seinem königlichen Auftraggeber, der wieder einmal die Geldmittel beschnitten hatte: »Ew. Majestät begreifen noch immer nicht das Geistreiche meiner Idee.«

Charlottenburg – die regulierte Natur

Im Jahr 1696 machte Kurfürstin Sophie Charlotte (1668 bis 1705) Simon Godeau (geb. 1632) zum Entwerfer und Leiter ihres Gartens Lützenburg/Lietzenburg.[1] Der aus Paris kommende Gärtner war ein Schüler von André

ground for a new visual experience. In the 14th century, Francesco Petrarca still needed to climb, with great difficulty, Mont Ventoux in Provence in order to be able to change his perspective of the world. On the other hand the visual appropriation introduced by Freydanck made it possible to fly over the gardens of the kings of Prussia. Panoramas became popular spectacles of illusionist 360-degree vistas. The circular vista made it possible to experience the landscape that was the world.

Frederick William IV introduced his intentions to beautify the landscape with the idea that he would turn the territory over which he ruled into a garden. Though his words sound simple, there is an overtone of the grandiose and visionary, fantastic elements that have been part and parcel of the development of Berlin and Potsdam as a locale of garden art since the first projects by Elector Frederick William of Brandenburg.

With an edition of the *Arabian Nights* in his luggage Frederick William IV began his first campaign. Inspired by the fairy-tale world, he told his sister Charlotte, in letters dated 1816/17, his own Oriental-style novella *Die Königin von Borneo* (*The Queen of Borneo*) about the first-person narrator borne on the wings of the bird Roc to Borneo in the Indian archipelago, where he finds himself in a fantasy landscape surrounded by equally fantastic buildings.

It was the theatre decorator Innocente Bellavita who designed Frederick's Ruinenberg following suggestions by Georg Wenzeslaus von Knobelsdorff (1699–1753). Karl Friedrich Schinkel (1781–1841), in collaboration with whom Lenné designed the Arcadian garden visions of Frederick William IV around Berlin and Potsdam, was also a scenographer. His second stage design sketch for the opera *Nurmahal, Tal von Kaschmir*, 1822 (illus. 6), may be considered the final chord of Prussian garden art: All the rulers of Prussia who took part in creating the artistic whole that constituted the Berlin-Potsdam gardens and parks imagined a kind of world landscape. But only time and the creative collaboration of Frederick William IV, Schinkel and Lenné took the utopia to its limit. It was decorative art that would take it beyond that limit.

From the garden terrace, similar to those he had often tried out, for instance in Potsdam in the Römische Bäder (Roman Baths), Charlottenhof, the Glienicke Stibadium, the set designer Schinkel left the subtropical proliferation of vegetation in the foreground to lead us over a collection of mythical structures, over wooded hills, bodies of water and waterworks to the snow-covered heights of the mountains in the background. As ephemeral as the backdrop of a play, the garden is only too transitory a work of art, subject to the constant alternation of times of day and seasons, growth and decay, the moods of fashions as well as the devastation and power struggles that characterize each period.

The texts and photographs in this volume are snapshots. They attempt to give an approximate sense of the »ingenuity of the idea« involved in the Prussian gardens and parks in Berlin and Potsdam. Somewhat impatient with the king, his patron, who had once more cut the funding, Lenné formulated the high standard he expected of royal landscape art: »Your Majesty still does not understand how ingenious my idea is.«

Charlottenburg – regulated nature

In 1696 Electress Sophia Charlotte (1668–1705) made Simon Godeau (b. 1632) the designer and director of her Lützenburg/Lietzenburg garden.[1] The gardener, who came from Paris, was a pupil of André Le Nôtre, Louis XIV's gardener. Responsible for the Lützenburg orchards was René Dahuron, a pupil of Jean de La Quintinie, the kitchen gardener of Versailles.

The plot of land originally named after the neighbouring village of Lützenburg and called Charlottenburg after 1705 became Sophia Charlotte's court of muses: After initially using Caputh near Potsdam, given to her upon her marriage, as her summer residence, the electress, and Prussian queen since 1701, had a new palace built northwest of Berlin and had a garden laid out (illus. 7). Johann Arnold Nering (1659–1695) built the small summer residence starting in 1695, Martin Grünberg (1655 to 1706) completed the work after the latter's death, and Nicodemus Tessin the Younger (1654–1728) had a part in drawing up the blueprints.

Together with the small castle of Friedrichsthal north of Oranienburg, designed by Nering, dated 1697, Lützenburg became the first palace built in northern Germany whose arrangement of rooms corresponded to the French principle of a *maison de plaisance* – a pleasure house that did not claim to be a residence, modeled after Louis le Vau's 1661 château Vaux-le-Vicomte: an upper story (*bel étage*), limited, symmetrically arranged space, an oval central hall that jutted out of the front of the building into the natural surroundings, and whose glass doors directed one's eyes from the courtyard into the garden.

Work on the garden began in the autumn of 1697. In 1705, after Sophia Charlotte's death, until an argument regarding the excessive pollarding of the linden trees in 1711, Godeau continued to work for Frederick (1657 to 1713), who reigned, beginning in 1688, as Elector Frederick III, and after 1701 at the same time ruled as the first king in Prussia. Johann Lohmann became Godeau's successor. After Lohmann's death in 1729 the master apprentice and grower Joachim Arndt Saltzmann (1691 to 1771) took on the care of the garden.

After 1701 the Swedish-German architect Johann Friedrich Eosander von Göthe (1669–1728) enlarged the park westward and expanded the castle by 1707 into a three-wing building. In 1708–12 it was further improved by adding a dome-shaped tower, an orangery in the west and forecourt. In 1740–42, when Georg Wenzeslaus von Knobelsdorff added the Neuer or Knobelsdorff-Flügel for Frederick II, the garden around the area in front of Knobelsdorff's addition was expanded and the pleasance in front of the castle was completely renewed.

From 1787 to 1833 Johann August Eyserbeck (1762 to 1801), Georg Steiner (1774–1834) and Lenné redesigned the garden to create a landscape park. Carl Gotthard Langhans (1732–1808) built a belvedere in the north part of the landscape garden in 1788 for Frederick William II; Heinrich Gentz (1766–1811) designed the mausoleum for Queen Louise of Prussia in 1810, and Schinkel was the architect of the Neuer Pavillon, 1824/1825. Several bridges were added as well.[2]

Axes

In the summer of 1699 Sophia Charlotte was able to move to Lützenburg. Frederick I, her husband as of

Le Nôtre, Gärtner Ludwigs XIV. Verantwortlich für die Lützenburger Obstzucht war René Dahuron, Schüler von Jean de La Quintinie, dem Versailler Küchengärtner.

Das zunächst nach dem Nachbardorf Lützenburg, seit 1705 Charlottenburg benannte Grundstück wurde Sophie Charlottes Musenhof: Nachdem ihr als Sommersitz bisher ihre Morgengabe Caputh bei Potsdam zur Verfügung gestanden hatte, ließ sich die Kurfürstin und seit 1701 preußische Königin nordwestlich vor Berlin ein neues Schloß errichten und einen Garten anlegen (Abb. 7). Johann Arnold Nering (1659–1695) erbaute die kleine Sommerresidenz ab 1695, Martin Grünberg (1655–1706) übernahm die Ausführung nach seinem Tod, Nicodemus Tessin d. J. (1654–1728) brachte sich mit Entwürfen ein.

Zusammen mit dem Nering-Schlößchen Friedrichsthal von 1697 nördlich von Oranienburg wurde Lützenburg das erste in Norddeutschland errichtete Schloß, dessen Raumprogramm dem französischen Prinzip eines *maison de plaisance* entsprach – eines Lusthauses ohne Residenzanspruch, vorgeprägt 1661 in Louis le Vaus Schloß Vaux-le-Vicomte: Obergeschoß (Beletage), knappes, symmetrisch angeordnetes Raumangebot, aus der Front in die Natur tretender, ovaler Mittelsaal, der durch Glastüren den Blick bereits vom Hof aus in den Garten lenkt.

Der Garten war seit Herbst 1697 im Entstehen. 1705, nach Sophie Charlottes Tod, arbeitete Godeau bis zu einem Streit um das zu kurze Beschneiden der Linden im Jahr 1711 weiter für Friedrich (1657–1713), der ab 1688 als Kurfürst Friedrich III. und ab 1701 zugleich als erster König in Preußen regierte. Johann Lohmann wurde Godeaus Nachfolger. Nach dessen Tod 1729 übernahm der Meistergeselle und Planteur Joachim Arndt Saltzmann (1691–1771) die Pflege des Gartens.

Ab 1701 vergrößerte der schwedisch-deutsche Architekt Johann Friedrich Eosander von Göthe (1669–1728) den Park in westlicher Richtung und erweiterte das Schloß bis 1707 zur Dreiflügelanlage. 1708–12 wurde es durch Kuppelturm, Orangerie im Westen und Vorhof weiter aufgewertet. 1740–42, als Knobelsdorff für Friedrich II. den Neuen oder Knobelsdorff-Flügel anfügte, wurden der Garten um das Gebiet vor Knobelsdorffs Anbau ausgedehnt und das Luststück vor dem Schloß gänzlich erneuert.

In den Jahren 1787 bis 1833 gestalteten Johann August Eyserbeck (1762–1801), Georg Steiner (1774–1834) und Lenné den Garten zu einem Landschaftspark um. Carl Gotthard Langhans (1732–1808) baute 1788 für Friedrich Wilhelm II. ein Belvedere im nördlichen Landschaftsgarten, von Heinrich Gentz (1766–1811) stammt das Mausoleum für Königin Luise von Preußen, 1810, und von Schinkel der Neue Pavillon, 1824/25. Hinzu kamen mehrere Brücken.[2]

Achsen

Im Sommer 1699 konnte Sophie Charlotte nach Lützenburg ziehen. Friedrich I., ihr Gemahl seit 1684, ließ ihr Zeit und Geld, ihre persönlichen Wünsche zu verwirklichen. Schließlich kam der Aufbau eines neuen Zentrums höfischer Kultur seinem Bestreben entgegen, sein Land, das sich noch in der Erholungsphase nach dem Dreißigjährigen Krieg befand, weiter auszuschmücken. Bereits Friedrichs Vater, der Große Kurfürst, hatte dem Berliner Stadtschloß das Fischerdorf Potsdam als Nebenresidenz hinzugesellt und mit dem umgebenden Ring seiner ländlichen Lustschlösser Caputh im Süden am Templiner See, Bornim im Norden, Glienicke an der Glienicker Lake die Glanzpunkte geschaffen, die kultivierte Lebensart und wirtschaftliche Blüte über Brandenburg-Preußens Grenzen hinaus verkündeten.[3]

Das stadtplanerische Strukturieren einer Landschaft mit Hilfe von Alleen und Architekturfixpunkten, Obstplantagen und landwirtschaftlichen Mustergütern hatte der Große Kurfürst von seinem Statthalter und Freund Johann Moritz von Nassau-Siegen in der brandenburgischen Residenzstadt Kleve an der Grenze zu den Niederlanden übernommen. Das Land mittels Schneisen und markanten Orten zu gliedern, fuhr Friedrich III./I. fort.[4] Berlin wurde zu einer prachtvollen Residenz des Barock. Schloß Köpenick, vom Niederländer Rutger van Langerfeld entworfen, erkor er zur Kurprinzenresidenz auf einer Spreeinsel vor den Toren Berlins. Schloß Oranienburg, den Landsitz seiner Mutter Luise Henriette von Oranien, ließ er ausbauen.

1703 entstand das Schlößchen Monbijou an der Spree. Die Landschlösser in Niederschönhausen (Schönhausen), Tegel, Hermsdorf, Rosenthal, Blankenfelde, Altlandsberg, Ruhleben und Friedrichsfelde mit ihren barocken Gartenanlagen bildeten weitere Akzente seiner Residenzlandschaft. Innerhalb des planvollen Achsensystems wurde das Schloß seiner Gemahlin zum Brennpunkt – im wörtlichen Sinne.

Augenfälligstes Merkmal des barocken Charlottenburger Gartens ist die Dominanz seiner durchlaufenden Süd–Nord-Perspektive (Abb. 8). Ausgehend von der Schloßarchitektur, trieb sie das Auge in einer Länge von 9 km durch seine Hauptelemente Parterre, Boskett und Wasserbecken (heute: »Karpfenteich«) bis zu einer Anhöhe von 50 m bei Tegel jenseits der Spree. Den Sog der durchlaufenden Achse veranschaulicht Eosanders Idealplan aus der Zeit Friedrich Wilhelms I., Nachfolger Friedrichs III./I. Umgesetzt wurden von diesem ausgreifenden Entwurf die Akzentuierung der Längsachse mit Hilfe eines breiten Rasenbands und die Verbreiterung des Parterre-Querwegs, der nun ebenfalls einen *tapis vert* aufnahm, ein schlichtes Rasenstück.

Auf die Süd–Nord-Perspektive stößt der von Osten nach Westen ausgerichtete Schloßbau. Vom Treffpunkt der Achsen im ovalen Mittelsaal des Charlottenburger Schlosses gingen beiderseits der süd–nördlichen zwei schräge Sichten aus und erweiterten das Strahlenmuster zum klassisch barocken Dreistrahl, dem *patte d'oie* (Gänsefuß). Die östliche führte zum 9,5 km entfernten Schloß Schönhausen, die westliche nach Ruhleben und zur Festung Spandau in 6 km Entfernung. Die von ihnen geschnittenen Bosketten nahmen in der Disposition ihrer raumbildenden Lichtungen, den *salles*, Rücksicht auf die durchziehenden Schneisen.

Godeau folgte seinem Wegbereiter Le Nôtre in der Zusammenführung von Baukörper und Garten entlang der Bewegung auf einer Mittelachse, in der Sammlung der Aufmerksamkeit im Gartensaal und im Ausstrahlen des Blicks entlang klar definierter Perspektiven. Le Nôtre war es mit diesem zuerst in Vaux-le-Vicomte verwirklichten Modell geglückt, dem abstrakten zentralistischen Herrschaftsgedanken des Absolutismus in den französischen Gartenanlagen des 17. Jahrhunderts anschauliche Gestalt zu geben.

Charlottenburg entwickelte das französische System jedoch weiter. In das Erleben des Gartens als Abbild ei-

7. Nach Johann Friedrich Eosander von Göthe, Schloß Charlottenburg, Gartenseite, um 1708. Radierung aus: *Theatrum Europaeum*, Bd. 16, Frankfurt am Main 1717. (SPSG, Potsdam.)
8. Martin Engelbrecht nach Johann Friedrich Eosander von Göthe, Schloß und Schloßgarten Charlottenburg, um 1717. Radierung aus: *Theatrum Europaeum*, Bd. 16, Frankfurt am Main 1717. (SPSG, Potsdam.)

7. After Johann Friedrich Eosander von Göthe, Schloß Charlottenburg, garden façade, ca. 1708. Etching from: *Theatrum Europaeum*, vol. 16, Frankfurt am Main, 1717. (SPSG, Potsdam.)
8. Martin Engelbrecht after Johann Friedrich Eosander von Göthe, Schloß and Schloßgarten Charlottenburg, ca. 1717. Etching from: *Theatrum Europaeum*, vol. 16, Frankfurt am Main, 1717. (SPSG, Potsdam.)

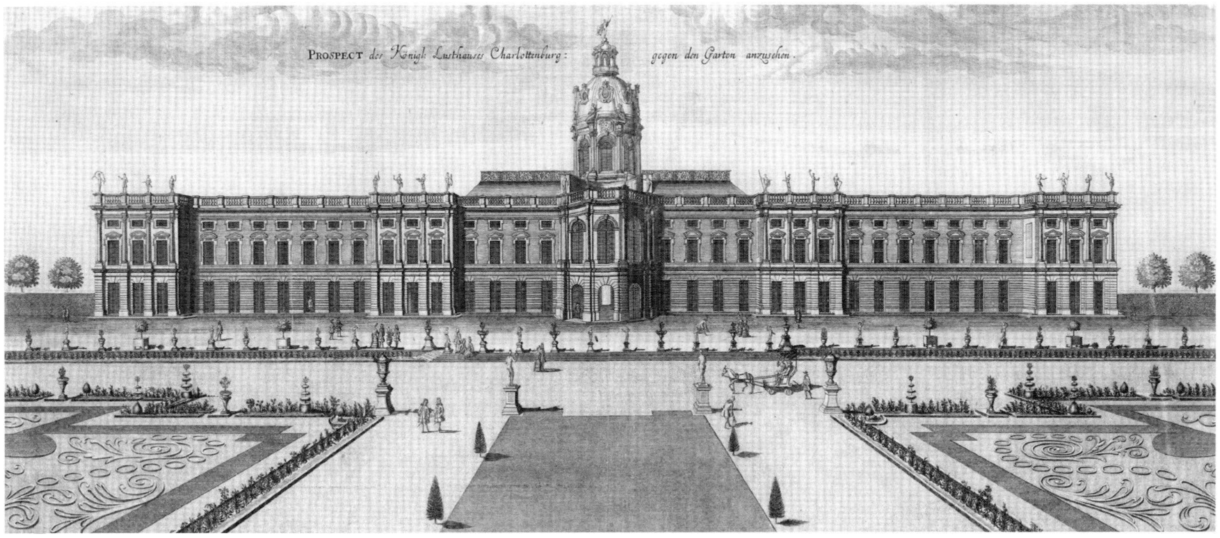

1684, let her have the time and money to fulfil her personal wishes. After all, the construction of a new centre of courtly culture was in line with his own endeavour to continue to embellish his country, which was still recovering from the Thirty Years' War. Already Frederick's father, the Great Elector, had added the secondary residence, the fishing village of Potsdam, to the Berlin city palace and with the surrounding ring of his country summer residences Caputh in the south by Templiner See, Bornim in the north and Glienicke on Glienicker Lake had created the highlights that proclaimed a cultivated lifestyle and economic prosperity beyond the borders of Brandenburg-Prussia.[3]

The urban development structuring of a landscape by means of avenues and architectural points of reference, orchards and agricultural model farms are ideas the Great Elector had adopted from his governor and friend Johann Moritz von Nassau-Siegen in the Brandenburg residence city of Cleves at the border to the Netherlands. Frederick III/I continued to structure the land by means of breaks and clearly defined places.[4] Berlin became a magnificent Baroque residence. He chose Schloß Köpenick, designed by the Netherlands architect Rutger van Langerfeld, to be the crown prince's residence on an island in the Spree before the gates of Berlin. He had Schloß Oranienburg, the country seat of his mother Louise Henriette of Orange, expanded.

The little Schloß Monbijou on the Spree was built in 1703. The rural palaces in Niederschönhausen (Schönhausen), Tegel, Hermsdorf, Rosenthal, Blankenfelde, Altlandsberg, Ruhleben and Friedrichsfelde with their Baroque gardens and grounds represented additional highlights of his landscape of residences. Within the planned system of axes, the palace of his wife became the – literal – focus.

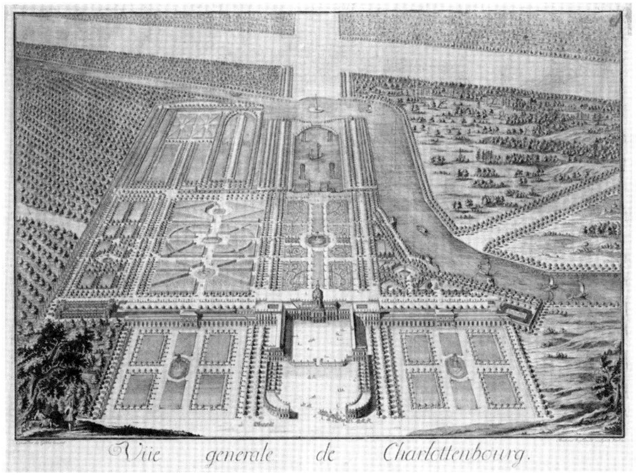

The most conspicuous characteristic of the Baroque garden of Charlottenburg is the dominance of its continuous south–north perspective (illus. 8). Starting from the palace building, it compelled the eye to move for 9 km through its main elements – the *parterre*, the *bosquet* and the pond (today referred to as the »Carp Pond«) to a 50-m-high hill near Tegel on the other side of the Spree. The pull of the continuous axis is illustrated by Eosander's ideal plan from the time of Frederick William I, the successor of Frederick III/I. The features of this far-reaching design that were implemented were the accentuation of the longitudinal axis by means of a wide swathe of lawn and the widening of the transverse path across the *parterre*, which now also came to include a *tapis vert*, a simple patch of lawn.

The palace, oriented east–west, runs counter to the south–north perspective. From the meeting point of the axes in the oval central hall of Schloß Charlottenburg two oblique views led off on both sides of the south–north view and expanded the pattern of rays into the classic Baroque triple-ray design, the *patte d'oie* (goosefoot). The eastern perspective led to Schloß Schönhausen, 9.5 km distant, while the western one led to Ruhleben and to the fortress of Spandau 6 km away. The disposition of the cleared avenues or *salles* in the *bosquets* intersected by the perspectives took into consideration the lanes or breaks that ran through them.

Godeau followed his predecessor Le Nôtre in merging the architectural structures and the gardens along the movement on a central axis, gathering attention in the garden hall and drawing the observer's eyes along clearly defined perspectives. Le Nôtre, with the model he first realized in Vaux-le-Vicomte, had succeeded in giving visible form in the French parks and gardens of the 17th century to the abstract centralistic concept of government represented by absolutism.

Charlottenburg, however, developed the French system even further. The garden is experienced as the representation of an overall order whose foundation was the absolutist ruler. The palace is so directly incorporated in this order that it initiates this domination of the open landscape by means of perspective alignments.

Mirror reflections that suggest windows and real window apertures of the Oval Hall produce the illusion that one is in a freestanding pavilion. The first-floor hall forces one, as it were, to gaze into the sheaf of rays. An ideal plan provided for fountains in all three of the axes framed by the arches of the windows; their soaring jets of water would have accompanied the dramatic view of appearances and disappearances, similar to the open hall »La Colonnade« in Versailles, with great effect.[5]

But that's not all. In the focal point, i.e., a few steps outside the centre, standing a little closer to the mirror-lined back wall of the hall in a diagonal cross, the observer experienced the elongation of the perspectives toward Schönhausen and Spandau in whichever mirror was located opposite the corresponding window. The perspective on one side, fixed to architectonic target points in the landscape, is extended out beyond the human visual faculty into infinity on the other side: the garden and Schloß Charlottenburg push the favorite theme

ner übergreifenden, im absolutistischen Fürsten fundierten Ordnung ist das Schloß so unmittelbar miteinbezogen, daß es die Beherrschung der freien Landschaft durch Perspektivfluchten selbst anleitet. Fenster suggerierende Verspiegelungen und reale Fensteröffnungen des Ovalen Saals erzeugen die Illusion, sich in einem frei stehenden Pavillon aufzuhalten. Der Saal in der Beletage zwingt den Blick gleichsam in das Strahlenbündel hinein. Eine ideale Planung sah Fontänen in allen drei von den Fensterbögen gerahmten Achsen vor, deren aufsteigende Wasserstrahlen die Inszenierung des Auftauchens und wieder Verschwindens ähnlich dem offenen Saal »La Colonnade« in Versailles effektvoll begleitet hätten.[5]

Doch damit nicht genug. Im Brennpunkt, das heißt einige Schritte aus der Mitte heraus, etwas näher an der verspiegelten Rückwand des Saals stehend, erlebte der Betrachter, in ein Andreaskreuz eingespannt, die Verlängerung der Perspektiven nach Schönhausen und Spandau in jeweils dem Spiegel, der dem entsprechenden Fenster gegenüberliegt. Die an architektonischen Zielpunkten in der Landschaft fixierte Perspektive auf der einen Seite wird auf der anderen Seite mittels Spiegel über das menschliche Sehvermögen hinaus in die Unendlichkeit gedehnt: Garten und Schloß Charlottenburg reizen das Lieblingsthema barocker Kunst aus, indem der Ellipse des Saalovals mit der Anordnung ihrer fünf auf landschaftliche Fixpunkte bezogenen Fensterausblicke gegenüber fünf Spiegeln die räumliche Darstellung des Unendlichen gelingt.

Sophie Charlotte

Sophie Charlottes Ideal war die Hofkultur Frankreichs und Italiens. Die gebildete Kurfürstin und Königin, die fließend Französisch, Italienisch sowie Englisch beherrschte und ausgezeichnet Cembalo spielen konnte, hielt einen Gesprächszirkel, veranstaltete Feste, Musik- und Theateraufführungen. Nahe dem Schloß errichtete Eosander im Südwesten ein hölzernes Theatergebäude samt Maschinerie für die Bühneneffekte. Ein Laubengang östlich des Schlosses umgab einen 20 x 30 m großen Hof, in dem Festspiele aufgeführt wurden (Abb. 9).

Neben der italienischen Oper mochte Sophie Charlotte chinesische Porzellane, deren mehrere hundert Stück sie im Schloß gern selbst anordnete. Nur durch das verschwenderische Porzellankabinett am Ende der Raumflucht im Westen des Schlosses war Sophie Charlottes »heimlicher Garten«, der private *jardin secret*, zugänglich, der besonders wertvolle Blumen wie zarte Kleinodien barg.

Sophie Charlottes Bewunderer war der Philosoph der Aufklärung Gottfried Wilhelm Leibniz (1646–1716), der häufiger Gast in Lützenburg war. Die Kurfürstin unterstützte ihn bei seiner Idee der Gründung einer Preußischen Akademie der Wissenschaften in Berlin, die 1700 Wirklichkeit wurde. Geprägt wurden Sophie Charlottes Interessen besonders von ihrer kulturell und politisch offenen und regen Mutter Sophie, Prinzessin von der Pfalz (auch Kurfürstin Sophie von Hannover, 1630–1714). Seit 1680 war Sophie Charlotte in Hannover aufgewachsen. Den Großen Garten von Herrenhausen ließ ihre Mutter dem Zeitgeschmack gemäß ausgestalten.

Neben der Mutter hatte Sophie Charlotte zeitlebens guten Kontakt zu ihrer Cousine Elisabeth Charlotte von Orléans (auch: Liselotte von der Pfalz), Schwägerin Ludwigs XIV. Wie die eigene Tochter war auch sie von Sophie erzogen worden. Liselotte hielt Sophie Charlotte beständig über die neuesten aristokratischen Moden in Frankreich auf dem Laufenden. Ihr Gemahl, Herzog Philipp I. von Orléans, hatte Le Nôtres Können mit der Anlage des Gartens von Saint-Cloud auf dem abfallenden linken Ufer der Seine herausgefordert. Die von Sophie Charlotte gewählten Ratgeber für Schloß- und Gartenbau, Hofbaumeister Giacomo Quirini, tätig in Hannover, und der von Liselotte von der Pfalz empfohlene Gartenkünstler Le Nôtre widerspiegeln die beiden Stränge ihrer Beeinflussung. Gepaart mit einem ihrem Gemahl ebenbürtigen Bestreben, höfische Pracht zur Schau zu stellen, ergaben sie den ersten Garten des Hochbarock im Duktus Le Nôtres in Brandenburg-Preußen.[6]

Der Barockgarten bis 1713 – modellierte Landschaft

Wohl ein Gärtner zeichnete 1696/97 den Grundriß des Gartens von Schloß Lützenburg (Abb. 10). Kriegsverluste machen ihn zu Charlottenburgs einzigem erhaltenen Gartenplan der Barockzeit. Er gibt den Stand der Überlegungen zur Gartenanlage wieder, kurz bevor der endgültige, heute verschollene Entwurf von Godeau, den Le Nôtre zur Begutachtung erhalten hatte, beschlossen wurde. Etwa acht Jahre später, 1704, veranschaulichen die detailreichen Zeichnungen im Tagebuch des Architekten Christoph Pitzler Sophie Charlottes Garten.[7]

Die Anlagen südlich des Schlosses und die Küchengärten wurden nicht verwirklicht. Zu dem von Pitzler gezeichneten Zierwerk gehörten bunt bemalte Holzpyramiden, Vasen auf Sockeln oder Postamenten und vergoldete Bleifiguren.

Die bildhauerische Modellierung des Geländes ist das Thema, das Godeau neben der Beherrschung der Perspektive mit Le Nôtre verbindet.[8] In drei hierarchisch gestuften Ebenen ließ Godeau das Gelände vom höchsten Punkt der Schloßterrasse bis hin zum Wasser abfallen.

Die Höhendifferenz lenkte die Ankunft im Garten von der Spree choreographisch, ähnlich dem Aufstieg vom Grand Canal zum Schloß Versailles. Auf dem Wasser bewegte man sich mit Treckschuten, die von Pferden gezogen wurden. Parallel zur Spree zog sich ein ufernaher Treidelweg. Hinter drei hölzernen Angelhäusern führte ein Kanal in das Charlottenburger Wasserbecken. Bei Windstille spiegelte sich darin das Schloß: Die erste Begegnung zwischen Mensch und Architektur schien als virtuell verdoppeltes Zauberbild auf. Am südlichen Ende des Beckens stiegen die Ankommenden auf dem Gang an Land, der direkt um die *pièce d'eau*, das Wasserstück, führte. Das Boot konnte derweil durch die Fortsetzung des Kanals in ein Gondelhaus an dessen Ende gebracht werden. Erst vom Land zeigte sich das höher gelegene Parterre. Eine Reihe im Wechsel stehender Taxuskegel und Vasen oder Hochstämme trennten es an der Rasenböschung vom Wasserbereich. Von der Seite betrat man das 100 x 250 m große Luststück, um es vom Zentrum aus überblicken zu können.

Südlicher und nördlicher Parterre-Abschnitt waren nahezu spiegelbildlich gestaltet – entgegen dem Brauch, den vom Schloß aus nicht einsehbaren hinteren Teil einfacher zu halten. Den vom Wasser Ankommenden empfing sogleich ein reiches ornamentales Bild: Die einzelnen Felder waren mehrfach durch eine *plate-bande*

9. Johann Friedrich Eosander von Göthe oder Hassan de Coron, *Zwei Divertissements in Lietzenburg*, 1702. Feder, aquarelliert. (Staatsbibliothek zu Berlin, Preußischer Kulturbesitz, Handschriftenabteilung – Reprographie aus: AKat. 1999 a.)
10. Unbekannter Zeichner, Garten Lietzenburg, Planentwurf, 1696/97. Feder, Tusche, laviert. (Sächsische Landesbibliothek, Staats- und Universitätsbibliothek Dresden – Reprographie aus: AKat. 1999 a.)

9. Johann Friedrich Eosander von Göthe or Hassan de Coron, *Zwei Divertissements in Lietzenburg*, 1702. Pen, painted in watercolours. (Staatsbibliothek zu Berlin, Preußischer Kulturbesitz, Handschriftenabteilung – reproduced from: AKat. 1999 a.)
10. Unknown graphic artist, Lietzenburg garden, plan draft, 1696/97. Pen, ink, washed. (Sächsische Landesbibliothek, Staats- und Universitätsbibliothek Dresden – reproduced from: AKat. 1999 a.)

of Baroque art to the limits, as the ellipsis of the oval hall, with its arrangement of the views out its five windows, oriented toward fixed points in the landscape and facing five mirrors, succeeds in spatially representing infinity.

Sophia Charlotte

Sophia Charlotte's ideal was the culture of the courts of France and Italy. The educated electress and queen, who fluently spoke French, Italian and English, and was an accomplished harpsichord player, held a discussion circle, and organized parties, musical and theatrical performances. Near the palace, on the southwest side, Eosander erected a wooden theatre building including machinery for stage effects. A pergola east of the palace surrounded a courtyard, 20 x 30 m large, in which pageants were performed (illus. 9).

In addition to Italian opera Sophia Charlotte liked Chinese porcelain, and enjoyed personally arranging the several hundred pieces of her collection in the palace. Only through the lavish china gallery at the end of the suite of rooms on the palace's west side was there access to Sophia Charlotte's private »secret garden« that concealed particularly valuable flowers like delicate jewels.

Sophia Charlotte's admirer was the Enlightenment philosopher Gottfried Wilhelm Leibniz (1646–1716), a frequent visitor in Lützenburg. The electress supported him in his plan to found a Prussian academy of sciences in Berlin, which became a reality in 1700. Sophia Charlotte's interests were shaped particularly by her culturally and politically open-minded and active mother Sophia, Princess of the Palatinate (also Electress Sophia of Hanover, 1630–1714). Since 1680 Sophia Charlotte had grown up in Hanover. The Great Garden of Herrenhausen had been laid out by her mother in accordance with the taste of the period.

In addition to her mother, Sophia Charlotte throughout her lifetime was close to her cousin Elisabeth Charlotte of Orléans (also referred to as Liselotte von der Pfalz), the sister-in-law of Louis XIV. She, too, had been raised by Sophia as though she were her own daughter. Liselotte kept Sophia Charlotte constantly informed about the newest aristocratic fashions in France. Her husband, Duke Philipp I of Orléans, had challenged Le Nôtre's skills by commissioning him with the layout of the garden of Saint-Cloud on the sloping left bank of the Seine. The consultants Sophia Charlotte chose for the construction of the palace and the landscaping of the garden, court architect Giacomo Quirini, active in Hanover, and garden designer Le Nôtre, recommended by Liselotte von der Pfalz, represent the two strands of influence in her life. Coupled with a desire equal to that of her husband to show off courtly splendour, they produced the first garden of the High Baroque in the characteristic style of Le Nôtre in Brandenburg-Prussia.[6]

The Baroque garden up to 1713 – a modelled landscape

It must have been a gardener who in 1696/97 drew up the blueprints for the garden of Schloß Lützenburg (illus. 10). Because of wartime losses, this is Charlottenburg's only garden plan to survive from the Baroque. It gives an account of the status of reflections regarding the layout of the garden, shortly before the definitive, now lost design by Godeau, about which Le Nôtre had been asked to give his expert opinion, was decided upon. About eight years later, in 1704, detailed drawings in the diary of architect Christoph Pitzler show what Sophia Charlotte's garden looked like.[7]

The gardens south of the palace and the kitchen gardens were not implemented. The decorative elements drawn by Pitzler included colourful painted wooden pyramids, vases on pedestals and gilded lead figures.

In addition to a mastery of perspective, sculptural modelling of the terrain is the theme that links Godeau with Le Nôtre.[8] In three hierarchically structured levels, Godeau had the landscape slope from the highest point of the palace terrace down to the water.

The difference in height choreographically directed arrival in the garden from the Spree, reminiscent of the climb from the Grand Canal to the Palace of Versailles. On the water people traveled on small horse-drawn wooden boats. Parallel to the Spree River, close to the bank, there was a towpath. Behind three wooden anglers' cabins a canal led into the Charlottenburg pond. When the weather was calm the palace was reflected in it: The first encounter between the visitor and the building appeared as a virtually doubled magic image. At the south end of the pond arriving visitors stepped ashore on the path that led directly around the *pièce d'eau*, the pond. In the meantime the boat could be brought along a continuation of the canal into a boathouse at its end. Only from the land did the higher *parterre* become visible. Near the slope of the lawn, a row of alternating conical yews and vases or tall trees separated it from the pond. From the side one entered the 100 x 250 m large pleasance, and was then able to have an overall view of it from its centre.

The south and north section of the *parterre* were almost mirror images of each other – contrary to the custom of keeping the rear section, which could not be seen from the palace, simpler. People who arrived from the direction of the water were immediately greeted by a rich, ornamental scene: The individual sections were repeatedly framed by a *plate-bande coupée*, a flower bed interrupted at intervals by vases or yews. A strip of lawn set off by sand from the flower bed surrounded them like leaf- and scrollwork and at the same time meshed with the embroidery elements outlined by dwarf box plants. The inner, darker ground of black or red material contrasted with the light-coloured outside sandy soil; on it, the ornamentation unfolded freely, without a centre and symmetrical repetition.

The palace terrace was reached after crossing the *parterre*. In front of its smooth wall, a flower bed was filled with a profusion of flowers. A flight of steps led to the terrace. A new high point of the structured promenade came from the concentration of standing still and gazing around that followed the movement through water and garden: For the first time, it was possible to have a view of the entire garden and to follow its perspectives as they radiated to the horizon.

From the Baroque to the landscape garden

Sophia Charlotte's garden had actually turned out too large: It was the courtyard that prescribed its dimension, not the garden façade of the Nering building stretching out directly in front of.

Not until the palace was enlarged were the proportions reconciled. The reconfigurations under Frederick I

coupée gerahmt, ein Blumenbeet, das in Abständen Vasen oder Eiben unterbrechen. Ein durch Sand davon abgesetztes Rasenband umspielte sie wie Bandlwerk und griff dabei in die von Zwergbuchs umrissenen Broderieornamente ein. Mit dem hellen äußeren Sandgrund kontrastierte der innere dunklere Grund aus schwarzem oder rotem Material, auf dem sich das Ornament frei, ohne Mittelpunkt und symmetrische Wiederholung entwickelte.

Das Parterre durchlaufend, wurde die Schloßterrasse erreicht. Vor ihrer glatten Mauer entfaltete sich der Blumenschmuck im vorgelagerten Beet. Eine Freitreppe führte auf die Terrasse. In der Konzentration des Stillstehens und Schauens, die auf die Bewegung durch Wasser und Garten folgte, fand die geordnete Gartenpromenade einen neuerlichen Höhepunkt: Erstmalig war es möglich, den gesamten Garten zu überschauen, dem Ausstrahlen seiner Perspektiven bis zum Horizont zu folgen.

Vom Barock- zum Landschaftsgarten

Sophie Charlottes Garten war eigentlich zu groß geraten: Der Hof gab sein Maß vor, nicht die Gartenfront des Nering-Baus, vor der er sich unmittelbar erstreckte.

Erst mit der Vergrößerung des Schlosses fanden die Proportionen zueinander. Die Umgestaltungen unter Friedrich I. zielten auf eine monumentalere Wirkung von Schloß und Garten, wie sie Eosanders Idealplan deutlich macht. Fasanerie und Küchengarten mit Teichen für Hecht- und Karpfenzucht erweiterten den Garten ebenso wie Anlagen für Gesellschaftsspiele.

Nachdem Friedrich Wilhelm I. (1688–1740) den Garten allein ob seines Nutzwerts beachtet hatte, behandelte Friedrichs II. Korrespondenz während seiner beiden ersten Schlesienkriege neben Fragen um den Bau des Berliner Opernhauses auch den Neuen Flügel in Charlottenburg. Die von Godeau geprägte Struktur des Gartens behielt Friedrich II. bei und erweiterte sie lediglich um ein Parterre vor dem Knobelsdorff-Flügel. Viele neu angeschaffte Pflanzen und Bäume füllten Lücken. Dem Obstanbau galt Friedrichs besondere Aufmerksamkeit. Schönfarbige Blumen in der Parterrebroderie, zahlreiche Statuen, viele Kindergruppen und 24 Büsten der julischen Kaiser und ihrer Gemahlinnen vor Orangerie und Neuem Flügel aus dem Charlottenburger Depotbestand umgaben die barocke Strenge mit dem spielerischen Hauch des Rokoko. Den Abstieg von der Schloßterrasse in den Garten begleitete an Stelle von Blumenvasen ein Sphingenpaar, wie es Friedrich auch in seinen anderen Gärten vom Oberen Belvedere in Wien übernommen hatte.

Erst mit Friedrichs Neffen, Friedrich Wilhelm II., wechselte der Charlottenburger Garten sein Gesicht, er wurde Landschaftspark.[9] Das Vorbild auf dem Kontinent hatte Fürst Leopold Franz von Dessau in der Auenlandschaft der Elbe mit seinem Gartenreich Wörlitz geschaffen. Der Sohn des Wörlitzer Gärtners, Eyserbeck, der zur gleichen Zeit Friedrich Wilhelms Neuen Garten am Heiligen See anlegte, begann Charlottenburg behutsam umzugestalten. Die gleichlaufenden Alleen blieben unberührt, während die Parterres zu einer geschlossenen Wiesenfläche gefügt wurden, besetzt mit Sträuchern und Baumgruppen. Im neu hinzugewonnenen Sumpfland im Nordwesten wurden Teiche und Gräben angelegt und Schlängelwege durch die Bosketten geführt.

Den beginnenden Stilpluralismus repräsentiert Langhans mit drei Angelhäusern in den Formen Urhütte, Gotik (Abb. 11) und Antike, wobei letzteres unausgeführt blieb. Das Otaheitische Korbhaus stand wie eine Hütte in der Südsee auf Holzpfählen im Wasser. Die Bretterzauneinhegung des Gartens wich einem Kanal und dem nun beliebten Graben. Dieser diente als sogenanntes Aha, zum Landschaftsgartenvokabular avancierter Ausdruck der Verwunderung ob der erst von nahem sichtbaren Gartengrenze. Der Landschaftspark Charlottenburg ging in der umliegenden Natur auf. Die Obstkultur wurde von Friedrich Wilhelm II. weitergepflegt und um ein neues Orangenhaus erweitert.

»Nicht ganz in dem Geist entworfen, wie die Gärten der Tuilerien usw. bei Paris«

Unter Friedrich Wilhelm III. führte Hofgärtner Steiner einige wohl noch von Eyserbeck geplante Änderungen durch, und es entstand ein zusammenhängendes, von der Spree gespeistes Wassersystem, das eine Insel, die spätere Luiseninsel, ausbildete. Das große Bassin erhielt eine scheinbar natürliche Teichform. Einzeln ausgestaltete Gartenschmuckräume, Blumen, italienische Topf- und Kübelpflanzen, Bildwerke und die malerische Umsäumung mit Sträuchern und Bäumen entsprachen dem Geschmack Friedrich Wilhelms III. Neben Paretz bei Potsdam wurde Charlottenburg zum bevorzugten Wohnort des Königs und seiner Gemahlin Luise von Mecklenburg-Strelitz. In ihrem Andenken ließ er im Todesjahr seiner Gemahlin 1810 ein Mausoleum in einem Tannenwäldchen nordwestlich des Schlosses erbauen. Friedrich Wilhelms im Jahr 1824 eingegangene morganatische Ehe mit der Gräfin Auguste von Harrach, erhoben zur Fürstin von Liegnitz, war Anlaß für eine betont bürgerliche neue Wohnung im Charlottenburger Park, gleich neben dem Schloß: Der Neue Pavillon von Schinkel ist ein schlichter villenartiger Kubus, der es erlaubt, von all seinen vier Seiten direkt in den Park zu treten.[10]

Erst nach dem Ende der Befreiungskriege trieb Lenné durch seinen mit Steiner ausgearbeiteten Idealplan die Umformung Charlottenburgs zu einer Parklandschaft weiter voran. Teile der Zeichnung wurden 1821 zögernd genehmigt. Wie Lenné im Begleitschreiben vorsichtig formulierte, sei der Verschönerungsvorschlag, wie »Se. Majestät bemerken [dürften], nicht ganz in dem Geist entworfen, wie die Gärten der Tuilerien usw. bei Paris«.[11]

Etwa 20 Jahre später vollendeten die Pappelpflanzungen des Hofgärtners Joachim Anton Ferdinand Fintelmann (1774–1863) auf dem neu angekauften Geländestück jenseits der Spree für einen kurzen Moment Lennés Vision des fließenden Übergangs vom Garten in die Landschaft. Die mit dem 1846 begonnenen Eisenbahnbau von Hamburg nach Berlin verbundene Aufschüttung eines Bahndamms an der Nordgrenze des Parks bedeutete dessen allmählichen Niedergang. Gleisanlagen und später Mietshäuser rückten an die Grenzen des Parks.

Mit Achtung vor dem Original: »Im Sinne des Barock«

In der Zwischenzeit stand Charlottenburg unter Friedrich Wilhelm (IV.) bis zu dessen Tod im Jahr 1861 noch einmal im Rampenlicht nostalgischer Aufmerksamkeit, die sich in der teilweisen Rückführung geometrischer Formen

11. Carl Gotthard Langhans, Gotisches Angelhaus im Schloßgarten Charlottenburg, um 1790. Aquarell. (SPSG, Potsdam.)

11. Carl Gotthard Langhans, Gothic anglers' cabin in Schloßgarten Charlottenburg, ca. 1790. Watercolour. (SPSG, Potsdam.)

aimed at a more monumental effect by the palace and grounds, as Eosander's ideal plan makes clear. A pheasantry and kitchen garden with ponds for raising pike and carp expanded the garden; also added were facilities for parlour games.

Frederick William I (1688–1740) had valued the garden solely because of its utilitarian value. Frederick II's correspondence during his first two Silesian wars, in addition to dealing with questions about the construction of the Berlin opera house also discussed the New Wing in Charlottenburg. Frederick II retained the structure of the garden planned by Godeau and merely expanded it by adding a *parterre* in front of the Knobelsdorff Wing. Many newly acquired plants and trees filled in the gaps. Frederick paid special attention to fruit growing. Flowers in beautiful colours in the *broderie* of the *parterre*, numerous statues, many groups of children and 24 busts of the Julian emperors and their consorts in front of the Orangery and New Wing from the Charlottenburg inventory surrounded Baroque severity with a playful suggestion of the Rococo. Instead of flower vases, a pair of sphinxes stood by the staircase leading down from the palace's terrace into the garden, a tradition Frederick II had adopted in his other gardens in imitation of the Upper Belvedere in Vienna.

Not until the reign of Frederick's nephew, Frederick William II, was the Charlottenburg garden transformed: it became a landscape park.[9] It was Prince Leopold Franz of Anhalt Dessau who created the model on the Continent – the garden realm of Wörlitz in the floodplain of the Elbe. The son of the Wörlitz gardener, Johann August Eyserbeck, who was laying out Frederick William's Neuer Garten on Heiliger See at the same time, cautiously began to redesign Charlottenburg. The parallel avenues remained intact while the *parterres* were joined together into a closed meadow area, scattered with shrubbery and groups of trees. In the newly added marshland in the northwest ponds and ditches were dug and winding paths made through the *bosquets*.

Langhans represents the beginning stylistic pluralism with three anglers' cabins – a primitive hut, a Gothic structure (illus. 11) and one inspired by antiquity that was never implemented. The Otaheite basket house stood in the water on wooden stilts like a hut in the South Sea. The picket fence of the garden was replaced by a canal and a ditch, now a favorite with visitors. The latter served as a so-called »ha-ha«, an expression of surprise that became part of landscape garden vocabulary, designating the garden's boundary, visible only when in close proximity to it. The landscape park of Charlottenburg merged with the surrounding natural landscape. Frederick William II continued the cultivation of fruit and added a new orangery.

»Not drawn up entirely in the same spirit as the gardens of the Tuileries etc. near Paris«

Under Frederick William III, court gardener Steiner carried out a few changes probably still planned by Eyserbeck, creating a connected water system fed by the Spree River that formed an island, later called Luiseninsel. The large pond was given the seemingly natural form of a pond. Individual spaces with garden ornaments, flowers, Italian potted plants and plants in tubs, statuary and picturesque borders with shrubbery and trees suited the taste of Frederick William III. Beside Paretz near Potsdam, Charlottenburg became the favourite residence of the king and his spouse, Louise of Mecklenburg-Strelitz. As a memorial to her he had a mausoleum built for her the year she died (1810) in a spruce forest northwest of the palace. Frederick William's 1824 morganatic marriage to Countess Augusta von Harrach, elevated in rank to Princess of Liegnitz, occasioned an emphatically middle-class new home in Charlottenburg park, immediately adjacent to the palace: Schinkel's Neuer Pavillon is a plain villa-like cube that makes it possible to enter the park directly from all its four sides.[10]

It was not after the end of the Wars of Liberation that Lenné pressed ahead with redesigning Charlottenburg as a park landscape, using the ideal plan he had worked out together with Steiner. Parts of the draft were hesitantly approved in 1821. As Lenné cautiously stated in an accompanying letter, the proposal for beautification, as »His Majesty would no doubt note«, was »not drawn up entirely in the same spirit as the gardens of the Tuileries etc. near Paris«.[11]

Some 20 years later, the poplars planted by court gardener Joachim Anton Ferdinand Fintelmann (1774 to 1863) on the newly purchased plot of land on the other side of the Spree for a brief moment completed Lenné's vision of the fluid transition from the garden into the landscape. At the north boundary of the park, a railroad embankment had been raised in connection with the construction, begun in 1846, of a railroad from Hamburg to Berlin, gradually putting an end to the vision. Railroad tracks and later blocks of flats moved close to the park's boundaries.

With respect for the original: »In the spirit of the Baroque«

In the meantime, Charlottenburg under Frederick William (IV) until his death in 1861 was once more in the limelight of nostalgic attention expressed by the fact that geometrical forms were brought back in part: The straight main avenue, now called »Königsweg«, and three tree-lined avenues or various reconstructions of flower beds were laid out in accordance with the king's childhood memories following new designs.

Frederick William admired his predecessor Frederick II and paid tribute to him, for instance, by re-erecting the busts of the emperors and by placing a cast zinc statue, *Adorant* (*Adorer*), in an unidentified location, reminiscent of the *Praying Boy* of Sanssouci.[12]

In the period until the end of the monarchy (1918) only the area immediately outside the palace was maintained. Here, ca. 1856, modern carpet beds were laid out or, in 1884 at the latest, a tuff island with a jet of water was installed in the carp pond. Georg Potente (1876–1945), court gardener in Charlottenburg from 1909 on, laid out a *parterre* in neo-Baroque forms with borders and topiaries in the open centre in front of the palace, for the royal household members who still visited Charlottenburg on festive occasions.

In the Second World War the palace and garden were badly damaged.[13] There were bomb craters scattered throughout the garden, which in the postwar period was used as vegetable garden and a source of firewood. Because there was no Baroque park in Berlin as a testimonial of the city's past as a royal seat and since there were only a few examples of such parks in Germany,

äußerte: Die gerade Hauptallee, nun »Königsweg«, und drei Boskettalleen oder verschiedene Beetrekonstruktionen wurden gemäß den Kindheitserinnerungen des Königs nach Neuentwürfen angelegt. Seinen von ihm verehrten Vorfahren Friedrich II. würdigte Friedrich Wilhelm beispielsweise mit der Wiederaufstellung der Kaiserbüsten und mit einem an unbekanntem Ort plazierten *Adorant* aus Zinkguß, der an den *Betenden Knaben* von Sanssouci erinnerte.[12]

In der Zeit bis zum Ende der Monarchie 1918 wurde allein die schloßnahe Umgebung gepflegt. Hier entstanden um 1856 zeitgenössische Teppichbeete oder spätestens 1884 eine Tuffsteininsel mit Wasserstrahl im Karpfenteich. Georg Potente (1876–1945), seit 1909 Hofgärtner in Charlottenburg, legte für den Hofstaat, der Charlottenburg noch zu festlichen Anlässen aufsuchte, in der freien Mitte vor dem Schloß ein Parterre in den Formen des Neobarock mit Rabatten und Formgehölzen an.

Im Zweiten Weltkrieg wurden Schloß und Garten schwer beschädigt.[13] Bombentrichter verteilten sich über den Garten, der nach dem Krieg als Gemüseacker und Brennholzquelle diente. Das Fehlen einer barocken Gartenanlage in Berlin als Zeugnis seiner residenzstädtischen Vergangenheit und nur wenige Beispiele in Deutschland bestimmten die von der Schlösserdirektorin Margarete Kühn formulierte Zielsetzung für den Wiederaufbau des fürstlichen Gartendenkmals nach 1950. Bis hin zum Teich gibt noch heute die Gartenkunst »im Sinne des Barock« den Ton an,[14] während sich im Norden der landschaftliche Gartenteil ohne die Lennéschen Sichten, Wegführungen und Baumsorten des 19. Jahrhunderts anschließt.

Unterschiedliche barocke französische Vorbilder von Jacques-François Blondel und Antoine-Joseph Dézallier bildeten den Fundus für die Neugestaltung der Kompartimente und Rasenbahnen des Parterres als Pastiche, ein nachahmender Ehrenerweis an den barocken Originalzustand. Im Westen des Schlosses wurde Sophie Charlottes Privatgarten in Anlehnung an einen Entwurf von Dézallier neu geschaffen. Der Springbrunnen von 1967/68 machte den Garten barocker, als er in Bezug auf sein unrealisiertes Wasserspiel je gewesen war. Die restaurierten Gartenskulpturen fanden neue Aufstellungen. Hinzu kamen neu geschaffene wie die Aluminiumputten der vier Jahreszeiten und der Elemente nach Vorbildern der KPM und die Eisenvasen von Harald Haacke (1924–2004) nach dem Knobelsdorff-Skizzenbuch auf der Balustrade am Teich. Die überkommenen Eisenbrücken wurden erneuert und neue Gartenzugänge geschaffen.

Rheinsberg

»Nun bin ich auf meinem Landsitz und genieße die ländlichen Freuden mit vollen Zügen.« Friedrich (II.) an seine Schwester Wilhelmine

Kronprinz Friedrich, der künftige König Friedrich II., erhielt 1734 von seinem Vater Friedrich Wilhelm I. Gut Rheinsberg zum Wohnsitz. Zusammen mit seiner Gemahlin Elisabeth Christine, die er 1733 geheiratet hatte, zog er zwei Jahre später in das Wasserschloß aus dem 16. Jahrhundert am Grienericksee. Das Schloß war von Johann Gottfried Kemmeter (gest. 1748), seit 1731 Baudirektor der kurmärkischen Kammer, barock umgebaut worden. Ab 1737 ließ Friedrich das Schloß durch Knobelsdorff weiter ausbauen sowie Nordflügel und Turm anfügen. Friedrich bestieg 1740 den Thron und schenkte Rheinsberg 1744 seinem Bruder Heinrich (1726–1802). Dieser bezog das Schloß 1752, nachdem er sich mit Wilhelmine von Hessen-Kassel vermählt und Friedrich ihm eine eigene Hofhaltung ermöglicht hatte. Von 1763 bis zu seinem Tod 1802 war Rheinsberg ständige Residenz von Heinrich.

Friedrichs Rheinsberg

Die Anlage des Rheinsberger Gartens begann 1734. Der Garten setzte sich anfangs aus einer rechteckigen Insel mit dem Schloßbau im Südosten des Grienericksees und dem Lustgarten im Süden zusammen. Den landschaftlichen Gegebenheiten angepaßt, schließt die Hauptallee des Rheinsberger Parks im rechten Winkel an die Ost–West-Ausrichtung des Schlosses an. Der Lustgarten liegt dem Mittelrisalit des Schloßseitenflügels gegenüber. Später wird Sanssouci diese neue Sprache der deaxialen Gartenerschließung fortsetzen. Der Garten der Kronprinzenzeit Friedrichs wurde von Knobelsdorff und Johann Samuel Sello (1715–1787) gestaltet, von etwa 1734 bis 1748 war dieser Leitender Gärtner in Rheinsberg. Das Inventar der Jahre 1746/47 beschreibt den Garten, Pläne fehlen.[15]

Flora und Pomona – Rheinsberg als Lust- und Nutzgarten

In Friedrichs Rheinsberg bildeten Nutz- und Lustgarten eine Einheit. So war es bereits im ersten von Friedrich geschaffenen Amalthea-Garten in Neuruppin (1732 bis 1736).[16] Und so wird es später auch in Sanssouci und Charlottenburg sein. Das Leitmotiv aller vier friderizianischen Gärten – »schön und nützlich« – formulieren die Göttinnen der Blüte und der Baumfrüchte, Flora und Pomona. Ihnen wurde ein zweifacher Auftritt gewährt: Sie standen am Eingang zur Stadt. Pomona ist erhalten, Flora gibt es seit 1899 nicht mehr. Und sie stehen noch heute seitens des Gartenportals an der von der Landstraße nach Ruppin im Süden zum Schloß führenden Allee. Das Gartenportal wurde 1741 von Knobelsdorff und Friedrich Christian Glume (1714–1752) geschaffen.

Die 300 m lange, von Linden- und Fichtendoppelreihen im Wechsel gesäumte Allee verbreitert sich an ihrem nördlichen Ende zum Oval des Parterres der Orangerie. Zu diesem tiefer gelegenen, zur Aufstellung von Pomeranzen nutzbaren Luststück geleitet eine von Sphingen flankierte Treppe. Sie wurde von Knobelsdorff entworfen und von Glume ausgeführt. Die Figurengruppen *Raub der Proserpina* und *Apoll und Daphne* von Glume akzentuieren das Parterre auf der nördlichen, dem Schloß zugewandten Seite. Regelmäßig geformte Gartenräume östlich und westlich der Hauptallee beherbergten Pfirsich-, Kirsch-, Apfel-, Birnen- und Pflaumenbäume. Vom Orangenhaus zeugt der zentralbauartige Architekturtorso seines Mittelpavillons. 1747 war es noch im Bau, 1753 wurden die begonnenen Flügel abgerissen. Durch den Mittelpavillon führt eine Querallee, die den Hauptweg schneidet.

Um bereits möglichst früh im Jahr Früchte ernten zu können, waren Treibhäuser und Orangeriegebäude auch

Margarete Kühn, director of palaces, planned the reconstruction of the royal garden memorial after 1950. Up to the pond, the predominant style of the garden is still the Baroque,[14] while in the north, the adjacent landscape part of the garden no longer has the 19th-century perspectives of Lenné, or the former paths and tree varieties.

Various French Baroque models by Jacques-François Blondel and Antoine-Joseph Dézallier formed the basis for the redesign of the compartments and strips of lawn of the *parterres* as a pastiche, an imitative homage to the original Baroque condition. West of the palace, Sophia Charlotte's private garden was recreated, modeled after a design by Dézallier. The 1967/68 fountain made the garden more Baroque than it had ever been before, since the waterworks of the original design had not been implemented. The restored garden sculptures were put back in the park. Added to these were new statues, such as the aluminium putti of the four seasons and of the elements, based on models of the KPM (Royal Porcelain Factory) and the cast-iron vases of Harald Haacke (1924–2004), based on the Knobelsdorff sketchbook, on the balustrade by the pond. The traditional cast-iron bridges were renovated and new access paths to the garden were created.

Rheinsberg

»Now I am at my country seat enjoying the rural pleasures to the full.« Frederick (II) to his sister Wilhelmina

Crown Prince Frederick, the future King Frederick II, received Gut Rheinsberg from his father Frederick William I as his residence in 1734. Together with his wife Elisabeth Christine, whom he had married in 1733, he moved into the moated 16th-century castle by Grienericksee two years later. The castle had been reconstructed in the Baroque style by Johann Gottfried Kemmeter (d. in 1748), director of building of the Chamber of Kurmark Brandenburg since 1731. As of 1737 Frederick had the palace further converted by Knobelsdorff, also adding the north wing and tower. In 1740 Frederick ascended the throne and, in 1744, gave Rheinsberg to his brother Henry (1726–1802). The latter moved into the palace in 1752 after he had married Wilhelmina of Hessen-Kassel and Frederick had made it possible for him to maintain his own court. From 1763 until his death in 1802 Rheinsberg was Henry's permanent residence.

Frederick's Rheinsberg

The formation of the Rheinsberg garden began in 1734. Initially the garden consisted of a rectangular island with the castle on the southeast shore of Grienericksee, and the pleasure garden in the south. Adapted to the situation of the landscape, the main avenue of the Rheinsberg park connects with the east–west alignment of the palace at a right angle. The pleasure garden is located opposite the central projection of the side wing of the palace. Later, Sanssouci will continue this new idiom of the non-axial development of the garden. The garden of the period when Frederick was crown prince was created by Knobelsdorff and Johann Samuel Sello (1715 to 1787); the latter was head gardener in Rheinsberg from roughly 1734 until 1748. The inventory of 1746/47 describes the garden, but there are no plans.[15]

Flora and Pomona – Rheinsberg, a garden combining pleasure and usefulness

In Frederick's Rheinsberg, the vegetable garden and pleasure garden were an integrated whole. This had already been true of the first garden created by Frederick, the Amalthea Garden in Neuruppin (1732–36).[16] And it would later be true of Sanssouci and Charlottenburg as well. This was the leitmotif of all four of Frederick's gardens – »beautiful and useful« – expressed by the goddesses of flowers and fruit trees, Flora and Pomona. They appeared twice: They stood at the entrance to the city (Pomona is still there, while Flora has been gone since 1899), and they still stand on the sides of the garden portal near the avenue that leads from the highway to Ruppin in the south to the palace. The portal was created in 1741 by Knobelsdorff and Friedrich Christian Glume (1714–1752).

The avenue, 300 m long and flanked by double rows of alternating linden and spruce trees, widens at its north end into the oval of the orangery *parterre*. Leading to this pleasance, which was located at a lower level and used for displaying orange trees, is a staircase flanked by sphinxes. It was designed by Knobelsdorff and implemented by Glume. The groups of figures Rape of Proserpina and Apollo and Daphne by Glume accentuate the *parterre* on the north side, which is turned toward the palace. Peach, cherry, apple, pear and plum trees grew in regularly shaped garden plots east and west of the main avenue. Of the orangery, the torso of its central pavilion, resembling the central building, still remains. In 1747 it was still being built, but in 1753 the wings that had been started were razed. A transverse avenue that intersects with the main road leads through the central pavilion.

In order to be able to harvest fruit as early as possible in the season, greenhouses and orangery buildings were also planned near the Ruppin road south of the main entrance. Grapes, peaches and apricots were grown against six espalier walls. Finally, beauty and usefulness were combined in the fruit-bearing and ornamental hedges that bordered the castle island: on the lake side, a beech hedge, interrupted in the middle by a gap that provided a view of the water. It stood between two chestnut trees planted by the Belville family, previous owners of the castle, and was accompanied by a row of plum trees. The bank of the tributary Rhin and the south moat of the castle were lined with plantings of currants and yews. Apple and pear trees formed small forests in the north and south as closely planted dwarf fruit trees, so-called Franzobst. Boxwood framed the main *parterre* on the lake side. The pleasance, which was relatively small since the lake was immediately next to it, was ornamented with regularly shaped beds of creeping vines and flowers.

Friedrichsruh – prerequisites for the Rococo in the era of Frederick

The symbols for rhetoric, music, painting and sculpture decorate the projecting entrance of the palace. Over the carriage entrance on the town side an inscription reads: »Friderico Tranquillitatem Colenti. MDCCXXXIX« (Property of Frederick, who cultivates tranquillity. 1739). Rheinsberg was not only a lovely locale for growing fruit but also the Friedrichsruh (Frederick's Rest) that followed the

an der Ruppiner Landstraße südlich des Haupteingangs geplant. An sechs Treibmauern wurden Wein, Pfirsiche und Aprikosen gezogen. Schönes und Nützliches verband sich schließlich in den Obst- und Zierhecken, die die Schloßinsel begrenzten: seeseitig eine mittig durch ein Sichtfenster zum Wasser hin unterbrochene Buchenhecke. Sie stand zwischen zwei Kastanien der Vorbesitzerfamilie Belville und wurde von einer Pflaumenbaumreihe begleitet. Das Ufer des Zuflusses Rhin und den südlichen Schloßgraben säumten Johannisbeer- und Taxuspflanzungen. Apfel- und Birnenbäume bildeten als eng stehendes Zwergobst, sogenanntes Franzobst, kleine Wälder im Norden und Süden. Buchsbaum faßte das seeseitige Hauptparterre. Das wegen des dicht daneben liegenden Sees relativ kleine Luststück ornamentierten regelmäßig geformte Ranken- und Blumenbeete.

Friedrichsruh – Voraussetzungen des friderizianischen Rokoko

Rhetorik, Musik, Malerei und Bildhauerei schmücken als Sinnbilder den Eingangsrisalit des Schlosses. Über der stadtseitigen Durchfahrt steht: »Friderico Tranquillitatem Colenti. MDCCXXXIX« (Friedrich zu eigen, der der Ruhe pflegt. 1739). Rheinsberg war nicht nur ein schöner Ort der Obsttreiberei, sondern das auf die Zeit der väterlichen Bevormundung und Zurechtweisung folgende Friedrichsruh des 20jährigen Kronprinzen.[17] Der heitere Überschwang dieser Jahre ist in dem von Friedrich Anfang 1740 skizzierten Monopteros spürbar (Abb. 12).

Auf seinem Dach stützt sich der dickbäuchige Gott des Weins halb liegend auf ein Faß. Mit der Rechten, die schwungvoll einen Pokal hebt, prostet er dem Betrachter zu. Der Bacchustempel sollte wohl östlich der Hauptallee aufgestellt werden, wurde aber nie ausgeführt.[18] In Sanssouci wird Friedrich das Bacchusthema erneut aufgreifen. Auch die Idee der muskulösen Hermen, die mit hochgereckten Armen das Tempeldach tragen, gefiel Friedrich offenbar so gut, daß er ihre Gestalt mit den Karyatiden der Gartenfassade von Schloß Sanssouci nachklingen läßt.

Lektüre und Komponieren, Austausch mit Gleichgesinnten, frühe Übungen als Bauherr und Gartengestalter bestimmten die Jahre des ruhigen Ausprobierens in Rheinsberg und wurden Lebensprogramm. Friedrichs Studium der Naturrechtslehre des Aufklärers Christian Wolff, *Vernünftige Gedanken von Gott, der Welt und der Seele des Menschen, auch allen Dingen überhaupt*, von 1719, führte zu eigenen Texten, wie dem Antimachiavell, *L'Antimachiavel, ou Examen du Prince de Machiavel*, von 1739/40. Friedrichs Korrespondenz mit François-Marie Arouet de Voltaire begann 1736. Der Bitte um Unterweisung und Gespräch, dem das in Briefen überlieferte, über mehr als 40 Jahre währende »epochale Zwiegespräch« der beiden folgte, entgegnete der Philosoph: »Die wirklich guten Könige sind nur die, welche wie Sie damit beginnen, sich zu bilden«.[19]

Die Schriften von Horaz, Lukrez und Cicero, die autobiographischen Gedanken von Marc Aurel und die zeitgenössischen Historiographien von Charles Rollin[20] und Montesquieu[21] formten Friedrichs teleologisches Bild der römischen Geschichte: Sie sei Beginn einer weltgeschichtlichen Entwicklung, die sich in einem *Grand Siècle* vollende. Der König gliederte seine Anstrengungen um den Aufstieg Preußens im Konzert der Mächte in diese Entwicklung ein.

»Verbesserungen des menschlichen Geistes in den Künsten und Wissenschaften«[22] gehörten zum königlichen Förderprogramm: »Kultur für den Staat und den Nachruhm«.[23] Rheinsberg bildete den Auftakt: Hiermit leiten Knobelsdorff, Antoine Pesne (1683–1757) und Glume als Baumeister, Bildnis- und Historienmaler sowie als Bildhauer – und vielleicht wichtiger noch: als Freunde – das friderizianische Rokoko ein.

Schauplatz ist die Landschaft der Mark Brandenburg: ihre bewaldeten Ebenen, Büsche, Laubbäume, Kiefern, leichten Anhöhen, ihre einfachen Bauerngehöfte, Dörfer und aufragenden Kirchtürme, die Oderniederung und die Seenlandschaft um Rheinsberg und Neuruppin im Norden. In zahlreichen Skizzen beschäftigte sich Knobelsdorff mit dieser Landschaft und schuf ein »Arkadien der Mark«.[24] Mit dem Blick des Landschaftsmalers hielt Knobelsdorff bereits um 1735 Schloß Rheinsberg vom Westufer des Grienericksees aus fest (Abb. 13). Die von der Hand Pesnes eingefügte friderizianische Hofgesellschaft belebt den Vordergrund.

Auch die Gestaltung der dem See zugewandten Seite von Schloß Rheinsberg ist einer malerisch-verklärten Annäherung an die Landschaft verpflichtet. Die Kolonnade, die Knobelsdorff zwischen das Rahmenwerk der Rundtürme spannte, verschleiert und öffnet wie ein Vorhang den Blick auf eine gemäldeartig in die Tiefe gestaffelte Szenerie. Vom schloßnahen Parterre über den Wasserspiegel bis hin zu den waldigen Höhen jenseits des Sees verliert sie mehr und mehr an Deutlichkeit. Das Erlebnis der märkischen Landschaft, dem Knobelsdorff in der Malerei folgt, wird mit der Kolonnade architektonisch-landschaftsgärtnerisch inszeniert.[25] Die Grundlage der solcherart arrangierten Gartenseite schuf Knobelsdorff mit der optisch wirksamen Erhebung der Schloßinsel über die Umgebung. Die Erhöhung der Insel und die Begradigung der mittelalterlichen, im Süden, Osten und Westen um die Insel führenden Gräben sowie der Mündung des von Süden einfließenden Rhin drängen die Insel wie eine Plattform tiefer in den See.

Im April 1737 kehrte Knobelsdorff von seiner Studienreise nach Italien zurück. Am Rheinsberger Gartenportal bringen die korinthischen Säulenpaare und klassisch gegliederten Gebälke römisch-antikes Formengut in die Mark. Aus der Kombination von Säulen und Gebälk sowie seitlich anschließenden Mauern schuf Knobelsdorff eine hoheitsvoll-elegante und zugleich intime Eröffnung des Gartenreichs. Zusammen mit dem auf leichter Anhöhe im Brennpunkt errichteten Obelisken und dem Vasen- und Figurenschmuck von Glume war diese Eröffnung so gelungen, daß beide Künstler die Portalfindung in Sanssouci wiederholen werden. Der Obelisk war zunächst aus Holz ausgeführt, 1761 dann in Stein, 1790 wurde er durch einen Wartturm ersetzt.

Glumes Kunst verdankt sich spätbarocker Tradition, sein Vater Johann Georg (1679–1765), seit 1736 Hofbildhauer, war Schüler von Schlüter. Eine Summe aus Antike und Barock sind die mit naturalistischem Reliefdetail reich verzierten Vasen, Flora und Pomona, die unter schwungvollem Gewand Spiel- und Standbein deutlich sichtbar werden lassen, sowie die aus Holz gearbeiteten Götterstatuen auf der Schloßbrücke und Glumes liebenswerte Putten,[26] von Speckfalten strotzend und voller Grübchen. »In der Note des Klassizismus im Rokoko mögen sich beide, Knobelsdorff und Glume, einig gewesen sein.«[27]

Pesnes Bilder sind geprägt von dessen Bewunderung für die Kunst von Antoine Watteau und seiner

12. Friedrich (II.), Bacchustempel in Rheinsberg, nicht verwirklichter Entwurf, Anfang 1740. Feder. (Hessische Hausstiftung, Archiv und Bibliothek Schloß Fasanerie Eichenzell – Reprographie aus: AKat. 1999 b.)
13. Georg Wenzeslaus von Knobelsdorff, Schloß Rheinsberg mit Böbereckensee, um 1737. Öl auf Leinwand. (SPSG, Schloß Rheinsberg.)

12. Friedrich (II.), Bacchus temple in Rheinsberg, unrealized draft, beginning of 1740. Pen. (Hessische Hausstiftung, Archiv und Bibliothek Schloß Fasanerie Eichenzell – reproduced from: AKat. 1999 b.)
13. Georg Wenzeslaus von Knobelsdorff, Schloß Rheinsberg with Böbereckensee, ca. 1737. Oil on canvas. (SPSG, Schloß Rheinsberg.)

period during which the 20-year-old crown prince was constantly belittled and reprimanded by his father.[17] The merry exuberance of these years is noticeable in the monopteros Frederick sketched in early 1740 (illus. 12).

On its roof the potbellied god of wine leans half recumbent against a barrel. With his right hand, which raises a goblet with a sweeping gesture, he toasts the onlooker. The temple of Bacchus was probably meant to be erected east of the main avenue but was never implemented.[18] In Sanssouci Frederick would once more take up the theme of Bacchus. Frederick obviously was so fond of the idea of muscular hermae supporting the temple roof with arms upraised that their figures are echoed in the caryatids of the garden façade of his Schloß Sanssouci.

Reading and composing, conversations with like-minded people, early practice as a builder and designer of gardens characterized the years during which Frederick peacefully tried out his ideas in Rheinsberg – ideas that became a programme for living. Frederick's studies of the doctrine of natural law of the Enlightenment philosopher Christian Wolff, *Vernünftige Gedanken von Gott, der Welt und der Seele des Menschen, auch allen Dingen überhaupt* (*Rational Thoughts on God, the World and the Soul of Man, and on All Things Whatsoever*), dated 1719, led to texts of his own, such as his Anti-Machiavelli, *L'Antimachiavel, ou Examen du Prince de Machiavel*, dated 1739/40. Frederick's correspondence with François-Marie Arouet de Voltaire began in 1736. To Frederick's request for instruction and conversation, followed by the two men's »epochal dialogue«, which has come down to us in letters and lasted more than 40 years, the philosopher responded: »The really good kings are only those who, like you, begin to educate themselves«.[19]

The writings of Horace, Lucretius and Cicero, the autobiographical reflections of Marcus Aurelius and the contemporary historiographies of Charles Rollin[20] and Montesquieu[21] formed Frederick's teleological view of Roman history: He believed it was the beginning of a development in world history that was being consummated in a Grand Siècle. The king felt that his efforts to bring about the rise of Prussia in the concert of powers were part of this development.

»Improvements of the human spirit in the arts and sciences«[22] were included in the royal promotional programme: »Culture for the state and posthumous fame«.[23] Rheinsberg was the prelude: With this project Knobelsdorff, Antoine Pesne (1683–1757) and Glume as builders, portrait and historical painters, and sculptors – and, perhaps more importantly, as friends – initiate the Fridertician Rococo.

The scene is the landscape of the Mark Brandenburg region: its wooded plains, bushes, deciduous trees, pines, gentle hills, its simple farmyards, villages and soaring church spires, the lowlands of the Oder River and the lake region around Rheinsberg and Neuruppin in the north. In numerous sketches Knobelsdorff depicted this landscape and created an »Arcadia of the Mark«.[24] With the eye of a landscape painter Knobelsdorff had already painted a view of Schloß Rheinsberg from the western shore of Grienericksee about 1735 (illus. 13). Members of Frederick's court, added to the painting by the hand of Pesne, make the foreground come to life.

The design of the side of Schloß Rheinsberg that is turned toward the lake is based on a picturesque and transfigured approach to the landscape. The colonnade that Knobelsdorff stretched into the framework of the round towers veils and reveals, like a curtain, the view of scenery graduated from front to back like a painting. From the *parterre* by the palace over the surface of the water to the wooded hills beyond the lake this scenery becomes less and less distinct. The experience of the landscape of Mark Brandenburg Knobelsdorff is looking for in his paintings is staged architectonically and also from a landscape gardener's point of view with the colonnade.[25] Knobelsdorff created the basis for the garden side arranged in this way by means of the visually effective raising of the castle island above its surroundings. The raising of the island and the straightening of the medieval moats that surrounded the island on the south, west and east sides, as well as of the mouth of the Rhin River, which flows into the lake from the south, push the island like a platform deeper into the lake.

In April 1737 Knobelsdorff returned from his study tour of Italy. At the entrance of the Rheinsberg grounds, the Corinthian pairs of columns and classically structured entablature bring ancient Roman forms to Mark Brandenburg. From a combination of columns and entablature, and adjoining lateral walls, Knobelsdorff created a majestic, elegant and at the same time intimate entrance to the garden realm. Together with the obelisk, placed at a focal point on a gentle slope, and Glume's ornamental vases and figures, this entrance was so successful that both artists would repeat the innovative portal in Sanssouci. The obelisk was initially made of wood, then, in 1761, of stone, and in 1790 it was replaced by a tower.

Glume's art comes out of the late Baroque tradition; his father Johann Georg (1679–1765), court sculptor from 1736 on, was a pupil of Schlüter. Here is the sum of classical antiquity and the Baroque: vases richly ornamented with naturalistic relief detail, Flora and Pomona, whose legs are clearly visible under their sweeping robes, and finally the wooden statues on the castle bridge and Glume's lovable putti,[26] chubby and full of dimples. »It is very likely that both Knobelsdorff and Glume were in agreement about preferring a touch of classicism in their Rococo.«[27]

Pesne's pictures are characterized by his admiration for the art of Antoine Watteau and his friendship with Nicolas Lancret, Watteau's most important successor. For the Rheinsberg interiors Pesne created bright mythological and allegorical paintings in light colours. Among his major works is a ceiling painting completed in 1740, *Apoll vertreibt die Finsternis* (*Apollo Drives Out Darkness*). Young Frederick owed his love of Watteau's art to Pesne. Using colours, Watteau records evanescent moods – serene, melancholy, dreamy – and soberly portrays mortality and loneliness. In the broadest sense, his art exactly portrays Frederick's constant conflict between power and morality, between being a king and the ethics of a philosopher. In Rheinsberg, Frederick writes to his sister Wilhelmina, he has two rooms with paintings »the majority of which are by Watteau or Lancret«.[28] Watteau's fêtes galantes decorated the walls in the palace interior, and in the garden they came to life.

Prince Henry's Rheinsberg

As an echo of his time as a crown prince in Rheinsberg, the opera house in Berlin, provisionally inaugurated on 7 December 1742, was King Frederick II's first represen-

Freundschaft zu Nicolas Lancret, Watteaus bedeutendstem Nachfolger. Für die Rheinsberger Innenräume schuf Pesne heitere mythologisch-allegorische Gemälde in lichten Farben. Zu seinen Hauptwerken zählt das 1740 vollendete Plafondgemälde *Apoll vertreibt die Finsternis*. Der junge Friedrich verdankte Pesne seine Vorliebe für Watteaus Kunst. Sie weiß flüchtige Stimmungen – heiter, melancholisch, träumerisch – und nüchterne Schilderung von Vergänglichkeit und Vereinsamung in Farben festzuhalten. In weitestem Sinne trifft sie Friedrichs beständigen Zwiespalt zwischen Macht und Moral, zwischen Königsein und Philosophenethos. Er habe in Rheinsberg zwei Zimmer mit Bildern, von denen »die Mehrzahl von Watteau oder Lancret« gemalt sei, schrieb Friedrich seiner Schwester Wilhelmine.[28] Watteaus *fêtes galantes* schmückten die Wände im Inneren des Schlosses, im Garten wurden sie lebendig.

Prinz Heinrichs Rheinsberg

Als Nachhall seiner Rheinsberger Kronprinzenzeit wurde am 7. Dezember 1742 mit dem Opernhaus in Berlin der erste Repräsentationsbau des Königs Friedrich II. und das erste Bauglied seines »Forum Fridericianum« provisorisch eingeweiht. Der Bau wurde 1741 bis 1743 errichtet und brannte 1843 ab. Wohl schon vor 1740 hatte Friedrich die zugrundeliegenden Baupläne Knobelsdorffs in Rheinsberg korrigiert. Zur Vollendung der Rheinsberger Gartenanlagen ließ seine Thronbesteigung keine Zeit mehr. Unter Prinz Heinrich vollzog sich der Übergang des kronprinzlichen Rokogartens zum frühen Landschaftsgarten. Heinrich respektierte aber weitgehend die friderizianischen Strukturen.[29]

Er konzentrierte sich auf die Einbeziehung der umliegenden Landschaft durch die westliche Erweiterung des Grundstücks jenseits des Grienericksees. Die Boberow-Kabeln, der Böbereckensee und das Gelände des späteren Boberow-Waldes wurden Teil des nun ausgedehnten Rheinsberger Gartenreichs. Auch die im Rheinsberger See gelegene Remusinsel ganz im Norden gehörte dazu, zu der bereits Friedrich gern Bootsfahrten unternommen hatte. Der mythologische Remus war der vermeintliche Gründer von Rheinsberg (auch: Remusberg).

Das im Westen vorgelagerte Schloßparterre wurde offener gegliedert, Boskette und Hecken entfernt. Statt dessen gab es zwei hölzerne Blumenkörbe, *corbeilles de fleurs*. Im zentralen Rondell kamen die von Heinrich beauftragten marmornen Bildwerke *Apoll* und die *Vier Elemente* des aus Carrara stammenden Giovanni Antonio Cybei (1706–1784) zur Aufstellung. Cybeis *Vier Jahreszeiten* stehen seit 1769 im Orangerierondell.[30] Im südlichen, jetzt als vertiefte Rasenstücke wie ein Boulingrin (oder: *bowling green*) angelegten Parterre standen die heute verschollenen Bildwerke von Christian Grunwald: *Venus, wie sie aus dem Bade steigt* sowie *Eine auf Knien liegende Figur, die durch ein Perspektiv sieht*. Nach dem Anbau zweier Pavillons an das Schloß 1786 ließ Heinrich einen gewundenen Pfad um die nun parterrelose Schloßinsel führen.

»Man schafft diesen Geschmack an Schnörkelei ab«

Ein bis heute erhaltenes sternförmiges Alleensystem im Boberow-Wald eröffnete Heinrichs landschaftsgärtnerische Arbeiten der Jahre 1753–64. Es sind dies acht Alleen, darunter die Vergil-Allee, die Allee zur Katakombe, die Warenthiner Allee, die Obelisk-Allee und die Meierei-Allee. Als optische Mittler zwischen dem Lustgarten des Schlosses und der freien Landschaft wurden Erdterrassen am südwestlichen Seeufer aufgeschüttet. Die Idee dazu stammte von Oberstallmeister Johann Georg von Reis(e)witz. Christian Friedrich Ekel hat sie 1762 ausgeführt. Auf den Wein- und Spalierobst tragenden Terrassen standen im Wechsel Vasen auf Postamenten und Fichten, sie ließen an die Weinbergterrassen des Bruders in Sanssouci denken. Von 1753 bis zum Beginn des Siebenjährigen Krieges 1756 arbeitete der Prinz eifrig selbst an den Gartenplanungen mit. Der Schriftsteller und seit 1748 Geheime Rat Jacob Friedrich von Bielfeld (1717–1770) leitete den Prinzen an. Hofgärtner Johann H. Müller (1748–1775) kümmerte sich um die Pflanzen. Bauleiter war Reis(e)witz, der ab 1757 als Intendant des Prinzen fungierte.

Gegen Ende der ersten Gestaltungsphase 1763 schrieb Bielfeld: »Der Garten ist sehr vergrößert worden, auch hat der Prinz ein Chinesisches Haus, eine Grotte am Ufer des Sees (1753) und eine Kolonnade, die einen Eiskeller bedeckt.«[31] Die Kolonnade von 1753 war Teil eines nicht erhaltenen, künstlichen Ruinenensembles. Zu den abbröckelnden Säulen gehörten das Remusgrab als Rundtempelruine mit einer Urne sowie ein 1759 von Johann Gottfried Büring (1723– nach 1788) entworfener, 1761 von Baurat Friedel ausgeführter Monopteros.

Dem wohl bereits 1753/54 begonnenen ersten Chinesischen Haus auf einem Hügel im äußersten Südosten der Rheinsberger Anlage folgten im Laufe der Zeit weitere asiatisch-exotische Architekturen, von denen keine überdauert hat. Heinrich erneuerte und vergrößerte 1753 Friedrichs verfallenes Treillagekabinett im Boberow am Ufer des Sees und errichtete nahebei eine heute verlorene Einsiedelei.

»Man schafft diesen Geschmack an Schnörkelei ab, man findet ihn nur noch bei den Kaufleuten und in den Gärten der alten Zeit«,[32] wird Heinrich am 12. September 1768 seinem Bruder Friedrich schreiben. Zu Beginn seiner Hinwendung zur neuen Gartenkunst ließ Heinrich Grotte, Ruine, Tempel, Eremitage und chinoise Bauten zu den abwechslungsreich kostümierten Akteuren seiner dreidimensionalen Landschaftsbühne werden. Musterbücher boten einen reichen Fundus solch dekorativer Kleinarchitekturen, mit denen es gelang, geheimnis- und gemütvolle, antik-zivilisatorische und exotische Gartenbilder im Einklang mit der Natur zu arrangieren. Die Rheinsberger »ornamental architecture« wurde dabei wohl ebenso von Bielfelds Begegnung mit dem neuen Gartenstil während seiner Englandreise 1735 inspiriert, wie sie sich mit Heinrichs Theaterleidenschaft traf.

Theater

Mit dem Heckentheater von 1753/54 setzte Heinrich diesem ihm liebsten Zeitvertreib ein Denkmal. Noch heute wird es bespielt. Hecken formen die natürliche Kulisse der Bühne mit Orchestergraben. Den geböschten Zuschauerraum in Hufeisenform hinterfängt ein mit Jungfernrebe und Reseda berankter Bogengang.

tational building and the first architectural structure of his »Forum Fridericianum«. The opera house was erected in 1741–43 and burned down in 1843. Probably already before 1740, in Rheinsberg, Frederick had corrected Knobelsdorff's architect's plans for the building. His ascension to the throne left him no time to complete the Rheinsberg grounds. It was under Prince Henry that the transition from the crown prince's Rococo garden to the early landscape garden took place. For the most part, though, Henry respected the Fridericiarn structures.[29]

He concentrated on integrating the surrounding landscape in the palace grounds by expanding the property in the west beyond Grienericksee. The Boberow-Kabeln, Böbereckensee and the terrain of the later Boberow Forest became part of the extended Rheinsberg garden realm. The Remusinsel, also located in Rheinsberg Lake, all the way north, was part of it as well. Frederick, too, had enjoyed boat rides to the island. The alleged founder of Rheinsberg (also known as Remusberg) was the mythological figure Remus.

The *parterre* on the west side of the palace was more openly structured, with the bosquets and hedges removed. In their place there were two wooden flower baskets, *corbeilles de fleurs*. In the central rondel were placed the marble sculptures commissioned by Henry, *Apoll und die Vier Elemente* (*Apollo and the Four Elements*), by Giovanni Antonio Cybei (1706–1784), who came from Carrara. Cybei's *Vier Jahreszeiten* (*Four Seasons*) have been standing in the orangery rondel since 1769.[30] In the south *parterre*, which is now laid out as sunken patches of grass like a bowling green, stood the now lost sculptures of Christian Grunwald: *Venus, wie sie aus dem Bade steigt* (*Venus Rising from Her Bath*) and *Eine auf Knien liegende Figur, die durch ein Perspektiv sieht* (*A Kneeling Figure Looking through a Telescope*). After adding two pavilions to the palace in 1786, Henry had a winding path laid out around the now *parterre*-less palace island.

»People are losing their taste for fancy curlicues«

A star-shaped system of avenues preserved to this day in the Boberow Forest was the first of Henry's landscape-gardening projects during the years 1753–64. There are a total of eight avenues, including Virgil Avenue, the Avenue to the Catacomb, Warenthin Avenue, Obelisk Avenue and Dairy Farm Avenue. As visual mediators between the castle's pleasance and the open landscape, earth terraces were banked on the southwest shore of the lake. The idea for this came from head equerry Johann Georg von Reis(e)witz. Christian Friedrich Ekel carried out the project in 1762. On the terraces where grapevines and espaliered fruit trees were grown, stood vases on pedestals alternating with spruce trees, reminding Henry of his brother's vineyard terraces in Sanssouci. From 1753 until the beginning of the Seven Years' War in 1756, the prince himself enthusiastically joined in planning the garden. The writer and, since 1748, privy councillor Jacob Friedrich von Bielfeld (1717 to 1770) instructed the prince. Court gardener Johann H. Müller (1748–1775) took care of the plants. The construction supervisor was Reis(e)witz, who from 1757 on acted as the prince's intendant.

Toward the end of the first phase of development, in 1763, Bielfeld wrote: »The garden has greatly increased in size, and the prince also has a Chinese house, a grotto on the lakeshore (1753) and a colonnade that conceals an ice cellar.«[31] The 1753 colonnade was part of an artificial collection of ruins that no longer exists. Among the crumbling columns was the grave of Remus, the ruin of a round temple with an urn, and a monopteros designed in 1759 by Johann Gottfried Büring (1723–after 1788) and built in 1761 by architect Friedel.

The first Chinese house, probably begun as early as 1753/54, on a hill in the furthermost southeastern part of the Rheinsberg grounds, was followed over time by other Asiatic, exotic structures, none of which has survived. In 1753 Henry renovated and enlarged Frederick's dilapidated latticework gallery in Boberow Forest on the shore of the lake, building a hermitage nearby that no longer exists.

»People are losing their taste for fancy curlicues; now you only find that in the houses of tradesmen and in old-time gardens«,[32] Henry would write to his brother Frederick on 12 September 1768. When he first became enamoured of the new garden design, Henry included a grotto, ruin, temple, hermitage and Chinese-style buildings – a motley crew of actors – on the stage of his three-dimensional landscape. Books of samples offered a rich treasure trove of decorative mini-architecture by means of which one could arrange, in harmony with nature, garden scenes that were full of mystery and feeling, classically civilising and exotic. Probably the Rheinsberg »ornamental architecture« was not only inspired by Bielfeld's encounter with the new style in gardens during his journey to England in 1735 but also coincided with Henry's passion for the theatre.

Theatre

With the hedge theatre, in 1753/54, Henry created a memorial to his favourite pastime. The theatre is still in use today. Hedges form the natural backdrop of the stage, which has an orchestra pit. The sloping horseshoe-shaped amphitheatre is framed by an arcade overgrown with Virginia creeper and mignonettes.

As soon as Henry was able to keep his own court, he had established an orchestra, and later he founded his own French theatre. The repertoire included divertissements, ballets, tragedies, comedies, lyrical dramas and operas. Henry acted himself, as a poet, artistic director and performer. Just as his garden realm followed the fashion of contemporary English landscape gardens, his theatre practice followed the development introduced by Christoph Willibald Gluck, modern stage music that was intended to be natural. Ceremonial posturing and declamatory recitation gave way to a performance style based on actual speech and facial expressions. In Rheinsberg, pastoral idylls were presented; the passions and blows of fate that affected lower middle-class lives became subjects for the stage, and middle-class audience members were just as welcome as the aristocracy.

Against the natural landscape scenery of Boberow Forest that had gradually been formed into a *ferme ornée* or ornamental farm, third estate and members of the court alike were invited to boisterous »farmyard« entertainments. As in the fêtes champêtres shown in the paintings in the anteroom of the Rheinsberg hall of mirrors, which was dedicated to music, the assembled guests disported themselves strolling about and amusing themselves to the sound of flutes, shawms and

Sobald Heinrich seinen eigenen Hof halten konnte, etablierte er eine Kapelle, der später ein eigenes französisches Theater folgte. Zum Repertoire gehörten Divertissements, Ballette, Tragödien, Komödien, Singspiele und Opern. Heinrich agierte selbst, als Dichter, Intendant und Schauspieler. So wie sein Gartenreich der Strömung des zeitgenössischen englischen Landschaftsgartens nachging, folgte seine Theaterpraxis der von Christoph Willibald Gluck eingeleiteten Entwicklung hin zu einer modernen, an der Natürlichkeit orientierten Bühnenmusik. Zeremonialposen und Deklamation wichen einem der wirklichen Sprache und Mimik verpflichteten Aufführungsstil. In Rheinsberg wurden Schäferidyllen dargeboten, Leidenschaften und Schicksalsschläge von Kleinbürgern zu Themen der Bühne, und die Bürgerschicht war als Zuschauer ebenso willkommen wie der Adel.

In den natürlichen, allmählich zu einer Zierfarm geformten Landschaftskulissen des Boberow waren dritter Stand und Hofstaat gleichfalls zu den ausgelassenen »Bauernwirtschaften« geladen. Ähnlich den *fêtes champêtres*, wie sie die Malereien im Vorzimmer zum der Musik geweihten Rheinsberger Spiegelsaal zeigen, erging sich die Gesellschaft bei Flöten-, Schalmeien- und Oboentönen in Spaziergängen und Belustigungen. Man trug zu diesem Anlaß Bauernhabit. Dem närrisch-pastoralen Treiben standen die barocken Rheinsberger Prunkdarbietungen gegenüber, die die legendären Gartenfeste des Sonnenkönigs Ludwigs XIV. wiederholten.

Feldherrenstolz

Mit der Heimkehr Prinz Heinrichs nach dem Frieden von Hubertusburg begann 1763 die zweite Phase der persönlich begleiteten intensiven Gartengestaltung. Heinrich war stolz auf seine Karriere als Feldherr, die mit seinem Oberbefehl über die preußischen Truppen im besetzten Kurfürstentum Sachsen 1758 ihren Anfang genommen hatte. Diesem Stolz verlieh er im Jahr 1765 mit der panoramaartigen Aufstellung ephemerer Siegeszeichenstaffagen Ausdruck – Staffagen, die Carl Friedrich Fechhelm (1723–1785) aus Holz und Malerei schuf. Es waren dies eine Trajanssäule, wohl mit Reliefs der dakischen kaiserlichen Feldzüge, ein Konstantinsbogen (nach Jean Barbault), eine römische Säule mit Kompositkapitell und schließlich Ruinen des Concordiatempels. All diese Staffagen konnten von der Schloßkolonnade aus auf der anderen Uferseite von den Erdterrassen bis hin zu den Höhenzügen der Boberow-Kabeln gesehen werden.

Im Zuge der Umformungen der Boberow-Kabeln zu einer *ferme ornée* mit Küchengärten wurde die auf eine Backsteinmauer aufgebrachte Monumentalmalerei des Concordiatempels der Meierei vorgeblendet, die 1766 von Kammerdirektor Hoffmann erbaut worden war. Gleichsam als Link zu den Siegesstaffagen nach römischen Denkmälern folgte 1771 oberhalb des Böbereckensees das nicht erhaltene Grabmal des römischen Dichters Vergil – ein hölzernes Aussichtsmonument in Form einer abgestuften Pyramide auf Kegelstumpf.

Karl Wilhelm Hennert

Karl Wilhelm Hennert (1739–1800), 1768 als Intendant des Schlosses eingesetzt, wirkte maßgeblich bis 1784 auf die Gestaltung des Rheinsberger Gartenreichs ein. Ekel und 1798 Johann Georg Wilhelm Steinert folgten ihm nach.[33] Den Forstmann und Leutnant der preußischen Artillerie Hennert hatte sein Bruder Johann Friedrich, Mathematiker und Astronom in Utrecht, in Ingenieurskunst und Mathematik eingewiesen. Kriegs- und Landbaukunst, Artilleriekenntnisse und Zeichnen vervollständigten seine Ausbildung, die es ihm ermöglichte, Gartenbauwerke zu entwerfen oder nach den prinzlichen Vorstellungen und Vorlagen auszuführen.

Hennert schreibt 1786: »Den Charakter, den die Gegend hat, oder den sie anzunehmen fähig ist, richtig zu bestimmen: ist die erste und vornehmste Regel seiner Kunst«.[34] Damit räumt er der freien Naturentfaltung den ersten Platz vor künstlicher Überformung ein. Er formuliert auf das knappste den Gedanken, dem sich die Dichter, Philosophen und Naturwissenschaftler verschrieben hatten, die die Entwicklung des Landschaftsgartens begleiteten: Salomon Geßner (1730–1788), dessen bukolisch gefärbte Prosastücke *Idyllen* 1756 anonym in Zürich erschienen, Jean-Jacques Rousseau (1712–1778), dessen Briefroman *La Nouvelle Héloïse* das Ideal der Harmonie von Kultur und Natur beschreibt, ebenso Albrecht von Haller (1708–1778) mit seinem philosophischen Lehrgedicht »Die Alpen« von 1732 und Johann Georg Sulzer (1720–1779), in dessen *Allgemeine Theorie der Schönen Künste* die Natur Lehrmeisterin der Gefühle und des Verstandes ist. Dazu gehört auch Christian Carl Lorenz Hirschfeld (1742–1792), der den englischen Gartenstil in Deutschland durchsetzen will und 1775 seine erste, als Streitschrift formulierte *Theorie der Gartenkunst* vorlegte. Auch laut Hirschfeld sind die natürlichen Gegebenheiten Voraussetzung für die Anlage eines Gartens. Es ist der Begriff der Schicklichkeit, das Decorum des Architekturtheoretikers Vitruv, den Hirschfeld auf den der jeweiligen landschaftlichen Situation innewohnenden Charakter anwendet, in welcher eine Gartenszene ausgeführt werden soll.

Die Darstellung der Natur nimmt bei Ekels Rheinsberg-Serie, 1773 von Heinrich beauftragt, den größten Raum ein. 1778 wurde Hennerts Beschreibung der Rheinsberger Residenz veröffentlicht.[35] In die Zeit von Hennerts Wirken im Park fielen Heinrichs Reise in die Niederlande vom 4. August bis Ende Oktober 1768 und sein Sommeraufenthalt 1770 bei seiner Schwester Königin Luise Ulrike von Schweden. Er erkundete planmäßig die Gartenkunst der niederländischen Landgüter und suchte alle als innovativ bekannten Anlagen auf. Der Zauber des Lustgartens, der Chinoiserien und des Bosketts »Stjärnan« (Stern) in Drottningholm erschlossen sich ihm im Zuge der für ihn veranstalteten Festlichkeiten, bei Theater und Illuminationsspektakeln. Im Garten von Schloß Karlberg in Stockholm wurde eigens aus Anlaß des Maskenballs für Prinz Heinrich ein grandioser Festpavillon errichtet, dessen Dach auf Palmstämmen ruhte, von denen Kandelaber hingen.[36]

Hennert schuf 1768 die Einsiedelei als Endpunkt der großen Querallee, nach einer Idee von Heinrich. Sie wurde 1790 durch den Nachbau der berühmten Egeriagrotte aus dem 2. Jahrhundert in Rom ersetzt, hier wie dort mit lagernder Nymphe, die aber nicht erhalten ist.

Um 1800

Nach 1789 erfolgte die letzte Phase der Rheinsberger Gartengestaltung. In der Zwischenzeit hatte Heinrich zwei Reisen nach Frankreich im Sommer und Herbst

oboes. Peasant costumes were worn on such occasions. In contrast to these droll pastoral carryings-on, the Baroque pomp and pageantry of Rheinsberg replicated the legendary garden festivals of the Sun King, Louis XIV.

A proud commander

Once Prince Henry returned home after the Peace of Hubertusburg, the second phase of intensive landscape design, which he personally supervised, began in 1763. Henry was proud of his career as a commander, which had begun with his supreme command over the Prussian troops in the occupied Electorate of Saxony in 1758. He expressed this pride in 1765 by putting up a panorama-like display of ephemeral victory trophies – created by Carl Friedrich Fechhelm (1723–1785) from wood and painting. They consisted of a Trajan Column, possibly with reliefs of the Dacian imperial campaigns, an Arch of Constantine (after Jean Barbault), a Roman Column with a composite capital, and finally ruins of the Concordia Temple. All these could be seen from the palace colonnade on the other shore, from the earth terraces all the way to the hills of the Boberow-Kabeln.

In the course of transforming the Boberow-Kabeln into an »ornamented farm«, a *ferme ornée*, with kitchen gardens, a monumental depiction of the Concordia Temple was painted on a brick wall to conceal the dairy farm that had been built in 1766 by Kammerdirektor Hoffmann. As a kind of link to the victory display based on Roman monuments, there followed, in 1771, above Böbereckensee, the no longer extant tomb of the Roman poet Virgil – a wooden lookout monument in the form of a stepped pyramid on the frustum of a cone.

Karl Wilhelm Hennert

Karl Wilhelm Hennert (1739–1800), appointed to the post of palace intendant in 1768, substantially influenced the design of the Rheinsberg garden realm up to 1784. Ekel and, in 1798, Johann Georg Wilhelm Steinert were his successors.[33] It was his brother Johann Friedrich, a mathematician and astronomer in Utrecht, who had introduced the forester and lieutenant of the Prussian artillery Hennert to engineering and mathematics. The art of warfare and agriculture, and a knowledge of artillery and drawing completed his education, which made it possible for him to design garden buildings or to build them in accordance with the prince's ideas and drafts.

Hennert writes in 1786: »To determine correctly the character that a region has or is capable of assuming is the first and foremost rule of one's art«.[34] He thus ranks the free unfolding of nature above its artificial modification. He puts in a nutshell the idea advocated by the poets, philosophers and natural scientists who had a part in the development of the landscape garden: Salomon Geßner (1730–1788), whose bucolically tinged prose pieces *Idyllen* appeared anonymously in Zurich in 1756, Jean-Jacques Rousseau (1712–1778), whose epistolary novel *La Nouvelle Héloïse* describes the ideal of the harmony of culture and nature, as well as Albrecht von Haller (1708–1778) with his philosophical didactic poem »Die Alpen«, dated 1732, and Johann Georg Sulzer (1720 to 1779), in whose *Allgemeine Theorie der Schönen Künste* Nature is the teacher of one's feelings and intellect. Among them also is Christian Carl Lorenz Hirschfeld (1742–1792), who wishes to gain acceptance for the style of English landscape parks in Germany and who in 1775 presented his first *Theorie der Gartenkunst* in the form of a polemic pamphlet. Hirschfeld, too, believes that natural conditions must be taken into account when laying out a garden. He applies the concept of seemliness, of decorousness advocated by the architectural theoretician Vitruvius to the character inherent in the specific situation in which a garden scene is to be implemented.

The depiction of nature is predominant in Ekel's Rheinsberg series, commissioned in 1773 by Henry. Hennert's description of the Rheinsberg residence was published in 1778.[35] It was during the period when Hennert was working in the park that Henry's journey to the Netherlands from 4 August until the end of October 1768 and his summer stay in 1770 with his sister Queen Louise Ulrike of Sweden took place. He methodically researched the garden art of Netherlands country estates and visited all parks and gardens known to be innovative. He discovered the magic of the pleasance, the chinoiseries and the *bosquet* »Stjärnan« (Star) in Drottningholm in the course of festivities, theatre and illumination entertainments organized in his honour. In the garden of Karlberg Palace in Stockholm a magnificent festival pavilion was erected specially for the occasion of the masked ball held for Prince Henry. Its roof rested on the trunks of palm trees from which candelabra were suspended.[36]

In 1768 Hennert created the Hermitage as the end point of the large transverse avenue, based on an idea of Henry's. It was replaced in 1790 by a copy of the renowned Egeria Grotto from 2nd-century Rome; both the original and the copy had a recumbent nymph, which has, however, not been preserved.

Ca. 1800

After 1789 came the last phase of the Rheinsberg garden landscaping. In the meantime Henry had undertaken two journeys to France in the summer and autumn of 1784 and in the winter of 1788/89. His letters do not indicate that he visited any gardens. Henry was now interested in conversation, theatre or Parisian porcelain manufacture.[37] Whatever the case may be, the prince might have seen the Anglo-Chinese park Désert de Retz in Chambourcy with its bizarre ornamental buildings for François Nicolas Henri Racine de Monville, and the Parisian Parc Monceau, inspired by England and dubbed the »Folie de Chartres«, created by Louis-Philippe-Joseph, Duke of Orléans and Chartres.

The plan by Johann Georg Wilhelm Steinert, son of head gardener Johannes Steinert, gives a detailed list of the vegetation and furnishings of Rheinsberg circa 1800 (illus. 14). The Boberow-Kabeln were landscaped. Once more the garden became a stage for Henry. Using art as a means, he faced personal traumas and conveyed political messages to posterity: As a younger son, Henry had always been denied the right to participate actively in affairs of state. He felt his royal brother's military intervention, his »wildcat attack«[38] of Silesia, was unjust and unnecessary. He believed Frederick's conduct of the war was unsatisfactory. Frederick never promoted him to the rank of field marshal he so desired – in spite of the fact that he recognized Henry's military achievements.[39]

1784 sowie im Winter 1788/89 unternommen. Seine Briefe belegen keinen Besuch von Gärten. Heinrich interessierten jetzt Konversation, Theater oder die Pariser Porzellanmanufaktur.[37] Immerhin könnte der Prinz den anglo-chinoisen Park Désert de Retz in Chambourcy mit seinen bizarren Zierbauten für François Nicolas Henri Racine de Monville gesehen haben und den von England inspirierten, als »Folie de Chartres« betitelten Pariser Garten Monceau von Louis-Philippe-Joseph, Herzog von Orléans und Chartres.

Der Plan von Johann Georg Wilhelm Steinert, Sohn des Obergärtners Johannes Steinert, gibt detailliert Vegetation und Möblierung von Rheinsberg um 1800 wieder (Abb. 14). Die Boberow-Kabeln wurden verlandschaftet. Noch einmal wurde für Heinrich der Garten zur Bühne. Mit Mitteln der Kunst begegnete er persönlichen Traumata und übermittelte der Nachwelt politische Botschaften: Als Nachgeborenem war es Heinrich stets verwehrt gewesen, sich aktiv in die Staatsgeschäfte einzubringen. Als ungerecht und unnötig empfand er den militärischen Zugriff des königlichen Bruders, seinen »Raubtiersprung«[38] auf Schlesien. Seine Kriegsführung hielt er für mangelhaft. Nie erhob ihn Friedrich in den so begehrten Rang des Feldmarschalls – trotz aller Anerkennung seiner militärischen Leistungen.[39]

Der Tempel für teure Verstorbene von 1790, auch als Katakombe bezeichnet und der an der Stelle der Trajanssäule 1791 errichtete Obelisk, den Georg Friedrich Boumann d. J. (1737–1812) entwarf, sind den nach Heinrichs Meinung zu Unrecht mißachteten Helden des Siebenjährigen Krieges gewidmet. Mit dem Obelisken nimmt Heinrich »eine gewisse Deutungshoheit über die Erinnerung an den Siebenjährigen Krieg für sich in Anspruch.«[40] (Abb. 15) Seine Einweihung wurde als Volksfest und militärische Feier zugleich zelebriert. »Ich habe das Denkmal zu Ehren meines verstorbenen Bruders und der ganzen preußischen Armee fertig gestellt«[41] – unter Auslassung all jener von Friedrich II. ernannten Marschälle!

Der geliebte Bruder August Wilhelm war 1757 von Friedrich in öffentlicher Ungnade von seiner Stellung als Infanteriegeneral der preußischen Armee entlassen worden. Er hatte sich einer militärischen Fehleinschätzung schuldig gemacht, die die Bombardierung Zittaus in Sachsen durch österreichische Truppen nach sich gezogen hatte. Heinrich machte die Kränkung für den Tod des Bruders im darauffolgenden Jahr verantwortlich und ließ 1758 westlich des Parterres der Orangerie inmitten der Lichtung einer Tannen- und Taxuspflanzung eine symbolische Ascheurne und eine Gedenkbüste aufstellen.[42]

Als letzten Akt in seinem Rheinsberger Gartenreich verfügte Heinrich, in einer Grabpyramide bestattet zu werden. Das von ihm gewählte Bild an ausgesuchtem Ort ist derart eindeutig, daß es geradezu mustergültig die Praxis der Landschaftsgärtnerei vorführt, Vorstellungsbilder zu kreieren, die von der Einbildungskraft des Betrachters mit Bedeutung aufgefüllt werden. Ohne Spitze sei die Pyramide an Stelle einer Schaukel zwischen Heckentheater und Hauptallee zu plazieren: ein den statisch-exakten Gesetzen der Geometrie folgendes Monument, das in seinem gewollten Mangel auf das Zeitliche und Unzulängliche allen Seins anspielt, statt des kindlichen Spielwerks, an dessen flüchtig-elegantem Schwung sich eine leichtlebige Adelsgesellschaft vergnügte. Die Pyramide wurde von Johann Georg Wilhelm Steinert 1802 ausgeführt.[43]

1802–13 gehörte Rheinsberg dem Bruder Heinrichs, Prinz Ferdinand und bis zu dessen Tod 1843 seinem Sohn, Prinz August. Im 19. Jahrhundert erfolgten keine größeren Umformungen. 1951 ging Rheinsberg von der Verwaltung der Staatlichen Schlösser und Gärten Potsdam-Sanssouci an die Sozialversicherung des Landes Brandenburg und war 1952–89 Sanatorium. Ab 1960 erfolgten denkmalpflegerische Maßnahmen, die nach der Übernahme durch die Stiftung Preußische Schlösser und Gärten Berlin-Brandenburg 1994 bis heute fortgesetzt werden.

Das friderizianische Sanssouci

»Ich betätige mich auch in der Gärtnerei.« Friedrich (II.) an seine Schwester Wilhelmine, 1735

Als geradezu imperialen Auftakt kündigt das stadtseitige Haupttor den königlichen Garten Sanssouci an, der ab 1744 für Friedrich II. angelegt wurde: gebildet von je vier korinthischen Säulen mit Gebälk, den Grundelementen antiker Baukunst (Abb. 16). Blumen-, Obst und Gartengerät ornamentieren den Fries und die bekrönenden Vasen und stimmen auf den Eintritt in das königliche Gartenreich ein. Halbrund geschwungene Mauern, die außen ein Graben begleitete, leiten in Verlängerung der Säulensockel auf die von Ost nach West verlaufende Hauptallee des friderizianischen Parks. Im Eröffnungsraum mit seinem schmückenden Rasenparterre zeigen sich zu Seiten der Torpfeiler Skulpturen, die Göttinnen der Blüte und der Baumfrüchte: Flora präsentiert im geschürzten Gewand ihre Blumen, Pomona hält ihr gefülltes Horn. An den acht auf der Mauer plazierten Vasen setzt sich die Blumen- und Früchtezier fort, bis die beiden Nymphen, die auf den Voluten am Ende der Mauer lagern, den von der Stadt her Kommenden in den Garten einlassen.

Knobelsdorff entwarf das Tor 1747. Nach dem Obelisken, der im Folgejahr von Steinmetz Johann Christian Angermann östlich von ihm aufgestellt wurde, heißt es Obeliskportal. In seiner Übereckstellung vermittelt der Obelisk zwischen Garten und Stadt. Mit dem Gartenportal verbanden ihn strahlenförmig gepflanzte Lindenreihen. Friedrich Christian Glume führte das Portal aus und schuf die Vasen sowie Flora und Pomona, die heute durch Kopien von 1963 und 1935 ersetzt sind.

Entlang des Hauptwegs reiht sich Rondell an Rondell, in Größe und Lage jeweils auf die ihnen zugeordnete Architektur abgestimmt. Sie bilden eine Folge verschieden gestalteter Gartenräume, die sich von der lichten Osthälfte, dem als erster Gartenteil 1744–50 angelegten Lustgartenbereich, zur etappenweise 1751–54 und 1763–70 ausgeführten baumreichen Westhälfte, dem »Rehgarten«, zieht. Vielfältig ist das Schmuckrepertoire aus Bassins und Fontänen, ebenerdigen Luststücken (Parterres), Blumenrabatten (*plates-bandes de fleurs*), heckengerahmten Obstquartieren, ornamental geformten Grünstreifen, eingefaßt mit Blumenrabatten (*compartiments/parterres de gazon*), Bogengängen (Treillagen) und den jeweils namengebenden Skulpturen (Abb. 17).

Aus einer schattigen Grünzone lugt die von Knobelsdorff 1751–57 geplante, in buntem Marmor geschmückte Neptungrotte hervor, bei der das Wasser in der Art eines *buffet d'eau* über muschelförmige Marmorschalen herabfällt. Die Najaden schuf Georg Franz Ebenhech

14. Johann Georg Wilhelm Steinert, Garten Rheinsberg, Plan, um 1800. Feder, aquarelliert. (SPSG, Potsdam.)
15. Unbekannter Zeichner, Obelisk im Garten Rheinsberg, 1790. Feder, aquarelliert. (SPSG, Potsdam.)
16. Johann Friedrich Nagel oder Johann Samuel Knüpfer, Obeliskportal im Park Sanssouci, um 1790. Kolorierte Radierung. (Stiftung Stadtmuseum Berlin – Reprographie aus: AKat. 1985.)
17. Georg Balthasar Probst, Terrassenanlage und Parterre im östlichen Teil des Parks Sanssouci, 1747/49. Kolorierter Kupferstich. (SPSG, Potsdam.)

14. Johann Georg Wilhelm Steinert, Rheinsberg garden, plan, ca. 1800. Pen, painted in watercolours. (SPSG, Potsdam.)
15. Unknown graphic artist, obelisk in the Rheinsberg garden, 1790. Pen, painted in watercolours. (SPSG, Potsdam.)
16. Johann Friedrich Nagel or Johann Samuel Knüpfer, Obeliskportal in Park Sanssouci, ca. 1790. Coloured etching. (Stiftung Stadtmuseum Berlin – reproduced from: AKat. 1985.)
17. Georg Balthasar Probst, terraced site and *parterre* in the eastern part of Park Sanssouci, 1747/49. Coloured copper engraving. (SPSG, Potsdam.)

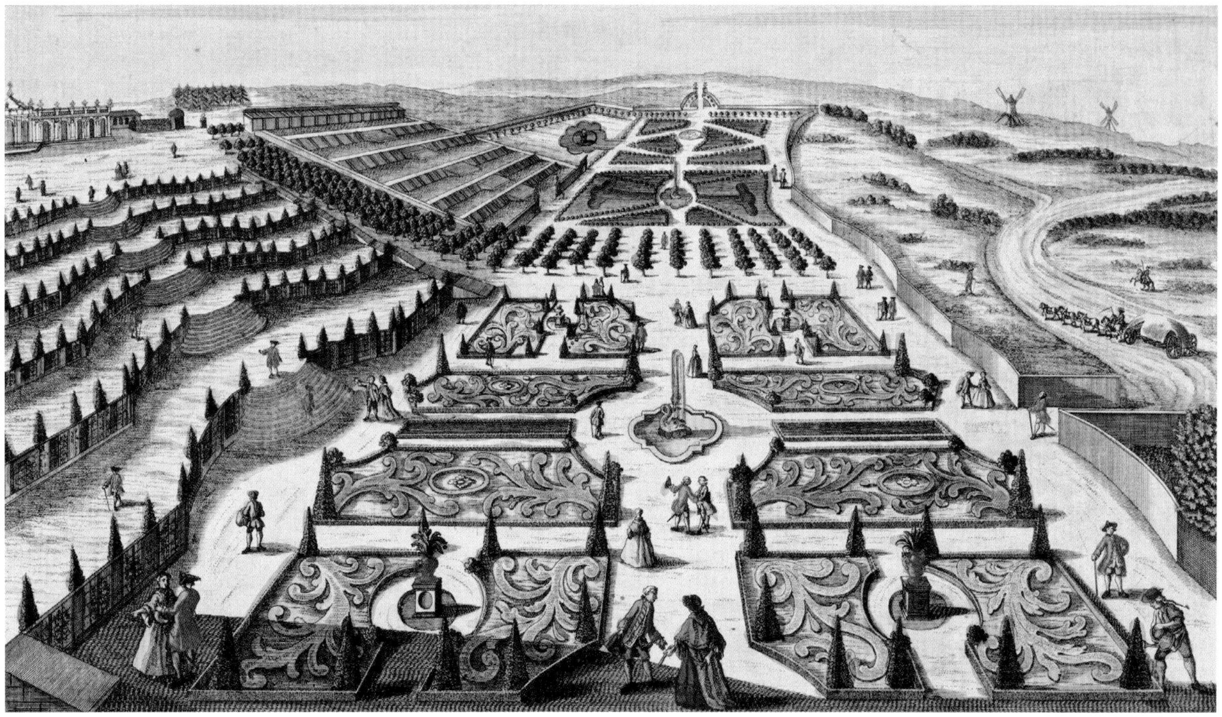

The 1790 Temple for the Dear Departed, also referred to as the Catacomb, and the obelisk erected on the site of the Trajan Column in 1791, designed by Georg Friedrich Boumann the Younger (1737–1812), are dedicated to the heroes of the Seven Years' War, who in Henry's opinion had been unjustly ignored. With the obelisk, Henry claims »a certain prerogative of interpretation regarding the memory of the Seven Years' War«.[40] (illus. 15) Its dedication was celebrated both as a public festival and a military ceremony. »I have built the memorial in honour of my late brother and the entire Prussian army«[41] – omitting all the marshals appointed by Frederick II!

In 1757 Frederick had dismissed his beloved brother Augustus William from his position as infantry general of the Prussian army. In public disgrace, Augustus William was guilty of a military misjudgment as a result of which Zittau in Saxony had been bombarded by Austrian troops. Henry blamed his brother's death in the following year on the insult, and in 1758 had a symbolic urn with ashes and a memorial bust set up west of the orangery *parterre* in the middle of the clearing in a plantation of firs and yews.[42]

As the last act in his Rheinsberg garden realm Henry decreed that he should be buried in a pyramid tomb. The image he chose in a selected spot is so unambiguous that, in a virtually exemplary fashion, it demonstrates the practice of landscape gardening of creating images that are filled with significance by the imagination of the observer. Henry wanted the pyramid, without a top, put up in place of a swing between the hedge theatre and the main avenue: a monument that followed the statically exact laws of geometry whose intentional defect would allude to the temporal and inadequate nature of all existence, instead of the childish toy that with its fleetingly elegant swinging motion amused a frivolous aristocracy. The pyramid was built by Johann Georg Wilhelm Steinert in 1802.[43]

From 1802 to 1813 Rheinsberg belonged to Henry's brother, Prince Ferdinand, and then to the son of the latter, Prince Augustus, until Augustus' death in 1843. In the 19th century there were no major remodeling projects. In 1951 Rheinsberg was transferred from the administration of the Staatliche Schlösser und Gärten Potsdam-Sanssouci to the Sozialversicherung des Landes Brandenburg, and was a sanatorium from 1952 to 1989. From 1960 on, conservation measures were carried out, and these have been continued from 1994 to the present day now that the property has been taken over by the Stiftung Preußische Schlösser und Gärten Berlin-Brandenburg.

Frederick's Sanssouci

»I am also busy gardening.« Frederick (II) to his sister Wilhelmina, 1735

The main portal on the city side announces the royal park of Sanssouci, laid out in 1744 for Frederick II, like an almost imperial prelude: formed by four Corinthian columns on each side with entablature, the basic elements of classical architecture (illus. 16). Flowers, fruit and gardening tools ornament the frieze and the vases that surmount it and put one in the right mood for the royal garden realm. Semicircular walls, paralleled by a moat outside, lead, in extension of the bases of the columns, toward the main avenue of the Fridericlan park, which runs from east to west. In the space immediately next to the entrance with its decorative *parterre* of lawn, sculptures stand on the sides of the pillars of the gate, the goddesses of flowers and of fruit trees: Flora presents her flowers in her gathered robe, and Pomona holds her cornucopia filled with fruit. On the eight vases placed on the walls, the ornamentation of flowers and fruit continues, until the two nymphs resting on the volutes at the end of the wall welcome visitors to the park arriving from the city.

Knobelsdorff designed the entrance in 1747. It is named the Obeliskportal after the obelisk erected east of it in the following year by stonemason Johann Christian Angermann. Positioned at a corner, the obelisk mediates between the garden and the city. It was connected to the garden's entrance by rows of linden trees that radiated outwards. Glume executed the portal and created

18. Johann Friedrich Schleuen, Schloß Sanssouci mit Terrassenanlage und Parterre, um 1756. Radierung. (SPSG, Potsdam.)

18. Johann Friedrich Schleuen, Schloß Sanssouci with terraced site and *parterre*, ca. 1756. Etching. (SPSG, Potsdam.)

1752, die namengebende Neptunfigur, deren Oberkörper 1963 als Kopie ersetzt wurde, Johann Peter Benckert 1760.

Zu den vor 1750 im Halbkreis aufgestellten vier Mohrenbüsten wurden vor 1772 zwei Kopien nach den Antiken Titus Vespasianus und Marc Aurel hinzugefügt. Zusammen formen sie das sogenannte Mohrenrondell, dessen Originale heute in Schloß Caputh stehen. In Potsdam wurden sie 1992–97 durch Kopien ersetzt.

Das sogenannte Oranierrondell ist der Bildergalerie vorgelagert, die Johann Gottfried Büring 1755–63 erbaute. Die 1992–98 in Marmor kopierten Büsten von Angehörigen des Hauses Oranien von François Dieussart, entstanden um 1647, reihen sich um ein Vierpaßbassin. Den zugehörigen Holländischen Garten umgeben Heckenquartiere mit Obstbäumen. Die Höhendifferenz zwischen Garten und Bildergalerie gleicht eine Terrassenmauer aus. 1764–66 wurde sie vom Hofgärtner Joachim Ludwig Heydert mit Perlmutt, Bergkristall und Korallen grottiert. Die Mauer bespielen Putten, die die Brüder Johann David und Johann Lorentz Räntz und andere Bildhauer schufen.

Im mittleren Lustgarten, dem Zentrum des friderizianischen Gartens, unterhalb von Schloß Sanssouci, verschmelzen Geometrie und Ikonographie.[44] Wo sich die Hauptachsen der Gesamtanlage kreuzen, ist das große Vorbild der Epoche und Friedrichs persönliches Ideal, Frankreich, mit den Geschenken Ludwigs XV. präsent: *Venus* (1748, Kopie 1904) und *Merkur* (1739, Kopie 1843) von Jean Baptiste Pigalle, die *Rückkehr von der Jagd* (auch: *Allegorie der Luft*, 1749) und das *Fischen im Meer* (auch: *Allegorie für das Wasser*, 1749) nach Modellen von Lambert Sigisbert Adam. 1752 trafen sie in Potsdam ein und wurden am Vierpaßbecken aufgestellt (1787 als Oval, 1841 als Kreis gestaltet).

Bis 1764 wurden die Elementebilder *Luft* und *Wasser* um *Feuer* (1756) und *Erde* (1758) vervollständigt. Dargestellt sind sie als Venus, die den von Vulkan für Äneas geschmiedeten Schild betrachtet, und als Ceres, die Triptolemos das Pflügen lehrt. Apoll (mit dem getöteten Python, 1752), Diana (im Bade, 1753), Juno (mit dem Pfau, 1753), Jupiter (mit Io, 1754), Mars (mit dem Speer, 1764) sowie Minerva (mit dem Grenzstein, 1760) bilden das Pantheon ab. Adam schuf es als Hofbildhauer Friedrichs II., Sigisbert-François Michel vollendete den Kriegsgott, als Adam nach Paris zurückgekehrt war. In der Beckenmitte illustrierten vergoldete Bleifiguren das Thema »Wasser«: Bis 1787 war es die Meeresnymphe Thetis mit Delphinen und Tritonen. 1820 wurde sie durch eine Galathea-Tritonen-Gruppe ersetzt.[45]

Sechs Terrassen, seitliche Rampen und eine mittige Freitreppe verbinden Schloß Sanssouci und den zentralen Lustgarten (Abb. 18). Talutmauern mit ihren verglasten und überdachten Nischen (frz. Talutage = Verdachung) begrenzen die Terrassen. Hier werden Weinreben und Spalierobst gezogen. Am Rand jeder Terrasse, je zwei Nischen verklammernd, standen Taxuspyramiden, denen im Sommer kugelig gestutzte Orangenbäume benachbart waren.[46] Den weiten Rückschwung der Mauern in der Mitte übernehmen die gegenläufig gekrümmten Treppenstufen. Sie wachsen gleichsam zum nach außen ausbuchtenden Marmorsaal des Schlosses auf und schwingen direkt unterhalb der Terrassenanlage in den gekrümmten Linien des Parterres aus.

Dieses war mit Astern, Anemonen, Bellis, Hyazinthen, Krokussen, Lilien, Goldlack, Malven, Jasmin, Levkojen, Iris, Aurikeln, Ranunkeln, Nelken, Rosen, Kaiserkronen und Tulpen reich und bunt bepflanzt.[47] Rahmen und Binnenzeichnung des Ziergartens formten geschnittener Buchs und farbiges Gestein. Zusätzlich schmückten die vergoldeten Bleigruppen *Dejanira und Nessus*, *Europa und Jupiter*, *Eurydike in der Unterwelt* sowie *Perseus und Andromeda* die vier Parterrefelder bis zum Ende des 18. Jahrhunderts. 1744–45 entstand die Terrassen-Nischen-Anlage. Schloß Sanssouci war 1747 fertig.

Auf der obersten Terrasse steht links und rechts des Schlosses je ein Treillagepavillon. Grün gestrichene, mit vergoldeten Schnitzereien verzierte Bogengänge stellen

the vases as well as Flora and Pomona, which have today been replaced by copies, dated 1963 and 1935.

Along the main road there is a series of rondels whose size and position are in tune with the architectural structure associated with each. They form a sequence of variously designed garden spaces running from the bright eastern half, the pleasance area laid out as the first part of the grounds in 1744–50, to the wooded western half, the »Rehgarten« (deer garden), implemented in 1751–54 and 1763–70. The varied repertory of ornamentation ranges from ponds and fountains, *parterres* at ground level, flower beds (*plates-bandes de fleurs*), orchards framed by hedges, ornamentally shaped grass strips bordered by flower beds (*compartiments/parterres de gazon*), arcades (latticework pergolas) and the sculptures for which each section was named (illus. 17).

From a shady green area peeks the Neptungrotte (Neptune Grotto), planned by Knobelsdorff in 1751–57, which is decorated with polychrome marble; in it, water falls in the manner of a buffet d'eau over shell-shaped marble basins. The naiads were created by Georg Franz Ebenhech in 1752, while the eponymous figure of Neptune, whose torso was replaced by a copy in 1963, was created by Johann Peter Benckert in 1760.

Added to the four busts of Moors, placed in a semicircle before 1750, were two reproductions of classical sculptures before 1772, representing Titus Vespasianus and Marcus Aurelius. Together they form the so-called Mohrenrondell, whose originals today stand in Schloß Caputh. In Sanssouci they were replaced by replicas in 1992–97.

Built by Johann Gottfried Büring between 1755 and 1763, the so-called Oranierrondell (House of Orange Rondel) is located in front of the picture gallery. François Dieussart's busts of members of the House of Orange, originally made ca. 1647 and copied in marble in 1992 to 1998, are lined up around a quatrefoil pond. The Dutch Garden associated with it is surrounded by shaded walkways with fruit trees. A terrace wall levels out the difference in height between the garden and the picture gallery. In 1764–66 it was grottoed by court gardener Joachim Ludwig Heydert with mother-of-pearl, rock crystal and corals. Playing on the wall are putti created by the brothers Johann David and Johann Lorentz Räntz, and other sculptors.

In the central pleasance, the centre of the Friderician garden, below Schloß Sanssouci, geometry and iconography merge.[44] Where the main axes of the park as a whole intersect, the great model of the epoch and Frederick's personal ideal, France, is present with the gifts of Louis XV: *Venus* (1748, copy 1904) and *Mercury* (1739, copy 1843) by Jean Baptiste Pigalle, *Rückkehr von der Jagd* (*Return from the Hunt*), also called *Allegorie der Luft* (*Allegory of the Air*), 1749, and *Fischen im Meer* (*Fishing in the Sea*), also called *Allegorie für das Wasser* (*Allegory for the Water*), 1749, based on models by Lambert Sigisbert Adam. In 1752 they arrived in Potsdam and were positioned by the quatrefoil pond (designed as an oval in 1787, and redesigned in 1841 as a circle).

By 1764 the set of statues that consisted of the elements *Air* and *Water* was completed by adding *Fire* (1756) and *Earth* (1758). The latter are represented as Venus gazing at the shield forged by Vulcan for Aeneas, and as Ceres teaching Triptolemos how to plough. Apollo (with the slain python, 1752), Diana (in the bath, 1753), Juno (with the peacock, 1753), Jupiter (with Io, 1754), Mars (with the spear, 1764) and Minerva (with the boundary stone, 1760) make up the Pantheon. Adam created it as the court sculptor of Frederick II; the god of war was completed by Sigisbert-François Michel when Adam had returned to Paris. In the middle of the pond gilded lead figures illustrated the theme »water«: until 1787 this was represented by the sea nymph Thetis with dolphins and Tritons. In 1820 she was replaced by a group of Galathea and Tritons.[45]

Six terraces, side ramps and a central open-air staircase connect Schloß Sanssouci and the central pleasance (illus. 18). Talut walls with their glazed and roofed-over recesses (Fr. talutage = projecting cover) form the boundaries of the terraces. Here grapevines and espaliered fruit trees are grown. At the edge of each terrace, linking pairs of recesses together, stood yew tree pyramids, and in summer these had orange trees next to them, trimmed into spherical shapes.[46] The wide backward swing of the walls in the middle is taken over by the steps, which curve in opposite directions. They grow upward, as it were, to the marble hall of the palace, which curves out, and swing outwards directly below the terrace in the curved lines of the *parterre*.

The latter was richly and colourfully planted with asters, anemones, English daisies, hyacinths, crocuses, lilies, wallflowers, mallows, jasmine, stock, irises, primroses, buttercups, carnations, roses, crown imperials and tulips.[47] The frame and interior outlines of the ornamental garden were formed by trimmed boxwood and coloured stones. In addition, until the end of the 18th century, the gilded lead figures *Dejanira und Nessus*, *Europa und Jupiter*, *Eurydice in der Unterwelt* and *Perseus und Andromeda* decorated the four fields of the *parterre*. The recesses of the terraces were created in 1744–45. Schloß Sanssouci was completed in 1747.

On the uppermost terrace, a latticework pavilion stands on the left and right of the palace. Arcades, painted green and ornamented with gilded carvings, create a connection to the palace. In the east pavilion a Hellenistic bronze sculpture that was famous in the time of Frederick once stood: the naked *Praying Boy*, praying for victory in contest, dated ca. 300 B.C.E. Frederick acquired it in 1747. The original is now located in the Pergamon Museum in Berlin, while a replica stands at Schloß Sanssouci. Plantings of larch trees reminiscent of Italian cypresses bordered the upper terrace on the sides. Among them were placed classical busts of rulers, Italian copies from the 18th century – as well as, on the west side, Cleopatra with a mourning Cupid and, on the east side, Flora with the spring wind Zephir by Adam (1750 and 1749, today in the form of a replica). Walnut trees and rows of chestnuts framed the terraces on the sides of the ramps all the way to the *parterre*, while in the south there was a moat lined with walls.

The central axis of the Friderician park runs into an avenue bordered by linden trees, and later by chestnut trees, flanked by ditches and two sphinxes created before 1754 by Ebenhech. Halfway, there was a replica of Gian Lorenzo Bernini's bust of Paolo Giordano II Orsini, Duke of Bracciano, which is currently being kept in the picture gallery. Two summerhouses formed the conclusion in the south before the Lord-Marschall-Haus, built 1764–66, formed the southern termination point. In the north there is a view from the Ehrenhof (Parade Court) through the opening of the colonnade to the backdrop of ruins 600 m away that was designed by Knobelsdorff, reworked by the Bayreuth theatre painter Innocente Bellavite and erected by Johann Boumann:

die Verbindung zum Schloß her. Im östlichen Pavillon stand eine zur Zeit Friedrichs berühmte hellenistische Bronzeplastik: der nackte, um den Sieg im Wettkampf *Betende Knabe* aus der Zeit um 300 v. Chr. Friedrich erwarb sie 1747. Das Original befindet sich heute im Pergamonmuseum in Berlin, vor Ort steht ein Nachguß. Lärchenpflanzungen, die an italienische Zypressen erinnern, begrenzten die oberste Terrasse seitlich. In ihnen waren antike Herrscherbüsten als italienische Kopien des 18. Jahrhunderts aufgestellt – dazu im Westen Kleopatra mit dem trauernden Amor und im Osten Flora mit dem Frühlingswind Zephir von Adam (1750 und 1749, heute als Kopie). Walnußbäume und Kastanienreihen rahmten die Terrassen zu Seiten der Rampen bis zum Parterre, während im Süden ein mauergefaßter Graben verlief.

Die Mittelachse der friderizianischen Anlage läuft in einer linden-, später kastaniengesäumten Allee aus, flankiert von Stichgräben und zwei bis 1754 von Ebenhech gearbeiteten Sphingen. Auf halbem Weg stand die Replik von Gian Lorenzo Berninis Büste von Paolo Giordano II. Orsini, Herzog von Bracciano, die zur Zeit in der Bildergalerie aufbewahrt wird. Zwei Gartenhäuser bildeten den Abschluß im Süden, bevor das 1764–66 erbaute Lord-Marschall-Haus den südlichen Schlußpunkt setzte. Im Norden geht der Blick vom Ehrenhof durch die Öffnung der Kolonnade zum 600 m weit entfernten Ruinenprospekt, der von Knobelsdorff entworfen, vom Bayreuther Theatermaler Innocente Bellavite überarbeitet und von Johann Boumann errichtet wurde: Eine hoch aufragende Säulengruppe, ein Rundtempel aus dorischen Säulen, eine Pyramide und eine Theaterwand nach römischem Muster verbergen das 1748 angelegte Wasserbecken. Es sollte das Wasser aus den Parkfontänen sprudeln lassen.[48]

Westlich von Schloß Sanssouci, vor der ehemaligen Orangerie, die 1771–74 von Georg Christian Unger zur Gästewohnung »Neue Kammern« umgestaltet wurde, liegt das Fontänenrondell. Hier standen acht vergoldete Bleifiguren aus der griechischen Mythologie von Ebenhech, die Ende des 18. Jahrhunderts durch Marmorskulpturen italienischer Künstler ersetzt wurden.

Das östliche Mohrenrondell findet im Westen seine Entsprechung im Musenrondell. Der von Glumes Marmorfiguren Polyhymnia, Terpsichore, Kalliope, Euterpe, Thalia, Melpomene und Klio (vor 1752) umstandene Platz bildet die Kreuzung von acht Wegachsen. Im Norden läuft eine Achse zur als Wasserspiel geplanten, nicht erhaltenen Thetisgrotte. Unter Friedrich Wilhelm IV. erfolgte der Umbau zum Felsentor. Im Westen führte eine Achse bis hin zu den Toren der Gartenmauer, die den Lustgartenbezirk abschloß. Die mittlere Achse verließ den Lustgartenbereich, um hinter der Mauer, durch das folgende Entführungsrondell, die Verbindung zur Waldzone des Rehgartens herzustellen. Paris und Helena, Römer und Sabinerin, Bacchus und Ariadne, Pluto und Proserpina sind die Protagonisten der Entführungsgruppen, die von Ebenhech um 1750 geschaffen wurden.

Zwei Architektur-Enklaven ganz eigener Art, öffneten den Rehgarten: Knobelsdorff gestaltete ein Wasserspiel als begehbare Kolonnade aus buntem Marmor, Vergoldungen und Durchblicken. Ihre Raffinesse zeigt das um 1792 gemalte Aquarell von Johann Friedrich Nagel (Abb. 19). Den 1764 eingeweihten, von Büring 1754–57 gebauten Chinesischen Teepavillon, der in seiner Vergoldung inmitten eines Tannenbosketts im Südwesten aufblitzt, verbindet ein Diagonalweg mit dem Musenrund. Lebensgroße vergoldete Sandsteinfiguren Tee und Kaffee trinkender, musizierender und Obst verzehrender Chinesen von Benckert und Johann Matthias Gottlieb Heymüller umringen das Teehaus.

Sein aus konzentrischen Kreisen entwickelter Grundriß suggeriert, es drehe sich samt seiner Besucher ausgelassen im Kreise. Selbst das Dach versetzen aufgemalte Spiralbänder in eine vermeintliche Rotation. Auf ihm thront ein Chinese im Schneidersitz vom Bildhauer Benjamin Giese und Kupferschmied Friedrich Jury. In der einen Hand hält er einen Schirm, in der anderen zwei Schlangen, die sich wie am Caduceus, dem Heroldsstab des Götterboten Hermes, winden. Der Beschwingtheit der Figuren und der Architektur antworteten die sich schlängelnden Wege der Umgebung. Ihr labyrinthisches Spiel beruhigte sich im Umfassungsweg, der nach Westen zum Neuen Palais führt.[49]

Mit dem Bau des Neuen Palais folgte 1763 eine weitere Sommerresidenz für Friedrich II. Diesmal galt es, Preußens Unerschöpflichkeit nach dem Siebenjährigen Krieg in einem Architekturdenkmal zu zelebrieren, in gewaltigen Ausmaßen und mit imposantem Figurenschmuck. Seine Ausführung und Innenausstattung lag bis 1769 in den Händen von Heinrich Ludwig Manger, Büring und Carl von Gontard (1731–1791).[50] Das neue Schloß ersetzte im Westen den ursprünglichen Sicht- und Endpunkt der 2 km langen Hauptallee, eine 1757 abgebrochene Felsengrotte.

Die Mauer um den Lustgarten wurde entfernt, der Rehgarten verband von nun an den Lustgarten und das geometrische, als Rasenparterre gestaltete Halbrondell vor dem Neuem Palais. Heinrich Christian Eckstein (1719–1796) und Planteur Johann Hartmann Burghoff gestalteten die Umgebung des Palais ab 1767. Im Norden und Süden dienten ein Heckentheater und ein Gartensalon höfischen Musikdarbietungen. Skulpturen, die die Gartenfassade nach Norden und Süden verlängern, die Aufstellung zahlreicher Antiken auf Postamenten am Halbrondell (aufgestellt bis 1827/28) und die kolossalen Marmorhermen entlang der Wege jenseits der Hauptallee paraphrasieren Friedrichs prahlerisches Bauwerk im Garten.[51]

Seit 1769 bilden die von Jean Laurent Le Geay und Gontard ab 1766 errichteten Wirtschaftshäuser, die Communs, mit ihren Tempelfronten, kuppelbekrönten Turmaufsätzen, Skulpturen und der zwischen ihnen liegenden Großen Kolonnade ein Gegengewicht zum langgestreckten Baukörper des Neuen Palais.

Der nahegelegene Antikentempel wurde während der Bauzeit des Neuen Palais zur Aufbewahrung der königlichen Antiken-, Gemmen- und Münzsammlung errichtet,[52] der Freundschaftstempel 1768–70 zum Gedenken an Friedrichs verstorbene Schwester Wilhelmine von Bayreuth. Der Architekt der beiden Bauten war Gontard.

Als letzte Gebäude des friderizianischen Sanssouci entstanden 1770–72 das Belvedere auf dem Klausberg von Unger als zweigeschossiger überkuppelter Rundbau und ein nahegelegenes Wohnhaus für den Weingärtner Werle von Gontard in Form einer chinesischen Pagode mit plastischer Drachenzier.

Gartenkunst auf friderizianisch

Die Kinder, die in schwindeliger Höhe die Vasen des Obeliskportals mit Blumengirlanden umkränzen, überschreiben den Eintritt ins Gartenreich gleichsam mit dem

19. Johann Friedrich Nagel, Rehgartenkolonnade im Park Sanssouci, um 1792. Gouache. (SPSG, Potsdam.)

19. Johann Friedrich Nagel, Rehgartenkolonnade in Park Sanssouci, ca. 1792. Gouache. (SPSG, Potsdam.)

A group of tall columns, a round temple of Doric columns, a pyramid and a Roman-style theatre wall conceal the water reservoir installed in 1748. Its purpose was to make it possible for water to bubble from the fountains of the park.[48]

West of Schloß Sanssouci, in front of the former orangery, which was remodelled in 1771–74 by Georg Christian Unger into the guest apartments »Neue Kammern«, is the Fontänenrondell. This is where eight gilded lead figures from Greek mythology by Ebenhech used to stand. These were replaced at the end of the 18th century with marble sculptures by Italian artists.

Corresponding to the Mohrenrondell (Rondel of the Moors) in the east, there is the Musenrondell (Rondel of the Muses) in the west. The square surrounded by Glume's marble figures Polyhymnia, Terpsichore, Calliope, Euterpe, Thalia, Melpomene and Clio (before 1752) forms the intersection of eight axis paths. In the north one axis runs towards the Thetisgrotte (Grotto of Thetis), planned as a water feature but no longer extant. Under Frederick William IV this was converted to a rock archway. In the west one axis led to the gates of the garden wall that encircled the pleasance. The central axis left the pleasance to create a connection, behind the wall and through the Entführungsrondell (Abduction Rondel) that followed, to the wooded area of the Rehgarten. Paris and Helena, a Roman and a Sabine woman, Bacchus and Ariadne, Pluto and Proserpina are the protagonists of the abduction groups created by Ebenhech ca. 1750.

Two architectural enclaves of a very special kind opened the Rehgarten: Knobelsdorff designed a waterwork that was an accessible colonnade of coloured marble, gilding and vistas. Its sophistication is shown by the watercolour painted ca. 1792 by Johann Friedrich Nagel (illus. 19). From the Chinese Teahaus, officially opened in 1764, and built by Büring in 1754–57, whose gilded columns shine in the middle of a spruce *bosquet* in the southwest of the park, a diagonal path goes to the muses' circle. Life-size gilded sandstone figures of Chinese men and women drinking tea and coffee, making music and eating fruit, by Benckert and Johann Matthias Gottlieb Heymüller, surround the teahouse.

Its ground plan, developed from concentric circles, suggests that the pavilion as well as its visitors are boisterously spinning around in a circle. Even the roof is seemingly set rotating by painted spiral ribbons. A Chinese man is enthroned cross-legged on the roof, the work of sculptor Benjamin Giese and coppersmith Friedrich Jury. In one hand he holds a parasol, in the other he has two snakes that are entwined as though on a caduceus, the herald's staff of Hermes, the messenger of the gods. The vibrancy of the figures and of the building is echoed by the meandering paths of the surroundings. Their labyrinthine interplay becomes sedate in the perimeter path that leads west to the Neues Palais (New Palace).[49]

The construction of the Neues Palais in 1763 provided an additional summer residence for Frederick II. This architectural monument celebrated Prussia's inexhaustible resources after the Seven Years' War, on a huge scale and ornamented with imposing statues. Its implementation and interior design up to 1769 were entrusted to Heinrich Ludwig Manger, Büring and Carl von Gontard (1731–1791).[50] The Neues Palais replaced, in the west, the original visual and terminal point of the 2-km-long main avenue, a grotto abandoned in 1757.

The wall around the pleasance was removed, and from then on the Rehgarten connected the pleasance and the geometric semi-rondel in front of the Neues Palais, designed as a grassy *parterre*. Heinrich Christian Eckstein (1719–1796) and court gardener Johann Hartmann Burghoff designed the environs of the Palais from 1767 on. In the north and south a hedge theatre and a garden salon provided venues for the court's musical performances. Sculptures that extend the garden façade toward the north and south, the numerous antiquities lined up on pedestals around the semi-rondel (placed there before 1827/28) and the colossal marble hermae along the paths on the other side of the main avenue paraphrase Frederick's ostentatious edifice in the gardens.[51]

The construction of the service buildings, or *communs,* with their temple façades, cupola-crowned tower storeys, sculptures and the Große Kolonnade located between them, by Jean Laurent Le Geay and Gontard, began in 1766. Since 1769 these have formed a counterbalance to the elongated building of the Neues Palais.

The nearby Antikentempel (Temple of Antiquities) was built during the construction of the Neues Palais to store the royal collection of antiquities, cameos and coins,[52] while the Freundschaftstempel (Temple of Friendship) was erected 1768–70 in memory of Frederick's late sister Wilhelmina of Bayreuth. The architect of both buildings was Gontard.

The last buildings of the Friderician Sanssouci to be erected (1770–72) were the Belvedere on Klausberg by Unger – a two-storey domed rotunda, and the nearby residence for the wine grower Werle by Gontard, in the form of a Chinese pagoda ornamented with sculptured dragons.

Garden art à la Frederick

Children at a dizzy height wreathe garlands of flowers around the vases of the Obeliskportal. They could be writing, above the entrance into the garden realm, the motto of courtly Rococo culture that is also the leitmotif of Frederick's garden: »sans souci«, free of care. This is how the palace is described with metal letters at the garden side entrance. In the palace's vestibule sits Mars, the god of war, who has laid down his arms, putti dangle their legs next to the depictions of weapons in the cupola and the first pictorial representation of the palace on the *sopraporta* in Charles Sylva Dubois' library, presumably built in early 1747, illustrates the motto »Et in Arcadia ego« – which translates as »Even in Arcady, there am I« (illus. 20).

Even before the building of the summer palace on the »Wüster Berg« outside the town of Potsdam that had previously been cleared of trees, Frederick's tomb had been completed on the east side of the upper terrace below Adam's Flora. When Frederick looked out the window of his library facing east, he faced the youthful figure of the *Praying Boy*. On the boy's pavilion the sun shines in gilt splendour. Sanssouci was the Arcadia of Frederick II, his idyll – beyond death.

For him it was the place of philosophy, of poetry and music in more ways than one: on the one hand, a place of retreat, on the other a place for staging his own person as a philosopher king. He signed his letters with »Hermit of Sanssouci« or »Philosopher of Sanssouci«. Here he grew the fruit he loved. The plants came from all over Europe – Portugal, Italy, France or even Algeria.

Motto, das die höfische Rokokokultur ebenso charakterisiert, wie es als Leitmotiv des friderizianischen Gartens gelten kann: lustvoll – oder eben »Sans, Souci.«, ohne Sorge. Im so mit Metallbuchstaben an der Gartenseite bezeichneten Schloß sitzt im Vestibül der Kriegsgott Mars mit niedergelegten Waffen, lassen Putten ihre Beine neben den Waffendarstellungen in der Kuppel baumeln und illustriert die erste bildliche Darstellung der Schloßanlage auf der Supraporte im Bibliothekszimmer von Charles Sylva Dubois, vermutlich Anfang 1747, den Leitspruch »Et in Arkadia ego« – sinngemäß: »Auch ich in Arkadien« (Abb. 20).

Noch vor der Erbauung des Sommerschlosses auf dem zuvor abgeholzten »Wüsten Berg« vor der Stadt Potsdam ist Friedrichs Grab auf der Ostseite der oberen Terrasse unter Adams Flora fertiggestellt worden. Blickte Friedrich aus dem Fenster seiner Bibliothek nach Osten, hatte er die jugendliche Gestalt des *Betenden Knaben* vor Augen. Am Pavillon des Jungen strahlt die Sonne im Glanz ihrer Vergoldung. Sanssouci war Friedrichs II. Arkadien, seine Idylle – über den Tod hinaus.

Es war ihm Ort der Philosophie, der Dichtkunst und der Musik in zweierlei Weise: einerseits als Ort des Rückzugs, andererseits als Ort der Inszenierung der eigenen Person als Philosophenkönig. Mit »Klausner von Sanssouci« oder »Philosoph von Sanssouci« unterschrieb er seine Briefe. Hier züchtete er das von ihm geliebte Obst, die Pflanzen kamen aus ganz Europa – Portugal, Italien, Frankreich oder gar Algerien.

Von der Freude am Leben im Einklang mit der Natur erzählen die kräftigen Körper der in Tanz und Gesang berauschten Faune und Nymphen. An der Gartenseite von Sanssouci lassen Glume und seine Werkstatt sie in Paaren die Last des Gebälks übernehmen. Sie entwachsen Pilastern, reich an bildhauerischer Zier: Früchte, Musikinstrumente, Masken, Gefäße und Zweige von Obst und Blumen verbinden sich mit der Bewegung des bacchantischen Gefolges. Die Verjüngung der mit Weinlaub geschmückten Wandpfeiler nach unten bindet Architektur und Skulptur.

Ganz Monarch seiner Zeit, war auch Friedrich II. das eigene Planen und Entwerfen angenehme Zerstreuung und autoritäre Einflußnahme. Von seinem Baumeister Knobelsdorff sind keine Gartenpläne bekannt, so daß Friedrich als Autor der Idee des Schlosses auf dem Weinberg mit seinem Lustgarten auftritt (Abb. 21). Dilettantisch und wie auf die Schnelle zeigen zwei vom König eigenhändig skizzierte Blätter die wesentlichen Züge des mittleren Quadrats von Garten und Schloß, das die barocken Gebäudetypen Orangerie und Maison de plaisance vereint: Terrassen, in vielen Rundbogen geöffnete Mauern, kegelförmige Baumpflanzung auf der oberen Terrasse, zentrale Fontäne mit Skulpturengruppe, Parterre sowie die Raumverteilung im Schloß.[53]

Knobelsdorff vermochte Friedrichs Vision bis zum Zerwürfnis 1746/47 Gestalt zu geben. Dessen persönliche Handschrift wußte klassizistische Strenge mit ornamental-pittoresker Verspieltheit zu verbinden: Mit dem *Vitruvius Britannicus* von Colen Campbell als englisches Nachfolgewerk auf die *Quattro libri* des italienischen Renaissancearchitekten Andrea Palladio waren die Bauten des englischen Palladianismus musterhaft vorgestellt. Die Ostfassade des Louvre von Claude Perrault, entstanden 1667–74, und die Gartenseite von Versailles, von Jules Hardouin Mansart 1678 begonnen, boten beispielhafte Gliederungssysteme großer Wandflächen des barocken Klassizismus in Frankreich.

Anregungen für die Rocaille- und Groteskenornamentik der Zeit gaben Antoine Watteau und die Vorlagenwerke von Juste Aurèle Meissonier und Jacques de Lajoue. Die Verbindung aus klarem, Halt gebendem Bezugssystem und heiter-ausschweifendem Dekor seiner Fassaden und Innenräume übertrug Knobelsdorff auf den Garten. Die entlang der ordnenden Hauptachse gereihten Rondellfiguren sowie die Rehgartenenklaven brechen die vom Hügelrücken vorgegebene Längsachse auf: Das zweidimensional entwickelte Achsengefüge beherbergt dreidimensionale »Handlungsräume«,[54] die den Aktionen der Skulpturen Platz bieten.

Friedrichs philosophisches Denken, das den Aufklärern seiner Epoche verpflichtet war, legt nahe, daß die Rondelle die Vorherrschaft barocker Achsen der Régencegärten zerbrechen sollten – gerade so, als inszenierten sie Friedrichs *Antimachiavel* (1740). »Nec pluribus impar« (Selbst mehreren Sonnen gleich) lautete die Devise Ludwigs XIV. Der in der Sonnensymbolik kulminierenden Selbstverherrlichung in Versailles steht in Sanssouci ein philosophischer Spannungsbogen entgegen, den Friedrich parallel zur Hauptachse von Ost nach West schlägt. Der Obelisk im Osten ist ein altägyptisches Zitat, das für die steingewordenen Strahlen des Sonnengottes steht. Seine Spitze spiegelt den Sonnenglanz als Sinnbild göttlicher Macht. Indem Friedrich die Spitze des Obelisken als Krönung seines starken Fundaments preist, gelang ihm die Vereinnahmung des Symbols absolutistischer Gewalt für das eigene, mit dem Signum der Aufklärung versehene Königtum. »Die Pyramide spricht zu dir [...] die höchste Spitze, überschaut und krönt das Ganze; aber trägt nicht, sondern wird getragen von allem, was unter ihr liegt [...] Das tragende Fundament ist das Volk in seiner Einheit. Halte es stets mit ihm, daß es dich liebe und vertraue; darin allein nur kannst du stark und glücklich sein.«[55]

Die vom Obelisken ausgehenden Lindenreihen fächerten sich wie Sonnenstrahlen auf. So wie die Sonne ihren täglichen Rundgang um das Schloß absolviert, begegnet das kosmologische Motiv erneut mit den Sonnen an den Pavillons im Osten und Westen. Die königliche Grablege, die die Blumengöttin Flora und der Westwind Zephir bekrönen, ist in den Gedanken des ewigen Kreislaufs ebenso eingebunden wie die Allegorien der vier Elemente im Parterre: Jugend, Blüte, Tod, Auf- und Untergang, Tag und Nacht, Feuer/Wasser und Erde/Luft. »Gern und ohne Klage gebe ich meinen Lebensodem der wohltätigen Natur zurück, die ihn mir gütig verliehen hat, und meinen Leib den Elementen, aus denen er besteht«, beginnt der König 1769 die Verfügung über sein Begräbnis, das er sich »ohne Gepränge, ohne feierlichen Pomp [...] in Sanssouci auf der Höhe der Terrassen in einer Gruft« wünschte. »Ich habe als Philosoph gelebt und will als solcher begraben werden«.[56]

Im zentralen Parterre entwerfen die französischen Bildwerke einen Kosmos der Götter und Elemente, der durch die Würdigung vorangegangener Epochen in den benachbarten Gartenkompartimenten fundamentiert wird: Mit dem aus Büsten von Angehörigen des Hauses Oranien gestalteten Oranierrondell im östlichen Lustgarten rücken die Niederlande ins Bild, das bereits seit der Zeit des Großen Kurfürsten Friedrich Wilhelm neben Frankreich aktuelle kulturelle Vorbild. Die Reihe der zwölf antiken Büsten, die das Obeliskportal hinterfängt, verlängerte das genealogische Thema des Oranierrondells bis ins Altertum: Jupiter und Tochter Diana, Septimus Severus mit Sohn Caracalla und Nichte Julia Ma-

20. Charles Sylva Dubois und Antoine Pesne, Schloß Sanssouci mit Figurenstaffage (Supraporte im Konzertzimmer von Schloß Sanssouci), um 1747. Öl auf Leinwand. (SPSG, Potsdam – Photo: Hillert Ibbeken.)
21. Friedrich II., Grundriß des Schlosses Sanssouci und Terrassenanlage, Entwurf, 1744. Feder. (Berlin, ehemal. Hohenzollernmuseum, verschollen.)

20. Charles Sylva Dubois and Antoine Pesne, Schloß Sanssouci with staffage of figures (sopraporta in the concert room of Schloß Sanssouci), ca. 1747. Oil on canvas. (SPSG, Potsdam – photo: Hillert Ibbeken.)
21. Frederick II, floor plan of Schloß Sanssouci and terraced site, draft, 1744. Pen. (Berlin, former Hohenzollernmuseum, lost.)

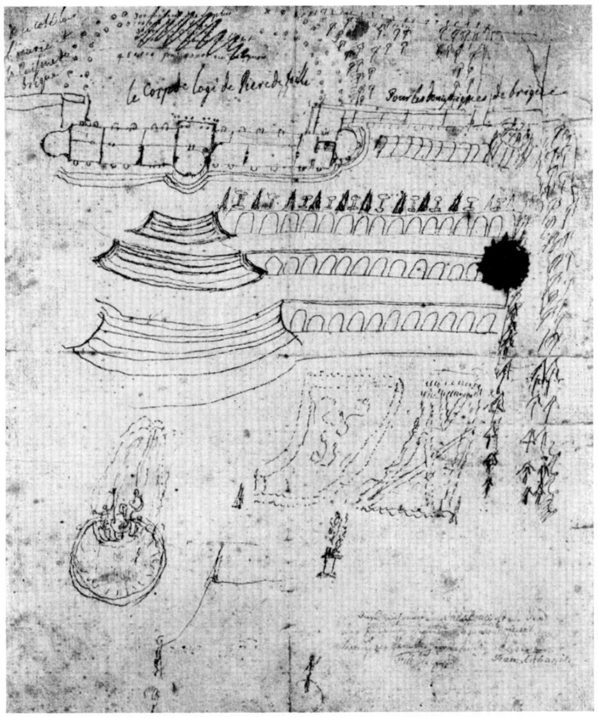

The strong bodies of the fauns and nymphs, intoxicated by dance and song, speak of joy in life in harmony with nature. On the garden side of Sanssouci, Glume and his studio create them in couples, enough to populate the entablatures of the buildings. They grow out of pilasters, abundant with sculptural ornaments: musical instruments, masks, vessels and branches laden with fruit and flowers commingle with the motion of the bacchanalian retinue. The tapering of the wall pillars, which are entwined with vine leaves, creates a bond between architecture and sculpture.

A typical monarch of his time, Frederick II enjoyed his own plans and designs as a pleasant distraction and an authoritarian exertion of influence. No plans of the garden are known to exist by his master builder Knobelsdorff, so that Frederick emerges as the author of the idea of the palace on the vineyard hill with its pleasance (illus. 21). Amateurish and seemingly sketched in a hurry, two pages by the king's own hand show the important features of the central square of the garden and palace, which combines the Baroque building types – orangery and *maison de plaisance*: terraces, walls with many open semicircular arches, a plantation of cone-shaped trees on the upper terrace, a central fountain with a group of sculptures, a *parterre*, and the layout of the rooms in the palace.[53]

Knobelsdorff was able to give form to Frederick's vision until their disagreement in 1746/47. In Frederick's personal manuscript, classicist severity was combined with ornamental, picturesque playfulness: With the *Vitruvius Britannicus* of Colen Campbell as the English follow-up to the *Quattro libri* of the Italian Renaissance architect Andrea Palladio, the buildings of English Palladianism were represented in an exemplary fashion. Claude Perrault's east façade of the Louvre, built in 1667–74, and the garden side of Versailles, begun by Jules Hardouin Mansart in 1678, offered model structuring systems of large wall surfaces of Baroque classicism in France.

Antoine Watteau and the collections of designs by Juste Aurèle Meissonier and Jacques de Lajoue gave suggestions for the *rocaille* and grotesque ornamentation of the period. Knobeldorff transferred to the garden the combination of a clear, stabilizing frame of reference and the gaily voluptuous décor of his façades and interiors. The rondel figures lined up along the central axis and the enclaves in the Rehgarten break up the longitudinal axis given by the ridge of the hill: The two-dimensionally developed structure of the axes harbours three-dimensional »spheres of action«[54] that provide room for the actions of the sculptures.

Frederick's philosophical thought, influenced by Enlightenment thinkers of his era, suggests that the rondels were meant to disrupt the supremacy of the Baroque axes of Regency gardens – exactly as if they were staging Frederick's *Antimachiavel* (1740). »Nec pluribus impar« (»Even equal to several suns«) was the motto of Louis XIV. While in Versailles self-glorification culminates in sun symbolism, Sanssouci contrasts with a philosophical arc of tension created by Frederick parallel to the main axis from east to west. The obelisk on the east side is an ancient Egyptian allusion that stands for the petrified rays of the sun god. Its tip reflects the brilliance of the sun, a symbol of divine power. By praising the tip of the obelisk as the culmination of its strong base, Frederick successfully adopts this symbol of absolutist power for his own kingdom, bearing the mark of the Enlightenment. »The pyramid speaks to you [...] the highest tip, which overlooks and crowns the entire structure, but does not support it; rather, it is supported by everything that is below it [...] The solid foundation is the people in its unity. Always be on the side of the people, that they may love you and trust you; only if you do that can you be strong and happy.«[55]

The rows of linden trees leading off from the obelisk fanned out like the rays of the sun. Just as the sun travels its daily round around the palace, the cosmological motif recurs repeatedly with the suns on the pavilions in the east and west of the park. The royal tomb, crowned by Flora, the goddess of flowers, and Zephir, the west wind, is just as fundamental to the idea of the eternal cycle as are the allegories of the four seasons in the *parterre*: youth, flowering, death, rise and fall, day and night, fire/water and earth/air. »Gladly and without lamentation I shall give back my life breath to benevolent Nature which generously lent it to me, and my body to the elements it consists of«, the king begins, in 1769, the testament instruction regarding his interment, which he wished to take place »without splendour, without solemn pomp [...] in Sanssouci at the level of the terraces in a tomb«. »I have lived as a philosopher and wish to be buried as one«.[56]

In the central *parterre* the French statues depict a cosmos of the gods and elements that is grounded by homage to past epochs in the adjacent *compartiments* of the garden: With the Oranierrondell in the eastern section of the pleasance, incorporating busts of members of the House of Orange, the Netherlands become part of the picture – next to France, the contemporary cultural model since the time of the Great Elector Frederick William. The series of twelve classical busts that frame the Obeliskportal extended the genealogical theme of the Oranierrondell to antiquity: Frederick had received Jupiter and his daughter Diana, Septimus Severus with his son Caracalla and niece Julia Mamaea, Faustina, Tiberius Antinous, three unknown figures, and a Roman councillor in 1742 together with the famous Paris collection of Cardinal Melchior de Polignac, whose praises Voltaire sang as a connoisseur of antiquities.[57] The busts of four Moors, which had been placed in a semicircle before 1750, expand the field of vision to include distant cultures, as do the Chinese figures that encircle the pavilion in the Rehgarten or the Drachenhaus pagoda.

The pavilion that holds the *Praying Boy* appears in one of the paintings Frederick liked so much and that he had assembled earlier in Rheinsberg, his residence as a crown prince, in Charlottenburg and now in the Little Gallery of Schloß Sanssouci: A comparable latticework pavilion appears in a park landscape in the right half of the picture *Le Moulinet*, by Watteau's pupil Nicolas Lancret, painted ca. 1730/35 and acquired by Frederick in 1744 (illus. 22). In front of it a group of Rococo courtiers amuse themselves dancing and making casual conversation.

Aside from the motifs borrowed here, to which one could add the nymphs at the Obeliskportal, reminiscent of Lancret, Frederick's garden breathes the atmosphere of the fairytale Baroque gardens painted in 1710–21 by Watteau: »Watteau painted dreams«[58] – Knobelsdorff designed dreams – to wit, Frederick II's dream of the kind of »spiritual home«[59] Rheinsberg had been for him. Within a Watteau scenery its sources are the traditions of Periclean and Alexandrine Greece and of the Rome of Caesar and Augustus, of Renaissance Italy during the pontificate of Leo X and absolutist France under

maea, Faustina, Tiberius Antinous, drei Unbekannte und einen römischen Ratsherrn hatte Friedrich 1742 mit der berühmten Pariser Sammlung des Kardinals Melchior de Polignac erhalten, den Voltaire als Antikenkenner rühmte.[57] Die vor 1750 im Halbkreis aufgestellten Büsten von vier Mohren erweitern das Blickfeld um ferne Kulturen ebenso wie die Chinesen, die den Pavillon im Rehgarten umringen oder die Drachenhauspagode.

Die Behausung des *Betenden Knaben* taucht in einem jener Gemälde auf, die Friedrich so mochte und die er bereits in seinem Kronprinzensitz Rheinsberg, in Charlottenburg und nun in der Kleinen Galerie von Schloß Sanssouci vereinte: *Le Moulinet* des Watteau-Schülers Nicolas Lancret, um 1730/35 entstanden, 1744 von Friedrich erworben, zeigt in der rechten Bildhälfte inmitten einer Parklandschaft einen vergleichbaren Treillagepavillon (Abb. 22). Davor ergeht sich eine höfische Rokokogesellschaft im lockeren Tanz und Gespräch.

Über die motivischen Übernahmen hinaus, denen sich die an Lancret erinnernden Nymphen am Obeliskportal hinzufügen ließen, ist es das Flair der in den Jahren 1710–21 gemalten märchenhaften Barockgärten von Watteau, das der friderizianische Garten atmet: »Watteau malte Träume«[58] – Knobelsdorff gestaltete Träume, nämlich Friedrichs II. Traum einer »geistigen Heimat«,[59] wie sie ihm Rheinsberg gewesen war. Innerhalb der Watteauschen Szenerie speist sie sich aus den Überlieferungen der als kulturelle Höhepunkte gefeierten Zeitalter des perikleischen und alexandrinischen Griechenlands sowie des cäsarischen und augusteischen Roms, des renaissancezeitlichen Italiens während des Pontifikats Leos X. und des absolutistischen Frankreichs unter Ludwig XIV. Die friderizianische Anlage erinnert an liebgewonnene Bauten aus dem eigenen Umfeld und adaptiert gezielt zeitgenössische Schöpfungen aus Kunst und Literatur, um sie in einem ganz individuellen Gartentraum zu vereinen.

Voraussetzungen

Bei der Wahl der entsprechenden Vorbilder ergänzten sich der König und sein Baumeister: Friedrich las vor allem die antiken römischen und französischen Autoren des 17. und 18. Jahrhunderts. Er kannte die aktuellen Vorlagenwerke. 1728 war er in Dresden der Prachtentfaltung Augusts des Starken als Gegensatz zum väterlichen »Grobianismus«[60] begegnet. Sein kulturelles Netzwerk ließ er in der Zusammenführung der französischen Geistesgrößen aus Philosophie und Naturwissenschaft als Mitspieler der berühmten Sanssouci-Tafelrunde kulminieren: Voltaire, Jean-Baptiste de Boyer, Marquis d'Argens, Julien Offray de La Mettrie, Pierre-Louis de Maupertuis und Francesco Algarotti. Der Wettstreit mit seinen Geschwistern Wilhelmine und Heinrich bei der Verschönerung ihrer Residenzen war ihm künstlerischer Ansporn. Knobelsdorff kannte verschiedenste Kunstdenkmäler aus eigener Anschauung, die er auf seinen Reisen 1736/37 nach Rom, Florenz, Venedig und Augsburg sowie 1740 nach Dresden, Wien, Paris und Flandern gesehen hatte. Beide begeisterten sich für die Gemälde der *fêtes galantes*.

Den antiken Topos der idealen Wohnlage an einem Hang hatte Plinius d. J. (62–113/115) mit der Beschreibung seiner toskanischen Villa Tuscum etabliert und Vitruv 33 v. Chr. im 6. seiner *10 Bücher über die Architektur* beschrieben. Leon Battista Alberti entdeckte ihn in *Über die Baukunst* (*De Re Aedeficatoria*, 1443–52) neu: »Ich wünschte es [das Haus vor der Stadt] ein bißchen höher gelegen«.[61] 1540 begründete Sebastiano Serlio mit einer Abbildung der Treppe von Donato Bramante in Form eines Amphitheaters im Nicchione des vatikanischen Belvedere in Rom im dritten Buch der *Architettura* die Tradition amphitheatralischer Stufenarchitektur, wie sie die Terrassen von Schloß Sanssouci zeigen. Wie ein Amphitheater angelegt, war auch der weithin bekannte Orangengarten des Handelsherrn Caspar Bose in Leipzig vom Ende des 17. Jahrhunderts.

Die hängenden, auf Terrassen angelegten Gärten der Semiramis in Babylon, um 600 v. Chr. entstanden, hatte Johann Bernhard Fischer von Erlach im *Entwurff einer historischen Architectur* 1705 in Wien publiziert. Die weit verbreitete Abhandlung *La Théorie et la pratique du jardinage* von Antoine Joseph Dézallier d'Argenville, Paris 1709, beschreibt mit »Hufeisentreppe« die Kombination Amphitheater und Terrassen.[62]

Direktes Vorbild war die als Gegenüber für Friedrichs Kronprinzensitz Schloß Rheinsberg geplante Terrassierung für einen Bacchustempel am Grienericksee. Etwa zeitgleich zu Sanssouci entstand der ebenfalls mit eingeschwungenem Mittelteil und axialen Freitreppen geformte Terrassengarten am Abteiberg im niederrheinischen Kamp, dem die in Klosterhöfe einbeschriebenen Gartenanlagen der fränkischen Zisterzienserabtei Ebrach vorausgegangen waren.[63] Die Verbindung von Terrassenanlage und Landsitz oder Schloß auf einem Hügel zeigen vor Sanssouci die von Pirro Ligorio 1560 begonnene Villa d'Este in Tivoli, Versailles ab 1661 und ein Entwurf Fischers von Erlach für Schönbrunn um 1690. Terrassen und Rampen verband Israël Silvestre 1674 auf seinem Stich *Vue du château de Versailles du côté de l'Orangerie*.

Als mögliche Anregung für die durch Podeste unterbrochene Treppe in Sanssouci wurde auf Francesco Antonio Muttonis Treppe vor der Palladio-Villa Piovene bei Vicenza (1539–40) verwiesen,[64] auf die Friedrich durch seinen in Venedig gebürtigen Freund Francesco Algarotti aufmerksam gemacht worden sein könnte.

Palladio und später Campbell schlossen Höfe gern mit Halbkreisen, wie es die griechische Antike bereits mit längsgerichteten Räumen und Bramante mit dem Belvederehof des Vatikan 1510 tat. Sanssouci zeigt den Halbkreisschluß an der vom Garten abgewandten Schloßseite mit den Kolonnaden, am Obeliskportal und mit den Kolonnaden zwischen den Communs. In diese Folge der Halbkreisabschlüsse mag man auch die konkaven Weinbergterrassen reihen. Aus zwei Halbkreisen wurde die Rehgartenkolonnade gebildet. Sie steht in einer Tradition mit der Havelkolonnade des Potsdamer Stadtschlosses und der Hofkolonnade von Sanssouci. Den Wechsel zwischen innerer Säulen- und äußerer Pfeilerstellung als Einfassung ihrer Umgänge könnte sich am Bosquet de la Colonnade von Mansart in Versailles, entstanden 1685, inspiriert haben. Ihre Durchlässigkeit aber schuldet sie dem Apollo-Tempel in Friedrichs Garten Amalthea im brandenburgischen Neuruppin, der 1735 als erstes Gebäude aus der Zusammenarbeit von Friedrich II. und Knobelsdorff hervorgegangen war.[65]

Das an der Hedwigskathedrale in Berlin erprobte Motiv des römischen Pantheons wird in Sanssouci in mehreren Variationen durchgespielt: Die Decke des Marmorsaals in Schloß Sanssouci zeigt es ebenso wie

22. Nicolas Lancret, *Le Moulinet*, um 1730/35. Öl auf Leinwand. (SPSG, Schloß Charlottenburg.)

22. Nicolas Lancret, *Le Moulinet*, ca. 1730/35. Oil on canvas. (SPSG, Schloß Charlottenburg.)

Louis XIV – ages celebrated as cultural pinnacles. Frederick's park reminds him of beloved buildings from his own milieu and intentionally adapts contemporary creations from art and literature, combining them in a wholly individual garden dream.

Premises

In their selection of appropriate models, the king and his master builder complemented each other: Frederick read primarily classical Roman authors and French 17th- and 18th-century authors. He knew the current collections of designs. In 1728, he had encountered the display of splendour of Augustus the Strong in Dresden, a complete contrast to his own father's »brutishness«[60]. As part of his cultural network he brought together to join the famous round table of Sanssouci the great French geniuses in philosophy and the natural sciences: Voltaire, Jean-Baptiste de Boyer, Marquis d'Argens, Julien Offray de La Mettrie, Pierre-Louis de Maupertuis and Francesco Algarotti. His competition with his sister Wilhelmina and brother Henry as all three beautified their residences was artistic motivation for him. Knobelsdorff had personally seen many different kinds of artworks during his journeys in 1736/37 to Rome, Florence, Venice and Augsburg, and, in 1740, to Dresden, Vienna, Paris and Flanders. Both were enthusiastic about the paintings of the *fêtes galantes*.

The classical topos according to which the ideal place to live was on a slope had been established by Pliny the Younger (62–113/115 C.E.) with the description of his Tuscan villa Tuscum, and had been described by Vitruvius in 33 B.C.E. in the sixth of his *Ten Books on Architecture*. Leon Battista Alberti rediscovered him in *On the Art of Building* (*De Re Aedeficatoria*, 1443–52): »I wanted it [the house outside the town] to be located on somewhat higher ground«.[61] In 1540 Sebastiano Serlio, with a depiction of the staircase of Donato Bramante in the form of an amphitheater in the Nicchione of the Vatican Belvedere in Rome, in the third book of his *Architettura*, established the tradition of amphitheatrical stair architecture of the type characteristic of the terraces of Schloß Sanssouci. Also laid out like an amphitheatre was the well-known orange garden of the merchant Caspar Bose in Leipzig, dating back to the end of the 17th century.

The hanging, terraced gardens of Semiramis in Babylon, created ca. 600 B.C.E., had been publicized by Johann Bernhard Fischer von Erlach in his *Entwurff einer historischen Architectur*, published in 1705 in Vienna. The widely distributed treatise *La Théorie et la pratique du jardinage* by Antoine Joseph Dézallier d'Argenville, Paris 1709, describes the combination of amphitheatre and terraces as a »horseshoe staircase«.[62]

A direct model was the terracing for a Bacchus temple by Grienericksee planned as a counterpart of Frederick's residence as a crown prince, Schloß Rheinsberg. Created at roughly the same time as Sanssouci was a terraced garden which also had a middle part that curved in and axial staircases on Abteiberg in Kamp (Lower Rhine), and its precedent was the gardens of the Cistercian abbey of Ebrach, which were inscribed in cloisters.[63] Before Sanssouci the combination of terracing and country seat or palace on a hill is found in the Villa d'Este in Tivoli begun by Pirro Ligorio in 1560, in Versailles after 1661 and in a design by Fischer von Erlach for Schönbrunn ca. 1690. Israël Silvestre in 1674 combined terraces and ramps in his engraving *Vue du château de Versailles du côté de l'Orangerie*.

It has been suggested that a possible inspiration for the staircase interrupted by landings in Sanssouci was Francesco Antonio Muttoni's staircase in front of the Palladian Villa Piovene near Vicenza (1539–40),[64] to which Frederick's friend Francesco Algarotti, who was born in Venice, might have drawn Frederick's attention.

Palladio and later Campbell liked to close courtyards with semicircles, a practice already common in classical Greece when there were longitudinally oriented rooms, and followed by Bramante in the Belvedere courtyard of the Vatican in 1510. In Sanssouci the semicircular closure appears on the side of the palace turned away from the garden that has the colonnades, in the Obeliskportal and where there are colonnades between the *communs* (service buildings). Concave vineyard terraces may also be included in this list of semicircular closures. The colonnade in the Rehgarten was formed out of two semicircles. It is part of the same tradition as the Havel colonnade of the Potsdam Stadtschloß and the courtyard colonnade of Sanssouci. The alternation between inside columns and outside pillars to frame its ambulatories might have been inspired by Mansart's Bosquet de la Colonnade in Versailles, built in 1685. However, it owes its permeability to the Apollo Temple in Frederick's Garden Amalthea in Neuruppin (Brandenburg), the first building to be produced, in 1735, by the collaboration between Frederick II and Knobelsdorff.[65]

The motif of the Roman Pantheon that had been tried out in St. Hedwig's Cathedral in Berlin is played through in Sanssouci in several variations: It appears on the ceiling of the Marble Hall in Schloß Sanssouci as well as in the Belvedere and the Antikentempel. The two-storey rotunda of the domed Belvedere on Klausberg, surrounded by Corinthian columns, is also a reference to Imperial Rome in that it follows Nero's Macellum (central market building) in Pompeii depicted in the engravings of the *Palazzi dei Cesari* by Francesco Bianchini, Verona 1738, which Frederick had at hand in his library. The unusual combination of the belvedere with a sweeping two-flight open-air staircase is typical of Baroque representational architecture: At the end of the 17th century it is found in Troja Palace near Prague, in the beginning of the 18th century in the Zwinger in Dresden, and after the turn of the century it appears in Schloß Solitude near Stuttgart. Knobelsdorff designed a kind of open-air staircase in the interior of the Stadtschloß, in 1746–48. Since 1763 an open-air staircase has led to the picture gallery of Sanssouci, and since 1769 to the *communs*.

It was Frederick's sister Wilhelmina who introduced the ruin or grotto theatre in her gardens in Bayreuth as a Rococo feature. This is the model for the Grotto of Thetis and of Neptune, and for the grotto at the west end of the main avenue, only the foundations of which were built, later to be replaced by the Neues Palais. Gontard's Grotto Hall in the Neues Palais today makes up the loss of this grotto, which was to be built of »scraps and druses of resin«.[66]

It is possible that during Knobelsdorff's Italian journey his impressions of Roman Baroque architecture – for instance, the façade of San Carlo alle Quattro Fontane by Francesco Borromini or Gian Lorenzo Bernini's oval space in Sant'Andrea al Quirinale and Nicola Salvi's competition blueprint for the Trevi Fountain (1732–62) – inspired him to use curved lines that set swinging the motif of the triumphal arch, in the Neptungrotte. The

das Belvedere und der Antikentempel. Der von korinthischen Säulen umstandene zweigeschossige überkuppelte Rundbau des Belvedere auf dem Klausberg erweist dem Rom der Kaiserzeit ebenfalls seine Referenz, indem er dem zentralen Marktgebäude Macellum de Nero in Pompeji folgt, abgebildet im Stichwerk der *Palazzi dei Cesari* von Francesco Bianchini, Verona 1738, das Friedrich in seiner Bibliothek zur Hand hatte. Die ungewöhnliche Kombination des Belvedere mit einer weit ausschwingenden zweiläufigen Freitreppe ist barocker Repräsentation verpflichtet: Ende des 17. Jahrhunderts zeigt sie Schloß Troja nahe Prag, Anfang des 18. der Zwinger in Dresden, nach der Jahrhundertmitte die Solitude bei Stuttgart. Knobelsdorff stattete das Stadtschloß 1746–48 im Inneren mit einer Art Freitreppe aus. Seit 1763 führt eine Freitreppe zur Bildergalerie von Sanssouci, seit 1769 zu den Communs.

Den Gebäudetyp des Ruinen- oder Grottentheaters hatte Friedrichs Schwester Wilhelmine in ihren Gärten in Bayreuth für das Rokoko begründet. Ihm sind Thetis- und Neptungrotte verpflichtet sowie die lediglich in ihren Fundamenten errichtete und später dem Neuen Palais gewichene Grotte am westlichen Ende der Hauptallee. Für diese aus »Werkstücken und Drusen vom Harze«[66] geplante Grotte entschädigt heute Gontards Grottensaal im Neuen Palais.

Zur gekurvten Linienführung und zum damit in Schwingung versetzten Triumphbogenmotiv der Neptungrotte mag Knobelsdorff während seiner Italienreise der Eindruck des römischen Barock angeregt haben, zum Beispiel die Fassade von S. Carlo alle Quattro Fontane von Francesco Borromini oder Gian Lorenzo Berninis Ovalraum in S. Andrea al Quirinale sowie Nicola Salvis Wettbewerbsentwurf zum Trevi-Brunnen (1732–62). Den Kontrast einer architektonisch regelgerechten Front und naturhafter Elemente, den die Neptungrotte mit ihren seitlich getürmten Felsquadern zeigt, hatten italienische Grotten- und Brunnenanlagen ausgereizt, seit vom 16. bis zum 17. Jahrhundert Aquäduktschlüsse als Triumphbogenschauwände (Mostra) inszeniert worden waren. Nischenbrunnen gehörten auch zum Repertoire des Gartens der Villa d'Este in Tivoli.

Die architektonische Grundgestalt der Grotte sowie Teile ihres Skulpturenschmucks wie die Neptunfigur und die rechts und links lagernden Najaden, die Knobelsdorff um 1750 skizzierte,[67] verdanken sich verschiedenen Blättern des einflußreichen Entwurfskatalogs für Dekorationen im Innenraum oder beweglicher Kunst mit dem klingenden Namen *Morceaux de fantaisie* von der Hand des Malers de Lajoue. Knobelsdorff lag er in einem von J. G. Hertel herausgegebenen Augsburger Nachstich von Jacob Wagner nach der zwischen 1738 bis 1745 entstandenen Pariser Folge vor. Die von Benckert ausgeführte Neptunfigur nähert sich dem Meeresgott der Fontana di Trevi und des Dresdener Neptunbrunnens, den Lorenzo Mattielli 1744 nach Plänen von Zacharias Longuelune für den Park des Palais Brühl-Marcolini schuf. Die Grottierung des Inneren ist abhängig von französischen Grottenpavillons bis hin zur berühmten Versailler Thetisgrotte (1664, 1684 abgetragen).

Für den Freundschaftstempel nahm sich Friedrich den von ihm selbst skizzierten, Apoll geweihten Tempel im Amalthea-Garten zum Muster[68] – ursprünglich durch Voltaires Dichtung *Le Temple de l'amitié* aus dem Jahr 1732 angeregt und nunmehr durch den 1761 von seinem Bruder Heinrich in Rheinsberg gebauten Erinnerungsrundtempel angestachelt. Mit dem Apollotempel, dem ersten nach den über Palladio vermittelten Regeln der Antike gebauten Monopteros auf dem Kontinent, war Friedrich und Knobelsdorff der »Schritt vom Bild in die Landschaft«[69] gelungen: Das Traumland Arkadien, das die französischen Landschaftsmaler seit Claude Lorrain, Nicolas Poussin und schließlich Watteau in der Fläche erschaffen hatten, eroberte nun den begehbaren Raum. Als Architekturpaten kommen der Sibyllentempel in Tivoli oder der Rundtempel auf Lancrets *Einschiffung nach Cythera* in Frage. 1719 war bereits im englischen Stowe durch John Vanbrugh der älteste erhaltene Gartenmonopteros am Ende einer Querallee entstanden, die die barocke Zentralachse schnitt.

Auch den Chinesischen Pavillon skizzierte der König selbst. Er inspirierte sich an den nach seinem Grundriß »Trèfle« (Kleeblatt) genannten Pavillon im Park von Lunéville in Lothringen, der 1742 von Emmanuel Héré de Corny für König Stanislaus Leszcynski von Polen errichtet wurde und den Friedrich aus Hérés Kupferstichwerk kannte. Vergoldete Palmen, wie sie den Pavillon umgeben, hatte Hoppenhaupt 1748 bereits für das Theater des Stadtschlosses verwendet. Das naturnahe Dekorelement könnte Friedrich durch Marc-Antoine Laugiers Erwähnung von »großen Palmenbäumen« anstelle von Säulen bekannt gewesen sein. Laugier (1713–1769) hatte 1753 ein Beispiel einer natürlichen, an der Urhütte orientierten Architektur beschrieben, die seine These der »Nachahmung« als »Mutter der Kunst« belebte: »Die kleine elende Bauernhütte, welche ich [Laugier] beschrieben habe, ist das Muster, von welchen man sich einen Abriß, von aller Pracht und Herrlichkeit der Baukunst gemacht hat.«[70]

Vermutlich hat Friedrich an der Palmenidee vor allem das exotische Moment gereizt. Laugiers imaginäre Urhütte als Prinzip für eine moderne Architektur wird erst für seinen Thronfolger von Interesse werden. 1763 erhielt Friedrich »trois plans [...] à la Chinoise«, Brückenentwürfe in chinesischer Manier des Architekten William Chambers (1728–1796). Im selben Jahr kam Chambers' Werk der Anlage von Kew Gardens in London heraus, *Plans, Elevations, Sections and Perspective Views of the Gardens and Buildings at Kew*. 1757 waren dessen *Designs of Chinese Buildings* erschienen. Chambers' Musterbücher wirkten ebenso auf das wenig später begonnene Drachenhaus, das die abgebildete Pagode am Ufer des Perlflusses nahe Guangzhou (Kanton) im Süden Chinas wiederholt.[71]

Die Hieroglyphen ähnlichen Reliefzeichen und Bildszenen von einem der Brüder Hoppenhaupt auf dem Obeliskenschaft bezeugen den gewollten Verweis auf Ägypten als Herkunftsland. Obelisken als Gartenstaffage führte Francesco Colonna in den Holzschnitten der *Hypnerotomachia Poliphili*, Venedig 1499, ein. Von Ägypten gelangten sie als Trophäen nach Rom. Den Theatergarten der Villa Mattei schmückte beispielsweise seit 1587 ein Obelisk Ramses II. In Landschaften und Städten bediente man sich ihrer hochaufragenden Gestalt fortan gern zur Akzentuierung von Blickpunkten. Athanasius Kircher und Joan Blaeu beförderten mit der Abbildung von Obelisken deren Rezeption.[72]

Sanssouci als Ort der Erinnerung

Bereits seinen Jugendsitz Rheinsberg eröffnete Friedrich mit einem Obelisken in Verbindung mit einem halbrunden Portal, das Flora und Pomona begleiten. Rheinsberg

designs of Italian grottoes and fountains had pushed to the limits the contrast between an architectonically regular façade and natural elements shown by the Neptungrotte, where rocks were piled along the sides; after all, aqueduct terminations had been used from the 16th to the 17th century as ornamental screens of triumphal arches (Mostra). Recessed fountains were also part of the repertory in the garden of the Villa d'Este in Tivoli.

The basic architectonic design of the grotto, and parts of its sculptural decoration, such as the figure of Neptune and the Naiads recumbent on the right and left, which Knobelsdorff sketched ca. 1750,[67] are based on various pages from the influential design catalogue for interior decorations or movable art, with the resounding name *Morceaux de fantaisie*, by the painter de Lajoue. Knobelsdorff saw the catalogue in the form of an Augsburg reproduction by Jacob Wagner published by J. G. Hertel, after the Paris series (1738–45). The figure of Neptune, executed by Benckert, resembles the sea god of the Trevi Fountain and of the Dresden Neptune Fountain, which Lorenzo Mattielli created in 1744 after plans by Zacharias Longuelune for the park of the Palais Brühl-Marcolini. The grottoing of the interior is influenced by French grotto pavilions up to and including the famous Thetis Grotto in Versailles (1664, torn down in 1684).

Frederick modelled the Freundschaftstempel on his own sketch of the temple in the Amalthea Garden, dedicated to Apollo[68] – originally inspired by Voltaire's 1732 poem »Le temple de l'amitié« and now spurred on by a memorial round temple built in 1761 by his brother Henry in Rheinsberg. With the Apollo Temple – the first monopteros to be built on the Continent according to the rules of classical antiquity mediated by Palladio – Frederick and Knobelsdorff had successfully taken the »step from the painting into the landscape«[69]: The dreamland of Arcadia that French landscape painters since Claude Lorrain, Nicolas Poussin and finally Watteau had created two-dimensionally now conquered a space one could walk into. Included among works that inspired architectural structures are the Temple of the Sibyl in Tivoli or the round temple on Lancret's *Embarkation for Cythera*. As early as 1719, the oldest still extant garden monopteros had been built in Stowe by John Vanbrugh; it was at the end of a transverse avenue that intersected with the Baroque central axis.

The Chinesisches Teehaus, too, was sketched by the king himself. He was inspired by the pavilion, named »Trèfle« (cloverleaf) for its ground plan, in the park of Lunéville in Lorraine, built in 1742 by Emmanuel Héré de Corny for King Stanislaus Lesczinsky of Poland, with which Frederick was familiar from Héré's copperplate engravings. Gilded palm trees, like those that surround the pavilion, had already been used in 1748 for the theatre of the Stadtschloß by Hoppenhaupt. The natural décor element might have been familiar to Frederick through Marc-Antoine Laugier's mention of »large palm trees« in lieu of columns. Laugier had been describing, in 1753, an example of a natural structure based on the primeval hut that supported his thesis that »imitation« was the »mother of art«: »The wretched little peasant hut [Laugier] have described is the model from which people have made a blueprint of all the splendour and glory of architecture.«[70]

Presumably it was primarily the exotic aspect of the idea of palm trees that excited Frederick. Laugier's imaginary primeval hut as a principle for modern architecture was to be of interest only to Frederick's successor to the throne. In 1763 Frederick received »trois plans [...] à la Chinoise«, Chinese-style designs of bridges by the architect William Chambers (1728–1796). In the same year Chambers' work about the layout of Kew Gardens in London, *Plans, Elevations, Sections and Perspective Views of the Gardens and Buildings at Kew*, was published. The latter's *Designs of Chinese Buildings* had appeared in 1757. Chambers' books of designs also influenced the Dragon House, begun soon thereafter, which replicates the pagoda depicted by him on the bank of the Pearl River near Guangzhou (Canton) in the south of China.[71]

The hieroglyph-like relief symbols and images by one of the Hoppenhaupt brothers on the shaft of the obelisk attest the intentional reference to Egypt as its country of origin. It was Francesco Colonna who introduced obelisks as garden decorations in the woodcuts of the *Hypnerotomachia Poliphili*, Venice 1499. From Egypt they were brought to Rome as trophies. For instance, since 1587 an obelisk of Ramses II had decorated the theatre garden of the Villa Mattei. Henceforth, because of their towering form, they were a favourite device for accentuating focal points in landscapes and cities. Athanasius Kircher and Joan Blaeu, by depicting obelisks, promoted their popularity.[72]

Sanssouci as a place of memory

Already the gate of the grounds of Rheinsberg, where Frederick lived in his youth, sported an obelisk in combination with a semicircular portal, and the figures of Flora and Pomona. Another allusion to Rheinsberg is the two sphinxes at the end of the avenue leading south. Their key positions at the entrances and exits make them the gatekeepers of the remembrance of his time as a crown prince in Rheinsberg. Finally, other features of the architecture of memory included a few old-fashioned details such as *parterres* laid out in a square, or the central Thetis group.

The meandering paths near the Chinesisches Teehaus, called »Englische Gänge« (English walkways) in view of the place of origin of the landscape garden, seem to be committed to the past rather than to the modern English garden style. Very similar path formations were first laid out in the *bosquet* of Louis XIV's private garden, Louveciennes in Marly,[73] so that Frederick may have included them here as a reminiscence of the kitchen garden, referred to jokingly by Frederick William I himself as »Marly«, on the site of the later Park Sanssouci. Perhaps it was a small courtesy toward his unloved, though respected, father?[74] The latter had invited his son to dine »on the hill« of his »Marly« (1743) – an occasion on which Frederick became aware of the beauty of the location: »on the hill [...], from which the view is delightful«.[75]

Neuer Garten and Pfaueninsel

»Call in the country.« Alexander Pope: Epistle to Richard Boyle, Earl of Burlington, 1731

Neuer Garten – the sentimental revolution

With the layout of the Neuer Garten King Frederick William II turned his back on the forms of the Rococo.

zitieren auch die beiden Sphingen am Ende der nach Süden führenden Allee. Ihre Schlüsselpositionen an den Ein- und Ausgängen lassen sie zu Torhütern des Gedenkens an die Rheinsberger Kronprinzenzeit werden. In die Erinnerungsarchitekturen reihten sich schließlich einige altmodische Details, wie die im Quadrat angelegten Parterres oder die zentrale Thetisgruppe.

Eher der Vergangenheit als dem modernen englischen Gartenstil verpflichtet, erscheinen die mit Blick auf den Entstehungsort des Landschaftsgartens mit »Englische Gänge« bezeichneten Schlängelpfade am Chinesischen Teehaus. Ganz ähnliche Wegformationen wurden erstmalig im Boskett des Privatgartens Ludwigs XIV., Louveciennes in Marly, angelegt,[73] so daß Friedrich sie hier durchaus als Reminiszenz an den von Friedrich Wilhelm I. selbst scherzhaft »Marly« betitelten Küchengarten an der Stelle des späteren Park Sanssouci eingefügt haben mag. Vielleicht war es eine kleine Aufmerksamkeit dem ungeliebten, gleichwohl geachteten Vater gegenüber?[74] Dieser hatte seinen Sohn eingeladen, »auf dem Berg« seines »Marly« zu speisen (1743) – eine Gelegenheit, bei der sich Friedrich der Schönheit der Lage bewußt wurde: »auf dem Berg [...], von dem die Aussicht entzückend ist«.[75]

Neuer Garten und Pfaueninsel

»Call in the country.« (Die Landschaft hereinrufen.)
Alexander Pope: Epistle to Richard Boyle, Earl of Burlington, 1731

Der Neue Garten – die sentimentale Revolution

Mit der Anlage des Neuen Gartens kehrte König Friedrich Wilhelm II. den Formen des Rokoko den Rücken zu. Ab 1787 entstand im Nordosten Potsdams ein dem neuen Geschmack folgender sentimentaler Landschaftsgarten. Er schmiegt sich an das Westufer des Heiligen Sees, dehnt sich im Norden bis hin zum Jungfernsee und nimmt zunächst verhalten Bezug zur Flußlandschaft der Havel. Im Garten setzt sich fort, was sich bereits im Todesjahr des alten Königs 1786 bei der frühklassizistischen Neugestaltung von dessen Arbeits- und Schlafzimmer in Schloß Sanssouci durch den führenden Architekten der neuen Richtung, Friedrich Wilhelm von Erdmannsdorff (1736–1800), angekündigt hatte: ein Verlangen nach einfachen Raum- und Schmuckformen, das sich in der Gartenkunst mit dem Wunsch nach romantisch-gefühlsbetonten Wirkungen paart. Entlang klar strukturierter Wegeführungen und Gehölzgruppierungen, die vorgeben, natürlichen Wuchses zu sein, entfalten dekorative Staffagen diverser Länder und Epochen ein begehbares, stimmungsvolles Bilderbuch.[76]

Vorbild für die Gestaltung des Neuen Gartens war das von Fürst Leopold III. Friedrich Franz von Anhalt-Dessau angelegte Gartenreich Wörlitz, das neben Harbke bei Helmstedt als erste deutsche Anlage den Grundsätzen englisch-sentimentaler Gärten folgte, wie sie etwa William Chambers' Kew Garden ab 1730 vorgab. In der Natur, in fernen Zeiten und bei fernen Völkern erblickten die Zeitgenossen Friedrich Wilhelms II. Gegenentwürfe zu Gesellschaft und Kunst des als dekadent und verkünstelt angesehenen Rokoko. Das Gotische, das Chinesische, das Ägyptische, das Holländische, das Maurische und das Antike aus griechischer und römischer Zeit waren Geschmacksrichtungen, die aufgrund ihrer Gemeinsamkeit, das Einfache und Ursprüngliche zu verkörpern, als Kleinarchitektur oder Schmuckelement im Garten des 18. Jahrhunderts Seite an Seite stehen konnten. Zur Nachahmung der abgebildeten Gebäude regten Musterbücher und Gartenpublikationen an. Die wichtigste deutsche Publikation war das von dem Leipziger Philosophieprofessor Johann Gottfried Grohmann herausgegebene *Ideenmagazin für Liebhaber von Gärten, Englischen Anlagen und für Besitzer von Landgütern um Gärten und ländlichen Gegenden, sowohl mit geringen als auch großem Geldaufwand nach den originellsten Englischen, Gothischen, Sienesischen Geschmacksmanieren zu verschönern und zu veredeln*. ([2]1797 ff.)

Wie bereits bei der Verwirklichung seiner Architekturideen fehlte es Friedrich Wilhelm II. auch für die Gartenkunst an einheimischen Kräften. Der neue König hatte während seiner Kronprinzenzeit die fortschrittlichen Kunstschöpfungen im Fürstentum Anhalt-Dessau verfolgt und den dort tätigen Erdmannsdorff später selber als künstlerischen Berater, Kunstagenten und Reiseführer eingestellt. Erdmannsdorff hatte Italien und England bereist. Johann August Eyserbeck (1762–1801), dessen Vater die Wörlitzer Anlagen geplant hatte, wurde mit der Gestaltung des Neuen Gartens betraut.

Eyserbeck begann 1791 mit der Pflanzung von 12 000 Bäumen. Weißdorn, Wacholder, Lärchen, Sumachbäume, Feldulmen, Fichten, Riesenwacholder, Schwarzpappeln, Trompetenbäume sowie exotische Sorten wie Weymouthskiefern, nordamerikanische Hemlocktannen, Geweihbäume, Schimmelfichten, kanadische Pappeln, Virginische Traubenkirschen und Robinien wurden aus heimischen Forstbaumschulen sowie aus Leipzig, Wörlitz, Dessau, Zerbst und Schlesien herbeigeschafft. Johann Georg Morsch (ca. 1750–1804) leitete die Ausführung der gärtnerischen Arbeiten.

Friedrich Wilhelms II. Reiseeindrücke prägten den Garten und seine Architekturen ebenso wie seine Vorlieben und Leidenschaften. 1780 reiste er nach St. Petersburg und besuchte das dortige holländische Dorf im Landschaftspark Zarin Katharinas II. 1788 fuhr er nach Kleve zum Besuch des Gartens des Hauses Bellevue und nach Het Loo in Holland, 1794 nach Warschau zum Besuch des Palais Lazienki (auch: Palast auf dem Wasser). Er las die Werke der französischen Aufklärer Voltaire und vor allem Jean-Jacques Rousseau sowie William Shakespeare und die Schriften des Altertumsforschers Johann Joachim Winckelmann (1717–1768). Er liebte die Frauen, vor allem aber seine Mätresse Wilhelmine Encke, seit 1794 Gräfin von Lichtenau (1753–1820).

Er mochte die Nähe seiner Residenzen zum Wasser, um sie mit dem Boot aufzusuchen, das Cellospiel, die Abgeschiedenheit und begeisterte sich für die Ideen der Freimaurer und des Ordens vom Gold- und Rosenkreuz. Angeregt und unterstützt durch Herzog Friedrich August von Braunschweig-Oels, Prinz Carl von Hessen und seinen Außenminister Johann Christoph von Woellner, trat Friedrich Wilhelm 1781 dem Orden bei. Die engsten Vertrauten des Königs waren Wilhelmine Encke, die 1795/96 Italien bereist hatte, und Friedrich Wilhelms Geheimer Kämmerer Johann Friedrich Ritz (1755–1809), der die Gotik favorisierte. Sie berieten ihn in künstlerischen Fragen und beeinflußten so die Anlage des Neuen Gartens unmittelbar. Erster Garteninspektor in Preußen war zwar Heinrich Ludwig Manger (1728–1790). Die Lieblingsgärten des Königs, Charlottenburg, der Neue Garten und die Pfaueninsel unterstanden jedoch nicht ihm, sondern Ritz.

From 1787 on, a sentimental landscape garden that followed the new trend was created northeast of Potsdam. It hugs the west bank of Heiliger See, extends as far as Jungfernsee in the north and refers back, cautiously at first, to the landscape of the Havel River. In the garden a trend that had already been in the air since 1786, when the old king died, is continued; that year, the king's study and bedroom in Schloß Sanssouci were renovated in the early classical style by the leading architect of the new movement, Friedrich Wilhelm von Erdmannsdorff (1736 to 1800). This trend is characterized by a desire for simple spatial and ornamental forms, coupled in the gardens with the wish for romantic, emotional effects. Along clearly structured paths and groupings of trees that profess to have evolved naturally, decorative accessories from various countries and eras unfold a walk-through picture book full of atmosphere.[76]

The model for the layout of the Neuer Garten was the Wörlitz Garden Realm created by Prince Leopold III Frederick Franz of Anhalt-Dessau. Besides Harbke near Helmstedt it was the first German park to follow the principles of English sentimental gardens, in the style modelled, for instance, by William Chambers' Kew Gardens after 1730. In nature, in the distant past and among faraway peoples, the contemporaries of Frederick William II saw alternatives to a Rococo society and art they viewed as decadent and artificial. The Gothic, Chinese, Egyptian, Dutch, Moorish and classical Greek and Roman cultures represented tastes that, on account of their common ground to embody what was simple and natural, could stand side by side in an 18th-century garden in the form of small-scale structures or decorative elements. Design books and garden publications prompted garden architects to imitate the buildings depicted in them. The most important German publication was the *Ideenmagazin für Liebhaber von Gärten, Englischen Anlagen und für Besitzer von Landgütern um Gärten und ländlichen Gegenden, sowohl mit geringen als auch großem Geldaufwand nach den originellsten Englischen, Gothischen, Sienesischen Geschmacksmanieren zu verschönern und zu veredeln*, published by the Leipzig professor of philosophy Johann Gottfried Grohmann. (^{2}1797 ff.)

Frederick William II lacked the local staff to help him realize not only his architectural plans but also his ideas about garden design. During his time as a crown prince the new king had followed the progressive artistic creations in the principality of Anhalt-Dessau. Later he himself hired Erdmannsdorff, who was working in Anhalt-Dessau, as an artistic advisor, art agent and travel guide. Erdmannsdorff had toured Italy and England. Johann August Eyserbeck, whose father had planned Wörlitz Park, was given the task of designing the Neuer Garten.

Eyserbeck began in 1791 by planting 12 000 trees. Hawthorn trees, junipers, larches, sumac, small-leaved elms, spruces, eastern red cedars, black poplars, catalpas as well as exotic species such as eastern white pines, North American hemlocks, Kentucky coffee trees, white spruces, eastern cottonwoods, chokecherries and black locusts were brought from local tree nurseries as well as from Leipzig, Wörlitz, Dessau, Zerbst and Silesia. Johann Georg Morsch (ca. 1750–1804) was in charge of the gardening work.

The travel impressions of Frederick William II shaped the garden and its architectural structures, as did his preferences and passions. In 1780 he traveled to St. Petersburg and visited the Dutch village there in the landscape park of Czarina Catherine II. In 1788 he went to Cleves to visit the garden of Bellevue House and to Het Loo in Holland. In 1794 he travelled to Warsaw to visit the Lazienki Palace (a.k.a. Palace on the Water). He read the works of French Enlightenment figures like Voltaire, and especially Jean-Jacques Rousseau and William Shakespeare and the writings of archeologist Johann Joachim Winckelmann (1717–1768). He loved women, but particularly his mistress Wilhelmine Encke, elevated to the rank of Countess of Lichtenau after 1794 (1753–1820).

He liked the fact that his residences were near water and that he could go there by boat; he loved playing the cello and solitude, and was thrilled by the ideas of the Freemasons and the Order of the Hermetic Gold and Rose Cross. Encouraged and supported by Duke Frederick Augustus of Braunschweig-Oels, Prince Charles of Hesse and his foreign minister, Johann Christoph von Woellner, Frederick William joined the order in 1781. The closest confidants of the king were Wilhelmine Encke, who had toured Italy in 1795/96, and Frederick William's privy chamberlain, Johann Friedrich Ritz (1755–1809), who favoured the Gothic style. They advised him in artistic matters and thus directly influenced the design of the Neuer Garten. To be sure, the head garden inspector in Prussia was Heinrich Ludwig Manger (1728–1790). However, not he but Ritz was responsible for the king's favourite gardens – Charlottenburg, the Neuer Garten and Pfaueninsel.

The location of the Neuer Garten, overlooking Heiliger See, the Havel River and Jungfernsee as well as the rural idyll of meadows, mills, vineyards, orchards and fields of grain on the eastern shore of Heiliger See had prompted Frederick William back when he was heir to the throne to purchase the land on the lake shore. Additional purchases of land expanded the park, up to 1793, to its present size of almost 74 ha. Eyserbeck incorporated in the new park the housee of the previous owners, called the Rotes, the Grünes and the Weißes Haus because of the colour they were painted, while the house by the lake was replaced by the early-classicist Marmorpalais begun in 1787 by Gontard (illus. 23).

In connection with this »New House« a group of architects beside Gontard – Andreas Ludwig Krüger (1743 to 1822) as building supervisor, Langhans from the Silesian province of Breslau and Michael Philipp Daniel Boumann (1747–1803) – created the smaller structures in the park. By the mid-1790s the garden and its decorations had been completed. In 1797 Boumann began to remodel the Marmorpalais; Ludwig Ferdinand Hesse (1795–1876) finished the work in 1843–48 according to plans by Ludwig Persius (1803–1845). The north and south wing, which were connected by quarter-circle galleries with the cube-shaped main building, were meant to provide additional space now that the king was spending more and more time in the Neuer Garten. However, when he died in the Marmorpalais on 16 November 1797, work on the interior had not begun yet.

As the oldest and only Chinese decoration, a copper parasol or umbrella protected the seat on the former Schneckenberg that briefly stood where the north wing of the Marmorpalais is now located. In 1798 it was moved. Along what is now the poplar avenue Gontard designed for members of the court the Dutch brick complex of servants' quarters, royal stables, outbuildings and Kavaliershaus, implemented by Krüger in 1789/90. In the tradition of model villages since Queen Marie

Die landschaftliche Lage mit ihren Ausblicken auf den Heiligen See, die Havel und den Jungfernsee sowie auf die ländliche Idylle aus Wiesen, Mühlen, Wein-, Obst- und Kornfeldern am Ostufer des Heiligen Sees hatten Friedrich Wilhelm bereits als Thronfolger veranlaßt, das Land am Seeufer zu erwerben. Der Zukauf von Grundstücken erweiterte den Park bis 1793 auf seine heutige Größe von nahezu 74 ha. Das nach ihrem Anstrich sogenannte Rote, Grüne und Weiße Haus der Grundstücksvorbesitzer integrierte Eyserbeck in die neue Anlage, das Haus am See wich dem 1787 von Gontard begonnenen frühklassizistischen Marmorpalais (Abb. 23).

Im Anschluß an dieses »Neue Haus« schufen außer Gontard die Architekten Andreas Ludwig Krüger (1743 bis 1822) als Bauleiter, Langhans aus der schlesischen Provinz Breslau und Michael Philipp Daniel Boumann (1747–1803) die Kleinbauten im Park. Bis zur Mitte der 1790er Jahre waren der Garten und seine Ausstattung vollendet. Boumann begann 1797 das Marmorpalais umzugestalten, Ludwig Ferdinand Hesse (1795–1876) vollendete es in den Jahren 1843–48 nach Plänen von Ludwig Persius (1803–1845). Nord- und Südflügel, die über Viertelkreisgalerien mit dem kubusartigen Hauptgebäude verbunden wurden, sollten den immer längeren Aufenthalten des Königs im Neuen Garten Raum bieten. Bei seinem Tod am 16. November 1797 im Marmorpalais hatte ihr Innenausbau jedoch noch nicht begonnen.

Als älteste und einzige chinesische Staffage schützte ein aus Kupfer gefertigter Sonnen- beziehungsweise Regenschirm den Sitzplatz auf dem ehemaligen Schneckenberg, der sich kurzzeitig an der Stelle des heutigen Nordflügels des Marmorpalais befunden hatte. 1798 wurde er versetzt. Entlang der heutigen Pappelallee entwarf Gontard für den Hofstaat das 1789–90 von Krüger ausgeführte holländische Backsteinensemble aus Domestikenhäusern, Marstall, Remisengehöft und Kavalierhaus. In der Tradition von Musterdörfern seit dem Hameau der Königin Marie Antoinette in Versailles stellte es ein ideales Abbild schlichten ländlichen Lebens dar. Einen ähnlichen Gegenentwurf zur höfischen Lebensführung zeigte beispielsweise auch die Holländerei von Zarskoje Selo.

Für Zusammenkünfte der Hofgesellschaft und ihrer Gäste schuf Krüger 1791/92 am Jungfernsee einen festlichen Ort in Grottengestalt, den dichter Wald hinterfing. Während das Äußere eine natürliche Felshöhle vermuten läßt, überraschten die drei Säle im Inneren durch ihre bunt glitzernde Wandgestaltung aus farbig unterlegtem Marienglas, grünem Serpentinit und Muscheln (Abb. 24). Spiegel vervielfachten ihre Wirkung. In einer lichten Landschaftspartie am Nordostufer des Heiligen Sees entstand 1792/93 ein Maurischer Tempel, von Langhans ausgeführt, der 1869 wegen Baufälligkeit abgerissen wurde.

Unter fremdem Gewand versteckten sich auch profane Nutzgebäude. Die Schloßküche von Gontard, entstanden 1788–90, präsentiert sich als halb versunkene Tempelruine mit ihren im Erdboden vergrabenen Säulenschäften, korinthischen Kapitellen, akanthusrankengeschmücktem Gebälk und Giebel. Ihre unvollendete Ausführung suggeriert Zerstörung.[77] Vorbild dürfte der verschüttet erhaltene Marstempel auf dem Forum Romanum in Rom gewesen sein. Küche und Marmorpalais blicken mit ihren Schauseiten auf den See. Nähert man sich ihnen am Seeufer von Süden her, taucht nach einer Wegkrümmung zunächst die Ruine auf, bevor sich hinter der Kulisse des Verfalls das Marmorpalais erhebt. Der Niedergang einstiger Größe und die Wiedergeburt klassischer Architektur wurden als Zusammenschau inszeniert.

Die Orangerie entwarf Langhans 1791–93. Darin überwintern noch heute Orangenbäume und andere exotische Pflanzen, während der mittlere der drei Säle als Konzertraum gestaltet wurde. In Architektur und Ausstattung bringt die Orangerie ägyptische, klassizistische und gotisierende Elemente zusammen – ein Gewächshaus der Stile als Antwort auf den Neuen Garten, der eben jene Stile unter freiem Himmel vereint.

Die Südseite gibt durch große Fenster und eine mittlere Tür den Blick zum Park frei. Die Innenausstattung des von Langhans entworfenen festlichen »Orange Saals«, des späteren Palmensaals (Abb. 25), variiert das Gartenthema: Die Wände sind aus einheimischen Hölzern boisiert. An ihnen wachsen grün gefaßte Palmen aus kannelierten Säulenstümpfen bis in den Deckenbereich empor, wobei sie sich als aufgelegtes Stabwerk in ein Wandgliederungssystem verwandeln. An der Decke umspielen licht gemalte Ranken und Blüten die Bilder musizierender Putten. Auf Konsolen und Podesten standen Topfpflanzen in *cache-pots* aus Porzellan.

Langhans' Schöpfung spiegelt die Rückkehr zur Natur wider, die im Kontext der Kulturkritik von Jean-Jacques Rousseau zum Schlagwort avanciert war. Rousseaus Idealvorstellung einer neuen Einfachheit hatte der französische Theoretiker Marc-Antoine Laugier auf die Baukunst übertragen und die Urhütte zum theoretischen Ideal und Maß der modernen Architektur bestimmt. Las Langhans Laugier? Die geregelte Natur des Palmensaals mit ihren Anklängen an gotische Kirchenräume scheint die folgende Passage aus Laugiers *Essai sur l'architecture* von 1753 gleichsam nachzubilden: »Ich stelle mir vor, wenn in einer Kirche die Säulen aus großen Palmenbäumen bestünden, die ihre Aeste rechts und links ausbreiteten, und dadurch den Bogen des Gewölbes vorstellten; so würde dieß eine erstaunliche Wirkung thun. [...] An den Rippen des Gewölbes lassen sich die gothischen Glieder in andere von besserer Wahl verwandeln: an dem inwendigen Gewölbe lassen sich [...] geflochtene Palmen machen [...] Eine solche Einrichtung wäre nichts als eine Nachahmung der Natur, die man sehr vollkommen und wichtig machen könnte; ich zweifle, ob es jemand gereuen würde diese Methode gewählt zu haben.«[78]

Laugiers Postulat der Urhütte folgt auch das zweite Küchengebäude, in Betrieb ab 1796, in der die Speisen für die Bewirtung in der Grotte vorbereitet wurden. Der gebotenen Einfachheit gehorchte sie als baumrindenverkleidetes Häuschen, 1958 wurde es abgebrochen, 2010/11 wieder aufgebaut. In unmittelbarer Nähe zu dieser Küche stand in dichtem Gehölz am nördlichsten Ende des Gartens eine Einsiedelei. Wieder entpuppte sich der Innenraum des in anrührender Schlichtheit getarnten Borkenpavillons als festlicher, kostbar vertäfelter Salon mit einer Deckenmalerei, die die sieben Planetengötter und die Tierkreiszeichen zeigte. Der Marmorboden stellte in schwarz-weißer Inkrustation eine Weltkarte dar. In vier Nischen des ovalen Raums standen Antikenabgüsse der Töchter des Lykomedes. Die Einsiedelei wurde 1961 bis auf die Fundamente abgetragen.

Die Bibliothek, die Meierei und ein seit etwa 1913 verlorenes gotisierendes Müllerhaus von 1795 deklinieren mit Maßwerk, Spitzbogenarkaden und -rahmungen, Rundfenstern und Rustizierung neogotisches Architek-

23. Unbekannter Zeichner, Marmorpalais im Neuen Garten, Gartenseite, um 1789. Feder, aquarelliert. (SPSG, Potsdam.)
24. Mittelsaal der Grotte im Neuen Garten, Zustand 1912. (SPSG, Potsdam.)
25. Palmensaal der Orangerie im Neuen Garten, Zustand 2003. (SPSG, Potsdam – Photo: Michael Bischoff.)

23. Unknown graphic artist, Marmorpalais in the Neuer Garten, garden façade, ca. 1789. Pen, painted in watercolours. (SPSG, Potsdam.)
24. Central hall of the grotto in the Neuer Garten, state in 1912. (SPSG, Potsdam.)
25. Palm hall of the Orangerie in the Neuer Garten, state in 2003. (SPSG, Potsdam – photo: Michael Bischoff.)

Antoinette's Hameau in Versailles it represented an ideal image of simple rustic life. An instance of a similar alternative to the courtly lifestyle was the dairy of Czarskoe Selo.

For gatherings of court society and their guests Krüger created, in 1791/92, a festive venue in the shape of a grotto by Jungfernsee, framed by dense woods. While the exterior leads one to expect a natural cave, the three halls in its interior surprised viewers by the colourful glittering design of the walls, which were made of isinglass on a coloured background, green serpentinite and seashells (illus. 24). Mirrors multiplied their effect. In a sunlit part of the landscape on the northeast bank of Heiliger See a Moorish temple was created in 1792/93, implemented by Langhans. It was torn down in 1869 due to its dilapidation.

Mundane utility buildings were also concealed in exotic guise. The palace kitchen, by Gontard, built in 1788 to 1790, presents itself as a half-sunken temple ruin with its columns buried in the ground, its Corinthian capitals and roof beams and gables wreathed with acanthus tendrils. The fact that the construction is unfinished suggests destruction.[77] It is probably modelled on the Temple of Mars on the Forum Romanum in Rome, preserved because it was buried. The front façades of the kitchen and the Marmorpalais face the lake. If one approaches them along the lakeshore from the south, the first to appear after a bend in the path is the ruin, before the Marmorpalais rises behind this scenery of disintegration. The decline of former greatness and the rebirth of classical architecture are staged as a simultaneous spectacle.

The Orangery was designed by Langhans in 1791–93. In it orange trees and other exotic plants overwinter to this day, while the middle one of the three halls was designed as a concert space. In its architecture and furnishings the orangery combines Egyptian, classicist and faux-Gothic elements – a hothouse of styles as a response to the Neuer Garten, which unites those very styles in the open air.

Large windows and a central door on the south side provide a view of the park. The interior design of the festive »Orange Hall« designed by Langhans, later known as the Hall of Palms (illus. 25), is a variation on the garden theme: The walls are panelled with native woods. Along them palm trees framed in green grow from fluted frustums of columns up to the ceiling, where they are transformed into a system of superimposed bars that structure the walls. On the ceiling brightly painted tendrils and blossoms twine around the figures of putti making music. Potted plants used to stand in porcelain *cache-pots* on brackets and pedestals.

Langhans' work reflects the return to nature that had become a catchword in the context of Jean-Jacques Rousseau's critique of civilisation. The French theoretician Marc-Antoine Laugier (1713–1769) had transferred Rousseau's ideal of a new simplicity to architecture and declared the primeval hut to be the theoretical ideal and measure of modern architecture. Had Langhans read Laugier? The regularity of the Hall of Palms with its allusions to Gothic churches seems to reproduce the following passage from Laugier's 1753 *Essai sur l'architecture*, as it were: »I imagine that if in a church the columns consisted of tall palm trees spreading their branches right and left, thus representing the arch of the vaulted ceiling, the effect would be amazing. [...] The Gothic sections of the ribs of the vault can be transformed to other, better alternatives: plaited palms can be created on the surface of the interior vault [...] Such an arrangement would be nothing but an imitation of nature, which could be carried out very perfectly and significantly; I doubt whether anyone would regret choosing this method.«[78]

Laugier's postulate of the primeval hut is observed by the second kitchen building as well; in operation as of 1796, it was the place where food was prepared to be served in the grotto. Clad with tree bark, the little house had the simplicity required by Laugier. In 1958 it was torn down, to be rebuilt once more in 2010/11. Directly next to this kitchen, a hermitage stood in a dense wood at the northernmost end of the garden. Once again the interior of the pavilion of a touchingly plain building camouflaged with tree bark turned out to be a festive salon, sumptuously panelled with a ceiling fresco showing the seven planet gods and the signs of the zodiac. The marble floor represented a map of the world in black-and-white incrustation. In four niches of the oval room stood casts of classical statues – the daughters of Lycomedes. The hermitage was razed in 1961 except for its foundations.

The architectural style of the library, the dairy und a Gothic-style miller's house dated 1795 and lost since ca. 1913 is neo-Gothic, with tracery, arcades of Gothic arches und frames, circular windows and rustication. The dairy was designed by Langhans in 1791, converted in 1843/44 to a pumping station in the Norman style to which a tower was added in 1847 by Persius. The building combines Gothic features with a villa façade whose portico, main and mezzanine floor follow the canon for villas advocated by the Italian Renaissance architect Andrea Palladio. Intimacy – the king had a private room here where he could enjoy drinking milk – and economic function (the breeding of animals and public sale of milk) complemented each other.

The »Gotischer Turm«, another name for the two-storey library at the south end of Heiliger See, was built in 1792–94 based on a design by Langhans (illus. 26).[79] It is located by the former road between Heiliger See and the northeast section of town and rises above the quay wall of a canal bridged by the Behlertsbrücke that flowed into Heiliger See from the direction of town. Arcades open the building toward the landscape.

The picturesque arrangement of canal, bridge, library and a cluster of trees consisting of weeping willows and Italian-looking cottonwoods against a backdrop of park and urban landscape creates a garden tableau whose charm lies in contrasts: compact, densely planted vegetation versus open space that garden artist Lenné would expand to a fan-shaped vista in the 19th century. Views across the lake in the direction of the Marmorpalais, Brauhausberg, the spire of the Heiligengeistkirche and the rural suburb Berliner Vorstadt as well as Babelsberg, Glienicke and Sacrow; plus curved lines – the branches of weeping willows, the arches of the bridge, the library's arched openings – as counterparts to the vertical accents of the tops of the towers of the library, the Marmorpalais and the Heiligengeistkirche.

The contrasting moods – melancholy and serene – correspond to the visual contrasts. The exposed site of the library is similar to the geographical situation of the library in Wörlitz Park. While the library – a Gothic tower pavilion – is a response to the classicism of the Marmorpalais, the all-encompassing arch in the north stretches as far as the Maurischer Tempel. The dairy and the

turvokabular. Die Meierei wurde 1791 von Langhans entworfen, 1843/44 im normannischen Stil zum Pumpwerk umgebaut und erhielt 1847 einen Turmanbau durch Persius. Sie verbindet das Gotische mit einer Villenfront, die mit Portikus, Haupt- und Mezzaningeschoß dem Villenkanon des italienischen Renaissancearchitekten Andrea Palladio folgt. Intimität – der König besaß hier ein privates Zimmer zum Genuß von Milch – und wirtschaftliche Funktion von Tieraufzucht und öffentlichem Milchverkauf ergänzten sich.

Der »Gothische Turm«, wie die zweigeschossige Bibliothek am südlichen Ende des Heiligen Sees auch genannt wurde, entstand in den Jahren 1792–94 nach einem Entwurf von Langhans (Abb. 26).[79] Sie erhebt sich an der einstigen Landstraße zwischen Heiligem See und nordöstlichem Stadtgebiet über der Kaimauer eines von der Behlertsbrücke überquerten Kanals, der von der Stadt her kommend in den Heiligen See mündete. Arkaden öffnen das Gebäude zur Landschaft.

Die malerische Anordnung von Kanal, Brücke, Bibliothek, Baumgruppe aus Trauerweiden und italienisch anmutenden Pyramidenpappeln vor der Kulisse der Park- und Stadtlandschaft ergeben ein Gartenbild, dessen Reiz in Kontrasten besteht: Gedrängtheit durch dichte Bepflanzung versus Weite, die der Gartenkünstler Lenné im 19. Jahrhundert zum Fächerblick dehnen wird. Blicke über den See zum Marmorpalais, zum Brauhausberg, zum Heiligengeistkirchturm und zur ländlichen Berliner Vorstadt sowie nach Babelsberg, Glienicke und Sacrow; dazu geschwungene Linien – Äste von Trauerweiden, Brückenbogen, Rundbogenöffnungen der Bibliothek – als Gegenstücke zu den vertikalen Akzenten der Turmspitzen von Bibliothek, Marmorpalais und Heiligengeistkirchturm.

Den bildlichen Kontrasten entsprechen die gegensätzlichen Stimmungswerte elegisch und heiter. Die exponierte Lage der Bibliothek gleicht der geographischen Situation der Bibliothek im Park Wörlitz. Während die Bibliothek als gotischer Turmpavillon eine Gegenantwort zum Klassizismus des Marmorpalais bietet, spannt sich der Bogen im Norden in enzyklopädischer Weite bis hin zum Maurischen Tempel. Meierei und Müllerhaus hingegen zeigen ländliche Idyllen, die als Ausblicke auf eine unverdorbene Welt dienten: Die auf der vorgelagerten Wiese gehaltenen Kühe, Ochsen und Schafe vervollständigten das Meiereibild. Die Rehbucht nahe bei Meierei und Grotte entwarf ein pastorales Stück, das bukolische Hirtenidyllen nachempfand. Das Müllerhaus akzentuierte das bäuerliche Panorama am Ostufer des Heiligen Sees gegenüber dem Marmorpalais.

Mehrfach läßt der Neue Garten das Ägyptenmotiv anklingen: Ein Eiskeller zum Kühlen von Speisen mit Hilfe von im Winter gewonnenem Eis aus dem See entstand in Form einer ägyptischen Pyramide, ausgeführt von Krüger 1791/92. Pseudohieroglyphen und Planetenzeichen schmücken sie. Eine Vorlage fand sich mit der von Georges-Louis Le Rouge in den *Heften zur Neuen Gartenkunst* publizierten Pyramide la Glacière im Garten Désert de Retz in der Île de France. Nahebei stand die in Sandstein nach ägyptischem Original kopierte Statue der Artemis Ephesia, umgeben von 12 Kanopen. Ihre Aufstellung mag von der Ägyptenkopiensammlung im Keller des Wörlitzer Pantheons angeregt worden sein.

Ein Sphingenpaar ruhte in den rustizierten Halbkreisnischen seitlich des Kanaldurchlaufs der Behlertsbrücke. Eine weitere Sphinx lagert auf dem Architrav des Bogens über dem Hauptportal der Orangerie. Alle drei stammen von Wohler. In den Wandnischen beiderseits des Orangerieportals stehen Wächterfiguren, die mit den Attributen eines Pharaos ausgestattet sind, mit Nemes-Kopftuch, Schendjut-Leinenschurz und Leinenrollen, dem Tuch der Wiedergeburt.[80] Den Obelisken vor dem Marmorpalais entwarf Langhans 1793–94, ihn schmücken Medaillons der vier Jahreszeiten von Johann Gottfried Schadow (1764–1850) und den Gebrüdern Johann Christoph und Michael Christoph Wohler (1748–99, 1754 bis 1802).

Die Aufstellung antiker Skulpturen befriedigte den Wunsch nach der Wiederbelebung des Altertums. Ein durch Erdmannsdorff angekaufter Hermenschaft aus der Villa Negroni in Rom mit der griechischen Aufschrift »Themistokles« fand 1798 auf der Landzunge im Norden am Jungfernsee seinen Platz.

Die sentimentalen Landschaftsgärten des 18. Jahrhunderts hielten auch das Erinnern wach. Im Neuen Garten standen zwei Gedächtnisurnen für Frühverstorbene: die Geliebte des Königs, Julie von Voß (gest. 1789), Gräfin von Ingenheim, sowie seinen unehelichen Lieblingssohn aus der Verbindung mit Wilhelmine Encke, Alexander Graf von der Mark (gest. 1787).

Hat Friedrich Wilhelm II. in Grotte, Einsiedelei und Maurischem Tempel geheime Seancen und Reinigungsrituale seines Ordens abgehalten? War die Pyramide gleichsam der Eingang in die Unterwelt, um mit den geliebten Verstorbenen in Zwiesprache treten zu können? Soll der griechische Feldherr Themistokles an die Kraft geheimer Orakel erinnern, da ihm doch der delphische Bescheid zum Sieg über die Perser verholfen hatte? Sind die Sphingen Hüter geheimnisvoller Dinge?[81] Den Garten auf ein eindeutiges, vielleicht rosenkreuzerisches Programm festzulegen oder ihn als Übertragung von Roman- oder Singspielvorlagen wie etwa *König Sethos* vom Abbé Terrasson oder *Die Zauberflöte* in die Natur zu verstehen, würde seinen zahlreichen Facetten nicht gerecht werden.

Der Neue Garten war Friedrich Wilhelms II. persönliche Ideallandschaft. Sichten und Gegensichten über weite Distanzen, Gegenüberstellungen im Detail bündelten die unbegrenzten Themen seiner Visionen. Gestaltung, Bepflanzung und Staffagen entsprachen dem Zeitstil, feierten den englischen Landschaftsgarten, der sinnliche Versenkung ermöglichte und im Sinne Rousseaus zudem auch ökonomisch war. Am ästhetischen Genuß konnten all diejenigen teilhaben, denen der herkömmliche Vorrat an Bildern aus dem gemeinsamen Gedächtnis ihrer Kultur geläufig war.

1913–17 wurde der Neue Garten Standort des letzten Schloßbaus der Hohenzollern. Im Stil englischer Landhäuser errichtete Paul Schultze-Naumburg (1869–1949) das Fachwerkgebäude für das letzte preußische Kronprinzenpaar des deutschen Kaiserreichs, Wilhelm und Cecilie Auguste Marie aus dem Haus Mecklenburg. Seinen Platz fand es inmitten der Gehölzmassen, die Lenné im Bereich der ehemaligen Rehbucht hatte pflanzen lassen. Harmonisch fügt es sich in das Bestehende ein.[82]

Die Pfaueninsel – »der Lage halber«

Friedrich Wilhelm II. begann 1793 mit der Erschließung entfernterer Grundstücke, deren landschaftsgärtnerische Gestaltung eine Erweiterung des Neuen Gartens mit sich brachte. Auf dem Pfingst-, damals Judenberg,

26. August Wilhelm Ferdinand Schirmer, Gotische Bibliothek mit Behlertsbrücke im Neuen Garten, 1824. Aquarell. (SPSG/KPM-Archiv, Potsdam.)

26. August Wilhelm Ferdinand Schirmer, Gotische Bibliothek with Behlertsbrücke in the Neuer Garten, 1824. Watercolour. (SPSG/KPM-Archiv, Potsdam.)

miller's house, on the other hand, present rustic idylls that showed courtiers a pristine world: The cows, oxen and sheep which were kept in the meadow in front of the dairy completed the image. The so-called Rehbucht near the dairy and grotto was a pastoral scene that recreated bucolic pastoral idylls. The miller's house accentuated the rustic panorama on the east shore of Heiliger See opposite the Marmorpalais.

Repeatedly, the Neuer Garten alludes to the motif of ancient Egypt: A cold cellar where food is kept cool by means of ice obtained from the lake in winter was built in the form of an Egyptian pyramid, implemented by Krüger in 1791/92. It is decorated with hieroglyphs and the symbols for the planets. Its model is a pyramid publicized by Georges-Louis Le Rouge in *Hefte zur Neuen Gartenkunst*, la Glacière in the garden Désert de Retz in Île de France. Nearby stood a statue of Artemis Ephesia copied in sandstone from an Egyptian original, surrounded by twelve canopic jars. The installation may have been inspired by the collection of Egyptian copies in the basement of the Wörlitz Pantheon.

A pair of sphinxes reclined in the rusticated semicircular recesses on the sides of the canal where it flowed under the Behlertsbrücke. Another sphinx lies on the architrave of the arch above the main portal of the Orangery. All three are by Wohler. In the wall niches on both sides of the orangery portal are guardian figures which have the attributes of a Pharaoh – a nemes headdress, shendyt linen kilt and linen rolls, the cloth of rebirth.[80] The obelisk in front of the Marmorpalais was designed by Langhans in 1793–94; it is decorated with medallions of the four seasons by Johann Gottfried Schadow (1764–1850) and the brothers Johann Christoph and Michael Christoph Wohler (1748–1799, 1754 to 1802).

The erection of classical sculptures satisfied the wish to bring to life the world of the ancient Greeks and Romans. The shaft of a herm purchased by Erdmannsdorff from the Villa Negroni in Rome with the Greek inscription »Themistocles« was placed on the promontory on the north side of Jungfernsee in 1798.

The sentimental landscape gardens of the 18th century also kept memories alive. In the Neuer Garten there were two memorial urns for people who had died prematurely: the king's mistress, Julie von Voß, Countess Ingenheim (d. 1789), and his illegitimate favourite son from his liaison with Wilhelmine Encke, Count Alexander von der Mark (d. 1787).

Did Frederick William II hold the secret séances and purification rituals of his order in the Grotto, Hermitage and Moorish Temple? Was the pyramid the entrance to the underworld, as it were, making it possible to converse with beloved people who had died? Is the Greek commander Themistocles meant to remind us of the power of secret oracles? After all, the reply of the Delphic oracle had helped him gain the victory over the Persians. Are the sphinxes the guardians of mysteries?[81] We would not do justice to the garden's many facets if we were to limit it to an unambiguous, possibly Rosicrucian, programme or interpret it as a rendering in terms of a natural landscape of novels or operas such as the Abbé Terrasson's *Life of Sethos* or Mozart's *Magic Flute*.

The Neuer Garten was Frederick William II's personal ideal landscape. Views across great distances and contrasting views in detail bundled together the unlimited themes of his visions. The design, the plants and trees, and the decorations were in keeping with period style, and celebrated the English landscape garden that made sensual immersion possible and, as Rousseau intended, was also economical. All those who were familiar with the traditional stock of images from the collective memory of their culture could share in the aesthetic enjoyment.

In 1913–17 Neuer Garten became the site of the last palace to be built by the Hohenzollerns. In the style of English country houses, Paul Schultze-Naumburg (1869–1949) built the half-timbered house for the last Prussian crown prince of the German Empire, William, and his wife, Cecilie Auguste Marie of the House of Mecklenburg. Harmoniously integrated in the landscape, it was located in the middle of dense woods planted according to Lenné's directions in the area of the former Rehbucht.[82]

The Pfaueninsel – »because of its location«

In 1793 Frederick William began developing more distant plots of land, and their landscaping brought with it an expansion of the Neuer Garten. On Pfingstberg, called Judenberg at the time, he planned an additional neo-Gothic eye-catcher, though the new Gothic house with its tower was never built. Instead, Frederick William II purchased Pfaueninsel »because of its location«,[83] called Kaninchenwerder at the time, and originally known as Pfauenwerder. The Havel River became part of the park landscape.[84]

In contrast to the terrain of the Neuer Garten, which had to be completely newly planted, Pfaueninsel owed its characteristic appearance to the oak trees planted several hundred years previously, probably ca. 1440 in memory of Elector Frederick I of Brandenburg. In the centre of the island, pasture oaks (*Hudeeichen*) stand together as a cluster with their spreading branches, while in the west isolated, majestically soaring trees accentuate the gently sloping meadows. »[...] Let not one more piece of wood be felled there«,[85] decreed Frederick William II on 12 November 1793. Johann Friedrich Morsch the Younger (1765–1834), the younger brother of Johann Georg Morsch, carried out the gardening work on Pfaueninsel in 1794–1804 under the direction of Eyserbeck.

From spring until autumn 1794 a small castle was built on the south shore in the westernmost part of the island as a destination for outings by boat. Once more the king was fascinated by the idea of staging decay. His architect was master carpenter Johann Gottlieb Brendel, who used exclusively local types of wood for the construction. Sandstone sand applied to a coat of oil paint gives the illusion of a stone structure. Two round towers frame the central, battlemented part of the building, above which a bridge connects the two towers.

If one looks from the Neuer Garten across the water, the little castle, painted white, flashes in the distance, 4 km away. Frederick William II could even catch a glimpse of the island paradise he had created for himself and his mistress Wilhelmine Encke from the Marmorpalais: From the Landscape Room on the top floor a line of sight leads directly over the Havel River to the island, the castle and even farther – now as a utopian line of longing that only someone who was in the know could pursue in his dreams – into the castle's interior, the Otaheitisches Kabinett (Tahitian Gallery) in the north tower, modelled on a bamboo hut.

plante er einen weiteren neogotischen Blickfang, doch wurde das neue gotische Haus mit Turm nie gebaut. Statt dessen erwarb Friedrich Wilhelm II. »der Lage halber«[83] die Pfaueninsel, damals Kaninchenwerder, ursprünglich Pfauenwerder genannt. Die Havel wurde Teil der Parklandschaft.[84]

Im Unterschied zum Gelände des Neuen Gartens, das komplett neu bepflanzt werden mußte, verlieh der Pfaueninsel ein mehrere hundert Jahre alter, wohl um 1440 zum Gedenken an Kurfürst Friedrich I. von Brandenburg gepflanzter Eichenbaumbestand ihr charakteristisches Gesicht. In der Inselmitte stehen die Hudeeichen mit ihrem ausladenden Geäst als Waldstück beieinander, im Westen akzentuieren einzelne, majestätisch aufragende Bäume die sanften Wiesenflächen. »[…] daß daselbst kein Stück Holz mehr gefället werde«,[85] verfügte Friedrich Wilhelm II. am 12. November 1793. Johann Friedrich Morsch d. J. (1765–1834), der jüngere Bruder von Johann Georg Morsch, führte 1794–1804, von Eyserbeck angeleitet, die Gartenarbeiten auf der Pfaueninsel aus.

Von Frühjahr bis Herbst 1794 entstand ein kleines Schloß als Ausflugsziel für Bootsfahrten am Südufer ganz im Westen der Insel. Wieder reizte den König die Inszenierung des Verfalls. Sein Architekt war der Zimmermeister Johann Gottlieb Brendel, der für den Bau ausschließlich einheimische Holzarten verwendete. Auf einem Ölfarbenanstrich aufgetragener Sandsteinsand täuscht einen Steinbau vor. Zwei Rundtürme rahmen den mittleren, zinnenbesetzten Baukörper, über dem eine Brücke beide Türme miteinander verbindet.

Läßt man den Blick vom Neuen Garten aus über das Wasser gleiten, blitzt das weiß gestrichene Schlößchen in der Ferne. Friedrich Wilhelm II. konnte gar aus dem Marmorpalais heraus einen Blick auf das für sich und seine Geliebte Wilhelmine Encke geschaffene, 4 km entfernte Inselparadies werfen: Vom Landschaftszimmer im Obergeschoß führt eine Blicklinie über das Havelwasser direkt zur Insel, zum Schloß und weiter noch – nun als utopische Sehnsuchtslinie, die nur der Wissende weiterträumen konnte – hinein ins Schloßinnere, in das Otaheitische Kabinett im Nordturm, das einer tahitischen Bambushütte nachempfunden ist.

Als kleiner Fingerzeig auf genau jene Verbindung erscheint hier das Marmorpalais inmitten einer Wandbemalung, die mit Palmen, Ananas, exotischen Tieren und Vögeln den Betrachter in die Inselwelt der Südsee eintauchen läßt (Abb. 27). Louis Antoine de Bougainville hatte in seiner Reisebeschreibung von der Entdeckung Tahitis 1768 gerade den Mythos der Südsee als Paradies des freien Lebens und der Liebe begründet. Die europäischen Höfe versorgte sein Ausruf mit Gesprächsstoff, er habe »la nouvelle Cythère« gefunden, also das neue Kythera, die Insel, deren Meeresschaum die Liebesgöttin Aphrodite gebar.

Landschaftszimmer und Otaheitisches Kabinett schufen subtile Wechselbeziehungen realer, gestalteter und gemalter Natur: Während das Innere des Marmorpalais die von Peter Ludwig Lütke 1790 geschaffenen italienischen Ideallandschaften darbot (seit 1945 verschollen) (Abb. 28) und im Pfaueninselschloß fremdländische Traumlandschaften aufscheinen, verknüpfen die Fensterausblicke in die Landschaft das Gemalte mit der realen Umgebung, wird Italien an das Ufer des Heiligen Sees verlagert, Tahiti auf die Pfaueninsel. Die gemalten Zäune im Kabinett, deren Spitzen enden, wo im nächsten Wandfeld der Fenstersims die tatsächliche Sicht nach draußen begrenzt, spielen mit der Täuschung, man könne über den Zaun hinweg ins offene Land blicken. Ein Vogel, der sich auf dem Zaun niedergelassen hat und in den Raum blickt, vermittelt vexierbildgleich zwischen innen und außen. Ähnliches vermögen die Spiegel im Landschaftszimmer, indem sie den Garten, den See, die Havel, die Hügel ins Innere holen, wo dann einst die wandfüllenden Lütke-Veduten neben dem gespiegelten Gartenwerk Friedrich Wilhelms II. den Vergleich zwischen den verschiedenen Graden der Naturaneignung anregten. Im Schloß Paretz, das David (1748–1808) und Friedrich Gilly (1772–1800) 1797 für Friedrich Wilhelm (III.) neu erbauten und dessen Landschaftsgarten Hofgärtner David Garmatter (1764–1821) ausführte, gaukeln die Wandtapeten ein ähnliches optisches Spiel vor. Auch hier vermischen sich in der aufgemalten Umzäunung Realität und Fiktion. Im Paretzer Gartensaal dürfen Marmorpalais und Pfaueninselschloß ihren Dialog als Veduten an zwei schmalen Wandstreifen zu Seiten der Fenster fortsetzen. Ihre Abbilder machen sie zu direkten Nachbarn, die sich frontal gegenüber stehen.

Im Anschluß an das Pfaueninselschloß wurde als Gegenstück am nördlichen Ufer im Osten der Insel die Meierei in gotischer Manier gebaut. Sie beherbergt Wohnräume und einen Stall. Dem künstlichen Verfall des Äußeren steht im Inneren ein prachtvoll mit Stuck, Wandmalereien und Parkettboden ausgestatteter Saal entgegen. Vor der Meierei breitete sich ein dem Wörlitzer Vorbild folgender, sogenannter Schöner Bauernhof aus, eine *ornamented farm* mit Karpfenteich. Wirtschaftlich genutzt, war das ländliche Gut doch gleichermaßen Teil des ansonsten zweckfrei ausgeschmückten Landschaftsgartens. Der Nivellierung der Gegensätze lag die Vision einer harmonischen Gesellschaft zugrunde, in der Arbeit und Erholung, private Belange und gemeinnütziges Schaffen in perfektem Einklang miteinander stehen. Mit der beginnenden Industrialisierung wurde die heile Natur, wie sie hier vorbildhaft zu sehen war, eine mehr und mehr geachtete, zu bewahrende Kostbarkeit. Eine Küche in holländischem Stil, ein Kastellanshaus und ein borkenbesetztes Häuschen auf hohem Sockel vervollständigten die Bebauung unter Friedrich Wilhelm II. Nur zwei Jahre lang konnte sich Friedrich Wilhelm II. an seinem Inselparadies erfreuen.

Nach seinem Tod führte Friedrich Wilhelm III. (1770 bis 1840) die unvollendete Gestaltung der Pfaueninsel weiter. Zusammen mit Gemahlin Luise bewohnte er die Insel in den Sommermonaten. Joachim Anton Ferdinand Fintelmann war 1804–34 Gärtner der Pfaueninsel. Ab 1816 arbeitete er zusammen mit Lenné.[86] Die Bäume des Eichenwalds verblieben nun als schmale, abgrenzende Streifen von fünf großen, unregelmäßig geformten Äckern einer Musterlandwirtschaft, deren Flächigkeit Gehölzgruppen, *clumbs*, strukturierten. Die Gebäude, die unter Friedrich Wilhelm II. entstanden waren, blieben bestehen. Zusätzlich wurde für die Landwirtschaft 1803/04 ein gotisierendes Kavalierhaus nach Plänen von Schinkel erbaut.

1825 wurde dem rechten Turm die spätgotische Front eines Danziger Patrizierhauses vorgeblendet. Im selben Jahr wurde auf dem höchsten Punkt der Insel ein Brunnen aus Gußeisen aufgestellt, als Reservoir für die Verteilung des Gießwassers im Garten mit Hilfe einer englischen Dampfmaschine. 1829/30 folgte das erste in einem Potsdam-Berliner Landschaftsgarten an alpine Holzbauweisen angelehnte Schweizerhaus als Unter-

27. Peter Ludwig Lütke und Peter Ludwig Burnat, exotische Landschaft mit Ansicht des Marmorpalais, Otaheitisches Kabinett im Schloß Pfaueninsel, 1794. Wandmalerei. (SPSG, Schloß Pfaueninsel.)
28. Landschaftszimmer mit Gemälden von Peter Ludwig Lütke im Marmorpalais, Zustand um 1932. (SPSG, Potsdam.)

27. Peter Ludwig Lütke and Peter Ludwig Burnat, exotic landscape with view of the Marmorpalais, Otaheitisches Kabinett in Schloß Pfaueninsel, 1794. Mural painting. (SPSG, Schloß Pfaueninsel.)
28. Landscape room with paintings by Peter Ludwig Lütke in the Marmorpalais, state ca. 1932. (SPSG, Potsdam.)

As a small hint at this connection, the Marmorpalais appears here in a mural whose palm trees, pineapples, exotic animals and birds immerse the viewer in the island world of the South Seas (illus. 27). Louis Antoine de Bougainville in his book of travels about the discovery of Tahiti in 1768 had recently created the myth of the South Seas as a paradise of free life and love. His claim that he had found »la nouvelle Cythère« – that is, the new Cythera, the island whose sea foam gave birth to Aphrodite, the goddess of love – provided European courts with food for conversation.

The Landschaftszimmer and the Otaheitisches Kabinett created subtle interrelations between real, man-made and painted nature: While the interior of the Marble Palace contained ideal Italian landscapes painted by Peter Ludwig Lütke in 1790 (lost since 1945) (illus. 28) and exotic dream landscapes appear in the Pfaueninsel castle, views of the landscape through the windows link painted vistas with the real environment. Italy is moved to the shore of Heiliger See, and Tahiti is relocated on Pfaueninsel. The painted fences in the Kabinett, whose tops end where in the next wall panel the window cornice marks the boundary of the actual view to the outside, play with the illusion that one can look over the fence into the open country. A bird that has alighted on the fence and looks into the room mediates between the inside and outside like something in a picture puzzle. The same is true of the mirrors in the Landschaftszimmer, which bring the garden, the lake, the Havel River, the hills into the interior, where Lütke's full-wall *veduta* paintings next to the mirrored landscaping of Frederick William II suggested a comparison between the various degrees of appropriating nature. In Schloß Paretz, the new palace that David (1748–1808) and Friedrich Gilly (1772–1800) built for Frederick William (III) in 1797 and whose landscape garden was laid out by David Garmatter (1764–1821), the wall-paper leads one to believe in a similar optical illusion. Here, too, reality and fiction intermingle in the painted enclosure. In the garden hall of Paretz, the Marmorpalais and the castle of Pfaueninsel continue their dialogue as *vedute* in two narrow strips of wall on the sides of the windows. Their images make them into direct neighbours that face each other frontally.

In connection with the castle on Pfaueninsel, as its counterpart, the dairy was built in the Gothic manner on the north shore in the eastern part of the island. It consists of living space and a stable. Contrasting with the artificial dilapidation of the exterior, the sumptuous design of a hall in its interior features stucco, murals and a parquet floor. In front of the dairy, following the model of Wörlitz, there was a so-called »ornamented farm« with a carp pond. While it was used commercially, the rural estate was nevertheless also part of the otherwise non-utilitarian decorative landscape garden. The levelling of opposites was based on the vision of a harmonious society, in which work and rest, private concerns and work for the public good are in perfect accord. With beginning industrialization, people began to hold pristine nature, seen here in exemplary fashion, in increasingly higher regard: it became something precious that must be preserved. A Dutch-style kitchen, a castellan's house and a little house clad with bark on a high foundation completed the list of structures built under Frederick William II. He was able to enjoy his island paradise for only two years.

After the latter's death, Frederick William III (1770 to 1840) continued the unfinished work of creating Pfaueninsel. Together with his wife Luise he lived on the island in the summer months. Joachim Anton Ferdinand Fintelmann was the gardener of Pfaueninsel in 1804–34. After 1816 he worked together with Lenné.[86] The trees of the oak forest now survived as narrow strips that formed the boundaries of five large, irregular-ly shaped fields of a model farm whose area was structured by clumps of trees. The buildings that had been erected under Frederick William II remained standing. In addition a Gothic-style »Kavalierhaus« was built for the farm in 1803/04 according to plans by Schinkel.

In 1825, the late-Gothic façade of a Danzig patrician house was superimposed on the façade of the right-hand tower. In the same year a cast-iron fountain was placed on the highest point of the island, as a reservoir for irrigating the garden with the help of an English steam engine. In 1829/30 followed the first Schweizerhaus to be built in a Potsdam-Berlin landscape garden; using a timber construction method typical in the Alps, it provided housing for the gardeners and court employees. Designed by Schinkel, it was implemented by Albert Dietrich Schadow (1797–1869).

With a palm house, Schinkel continued the tradition of exotic tropical fictions. The palm house was built by Schadow in 1830/31; it burned down in 1880. The foundations, and the palm trees now placed there in summer recall its location. A painting by Carl Blechen dated 1834 gives an idea of its interior décor.[87]

Because Frederick William III loved animals, a large menagerie was set up. It started with kennels and stables for buffaloes and Bengal deer. Soon a bear pit and a beaver's lodge, a lama house styled like an Italian villa with a balcony for macaws and cockatoos, and a place for reindeer were added. In 1832 the menagerie totalled 847 indigenous and exotic animals. Frederick William IV presented them to the Berlin Zoo in 1842. Of the fancifully designed animal houses only the aviary still survives.

An additional high point in the beautification of the island was the first rose garden to be planted in a Potsdam-Berlin garden: begun in 1821, the garden was laid out as a labyrinth by Lenné, and its basic stock consisted of 2100 standard roses and 9 000 shrub roses from a private Berlin collection.[88] At the same time 1821 marked the beginning of extensive design changes by Lenné and Fintelmann. By 1834 their work had been concluded for the most part. Frederick William IV preserved the memory of Pfaueninsel in the time of his predecessors.

Belriguardo – Frederick William IV and garden design

»If we make the garden more beautiful, we do no wrong.«
Frederick William IV, 1845

The word »Belriguardo« – a beautiful sight and/or beautiful view – condenses in one mellifluous Italian expression the yearning felt by Frederick William IV when he assumed the care of the landscape of a Berlin-Brandenburg shaped by his forebears. From Frederick William of Brandenburg, Frederick III/I, Frederick William I, Frederick II, William II and Frederick William III he had inherited the residences of Berlin and Potsdam with their national architectural monuments, summer residences and gardens, though also surrounded by many miles of Bran-

kunft für Gärtner und Hofbedienstete. Schinkel entwarf es, Albert Dietrich Schadow (1797–1869) führte es aus.

Mit einem Palmenhaus setzte Schinkel die Tradition exotisch-tropischer Fiktionen fort. Den Bau führte 1830/1831 Schadow aus, 1880 brannte er ab. Postamente und im Sommer aufgestellte Palmen erinnern an seinen Standort. Ein Gemälde von Carl Blechen von 1834 vermittelt eine Vorstellung seiner Innenausstattung.[87]

Die Tierliebe Friedrich Wilhelms III. führte zur Einrichtung einer umfangreichen Menagerie. Ihren Auftakt bildeten Zwinger und Ställe für Büffel und Bengalische Hirsche. Bald kam es zu einer Bärengrube und einer Biberburg, einem Lamahaus im italienischen Villenstil mit einem Balkon für Aras und Kakadus sowie einem Platz für Rentiere. 847 einheimische und exotische Tiere wurden 1832 gezählt. Friedrich Wilhelm IV. übergab sie 1842 dem Berliner Zoo. Von ihren phantasievoll gestalteten Behausungen erhielt sich allein die Volière.

Als weiterer Höhepunkt der Inselverschönerung entstand ab 1821 der erste Rosengarten in einem Potsdam-Berliner Garten: 2100 Rosenhochstämme und 9 000 Strauchrosen aus einer Berliner Privatsammlung bildeten den Grundstock für den von Lenné labyrinthisch angelegten Garten.[88] Das Jahr 1821 markierte zugleich den Beginn umfassender Umgestaltungen durch Lenné und Fintelmann. 1834 waren ihre Arbeiten weitgehend abgeschlossen. Friedrich Wilhelm IV. wahrte das Andenken an die Pfaueninsel zur Zeit seiner Vorgänger.

Belriguardo – Friedrich Wilhelm IV. und die Gartenkunst

»Machen wir den Garten schöner, so tun wir kein Unrecht.« Friedrich Wilhelm IV., 1845

»Belriguardo« – der schöne An- und Ausblick – verdichtet in einem wohlklingenden italienischen Begriff das Verlangen, mit dem Friedrich Wilhelm IV. sich der von seinen Vorfahren gestalteten Landschaft Berlin-Brandenburg annahm. Von Friedrich Wilhelm von Brandenburg, Friedrich III./I., Friedrich Wilhelm I., Friedrich II., Wilhelm II. und Friedrich Wilhelm III. waren ihm die Residenzen Berlin und Potsdam mit ihren Staatsarchitekturen, Lustschlössern und Gärten geblieben, drumherum aber auch viel märkischer Sand und eintönige Kiefernwälder. Unter seiner dilettantisch-schöpferischen Hand sollte alles – das bereits Gestaltete und das noch Ungestaltete – in einer idealen Kulturlandschaft aufgehen.[89]

Exakt in der Verlängerung der Achse Sanssouci-Terrassen–Lustgarten auf dem Geländesporn der Halbinsel des Tornow (heute: Hermannswerder) am gegenüberliegenden Havelufer erträumte sich der junge Kronprinz mit »Belriguardo« (Abb. 29) in etwa sechzig eigenhändigen Skizzenblättern wohl bereits seit 1815 eine von der griechischen Baukunst inspirierte Schloßanlage auf gewaltigen Substruktionen, Freitreppen und Aquädukt mit vorgelagertem geometrischem Parterre und Hippodrom. Sie hätte über Sanssouci hinaus im Norden in einer Sichtverbindung mit dem Ruinenberg gelegen. Mit Belriguardo ließ der Urgroßneffe Friedrichs II. unausgeführten, 1755 im Plan entworfenen Wunsch eines terrassenerhöhten Pavillons an eben jenem Ort wiederaufleben.

Das ungebaute Schloß auf dem Tornow war Gipfel einer Anzahl von Schaugebäuden, die Friedrich Wilhelm als An- und Aussichtspunkte auf den landschaftlichen Erhebungen rund um Potsdam mit seinem inneren Kern Park Sanssouci vorsah: Eine Klosteranlage auf dem Brauhausberg im Südosten wäre Schloß Belriguardo direkt untergeordnet gewesen. Sie blieb ebenfalls unrealisiert. Den Babelsberg im Osten bekrönt ein Burgenschloß für Prinz Wilhelm: Babelsberg wurde in einem ersten Bauabschnitt 1834–45 nach einem Entwurf von Schinkel errichtet und 1845–49 von Persius vollendet. Es gehört zusammen mit Schloß Glienicke, 1824–29 für Prinz Carl durch Schinkel um- und ausgebaut, und dem Marmorpalais, dessen nördlichen Seitenflügel Prinz Albrecht nach dem Ausbau durch Hesse 1834–48 bewohnte, zum Kreis der Bruderschlösser Friedrich Wilhelms nahe der Havel.

Den Pfingstberg im Nordosten besetzt das Belvedere (Abb. 30). Es stellt einen Architekturrahmen um ein Wasserreservoir dar, den Hesse 1847–52 baute. Weitere projektierte Teile der Anlage, Kasino, Kaskaden, Fontänen und Treppen am Hang, blieben ebenso unausgeführt wie der Übergang zum Neuen Garten. Weite Sichten lassen von den Türmen und den Umgängen des Pfingstberg-Belvederes im Süden die ganze Stadt überblicken, bis hin zur Havel und gar bis nach Caputh. Im Westen breitet sich der Potsdamer Werder vor dem Beschauer aus, und im Nordosten geht der Blick über den Jungfernsee nach Sacrow und zur Pfaueninsel.

Den krönenden Abschluß der im Norden um den Park Sanssouci herumführenden Höhenstraße bildet das Orangerieschloß aus den Jahren 1851–60 von Friedrich August Stüler (1800–1865) und Hesse. Zusammen mit der Friedenskirche im Park Sanssouci ist es eines der beiden verwirklichten Großbauprojekte des Königs.

Die nur in Teilen realisierte triumphale Höhenstraße wurde durch Hesses 1851 eingeweihtes Portal nördlich des friderizianischen Obelisken vor dem Park Sanssouci eröffnet und sollte über ein Viadukt auf die Höhe der Bildergalerie geführt werden. An die Orangerie sollten sich ein Kasino und die römisch inspirierte Grottenarchitektur eines Nymphäums reihen, das durch die 1843 zum Felsentor umgebaute Thetis-Grotte erreichbar gewesen wäre. Das Orangerieschloß stand in einer Linie mit dem Klausberg-Belvedere Friedrichs II. und der Heiligengeistkirche in der Stadt Potsdam. An der Stelle der ehrgeizigen Ausschmückung der Höhenstraße zeugen heute von Friedrich Wilhelms Wirken in diesem Areal des friderizianischen Parks allein der Nordische Garten mit seinen immergrünen Gehölzen westlich des Felsentors und sein durch die Maulbeerallee getrenntes Pendant, der Sizilianische Garten, in dem Palmen und andere Mittelmeerpflanzen wachsen – beide 1857–60 nach Plänen Lennés angelegt. Wo einst im Nordischen Garten ein Rasenoval mit mittigem Beet von Blumenbändern umgeben war, ragen heute zwei Ginkgobäume auf.[90]

Der nördliche Mühlenberg, neben der Orangerie im Westen von Schloß Sanssouci, wurde in die Überlegungen zu den Blickbeziehungen zwischen entfernten Architekturen miteinbezogen. Er wurde als möglicher Standort eines seit 1779 diskutierten Denkmals für Friedrich II. vorgeschlagen, das schließlich als Reiterdenkmal in Berlin Unter den Linden 1851 seine Realisierung fand. Friedrich Wilhelms Überlegungen verbanden das dem Parthenon-Tempel auf der Athener Akropolis ähnliche Monument des von ihm verehrten Herrschers mit dessen daneben liegendem Lieblingsschloß Sanssouci, seiner Fanfaronade »Neues Palais« im Westen und Friedrich Wilhelms die Genealogie der Fürstensitze fortsetzendes Belriguardo im Süden.

29. Unbekannter Zeichner, Schloß Belriguardo, nicht verwirklichter Entwurf nach Skizzen von Friedrich Wilhelm (IV.), um 1830. Aquarell. (SPSG, Potsdam.)
30. Franz Michelis, Belvedere auf dem Pfingstberg aus der Vogelschau, 1861. Öl auf Leinwand. (SPSG, Potsdam.)

29. Unknown graphic artist, Schloß Belriguardo, unrealized draft after sketches by Frederick Wiliam (IV), ca. 1830. Watercolour. (SPSG, Potsdam.)
30. Franz Michelis, Belvedere on the Pfingstberg looked at from a bird's-eye view, 1861. Oil on canvas. (SPSG, Potsdam.)

denburg sand and monotonous pine forests. Under his amateurish but creative direction all of these projects – those completed and those yet-to-be-completed – were to be incorporated in one ideal cultivated landscape.[89]

Probably as early as 1815, in roughly 60 sketches from his own hand, the young crown prince visualized »Belriguardo« (illus. 29) precisely in the extension of the axis Sanssouci–terraces–pleasance on the promontory of the Tornow (known as Hermannswerder today) on the opposite bank of the Havel. His vision was a palace inspired by Greek architecture on massive substructures, flights of stairs and an aqueduct, with a geometrical *parterre* in front of it and a hippodrome. It would have been located in a line of sight connecting it beyond Sanssouci in the north with Ruinenberg. With Belriguardo, Frederick II's great-grandnephew revived his forebear's wish for a pavilion raised on a terrace on that very site, which the latter had planned in 1755 but never implemented.

The unbuilt palace on Tornow was the culmination of a number of buildings Frederick William had in mind as sights and lookout points on the elevated sites around Potsdam, their central core being Park Sanssouci: A monastery on Brauhausberg in the southeast would have been directly subordinated to Belriguardo Palace. It, too, was never built. Babelsberg in the east is crowned by a fortress castle for Prince William: Babelsberg was built in an initial construction stage in 1834 to 1845 according to a design by Schinkel and completed in 1845–49 by Persius. Together with Schloß Glienicke, renovated and completed for Prince Charles by Schinkel in 1824–29, and the Marmorpalais, whose north side wing was inhabited by Prince Albrecht in 1834–48 after being completed by Hesse, it is one of the circle of Frederick William's brother palaces near the Havel River.

Pfingstberg in the northeast was occupied by the Belvedere (illus. 30). It is an architectural frame around a water reservoir and was built by Hesse in 1847–52. Additional projected sections of the complex, casino, cascades, fountains and flights of stairs along the slope, were not implemented, and neither was the transition to Neuer Garten. From the towers and the ambulatories of the Pfingstberg Belvedere, there is a distant view of the entire town in the south, all the way to the Havel River and even to Caputh. In the west Werder spreads out before the viewer, and in the northeast one can see Sacrow and Pfaueninsel on the other side of Jungfernsee.

The crowning glory of the Höhenstraße that leads around Park Sanssouci in the north is the Orangerieschloß, built in 1851–60 by Friedrich August Stüler (1800 to 1865) and Hesse. Together with the Friedenskirche in Park Sanssouci it is one of the king's two large-scale projects that were implemented.

Access to the triumphal Höhenstraße, only sections of which were realized, was through Hesse's portal, dedicated in 1851, north of Frederick II's obelisk in front of Park Sanssouci. The road was to run over a viaduct to the level of the picture gallery. A casino and the Roman-inspired grotto of a nymphaeum were to be lined up next to the orangery. The nymphaeum would have been entered through the Thetisgrotte, converted in 1843 into a rocky arch. The Orangerieschloß was in alignment with the Klausberg Belvedere of Frederick II and the Heiligengeistkirche in the town of Potsdam. In lieu of the ambitious decoration of the Höhenstraße, the only witnesses today to Frederick William's work in this section of Frederick II's park are the Nordischer Garten with its evergreen woods west of the rocky gate, and its counterpart, the Sizilianischer Garten, where palm trees and other Mediterranean plants grow, separated from the Nordischer Garten by an avenue of mulberry trees – both created in 1857–60 according to the plans of Lenné. Where once in the Nordischer Garten an oval lawn with a central bed was surrounded by strips of flowers, two ginkgo trees grow today.[90]

Mühlenberg in the north, next to the orangery west of Schloß Sanssouci, was taken into account when visual connections between distant buildings were considered. It was proposed as the possible site of a memorial for Frederick II that had been under discussion since 1779. The memorial was finally implemented in 1851 as an equestrian statue on Unter den Linden in Berlin. Frederick William's plans linked the monument of the ruler he adored, which resembled the Parthenon Temple on the Acropolis in Athens, with Frederick II's favourite palace of Sanssouci, which was located next to it, his *fanfaronade* »Neues Palais« in the west and Frederick William's Belriguardo in the south, which continued the genealogy of the royal residences.

Landscape mosaics

Johann Moritz von Nassau-Siegen, in a letter on 20 August 1664, had urged the Great Elector to transform the Potsdam »island (Eyland)« into a paradise. Years later Frederick William IV transformed »the entire island of Potsdam [...] into the most magnificent and grandiose [...] living landscape painting«, as Carl Ludwig Häberlin wrote in 1855.[91] »Everything he had built or laid out in the form of gardens can be compared to a piece in a mosaic that completes the great picture conceived earlier.«[92]

While heights occupied by realistic or phantastic architectural structures surround Sanssouci, the mosaic pieces at the borders of Frederic II's park, though less triumphal, were no less glittering in their subtle coordination of architecture and landscape, of interior and exterior space in the midst of a park and garden landscape created by Lenné.

The first of these, in 1825, was Schloß Charlottenhof in the south, whose garden layout was completed in 1835 with a rose garden and hippodrome (illus. 31). Following plans by Schinkel, Charlottenhof was converted in 1826–29 for the crown prince. The latter, who knew Sanskrit, called his summer residence »Siam«, after a southeast Asian kingdom at the time.[93] Next came the complex of the Römische Bäder northeast of Charlottenhof by the man-made engine pond, in 1829 to 1840. Schinkel was the architect, while Persius supervised the construction of this complex, which consists of the 1829/30 gardener's house, the 1830 tea pavilion, the 1832 house for assistant gardeners and the 1834–40 Römische Bäder, and which is loosely connected by arcades and pergolas.

All the way in the north, the municipality of Bornstedt adjoins Park Sanssouci. Because it was close to the grounds of the royal palace, it was taken into account early on when plans were made to beautify the surroundings.[94] In 1842 the king began having the fields between Ruinenberg and Bornstedter See enclosed

Landschaftsmosaike

Dem Großen Kurfürsten hatte Johann Moritz von Nassau-Siegen im Brief am 20. August 1664 die Umwandlung des Potsdamer »Eylands« in ein Paradies nahegelegt. Jahre später verwandelte Friedrich Wilhelm IV. »die ganze Insel Potsdam [...] in das herrlichste und grandioseste [...] lebende Landschaftsgemälde«, wie es Carl Ludwig Häberlin 1855 formulierte.[91] »Alles was er bauen oder gärtnerisch anlegen ließ, ist einem Mosaikstein zu vergleichen, der das große vorgedachte Bild vervollständigt.«[92]

Während die mit realen oder phantastischen Architekturen besetzten Höhen Sanssouci umringen, folgten an den Grenzen des friderizianischen Parks weniger triumphale, in ihrer subtilen Abstimmung von Architektur und Landschaft, von Innen- und Außenraum aber nicht minder glitzernde Mosaiksteinchen inmitten der von Lenné gestalteten Park- und Gartenlandschaft.

Den Anfang machte 1825 Schloß Charlottenhof im Süden, dessen Gartenanlage mit Rosengarten und Hippodrom 1835 ihren Abschluß fand (Abb. 31). Nach Plänen von Schinkel wurde der Charlottenhof 1826–29 für den Kronprinzen umgestaltet. Mit »Siam«, einem damaligen Königreich in Hinterindien, bezeichnete der das Sanskrit beherrschende Hohenzoller sein Sommerschlößchen.[93] 1829–40 folgte der Komplex der Römischen Bäder im Nordosten von Charlottenhof am künstlich angelegten Maschinenteich. Schinkel war der Architekt, Persius der Bauleiter dieses Ensembles, das sich aus Gärtnerhaus von 1829/30, Teepavillon von 1830, Gärtnergehilfenhaus von 1832 und den Römischen Bädern von 1834–40 zusammensetzt und das Arkaden und Pergolen locker miteinander verbinden.

Ganz im Norden schließt sich der Ortsteil Bornstedt an Park Sanssouci an. Durch seine Nähe zu den königlichen Gärten wurde es schon früh in die Überlegungen zur Verschönerung der Umgebung einbezogen.[94] 1842 begann der König, die Ackerflächen zwischen Ruinenberg und Bornstedter See mit Hecken einfassen zu lassen, die neben dem Schutz vor Verdunstung zugleich einen schönen Anblick boten. Bis 1855 wurde der Raubfanghügel zum Aussichtsberg. Der Plan fand seine Fortsetzung im Wartturm, den Ferdinand von Arnim (1814 bis 1866) nach einem Entwurf von Persius 1845 neben der Ruinenbergarchitektur Friedrichs errichtete. Der quadratische, mit Zinnen besetzte Turm folgt mittelalterlicher Baukunst. Sein Beiname »Normannischer Turm« ist dabei eher seinem fortifikatorischen Charakter zuzuschreiben denn dem normannischen Stil, wie er nach dem Sieg Wilhelms des Eroberers bei Senlac Hill 1066 in der englischen Baukunst als Übertragung der romanischen Architektursprache der Normandie vorherrschte.[95]

Über den Bornstedter See erstreckt sich eine Sicht vom Wartturm bis hin zur 1855/56 umgebauten Bornstedter Dorfkirche. Sie ist Teil der unter Friedrich Wilhelm gestalteten Gutsanlage mit einem geometrischen Garten von Hofbaurat Johann Heinrich Haeberlin (1799 bis 1866). Das Bornstedter Ensemble zeigt sich ebenfalls von den Sanssouci-Kolonnaden und von der Orangerie sowie in unterschiedlichen Blickwinkeln von der Ribbeckstraße. Der langgestreckte See bietet nicht nur wechselnde Ansichten von seinem östlichen und südlichen Uferweg auf Gut Bornstedt, sondern zaubert auch eins der königlichen Schlösser in die dörfliche Umgebung: In ihm spiegelt sich das Orangerieschloß (Abb. 32).

Nahe der Bornstedter Eichenallee ließ Persius 1843 die bereits für die Höhenstraße geplante Idee eines Viadukts, nunmehr in verkleinertem Maßstab, Wirklichkeit werden: Die fünfbogige Teufelsbrücke aus Sandstein überquert den Teufelsgraben, der bereits unter Friedrich II. das Hochwasser des Bornstedter Sees ins Luch von Golm ableitete.[96]

Unterhalb des Westpavillons des Orangerieschlosses wurde der Paradiesgarten, der seinen Namen nach einem kleinen kaiserlichen Garten bei Wien erhielt, in den Jahren 1841–45 nach Plänen von Lenné durch Hofgärtner Ludwig Hermann Sello (1800–1876) angelegt. 1937 wurde unter Gartendirektor Paul Julius Emanuel Kache (1882–1945) der Garten zum Schaugarten umgestaltet, der später zum Botanischen Garten der Universität Potsdam wurde. Die Kleinarchitekturen hatten Persius und Hesse geschaffen: Im Nordwesten war der Garten durch eine Sandsteinpergola eingefriedet (1842–44), den Haupteingang an der friderizianischen Maulbeerallee markierten eine Pergola auf Terrakottasäulen und eine Wanne mit wasserspeienden Masken. Weitere Wasserspiele waren ein Brunnen (als Atrium oder Stibadium bezeichnet, 1845/46) und eine Wasserkaskade (1846).

Im Südosten von Sanssouci, am Rand des Küchengartens »Marly« aus der Zeit Friedrich Wilhelms I., wurden Kirche und Atrium der Friedenskirche 1845–48 nach Plänen von Ludwig Persius durch von Arnim verwirklicht. Bis 1854 folgten Glockenturm und Kreuzgang durch Stüler, Hesse und von Arnim. Der Gästetrakt »Schloß Marly«, Pfarrhaus, Schule und Pförtnerhaus reihten sich an.

Im Nordwesten des Neuen Palais an der Straße nach Bornim erwarb der Kronprinz 1828 das friderizianische Gehöft des unter anderem für die Hasenhege und Karpfenzucht zuständigen Land- und Oberjägers Achatius Daniel Lindstedt. Seit Lennés erstem unrealisierten Idealplan und dem ersten Blatt von 1832 aus einer Reihe von über 100 kronprinzlichen Zeichnungen wurde es unter der Mitwirkung von Persius, Hesse, Stüler und von Arnim inmitten eines Lenné-Gartens entwickelt und schließlich 1858–61 ausgeführt. Lindstedt markiert den Endpunkt der unter Friedrich Wilhelm IV. geschaffenen Reihe kleinteiliger Schloß- und Gartenanlagen im Villenformat. Wie auf einer Vedute fügen sie sich in die Umgebung, der sie ihrerseits den jeweils eigenen Ton aufprägen: schöner An- und Ausblick in einem.

Mittelalter und Antike

Zwei ungleiche Stilvorbilder bestimmten den Geschmack seit dem 18. Jahrhundert: mittelalterliches und klassisch-antikes Kunstschaffen. Beide Ideen wirkten auf die Kulturlandschaft Friedrich Wilhelms IV. ein. Die Regierung des Hohenzollern fiel in die Zeit nach der Befreiung von der napoleonischen Herrschaft, an denen der 18jährige Kronprinz an der Seite seines Vaters begeistert teilgenommen hatte. 1840 wurde Friedrich Wilhelm preußischer König. 1848 griffen die revolutionären Märzunruhen auf Preußen über. Der König löste die Reste der preußischen Nationalversammlung auf und setzte eine Verfassung für die preußische Monarchie durch.

Die Wiederherstellung der Macht des Königs ging mit einem neuen Bewußtsein der eigenen Geschichtlichkeit einher. Die Rückbesinnung auf die als deutsch angesehene Leistung der Gotik und das Christentum als Idee, Historie zu überdauern, wurden zentrale Themen. Der Lutheraner Friedrich Wilhelm beförderte das als natio-

31. August Wilhelm Ferdinand Schirmer, Schloß Charlottenhof, Blick von der Pergola auf die Römischen Bäder, 1831. Öl auf Leinwand. (SPSG, Potsdam.)
32. Julius Schlegel, Orangerie im Park Sanssouci, Nordseite mit Bornstedter See, 1858. Bleistift, weiß gehöht. (SPSG, Potsdam.)

31. August Wilhelm Ferdinand Schirmer, Schloß Charlottenhof, view of the Römische Bäder from the pergola, 1831. Oil on canvas. (SPSG, Potsdam.)
32. Julius Schlegel, orangery in Park Sanssouci, north side with Bornstedter See, 1858. Pencil, heightened with white. (SPSG, Potsdam.)

with hedges that not only protected them from evaporation but were also beautiful. By 1855 Raubfang hill had become a lookout hill. The plan was developed further with the building of the watchtower that Ferdinand von Arnim (1814–1866) erected next to Frederick's Ruinenberg structure based on an 1845 sketch by Persius. The square, battlemented tower is medieval in style. Its nickname »Normannischer Turm« is due more to the fact that it is like a fortification than to its being built in the Norman style typical of English architecture after William the Conqueror's victory at Senlac Hill in 1066, a rendering of the Romanesque architectural idiom of Normandy.[95]

Across Bornstedter See there is a view from the watchtower of the Bornstedt village church that was renovated in 1855/56. It is part of the estate created by Frederick William with a geometrical garden by court architect Johann Heinrich Haeberlin (1799–1866). The Bornstedt complex is also visible from the Sanssouci colonnades and from the orangery, as well as in different perspectives from Ribbeckstraße. Not only are there changing views of Bornstedt estate from the path along the east and south shore of the long lake but, as though by magic, the lake conjures up one of the royal palaces in a village setting: it shows a reflection of the Orangerie Palace (illus. 32).

Near the oak avenue of Bornstedt, in 1843, Persius built, though on a smaller scale, the viaduct that had already been planned for the Höhenstraße: The five-arch sandstone Teufelsbrücke (Devil's Bridge) crosses the Teufelsgraben (Devil's Ditch), which even in the time of Frederick II had diverted flood water from Bornstedter See into the marsh of Golm.[96]

Below the west pavilion of the Orangerieschloß, the Paradiesgarten (Garden of Paradise), whose name comes from a small imperial garden near Vienna, was laid out in 1841–45 by court gardener Ludwig Hermann Sello (1800–1876) according to plans by Lenné. In 1937, under garden director Paul Julius Emanuel Kache (1882–1945), the garden was redesigned into a display garden that later became the botanical garden of Potsdam University. The small structures had been created by Persius and Hesse: In the northwest the garden was enclosed by a sandstone pergola (1842–44), while a pergola on terracotta columns and a tub with masks that spouted water marked the main entrance by the Maulbeerallee from the time of Frederick II. Further water features were a fountain (called atrium or stibadium, 1845/46) and a water cascade (1846).

Southeast of Sanssouci, along the edge of the »Marly« kitchen garden from the time of Frederick William I, the church and atrium of the Friedenskirche were realized in 1845–48 by von Arnim according to plans by Persius. These were followed in the period up to 1854 by a belltower and cloister by Stüler, Hesse and von Arnim. Then came the »Schloß Marly« guest wing, the rectory, school and gatehouse.

Northwest of the Neues Palais by the road to Bornim, in 1828, the crown prince purchased the Fridirician farmstead of police constable and head gamekeeper Achatius Daniel Lindstedt, who was in charge, among other things, of protecting the hare population and of breeding carps. Since Lenné's first, unrealized ideal plan and the first of a series of over 100 drawings by the crown prince in 1832, the land was developed in the middle of a Lenné garden by a team of architects – Persius, Hesse, Stüler, Schinkel and von Arnim – and the plan was finally implemented in 1858–61. Lindstedt marks the final stage of a series of small-scale castle and garden projects in villa format created under Frederick William IV. As though on a *veduta* they are integrated in the environment, on which they in turn imprint their own particular atmosphere: fine lookout spots and lovely views rolled into one.

The Middle Ages and classical antiquity

Two dissimilar stylistic models had determined public taste since the 18th century: medieval and ancient classical art forms. Both had an effect on Frederick William IV's cultural landscape. The reign of the Hohenzollerns fell into the period after the liberation from Napoleonic rule, in which the 18-year-old crown prince had enthusiastically taken part at his father's side. In 1840 Frederick William became the king of Prussia. In 1848 the revolutionary March riots spread to Prussia. The king dissolved what remained of the Prussian National Assembly and imposed a monarchist constitution on Prussia.

The restoration of the king's power was accompanied by a new awareness of his own historicity. Now the central themes became the return to the Gothic style, seen as a German achievement, and Christianity as an idea that would outlive history. The Lutheran Frederick William promoted the project that was regarded as a national priority – to continue the construction of the half-finished Cologne Cathedral in Catholic Rhineland, annexed by Prussia. Gothic churches, but also the fortresses of the German Middle Ages and of the English Gothic period sparked ideas of illusionary fairy-tale worlds. In 1814 Frederick William had accompanied his father to England and seen examples of Norman architecture.

On Kälberwerder near Pfaueninsel Frederick William imagined the medieval complex of St. Georgen – a knight's castle, monastery and chapel – that he sketched in 1816. In 1840–42 he had Stüler restore the fortress of Stolzenfels on the Rhine River, and in 1850 the cornerstone was laid for the family seat of his dynasty, Hohenzollern Castle, newly built in an act of demonstrative preservation of a historical monument.

Beside his fortress phantasies, it is primarily the churches built by Frederick William that appear in medieval, i.e., early Christian and early Byzantine forms, intermingled with Carolingian, northern Italian-Romanesque and French-Gothic elements. Instructed by the king, architect Wilhelm Salzenberg (1803–1887) had since 1847 been taking pictures of the Byzantine churches of Constantinople of the period from the 5th to the 12th century, and the volume of pictures was published in 1854. The secretary of the Prussian embassy to the Vatican, Christian Carl Josias Bunsen, a close friend of the king, publicizes the diagram of early Christian church buildings in his 1842–44 commentary on a book of engravings of early Christian churches in Rome by the architects Johann Michael Knapp and Johann Gottfried Gutensohn.

The semicircular choir termination of the Heilandskirche (Church of Our Saviour) on Sacrow peninsula north of Potsdam, built in 1841–44 by Persius, almost thrusts its way into the Havel. It is mirrored in the river as though it were a small ship in the wide ocean. Arcades surround the hall church, which has no transept, giving the impression of a basilica. It is tall enough to look across the water. The open round arches on delicate

nale Aufgabe ersten Ranges angesehene Projekt, den halbfertigen Kölner Dom im von Preußen annektierten katholischen Rheinland weiterzubauen. Gotische Kirchen, aber auch die Burgen des deutschen Mittelalters und der englischen Gotik entzündeten Vorstellungen illusionärer Märchenwelten. 1814 hatte Friedrich Wilhelm seinen Vater nach England begleitet und Beispiele normannischer Architektur gesehen.

Auf dem Kälberwerder nahe der Pfaueninsel erträumte sich Friedrich Wilhelm das Mittelalterarrangement St. Georgen aus Ritterburg, Stift und Kapelle, das er 1816 zu Papier brachte. 1840–42 ließ er die Burg Stolzenfels am Rhein durch Stüler restaurieren, und 1850 erfolgte die Grundsteinlegung für die in einem Akt demonstrativer Denkmalpflege neu errichtete Stammburg seines Herrschergeschlechts, Burg Hohenzollern.

Neben den Burgenphantasien präsentieren sich vor allem Friedrich Wilhelms Kirchenbauten in mittelalterlichen, das heißt altchristlich-frühbyzantinischen Formen unter die sich Karolingisches, Oberitalienisch-Romanisches und Französisch-Gotisches mischt. Architekt Wilhelm Salzenberg (1803–1887) nahm, vom König dazu angewiesen, seit 1847 die byzantinischen Kirchen von Konstantinopel der Zeit vom 5. bis zum 12. Jahrhundert auf, das Tafelwerk erschien 1854. Christian Carl Josias Bunsen, Sekretär der Preußischen Vatikanbotschaft und enger Freund des König, propagiert das altchristliche Kirchenbauschema in seinem 1842–44 erschienenen Kommentar zu dem Stichwerk der frühchristlichen Kirchen in Rom der Architekten Johann Michael Knapp und Johann Gottfried Gutensohn.

Die Heilandskirche auf der nördlich von Potsdam gelegenen Halbinsel Sacrow, 1841–44 von Persius erbaut, drängt sich mit ihrem halbrunden Chorschluß geradezu in die Havel. In ihrem Wasser spiegelt sie sich, als sei sie ein kleines Schiff im weiten Meer. Die querschifflose, hoch über das Wasser ragende Saalkirche umgeben Arkaden in basilikaler Anmutung. Die offenen Rundbögen auf grazilen Säulen lassen die Natur dicht an die Architektur heranrücken. Glienicke, Babelsberg, Neuer Garten und Nedlitz schlagen das Sichtenrad um Sacrow. Das horizontale Streifenmuster der Außenwände als Wechsel aus blau glasierter Terrakotta und Mauerwerk mag sich am gleichzeitigen Bau der »Moschee« (von Persius 1841/43 erbaut), Pumpstation der friderizianischen Wasserspiele an der Neustädter Havelbucht, inspiriert haben. Es überzieht die Kirche mit einer feinen südlichen Note. Frei steht der Campanile, wie es in frühchristlicher Zeit üblich war.

Schon die frühesten Änderungsvorschläge des Kronprinzen für den Berliner Dom im Lustgarten aus den 1820er Jahren beinhalten die Sacrower Merkmale: halbrunder Chorabschluß und offener Säulenumgang, die der Monarch zusammen mit den Motiven freier Glockenturm, Apsiden, Rundbogen, Blendarkaden, hier und da ein Westriegel, eine Rosette wieder und wieder deklinierte. Vor allem aber sind es die illusionären Spiegelungen im Wasser, die Friedrich Wilhelm auszukosten nie müde wurde. Der Berliner Dom sollte sich mit seinem Chor in der Spree spiegeln, die Heiligengeistkirche von Potsdam stand an der Havel, das Spiegelbild der Friedenskirche erscheint im Friedensteich.

Aus dem Ensemble Friedenskirche spricht die tiefe Religiosität des Königs. Den bis 1845 unveränderten, schiefwinklig geschnittenen Marlygarten mit seiner zentralen Schießbahn erweiterte Friedrich Wilhelms östlicher Grundstückszukauf zu einem langgestreckten Gelände. Es wird nach wie vor durch seinen rechtwinklig zur Nord–Süd-Achse von Sanssouci gelegenen Haupteingang betreten. In sanfter Biegung führt der Weg entlang einer Wiesenmulde vorbei an persönlichen, genrehaften Bildwerken. Sie bilden den Auftakt zum östlichen Friedenskirchenabschnitt, der von der Gottesfürchtigkeit des Königs zeugt.

Das kleine Mädchen, das einem Papagei auf ihrer Schulter ein paar Körner aus der hohlen Hand anbietet, schuf Heinrich Berges 1847. Die Farbgebung der weißblauen Glassäule, auf der sie steht, erinnert an die bayerische Heimat von Friedrich Wilhelms Gemahlin, Königin Elisabeth. Ebenso bezaubernd wirkt Eduard Mayers nackter Knabe (1838), der mit angezogenen überkreuzten Beinen dicht an ein Vogelnest am Boden gerückt ist, das er behutsam mit der Linken berührt.

Bereits am Eingang weist der aus der Mitte gerückte Campanile den Weg. Zu Friedrichs Schloß Sanssouci auf dem Weinberg formt er den Gegenpol, um »[…] so das weltlich Negative: ›ohne Sorge‹, dem geistlich Positiven: ›Frieden‹ entgegen oder vielmehr gegenüberzustellen«.[97] An der östlichen Seite des Campanile malte Eduard Steinbrück (1802–1882) 1849 nach einer Skizze des Königs das Fresko mit Christus am Ölberg. Nachdem die Reliefwand im Kreuzgang Themen der Christusgeschichte vorstellt – etwa Christus mit Maria und Johannes, Taufe, Segnung der Kinder –, begegnet uns der Heiland überlebensgroß in der Mitte des Atriums wieder. Als Reproduktion von Bertel Thorvaldsens Marmororiginal (1851, Original 1821) ragt er aus dem vierpaßförmigen Vierströmebrunnen auf. Den ehemaligen Kugelfang von 1714 am Fuß des Campanile nutzte Friedrich Wilhelm zur Anbringung spätantiker und romanischer Spolien mit religiöser Thematik. Im Norden endet die Folge von Kreuzgang, Atrium und Säulengang, ursprünglich mit mittelalterlichen Bildwerken ausgestattet, jäh am Friedensteich, dem Altan auf der anderen Seite gegenüber.

Nachdem Christus in vielerlei Darstellungen den Gang durch die Anlagen der Friedenskirche begleitet hatte, muß man die schmale Erlöserpforte suchen, die in den östlichen Lustgarten Friedrichs II. führt. Auf der Lustgartenseite erscheint über dem Rundbogen der Pforte auf goldenem Grund das von August Kloeber (1793 bis 1864) gemalte Bild Christi. Den aus beiden Richtungen – vom Lustgarten wie vom Friedenkirchenensemble – gleichermaßen versteckten Weg bevorzugte der König, um zum Gottesdienst zu gehen.

Neben dem Mittelalter wurde die Kunst des Altertums als vorbildlich empfunden. Erdmannsdorff, Langhans sowie Vater Friedrich und Sohn David Gilly hatten seit Friedrich Wilhelm II. einen antikischen Stil geschaffen, dem Langhans' Brandenburger Tor 1788 ein Denkmal des Frühklassizismus setzte. Der Beginn der Ausgrabungen in Herculaneum und Pompeji 1738, die Reise der Architekten James Stuart und Nicholas Revett nach Athen und die von Winckelmann formulierten Grundlagen für die Bildvorstellungen vom Schönen und der Antike 1755/56 und 1764[98] hatten die Rückgriffe auf den Formenschatz des Altertums angeregt und die Vorbildlichkeit antiker Ethik deklariert.

Vor allem Friedrich Wilhelms Villenschlösser zeigen antike Formen. Klassische Strenge ist Glienicke, Charlottenhof und den Römischen Bädern eigen. Das Schlößchen Sacrow zwischen Jungfernsee und Havel blickt mit einer klassizistischen Fassade auf den Schloßpark. Schloß Lindstedt prägen sein hochgesetzter, prostyler Tempelanbau, Atrien, Pergola und Belvedere.

columns allow nature to move close to the building. Glienicke, Babelsberg, Neuer Garten and Nedlitz provide a full circle of vistas around Sacrow. The pattern of horizontal stripes of the exterior walls, an alternation of blue glazed terracotta and masonry, may have been inspired by the »Mosque« (built during the same period by Persius, in 1841/43), the pumping station of Frederick II's waterworks on the Havel bay in Neustadt. It gives the church a subtle Mediterranean flavour. The bell tower is freestanding, as was customary in the early Christian period.

Even the crown prince's earliest proposals of changes for the Berlin Cathedral in the pleasance, from the 1820s, contain the characteristic features of Sacrow: a semicircular choir termination and open peristyle, which the monarch reiterated again and again together with such motifs as a freestanding bell tower, apsides, round arches, blind arcades, an occasional west front, a rosette. But above all it was the illusionary mirror reflections in the water in which Frederick William continued to take great pleasure. The choir of the Berlin Cathedral was intended to be mirrored in the Spree, the Heiligengeistkirche of Potsdam stood on the bank of the Havel, while the reflection of the Friedenskirche appears in the Friedensteich pond.

The Friedenskirche complex of buildings expresses the king's deep religiosity. The Marly Garden had remained unchanged until 1845, cut at an oblique angle, with a shooting range in its centre. Frederick William's purchase of land on the east side expanded it into an elongated terrain. It was still accessed through the main entrance, located at a right angle to the north–south axis of Sanssouci. In a gentle curve the road leads along a dip in the meadow past personal, genre sculptures. They are the prelude to the east section of the Friedenskirche, which attests to the king's piety.

The little girl who offers a parrot on her shoulder a few grains from the palm of her hand was the work of Heinrich Berges, in 1847. The colouration of the white and blue glass column on which she is standing recalls the Bavarian homeland of Frederick William's wife, Queen Elisabeth. Equally enchanting is Eduard Mayer's nude boy (1838), sitting with his legs drawn up and crossed, and gently touching a bird's nest on the ground with his left hand.

Already at the entrance to the grounds the campanile, moved from the centre, points the way. It is the antithesis of Frederick's Schloß Sanssouci in the vineyard, thus juxtaposing »[...] what is worldly and negative: ›carefree‹, with the spiritual and positive: ›peace‹«.[97] In 1849, east of the campanile, Eduard Steinbrück (1802–1882) painted the fresco of Christ on the Mount of Olives based on one of the king's sketches. The relief wall in the cloister presents themes from the life of Christ – for instance, Christ with Mary and John, the baptism, the blessing of the children –, but the Saviour, larger than life, meets us again in the middle of the atrium. A reproduction of Bertel Thorvaldsen's marble original (1851, original in 1821), he rises from the quatrefoil-shaped Vierströmebrunnen. The former backstop of 1714 at the foot of the campanile was used by Frederick William to mount late classical and Romanesque spolia illustrating religious themes. In the north the sequence of cloister, atrium and colonnade, originally containing medieval statues, abruptly ends at the Friedensteich pond, opposite the gallery on the other side.

While many different images of Christ accompany the walk through the grounds of the Friedenskirche, one has to search for the narrow Erlöserpforte (Portal of the Redeemer) that leads into the eastern pleasance of Frederick II. On the side of the pleasance a picture of Christ painted by August Kloeber (1793–1864) appears on a golden ground above the round arch of the portal. The king preferred to take this path, equally concealed from both directions – the pleasance and the Friedenskirche buildings – when he walked to church.

Beside the Middle Ages, the art of classical antiquity was also considered to be exemplary. Erdmannsdorff, Langhans, and father Friedrich and son David Gilly had created an antique style since the time of Frederick William II; Langhans' Brandenburg Gate in 1788 was a memorial to early classicism. The beginning of excavations in Herculaneum and Pompeii in 1738, the journey of architects James Stuart and Nicholas Revett to Athens, and the principles formulated by Johann Joachim Winckelmann regarding the concept of the beautiful and the essence of classical art in 1755/56 and 1764[98] had inspired artists and architects to borrow from the treasure trove of forms found in antiquity, and classical ethics were declared to be exemplary.

It is primarily Frederick William's villa palaces that have classical forms. Classical severity is characteristic of Glienicke, Charlottenhof and the Römische Bäder. The small castle of Sacrow between Jungfernsee and Havel looks out upon the castle's grounds with a classicist façade. Schloß Lindstedt is characterized by its raised, prostyle temple addition, atria, pergola and belvedere.

Prince Charles purchased Glienicke in 1824. Drawings attest to the fact that the crown prince participated in the brainstorming that left its mark on the many design sketches for his own castle villa of Charlottenhof. Schinkel converted the early classicist country house of Glienicke into a castle that, with the already existing »Kavalierhaus«, is built around a courtyard garden. On one side, in 1832, Schinkel erected a tower. The projection of the main façade has a view of the Löwenfontäne of 1837: Doric columns on pedestals with gilded lion sculptures on their capitals flank the round basin of the fountain. On a terrace above the Havel River is the Casino, developed in 1824/25 from a small gaming house.[99] Additional lookout points are the »Kleine Neugierde« (»Small Curiosity«) (1825) and the »Große Neugierde« (»Big Curiosity«), built opposite the former in 1835–37 and moved in 1938, a round building crowned by a copy of the Monument of Lysicrates in Athens (335/34 B.C.E.).[100] The hustle and bustle of the road connecting Berlin and Potsdam, on which the Kleine and Große Neugierde are situated, unfolds like pictures on a roll of film. From the bench surrounding the building curious observers could watch the constantly changing scene, sectioned by the columns.

A fusion of the two contrary styles did not represent a contradiction, a fact demonstrated by Schinkel, for whom the synthesis of the Middle Ages and classical antiquity was a personal means of expression: In his painting *Der Morgen* (*Morning*) from the year 1813 (illus. 34) we are struck by the fact that he has placed Central-European trees, people in traditional German costumes of the time of Dürer, scattered classical ruins and a Mediterranean town side by side in the morning mist. Schinkel's *Blick in Griechenlands Blüte* (*A Glance into the Golden Age of Greece*) (1825) is Schinkel's classicist programme formulated in painterly terms.

The painter and architect Schinkel had been active in the Prussian State Construction Commission since 1810.

Prinz Carl kaufte Glienicke 1824. Zeichnungen belegen die Anteilnahme des Kronprinzen an der Ideenfindung, die auf die zahlreichen Entwurfsskizzen zur eigenen Schloßvilla Charlottenhof abfärbte. Schinkel baute das frühklassizistische Glienicker Landhaus zu einem Schloß um, das mit dem bereits bestehenden Kavalierhaus um einen Gartenhof herumgeführt ist. Seitlich errichtete Schinkel 1832 einen Turm. Der Risalit der Hauptfassade nimmt die Löwenfontäne aus dem Jahr 1837 in den Blick: Dorische Säulen auf Postamenten mit vergoldeten Löwenskulpturen auf ihren Kapitellen flankieren das runde Brunnenbecken. Auf einer Terrasse über der Havel steht das Kasino, 1824/25 aus einem kleinen Spielhaus entwickelt.[99] Weitere Aussichtsplätze sind die »Kleine Neugierde« (1825) und die 1835–37 ihr gegenüber errichtete, 1938 verschobene »Große Neugierde«, ein Rundbau, den das nachgebildete Lysikrates-Monument in Athen (335/34 v. Chr.) bekrönt.[100] Wie die Bilder auf einer Filmrolle läßt die Verbindungsstraße zwischen Berlin und Potsdam, an der die Kleine und die Große Neugierde liegen, das Straßentreiben vorbeiziehen. Von der umlaufenden Bank aus konnten die Neugierigen es als ständigen, durch die Interkolumnien in Abschnitte gegliederten Bildwechsel beobachten.

Daß die Zusammenschau der beiden konträren Stilrichtungen keinen Widerspruch darstellt, zeigt Schinkel, zu dessen persönlichem Ausdrucksmittel die Synthese von Mittelalter und Antike gehört: In seinem Gemälde *Der Morgen* aus dem Jahr 1813 (Abb. 34) fällt das Nebeneinander von mitteleuropäischem Baumbewuchs, Leuten in deutscher Tracht der Dürerzeit, verstreut liegenden antiken Trümmern und von einer südländischen Stadt auf, die aus dem Morgendunst auftaucht. *Blick in Griechenlands Blüte* ist Schinkels 1825 malerisch formuliertes Programm des Klassizismus.

Der Maler und Architekt Schinkel war seit 1810 in der preußischen Oberbaudeputation tätig. Während Friedrich Wilhelms Kronprinzenzeit entwickelte sich eine enge Zusammenarbeit zwischen dem kreativen königlichen Dilettanten und dem an Bauschule und -akademie durch David und Friedrich Gilly geschulten Schinkel, der den künstlerischen Stil der ersten Hälfte des 19. Jahrhunderts mit Neuer Wache, Schauspielhaus, Museum, Schloß Glienicke und Charlottenhof bestimmte.

Die romantisch-neugriechische Architektursprache des Klassizisten Schinkel traf sich mit Friedrich Wilhelms künstlerischen Vorstellungen. Sie dienten der Veranschaulichung seiner konservativen, schließlich in der 1848er Revolution angegriffenen Staatsidee, sein Königtum sei legitime Alleinherrschaft von Gottes Gnaden. Beide hatten Italien bereist, Schinkel 1803, der Kronprinz 1828. Schinkel war dem König seit 1815 als preußischer Oberbaudirektor verpflichtet. Die aus seiner Schule hervorgegangenen Architekten Persius und Stüler – 1842 wurden beide »Architekten des Königs« – sowie Hesse und von Arnim gaben Friedrich Wilhelms Phantasien Gestalt, Lenné schuf dazu die passenden Landschaftsrahmen.

Italien

Die große Klammer um die Schöpfungen Friedrich Wilhelms IV. bildet Italien. Der Paradiesgarten stellt ein Weingut in Italien vor. Glienicke, die doppeltürmigen Bauten Pfingstberg-Belvedere und Orangerie wurden von der Villa Medici in Rom inspiriert. Charlottenhof orientierte sich an der römischen Villa des Kardinals Alessandro Albani, in der dieser griechische und römische Kunst sammelte. Ebenso vorbildlich wirkten vor allem die Villa Raffael und das Gärtnerhaus Casa Cenci nahe der Villa Borghese in Rom. Die Gebäudegruppe Römische Bäder atmet italienisches Flair: Die antike Villenarchitektur umgibt eine südländische Gartengestaltung, zu der Weinpergolen und Kübelpflanzen gehören, oder das im Westen von Sello angelegte italienische Kulturstück, auf dem mediterrane Gewächse wie Mais, Artischocken, die distelähnliche Karde und Kürbis angebaut wurden.

Als charakteristische Architekturzitate des Landes seiner Sehnsucht sind Renaissanceformen, Rundtempel, Stibadien, Exedren oder die Elemente des Landhausbaus in lockerer, oft asymmetrischer Kombination ins Potsdamer Terrain einbeschrieben. In dessen Höhenzügen erblickte Friedrich Wilhelm IV. die Formationen der Sabiner und Albaner Berge bei Rom. Küsten und Flußläufe des Südens setzte er mit den Ausbuchtungen der Havel gleich. Ebenen erinnerten an die flache Gegend um Florenz.

»Du würdest keine wirkliche, sondern eine idealisch schön gemalte Gegend [formam pictam] zu sehen glauben, so sehr wird das Auge, wohin es sich wendet, durch Abwechselung und Gruppirung [varietate, discriptione] erquickt«, beschreibt Plinius d. J. in seinen Briefen seine Villa Tuscum und fährt fort, die enge Verwebung von Gebäude, Landschaft und Garten auszuführen.[101]

Daneben fand Friedrich Wilhelm Anregungen für die eigene Kreativität bei dem Eklektiker Charles Percier, der spätrömische und renaissancezeitliche Architekturversatzstücke neu verknüpfte, und bei dessen Kollegen Pierre-François-Léonard Fontaine, der dem dorisch-römischen Stil ebenso anhing. Das Lehrbuch *Précis des leçons d'architecture* (1802/05, [2]1813) von Jean-Nicolas-Louis Durand hielt freie architektonische Elemente bereit, die zu Bildern unterschiedlicher Wirkung kombiniert werden konnten. Pergolen, Treppen und Vorbauten oder der Kreuzgang der Friedenskirche verknüpfen Architektur und Garten. Sie schaffen abwechslungsreiche An-, Aus- und Durchblicke. Überschneidungen dienen ebenso der malerischen Komposition wie harmonische Gruppierungen von Baukörpern, Flächen, Farben, Material, Vegetation. Das Ergebnis der solchermaßen inspirierten Skizzen Friedrich Wilhelms IV. sind mit Bedacht proportionierte, stimmungsvolle, italienisch anmutende Zusammenspiele von Architektur und Landschaft (Abb. 33).

Babelsberg – »hier oder nirgends«

Seit 1826 hatte Prinz Wilhelm (1797–1888, ab 1861 preußischer König Wilhelm I., ab 1871 deutscher Kaiser) seinen Vater, Friedrich Wilhelm III., um einen eigenen Bauplatz auf dem Babelsberg gebeten. Das Gelände hatte er bereits 1811, 14jährig, während eines Garnisonsmanövers kennengelernt. Zehn Jahre später lobte er die Aussicht. »Hier oder nirgends«[102] sei der ideale Ort für Schloß und Garten. Möglicherweise hatte Lenné im Sommer 1828 dem Prinzen die gestalterischen Möglichkeiten des Geländes erläutert und das Stichwort »Rheinburg« gegeben, das zum Landschaft und Architektur verbindenden Leitbild werden sollte.[103] Den an seinem höchsten Punkt 48 m über der Havel messenden eiszeitlichen Moränenhügel »Buberow«, »Biberberg« oder

33. Friedrich Wilhelm (IV.), arkadische Landschaft, 1825. Feder, Bleistift. (SPSG, Potsdam.)
34. Karl Friedrich Schinkel, *Der Morgen*, 1813. Öl auf Leinwand. (Staatliche Museen zu Berlin, Preußischer Kulturbesitz, Alte Nationalgalerie – Wikimedia Commons.)

33. Friedrich William (IV), arcadian landscape, 1825. Pen, pencil. (SPSG, Potsdam.)
34. Karl Friedrich Schinkel, *Der Morgen*, 1813. Oil on canvas. (Staatliche Museen zu Berlin, Preußischer Kulturbesitz, Alte Nationalgalerie – Wikimedia Commons.)

During the period when Frederick William was crown prince, a close collaboration developed between the royal amateur and Schinkel, trained by David and Friedrich Gilly at the academy of architecture. It was Schinkel who defined the artistic style during the first half of the 19th century with the Neue Wache (New Guardhouse), theatre, museum, Schloß Glienicke and Charlottenhof.

The romantic, neo-Greek architectural idiom of the classicist Schinkel was along the same lines as Frederick William's artistic ideas. These illustrated the prince's conservative conception of the state – eventually attacked in the revolution of 1848 – that his kingship was legitimate autocratic rule by the grace of God. Both men had toured Italy, Schinkel in 1803 and the crown prince in 1828. As head of the State Construction Commission Schinkel had been under obligation to the king since 1815. Persius und Stüler, architects who had come from his school – in 1842 both became »architects of the king« – as well as Hesse and von Arnim gave shape to Frederick William's phantasies, while Lenné created the appropriate landscapes that framed them.

Italy

The largest common factor of Frederick William IV's creations is Italy. The Paradiesgarten represents a vineyard in Italy. Glienicke, the double-towered buildings of Pfingstberg Belvedere and the orangery were inspired by the Villa Medici in Rome. Charlottenhof was based on the Roman villa of Cardinal Alessandro Albani, in which the latter collected Greek and Roman art. Equally exemplary and influential were the Villa Raffael and the gardener's house Casa Cenci near the Villa Borghese in Rome. The buildings of the Römische Bäder have an Italian aura about them: The classical villa is surrounded by a garden designed in the Mediterranean style that includes vine pergolas and plants in tubs, or the Italian vegetable garden laid out on the west side by Sello, where Mediterranean plants such as maize, artichokes, the thistle-like cardoons, and pumpkins were grown.

Characteristic architectural quotations of the land of his longing – Renaissance forms, round temples, stibadia, exedrae or the elements of country-house construction – are inscribed in the terrain of Potsdam in loose, often asymmetrical combination. In the hills around Potsdam Frederick William IV saw the formations of the Sabine and Alban Hills near Rome. He equated the coasts and rivers of the Mediterranean region with the coves of the Havel River. Plains reminded him of the flat region around Florence.

»You would believe you are not seeing a real landscape, but an ideally painted one (*formam pictam*), for wherever your eye turns, it is so greatly refreshed by variety and configuration (*varietate, discriptione*)«, Pliny the Younger describes his Villa Tuscum and continues to link the building, landscape and garden closely.[101]

At the same time Frederick William found ideas to inspire his own creativity in the work of the eclectic Charles Percier, who combined late Roman and Renaissance architectural components in a new way, and in that of the latter's colleague Pierre-François-Léonard Fontaine, who was also attached to the Doric Roman style. The textbook *Précis des leçons d'architecture* (1802/05, [2]1813), by Jean-Nicolas-Louis Durand, contained independent architectonic elements that could be combined to form scenes that had different effects. Pergolas, staircases and projecting structures, or the cloister of the Friedenskirche, link the architectural structure and the garden. They create interesting and varied views, perspectives and cross-vistas. Overlapping serves both painterly composition and harmonic groupings of buildings, surfaces, colours, material and vegetation. The result of sketches by Frederick William IV inspired by such ideas is an interplay of architecture and landscape that is carefully proportioned, full of atmosphere, and reminiscent of Italy (illus. 33).

Babelsberg – »here or nowhere«

Since 1826 Prince William (1797–1888, from 1861 King of Prussia William I, from 1871 German Emperor) had begged his father, Frederick William III, for a building site of his own on Babelsberg hill. He had become familiar with the terrain as early as 1811, at the age of 14, during a garrison manoeuvre. Ten years later he praised the view. »Here or nowhere«[102] was the ideal place for a palace and garden. Possibly Lenné in the summer of 1828 had explained the creative potential of the terrain to the prince and struck the keynote »Rheinburg« that was to become the monarch's mission statement, combining landscape and architecture.[103] »Buberow«, »Biberberg« or »Babertberg«, an Ice Age moraine hill that rises 48 m above the Havel at its highest point and has a clearly defined indentation between the later park buildings Flatowturm and Gerichtslaube, is framed in the east by Tiefer See, a lake through which the Havel River flows, and in the south and southwest by the avenue to Glienicke, and Mühlenstraße.

Panorama drawings by Julius Hennicke and Julius Schlegel record the vistas from Babelsberg to Potsdam around the middle of the 19th century: one from Wilhelmshöhe (ca. 1855) (illus. 35) and one from the Bildstöckl, a wayside shrine with benches along its sides erected in 1850 on the bank of the Havel River (illus. 36). Visible from south to north are the suburb of Teltow with the belvedere on Brauhausberg, the Heiligengeistkirche, the dome of the Nikolaikirche and the Garnisonkirche. The silhouette of Schloß Babelsberg itself, in Hennicke's *Blick von der Birkenbank zu Glienicke auf Potsdam* (*View of Potsdam from the Glienicke Birch Tree Bench*), ca. 1850, is on the left edge of his watercolour (illus. 37).

As a result of William's marriage to Princess Augusta of Saxe-Weimar (1811–1890) in 1829, the Babelsberg construction project was brought to completion. Ever since the couple's Rhine journey in the summer of 1830 they vividly remembered the exemplary building of Burg Rheinstein, a former customs station of the Electorate of Mainz rebuilt in a historicist style in the previous year by their cousin Prince Frederick (Ludwig) of Prussia.[104]

Staging the past – Rhine Romanticism and Gothic Revival

Along the banks of the Rhine there were many medieval fortresses and churches, many of which were dilapidated. A small circle of poets had exalted the beauty of the landscape and of its somber artistic monuments in their literary and aesthetic writings. With the patriotic enthusiasm triggered by the Wars of Liberation, the romantic passion for the Rhine region ignited by Achim von Arnim

»Babertberg« mit seinem markanten Oberflächeneinschnitt zwischen den späteren Parkbauten Flatowturm und Gerichtslaube fassen im Osten der von der Havel durchflossene Tiefe See, im Süden und Südwesten die Allee nach Glienicke und die Mühlenstraße ein.

Panoramazeichnungen von Julius Hennicke und Julius Schlegel halten die Babelsberger Fernblicke auf Potsdam um die Mitte des 19. Jahrhunderts fest: einmal von der Wilhelmshöhe (um 1855) (Abb. 35) und einmal vom 1850 aufgestellten Bildstöckl mit seinen seitlichen Bänken am Ufer der Havel (Abb. 36). Von Süd nach Nord erscheinen die Teltower Vorstadt mit dem Belvedere auf dem Brauhausberg, die Heiligengeistkirche, die Kuppel der Nikolaikirche und die Garnisonkirche. Die Silhouette von Schloß Babelsberg selbst rückt auf Hennickes *Blick von der Birkenbank zu Glienicke auf Potsdam*, um 1850, an den linken Rand seines Aquarells (Abb. 37).

Wilhelms Heirat mit Prinzessin Augusta von Sachsen-Weimar (1811–1890) im Jahr 1829 brachte das Bauvorhaben Babelsberg zur Ausführung. Seit ihrer Rheinreise im Sommer 1830 stand dem Paar mit der im Jahr zuvor in historisierendem Geschmack wieder aufgebauten Burg Rheinstein des Vetters Prinz Friedrich (Ludwig) von Preußen, ehemalige kurmainzische Zollstätte, ein vorbildhafter Bau vor Augen.[104]

Staging the past – Rheinromantik und Neogotik

Das Ufer des Rheins war reich an mittelalterlichen Burgen und Kirchen, viele baufällig. Ein kleiner Kreis von Dichtern hatte die schöne Geographie und ihre morbiden Kunstdenkmäler literarisch-ästhetisch überhöht. Mit der vaterländischen Begeisterung, die die Befreiungskriege ausgelöst hatten, ergriff der von Achim von Arnim (1781–1831), Clemens Brentano (1778–1822) und Joseph von Eichendorff (1788–1857) entzündete Funke romantischer Schwärmerei für die Rheingegend ganz Preußen. Die Schönheit des deutschen Rheins wurde gepriesen, der Reichtum seiner Sagen und Legenden wie ein Schatz gehoben und künstlerisch verarbeitet. Nach 1820 entstanden zahlreiche, weitgehend von Schinkel beeinflußte Profan- und Kirchenbauten in den rheinnahen Gebieten, die seit 1816 zu Preußen gehörten. Die Neugotik wurde zum bevorzugten Stil der Kirchenbaukunst, inspiriert von romantischer Dichtung und dem Gothic Revival in England. Über dem Rhein bei Remagen baute Ernst Zwirner 1839–43 die berühmte Apollinariskirche mit ihren graziösen Turmgruppen, Wimpergen und Fialen über festungsartigem Unterbau. Auf Burg Rheinstein »[gehen wir], wenn der Prinz da sind, […] alle im Mittelalter«,[105] das in Kulisse und Kostüm zum Zweck der idealen Verklärung in Szene gesetzt wurde.

In Potsdam bot die Havel eine gewisse Analogie zum Rhein: ein Fluß, der sich durch anmutig bewegte Landschaft windet, an seinen Ufern stolz aufragende Bauwerke, hier und da eine Burg. Was nicht schon stand, konnte im entsprechenden Stilkleid gebaut werden. Humphry Repton (1752–1818) zeigt 1816 die idealtypische Darstellung für ein Schloß im Stil der »castle-gothic« (Abb. 38) und bemerkt dazu, daß es mehr die »irregularity of outline«, also der unregelmäßige Umriß gotischer Gebäude wäre, die ihren pittoresken Effekt ausmachten, als der gotische Stil an sich.[106]

Das ästhetische Gefallen am gotischen Formengut und das Interesse am Mittelalter, das der patriotische Jubel für die als deutsch angesehene »Heldentat« der Gotik entzünden half, leiteten die zweckbestimmte Verwendung gotisierender Formen. Daß die Wurzeln der Gotik in Frankreich liegen, blieb der Erkenntnis einer späteren Zeit vorbehalten. Schinkels unausgeführter neugotischer Entwurf für das Grabmal der Königin Luise von 1810 faßt die Facetten des Gotikenthusiasmus zusammen: Er ist patriotisch, religiös, natursymbolisch.

Horace Walpole (1717–1797) schuf seit 1748 mit seinem Landsitz Strawberry Hill in Twickenham einen der Gründungsbauten der englischen Neugotik. Als Verfasser des Schauerromans *The Castle of Otranto* legte er den literarischen Grundstein für die über den Mittelalterstil transportierten düster-unheimlichen Stimmungswert der Gotik, der seit der von Edmund Burke (1729 bis 1797) eingeführten ästhetischen Kategorie des Sublimen 1757 prickelnde Sinnenfreude bieten konnte.[107] Die Ursprünge der Obsession »Neugotik« finden sich im frühen englischen Landschaftsgarten. In seiner Modellwelt wurde sie als Stil des Historismus für poetische Staffagebauten seit den 1720er Jahren entwickelt und über das Medium Garten verbreitet.

Neugotische Formen, die sich wegen ihres Schmuckcharakters als ästhetische Applikationen von der Werktradition gotischer Steinmetze weit entfernt hatten, propagierte Batty Langley (1696–1751) in seinen Musterbüchern.[108] Das Nauener Tor von Johann Gottfried Büring in Potsdam brachte sie schon 1754–55 auf den Kontinent.[109] Friedrichs II. 1769 geplantes gotisches Gasthaus nahe dem Neuen Palais blieb ungebaut.

Unter Friedrich Wilhelm II. wurden 40 Jahre nach dem Nauener Tor die Gotische Bibliothek sowie – als künstliche Ruinen – Schloß und Meierei auf der Pfaueninsel (1792/94, 1794 und 1796) gotisierend gebaut. Für den Pfingstberg ließ er 1793 durch Georg Friedrich Boumann d. J. ein kathedralgotisches Belvedere entwerfen, das zugunsten der Pfaueninselbebauung aufgegeben wurde. Im Paretzer Schloßpark entstand 1799 das Gotische Rohrhaus von Friedrich Gilly.[110] Als Flechtwerktempel trat es zur klaren klassizistischen Schloßarchitektur (1796–97 von David Gilly) in ein ähnliches Spannungsverhältnis wie die Gotische Bibliothek zum Marmorpalais im Neuen Garten. Schloß und Park Babelsberg setzten die Reihe der antithetischen Gegenüberstellungen von Gotik und Klassik in der Nachbarschaft mit der italianisierenden Anlage von Schloß Glienicke oder im Gegenüber von mittelalterlichem Flatowturm und vermeintlich renaissancezeitlichem Pfingstberg-Belvedere fort.

Vorbildcharakter kam der breiten Palette der gotischen Formen an der Kanalfront des Gotischen Hauses in Wörlitz aus der Zeit von 1773 bis 1813 zu, das wohl unter Beteiligung von Friedrich Wilhelm von Erdmannsdorff von Georg Christoph Hesekiel ausgeführt worden war. Für Friedrich Wilhelm III. folgte 1804 das Belvedere auf dem Brauhausberg. 1828 wurde im Glienicker Schloßpark für Prinz Carl der Jägerhof gebaut, den Schinkel in den Formen englischer Cottage-Gotik entworfen hatte.[111]

Bereits in Weimar war Augusta dem für das Babelsberger Burgenschloß in Frage kommenden neugotischen Stil begegnet: In gotischen Formen zeigte sich ihr das Tempelherrenhaus, das 1786/87 als Umbau des Alten Orangenhauses zum »Salon« durch den Weimarer Hofarchitekten und Baurat Johann Friedrich Rudolf Steiner im Weimarer Park entstanden war. Innerhalb der klassizistischen Ausstattung des Residenzschlosses stellte das vermutlich von Gentz entworfene Bern-

35. Julius Hennicke, Potsdam von der Wilhelmshöhe im Garten Babelsberg, um 1855. Aquarell. (SPSG, Potsdam.)
36. Julius Schlegel, Potsdam vom Bildstöckl im Park Babelsberg, 1862. Bleistift, Deckfarben. (SPSG, Potsdam.)
37. Julius Hennicke, Potsdam von der Birkenbank im Park Glienicke, um 1850. Aquarell. (SPSG, Potsdam.)
38. Humphry Repton, Schloß im Stil der Castle-gothic, 1816. Holzstich. (Reprographie aus: Humphry Repton, *Fragments on the Theory and Practice of Landscape Gardening*, London 1816.)

35. Julius Hennicke, Potsdam from the Wilhelmshöhe in the Babelsberg garden, ca. 1855. Watercolour. (SPSG, Potsdam.)
36. Julius Schlegel, Potsdam from the Bildstöckl in Park Babelsberg, 1862. Pencil, opaque colours. (SPSG, Potsdam.)
37. Julius Hennicke, Potsdam from the Birkenbank in Park Glienicke, ca. 1850. Watercolour. (SPSG, Potsdam.)
38. Humphry Repton, palace in the castle-gothic style, 1816. Wood engraving. (Reproduced from: Humphry Repton, *Fragments on the Theory and Practice of Landscape Gardening*, London, 1816.)

(1781–1831), Clemens Brentano (1778–1822) and Joseph von Eichendorff (1788–1857) took hold of all of Prussia. People praised the loveliness of the German Rhine. The wealth of its myths and legends was treasured and became the basis for works of art. After 1820 numerous secular and ecclesiastical buildings, largely influenced by Schinkel, were built in the regions near the Rhine that had belonged to Prussia since 1816. The neo-Gothic style became the preferred style of church architecture, inspired by Romantic poetry and the Gothic revival in England. Above the Rhine near Remagen, in 1839–43, Ernst Zwirner built the famous Apollinariskirche with its graceful groups of towers, Gothic gables and pinnacles above a fortress-style substructure. »[We go to Burg Rheinstein], when His Majesty the Prince is there, [...] all in the Middle Ages«,[105] staged in backdrop and costumes to idealize and transfigure the present.

In Potsdam the Havel River had a certain resemblance to the Rhine: a river winding through a gracefully vibrant landscape, with proud buildings on its banks, and an occasional fortress. If a building was not already there, it could be built in the appropriate style. In 1816 Humphry Repton (1752–1818) shows a depiction of the ideal type of palace in the »castle-gothic« style (illus. 38) and notes that it is more the »irregularity of outline« of Gothic buildings that creates their picturesque effect than Gothic style per se.[106]

Aesthetic pleasure in all things Gothic and interest in the Middle Ages, which patriotic passion for Gothic art and architecture – seen as the »heroic achievement« of the Germans – helped ignite, were behind the use of Gothic forms. It was left to a later period to recognize that the roots of Gothic art and architecture are in France. Schinkel's unrealized 1810 neo-Gothic design for the tomb of Queen Louise sums up the various facets of this enthusiasm for everything that is Gothic: It is patriotic, religious, full of natural symbolism.

Beginning in 1748, with his country seat Strawberry Hill in Twickenham, Horace Walpole (1717–1797) had created one of the original buildings of English Gothic revival. As the author of the Gothic novel *The Castle of Otranto*, he laid the literary cornerstone for somber and eerie Gothic moods conveyed by way of the medieval style; Edmund Burke (1729–1797) had introduced the aesthetic category of the sublime, in 1757, and Walpole contributed the added thrill of the enjoyment of life's pleasures.[107] The origins of the obsession with »neo-Gothic style« are found in the early English landscape garden. It was in its model world, starting in the 1720s, that Gothic style was developed as the historicist style for decorative poetic buildings, and it was disseminated through the medium of the garden.

Neo-Gothic forms that were now applied as aesthetic decorations and were far removed from the working tradition of Gothic stonemasons were publicized by Batty Langley (1696–1751) in his architectural pattern books.[108] Johann Gottfried Büring's Nauener Tor in Potsdam brought these to the Continent as early as 1754–55.[109] Frederick II's Gothic inn near the Neues Palais, which he planned in 1769, remained unbuilt.

Under Frederick William II, 40 years after the Nauener Tor, the Gotische Bibliothek and – as faux ruins – the castle and dairy on Pfaueninsel (in 1792/94, 1794 and 1796) were built in the Gothic style. In 1793, for Pfingstberg hill, the monarch had Georg Friedrich Boumann the Younger design a belvedere resembling a Gothic cathedral that was later abandoned in favour of construction on Pfaueninsel. In the palace grounds of Paretz, in 1799, the Gothic Rohrhaus (Wicker House) was created by Friedrich Gilly.[110] The same tension existed between this wickerwork temple and the clear, neoclassical palace (1796–97 by David Gilly) as did between the Gotische Bibliothek and the Marmorpalais. The palace and park of Babelsberg continued the series of antithetical juxtapositions of Gothic and classical style in close proximity with the Italian-style grounds of Schloß Glienicke or in the vis-à-vis of the medieval Flatowturm and the supposed Renaissance style of the Pfingstberg Belvedere.

The broad palette of Gothic forms on the canal façade of the Gotisches Haus in Wörlitz, from the period between 1773 and 1813, served as a model; it was built by Georg Christoph Hesekiel, probably with the participation of Friedrich Wilhelm von Erdmannsdorff. The belvedere on Brauhausberg for Frederick William III followed in 1804. In 1828, Jägerhof castle was built in the grounds of Schloß Glienicke for Prince Charles, designed by Schinkel using the forms of English Cottage Gothic style.[111]

Already back in Weimar Augusta had encountered the neo-Gothic style which would be considered for the Babelsberg fortress castle project: It was in Gothic forms that she visualised the Tempelherrenhaus (House of the Templars), created in 1786/87 when the Altes Orangenhaus (Old House of Orange) in the Weimar park was converted into a »salon« by Weimar court architect and head of planning Johann Friedrich Rudolf Steiner. Within the framework of the classicist interior design of the castle, the Bernhardzimmer (Bernhard Room), presumably designed by Heinrich Gentz, with its neo-Gothic panelling, was an anomaly.[112] The writings of Robert Lugar (1773–1855) and his design of a small cottage, which immediately became a model, as well as texts by James Thomson (1700–1748), Repton and John Buonarotti Papworth (1775–1847)[113] inspired Augusta to choose the English Gothic style over others. The castles of Windsor near London, built in 1826, and Kórnik (Kurnik) near Poznan, converted in 1834 by Schinkel, offered a treasure trove of forms. Augusta's drawings, of which court building inspector Persius made clean copies, prepared the way for the construction of Babelsberg and influenced the carrying out of the Schinkel design according to her wishes.

Schloß Babelsberg is a continuation of the series of pseudo-stronghold park fortresses brought into idyllic unity with the landscape, precursors of Burg Rheinstein: the castle built in 1779 in the park of Wilhelmsbad near Hanau; Löwenburg, built ca. 1800 next to the castle in Kassel; Franzenfeste, built in 1801 in the park of Laxenburg near Vienna; and Mosburg, built in 1805 in the park of Wiesbaden Castle in Biebrich. What they all have in common is the aesthetic appeal of the genius loci, to which Schinkel's teacher Friedrich Gilly had already drawn attention in his wildly successful views of Marienburg (13th–15th century) in West Prussia, which he published in 1799–1803 (illus. 39).

Repton's and Lugar's remarks about how there is a correspondence between the nature of the landscape and the choice of style were confirmed by the features of the Babelsberg landscape: The Tiefer See of the Havel River adjoined hilly and mountainous terrain covered with a dense forest of pines and oaks.

hardzimmer mit seiner neugotischen Vertäfelung eine Besonderheit dar.[112] Die Schriften von Robert Lugar (1773–1855) mit dessen unmittelbar vorbildhaftem Entwurf eines kleinen Cottage sowie Texte von James Thomson (1700–1748), Repton und John Buonarotti Papworth (1775–1847)[113] regten Augusta an, die englische Gotik zu favorisieren. Die Schlösser Windsor bei London, 1826 errichtet, und Kórnik (Kurnik) bei Posen, 1834 durch Schinkel umgebaut, boten eine Fundgrube des Formenschatzes. Augustas Abzeichnungen, die Hofbauinspektor Persius ins reine übertrug, bereiteten die Errichtung von Babelsberg vor und beeinflußten die Ausführung des Schinkel-Entwurfs in ihrem Sinne.

Mit Schloß Babelsberg setzt sich die Reihe der in stimmungsvolle Einheit mit der Landschaft gebrachten pseudo-fortifikatorischen Parkburgen fort, wie sie von 1779 an im Park von Wilhelmsbad bei Hanau, um 1800 mit der Löwenburg beim Schloß in Kassel, 1801 mit der Franzenfeste im Park von Laxenburg bei Wien und mit der 1805 gebauten Mosburg im Park des Wiesbadener Schlosses zu Biebrich als Vorstufen zu Burg Rheinstein entstanden waren. Ihnen allen gemein ist der ästhetische Reiz am Genius loci, den bereits der Schinkel-Lehrer Friedrich Gilly in seinen Furore machenden, 1799 bis 1803 veröffentlichten Raumansichten der Marienburg in Westpreußen aus dem 13. bis 15. Jahrhundert in Szene setzte (Abb. 39).

Reptons und Lugars Ausführungen zur Übereinstimmung zwischen den Charakteren von Landschaft und Stilwahl trafen sich mit den landschaftlichen Gegebenheiten in Babelsberg: An den Tiefen See der Havel schloß sich hügelig-bergiges Terrain mit einem reichen Bewuchs von Kiefern- und Eichenwald an.

Neogotik im Sperrgebiet

Schinkel, der die Rekonstruktion der Ruine Rheinstein durch Johann Claudius von Lassaulx angeleitet hatte, erhielt 1833 den Auftrag, das Schloß auf dem Berg für Prinz Wilhelm englisch-neugotisch zu konzipieren. Im selben Jahr wurde Lenné mit der Anlage des Gartens betraut.

1835 konnte das von Prinz Wilhelm verniedlichend »Cottage« betitelte Schloß, zu diesem Zeitpunkt noch ein unfertiger Ziegelrohbau, vorläufig eingeweiht werden. Lennés Plan von etwa 1835, der das Schloß locker in ein Wegesystem einbindet, das die Berghöhen miteinander verknüpft, kam ebenfalls zur Ausführung. Hofgärtner seit 1836 war Christoph Ferdinand Kindermann (1805 bis 1865).

Nach einer Baupause, während der die Errichtung des prinzlichen Stadtpalais in Berlin Vorrang hatte, wurde Babelsberg ab 1838 weitergebaut. Bauinspektor Eduard Gebhardt (1803–1869) brachte die neuen Entwürfe zu Papier, die sich an den Ideen Pücklers orientierten: Der bereits durch seine *Andeutungen über die Landschaftsgärtnerei* (1834) sowie seine Kreation des Parks Muskau hochgeschätzte Pückler verurteilte nach einem zweiwöchigen Potsdam-Aufenthalt in einer Denkschrift von 1842 – »Unterthänigste Promemoria«[114] – Lennés Wirken, das dieser aufgrund fehlender Gelder 1839 aufgegeben hatte. Pückler erreichte, daß die weitere Gestaltung des Gartens in seine Hände gelegt wurde. Mit dem Abtritt Lennés wurde zugleich die Mitwirkung des königlichen Bruders und Schwagers, Friedrich Wilhelm (IV.), gebremst. Nach nur fünf Jahren war Pücklers Babelsberger Schöpfung als Landschaftsraum wahrnehmbar.[115]

Bis 1842 wurden überkommene Parkbauwerke neugotisch umgearbeitet. Die aus dem Gartenhaus eines Webers umgebaute »Prinzenburg«, in den 1840er Jahren Wohnung des späteren Kaiser Friedrichs, wurde 1850 zum tudorgotischen Haus für die Hofdamen (heute: »Kleines Schloß«). Charakteristisch sind seine von Lugar übernommenen grazilen Ecktürmchen. Neu errichtet wurden 1834–39 der Marstall durch Gebhardt, 1861 umgebaut und vergrößert, und 1843 das nordöstliche, »Steintor« genannte Pförtnerhaus: eine gedrungene Bastion, zinnenbewehrt, mit Treppenturm und Außentreppe. Entwürfe von Gebhardt, Langhans, Persius und Johann Heinrich Strack (1805–1880) zeugen von der unausgeführten Idee, dem Pförtnerhaus entlang der Straße nach Glienicke zinnenbekrönte Mauern und Türmchen ankündigend vorauszuschicken.

Nach Schinkels Tod setzte Persius auf dessen Grundlage den Schloßbau fort, starb jedoch noch im Jahr der Beauftragung, 1845. Hofbaurat Strack leitete die Arbeiten weiter, Hofbauinspektor Martin Gottgetreu (1813–1885) führte das zu einem Burgenkomplex erweiterte Schloß bis zur neuerlichen Einweihung 1849 aus. Zusätzlich zur Schinkelfassade, deren Hauptansicht von der Glienicker Brücke aus zu sehen ist, bot nun das Oktogon mit seinem Festsaal eine weitere Ansicht vom Fahrweg im Süden.

An der Glienicker Lake wurde 1843–45 nach den Entwürfen von Persius das normannischem Burgenstil verpflichtete Dampfmaschinenhaus wirkungsvoll in die vom Wasser sanft ansteigende Hanglage eingefügt. Schräg gegenüber der Glienicker Brücke gelegen, erscheint das Maschinenhaus aus der Glienicker Richtung dem Schloß als Auftakt. Die Pergola um den Schornsteinturm, die das Sich-Hochschrauben des Turmes aus dem Wasser über den Sockel in die Höhe mit seinen spiralförmigen, im oberen Teil horizontalen Ziegelbändern vermittelt, antwortet der Pergola am Schloß. Deren Durchblick gestattet die ferne Wahrnehmung des Dampfmaschinenhauses, dessen Schornsteinende mit der aufsteigenden Rauchsäule gerade noch im Fokus liegt.[116] Der zinnenbesetzte Umgang um den hochaufragenden Schornsteinturm ist geistreicher Fingerzeig auf das Babelsberger Thema der vielfältigen Aussichten, indem er, selbst nur unbetretbares Zierwerk, den Fernblick lediglich ahnen läßt. Mit der farbig glasierten Ziegelornamentik fand die norddeutsche Backsteingotik ihren Weg an die Havel. Die Erweiterung des Dampfhauses um eine Maschinenhalle und das Wasserbassin (später »Achterbecken« genannt) plante Gottgetreu um 1865.

Die Dampfmaschine pumpte Wasser der Havel in ein Staubecken oberhalb des Schlosses. Dessen Überlauf speiste den von Pückler 1844 künstlich geschaffenen, »Schwarzes Meer« bezeichneten Waldsee mit Bachlauf. Mit kleinen Inseln, Wasserfall und Kleinfontänen in abgeschiedener Waldestiefe bediente er romantische Vorstellungen der Versenkung in die Natur.

Um 1850 wurde das älteste Parkgebäude, das Kutscherhaus, so verändert, daß sein nun schräg gestellter Westgiebel, den Holzapplikationen schmücken, vom Fahrweg im Süden erblickt werden kann. Auf der Augustasicht am Südwesthang des Babelsbergs stand von 1853 bis in die 1950er Jahre ein als Teehaus genutztes Borkenhäuschen. Am südlichen Ausläufer des Berges erbaute Strack 1853–56 den Flatow-Rundturm, dem Pfeiler- und Flankentürmchen etwas von seiner Behäbig-

39. Johann Friedrich Frick nach Friedrich Gilly, Marienburg, Kapitel-Saal, 1799. Aquatinta. (Reprographie aus: Wilhelm Salewski (Hrsg.), *Schloß Marienburg in Preußen*, Düsseldorf 1965.)

39. Johann Friedrich Frick after Friedrich Gilly, Marienburg, chapter house, 1799. Aquatint. (Reproduced from: Wilhelm Salewski (ed.), *Schloß Marienburg in Preußen*, Düsseldorf, 1965.)

Neo-Gothic architecture in the prohibited zone

Schinkel, who had been in charge of the reconstruction of the Rheinstein ruin by Johann Claudius von Lassaulx, was commissioned in 1833 to develop an English Gothic revival concept for the castle on the hill for Prince William. In the same year Lenné was entrusted with the layout of the grounds.

In 1835 the castle whose importance Prince William played down by calling it a »cottage«, which at that point was still an unfinished brick shell, could be provisionally opened. Lenné's plan, dated ca. 1835, which loosely integrates the castle in a system of roads linking the crests of the hills, was also implemented. The court gardener from 1836 on was Christoph Ferdinand Kindermann (1805–1865).

After a construction pause during which the erection of the Prince's city palace in Berlin took priority, work on Babelsberg continued as of 1838. Building inspector Eduard Gebhardt (1803–1869) drew up the new blueprints that were based on the ideas of Prince Hermann Ludwig Heinrich von Pückler-Muskau (1785–1871): After spending a fortnight in Potsdam, Pückler, already highly esteemed because of his *Andeutungen über die Landschaftsgärtnerei* (*Notes on landscape gardening*) (1834) and Muskau Park, which he had created, wrote a memorandum – »Unterthänigste Promemoria« (1842)[114] – condemning Lenné's work, which the latter had abandoned for lack of funds in 1839. Pückler managed to get himself put in charge of the remaining layout of the garden. With Lenné no longer in the picture, Prince William's royal brother and brother-in-law, Frederick William (IV), played a far less significant role in shaping the garden. After only five years Pückler's contribution to creating the landscape of Babelsberg was noticeable.[115]

By 1842 traditional park buildings were renovated in the neo-Gothic style. »Prinzenburg«, converted from the summerhouse of a weaver, where the later Emperor Frederick lived in the 1840s, became a Tudor Gothic house for the ladies-in-waiting in 1850 (known today as the »Kleines Schloß«). Characteristic are its slender corner turrets adopted from Lugar. New buildings were the court stables (1834–39) built by Gebhardt, renovated and enlarged in 1861, and, on the northeast side, the gatehouse (1843), called »Steintor« (Stone Gate): a squat, crenellated bastion with a stair turret and an exterior stair. Blueprints by Gebhardt, Langhans, Persius and Johann Heinrich Strack (1805–1880) testify to the unrealized idea to build battlemented walls and turrets that would prefigure the gatehouse along the road to Glienicke.

After Schinkel's death Persius continued building the castle on Schinkel's foundation, but died in the very year he was commissioned to do the work (1845). Court architect Strack was subsequently in charge of the work, and court building inspector Martin Gottgetreu (1813 to 1885) continued the construction of the castle, now expanded into a fortress complex, until its rededication in 1849. In addition to the Schinkel façade, whose main view can be seen from the Glienickee Brücke, there was now an additional view of the octagon and its festival hall from the road in the south.

By Glienicker Lake, a steam-powered pump house based on Norman fortress-style designs by Persius was built in 1843–45, effectively set into the gentle slope ascending from the water. Diagonally opposite Glienicker Brücke, the pump house appears like a prelude to the castle as one approaches from the direction of Glienicke. The pergola around the chimney tower reveals the tower rising from the water above its foundation with its spiralling bands of brick, which become horizontal at the top. A vista through its counterpart, the pergola by the castle, shows the distant pump house, the top of whose chimney and rising column of smoke are barely in focus.[116] The crenellated ambulatory around the tall chimney tower is a witty reminder of the Babelsberg theme of numerous varied views: decorative and inaccessible, it merely suggests the distant view. With coloured glazed brick ornamentation, North German brick-Gothic architecture had now arrived in the Havel region. The expansion of the steam-powered pump house by an added engine hall and pond (later called »Achterbecken«) was planned by Gottgetreu ca. 1865.

The steam engine pumped the water of the Havel into a reservoir above the palace. The overflow from the reservoir fed the artificial forest lake and brook created by Pückler in 1844, referred to as the »Black Sea«. With its little islands, waterfall and small fountains in the seclusion of the forest, the lake was the ideal place to contemplate nature, a romantic notion.

Ca. 1850 the oldest park building, the Kutscherhaus (coachman's house), decorated with wood applications, was altered in such a way that its west gable, which is now placed at an angle, could be seen from the south road. A little bark-clad house used as a teahouse stood at the Augustasicht (a lookout point) on the southwest slope of Babelsberg hill from 1853 until well into the 1950s. On the southern foothill of Babelsberg, Strack built the round Flatowturm (1853–56), which its turrets keep from looking overly stolid. With its six storeys and the ambulatory at the top, Flatowturm is a belvedere at its best: It stands exactly on the axis Pfingstberg–Belvedere–Marmorpalais. There was formerly a drawbridge over the moat that surrounds the tower. The tower is modelled on the late medieval Eschenheimer Turm (1400 to 1428) in Frankfurt am Main. The gate, which William had seen personally, represents a mental association with the Hohenzollern ruler's dynastic prehistory. In 1376 and 1400 it was in Frankfurt, whose emblem is the Eschenheimer Turm, that the electors of Brandenburg participated in the election of the emperors of the Holy Roman Empire.

From Flatowturm there is a magnificent panorama of the city of Potsdam, which in genealogical overview includes the buildings of the Hohenzollern rulers – Frederick William I's Jagdschloß Stern (Stern Hunting Lodge), Frederick II's Schloß Sanssouci and Neues Palais, Frederick William II's Marmorpalais and Frederick William IV's Pfingstberg Belvedere. Contrary to its purpose, which is to turn in the wind, the weathervane of the tower and with it the eagle of the Prussian coat of arms at its top are firmly preset to point in the direction of Schloß Sanssouci.[117]

It was Gottgetreu who designed the castle kitchen (1859–60), whose building site, half concealed in the hillside, had already been decided on by Pückler. In 1861 to 1865 the new court gardener's house was built by Strack. The terrace and pergola are reminiscent of the Gebhardt building, while certain chalet-style features give the design a rustic flavour.

In 1865 Pückler handed the Babelsberg projects over to his pupil Otto Ferdinand Kindermann (1843–1918), who was in charge of them until his retirement in 1898. During his tenure the park was expanded southward to Nowawes by additional purchases of land. The gatehouse fac-

keit nehmen. Mit seinen sechs Etagen und dem Umgang in der Höhe ist der Flatowturm ein Belvedere at its best: Er steht genau auf der Achse Pfingstberg–Belvedere–Marmorpalais. Eine Zugbrücke half ehemals den um den Turm laufenden Wassergraben zu überwinden. Vorbildhaft war das spätmittelalterliche Eschenheimer Tor (1400–28) in Frankfurt am Main. Das Wilhelm aus eigener Anschauung bekannte Tor stellt die gedankliche Verbindung zur dynastischen Vorzeit des Hohenzollern her. Die brandenburgischen Kurfürsten hatten in Frankfurt, dessen Wahrzeichen das Eschenheimer Tor ist, 1376 und 1400 an der Abstimmung zur Wahl der Kaiser des Heiligen Römischen Reiches teilgenommen.

Vom Flatowturm bietet sich ein grandioses Panorama auf die Stadt Potsdam, das in genealogischer Überschau die Bauten der Hohenzollernherrscher in den Blick nimmt – Jagdschloß Stern Friedrich Wilhelms I., Schloß Sanssouci und das Neue Palais Friedrichs II., das Marmorpalais Friedrich Wilhelms II. und das Pfingstberg-Belvedere Friedrich Wilhelms IV. Entgegen ihrer Bestimmung, sich im Wind zu drehen, ist die Wetterfahne des Turms und mit ihr der preußische Wappenadler auf ihrer Spitze fest in Richtung Schloß Sanssouci eingestellt.[117]

Von Gottgetreu stammt die Schloßküche aus den Jahren 1859/60, deren halb im Berg verborgenen Bauplatz bereits Pückler bestimmt hatte. 1861–65 entstand durch Strack das neue Hofgärtnerhaus. Terrasse und Pergola erinnern an den Gebhardt-Bau, während Merkmale des Schweizerhaus-Stils ihn bäuerlich gestalten.

1865 übergab Pückler die Babelsberger Arbeiten seinem Schüler Otto Ferdinand Kindermann (1843–1918), der die Anlage bis zur Pensionierung 1898 betreute. Während seiner Schaffenszeit wurde der Park durch Grundstückszukäufe nach Süden bis Nowawes erweitert. Das Torhaus nach Nowawes und das Mühlentor (nach 1945 abgetragen) wurden 1866 errichtet. 1868 baute Strack das Matrosenhaus um, das noch aus der Zeit stammt, als eine Fabrik auf dem späteren Parkgelände gestanden hatte. Dem Matrosen und seinen Gehilfen, die die königliche Flotte warteten, diente es als Wohnhaus. Mit seinem vom Rathaus in Stendal aus dem 15. Jahrhundert inspirierten Staffelgiebel zeigt es Formen der norddeutschen Gotik. Diese sind auch der 1871/72 von Strack auf einer Anhöhe wiedererrichteten Gerichtslaube aus dem 13. Jahrhundert eigen, die zum 1872 abgerissenen Rathaus in Berlin gehörte.

In das 19. Jahrhundert fällt die Aufstellung von Denkmälern wie dem Bildstöckel. Es war Wilhelm zur Erinnerung an seinen badischen Feldzug im Jahr 1849 vom Großherzog Leopold von Baden geschenkt worden, da es ihm angeblich bei einer Schießerei als Kugelfang das Leben gerettet hatte. An die Niederschlagung der badischen Freiheitsbewegung erinnert auch ein neogotischer Sandsteinbau mit dem drachentötenden Erzengel Michael von August Kiss (1802–1865). Diese Replik des von Kiss ursprünglich für die gefallenen preußischen Soldaten auf dem Karlsruher Friedhof geschaffenen Mahnmals machte Friedrich Wilhelm IV. seinem Bruder zum anklagenden Geschenk: Er zwang ihn, es auf einer Erhebung hinter dem Schloß als ständigen Blickpunkt aus den Gesellschaftsräumen Teesalon und Tanzsaal aufzustellen. Der Einigungskriege 1864, 1866 und 1870/71 wurde mit den nachgebildeten Kriegsgedenkmünzen am Sockel der Siegessäule gedacht, die seit 1866 den höchsten Punkt des Babelsbergs, die Victoriahöhe, bekrönt. Unterhalb der Siegessäule kam 1882 die Feldherrenbank hinzu, die mit Bronzebüsten die Heerführer aus dem Krieg von 1870/71 ehrte.

1872 wurde der Park um die Nuthewiesen im Bereich des heutigen Kindermannsees erweitert, bevor er 1875 ein letztes Mal, nun jenseits der Allee nach Glienicke, auf insgesamt 150 ha vergrößert wurde. Im Osten an der Allee nach Glienicke entstand 1880 ein weiteres Torhaus, das, nachdem der jüngst hinzugewonnene Parkteil 1912 abgetrennt wurde, als Sternwarte dient. Bis zu seinem Tod blieb Babelsberg der bevorzugte Wohnsitz Wilhelms I.

1908 wurde begonnen, Gelände östlich des Schlosses für den geplanten, nicht ausgeführten Anbau eines weiteren Gebäudeflügels abzutragen. Fremdnutzungen, Einbauten und die Abtrennung von Gebieten bestimmten die Zeit nach dem Zweiten Weltkrieg: Das Schloß wurde Volksrichterschule, später Akademie für Staats- und Rechtswissenschaften sowie Internat der Filmhochschule. Seit 1963 nutzte es das Museum für Ur- und Frühgeschichte. Im Osten des Parks wurden Internatsgebäude errichtet. Der Park diente der paramilitärischen »Gesellschaft für Sport und Technik« als Trainingsplatz mit Schießplatz, Rodelbahn, Seestützpunkt und Reitsportanlage. In Teilen wurde die Umwandlung des Landschaftsgartens in einen Sport- und Kulturpark durch die Landschaftsarchitekten Walter Funcke (1907–1987) und Henrik Fischer verwirklicht. Hans Scharoun (1893–1972) war in den Jahren 1949/50 durch Standortgutachten und Skizzen für einen Mensabau an den Planungen für Babelsberg beteiligt.[118]

Die 1960 unter Gartendirektor Harri Günther (geb. 1928) begonnenen Wiederherstellungen mußten durch den Bau der Berliner Mauer aufgegeben werden, das Havelufer wurde Grenz- und Sperrgebiet.[119] Seit 1989 wird an der Wiederherstellung der Parklandschaft im Sinne von Lenné und Pückler-Muskau gearbeitet.

Hermann Fürst von Pückler-Muskau

Die Tatsache, daß mit dem Maschinenhaus für die Bewässerung des Parks gesorgt war, bot die wesentliche Voraussetzung der Arbeiten des Fürsten Pückler-Muskau. Die langlebigen Linden und Eichen wählte Pückler, um ein Gefüge aus Großbäumen zu gestalten, das Landschaftsbilder rahmt und Parkräume markiert.[120]

Die Lage am Hang, die vorgelagerte Residenzstadt Potsdam, Glienicke und die nahe Havel hatten Schinkel veranlaßt, Babelsberg als Belvedere zu konzipieren. Ausgehend von der Pergola am Schloß im Osten, die von der Natur zum Bauwerk führt, steigern sich die Aussichtsmöglichkeiten auf das Wasser über die großfenstrigen Gesellschafts- und Arbeitsräume der Beletage bis hin zum Zinnenkranz des westlichen Rundturms und zum schlanken Fahnenturm.

Analog zum Schloß zielten die Gartengestaltungen Lennés und Pückler-Muskaus im Wortsinne auf die Wegbereitung ausgewählter Sichten:[121] Die Anlage und Formung von Wegen erschließt den Landschaftsraum. Sie ermöglicht die Bewegung und erreicht Konzentrierung an ausgewählten Orten, die Bänke oder Kleinarchitekturen zusätzlich kennzeichnen. Von ihnen bieten sich An- und Gegensichten sowie Durch- und Aussichten in die freie, wegen ihres gemäldeähnlichen Charakters als Sichtziel prädestinierte Landschaft. Gestaltete Gärten und Umgegend aus Dörfern, Äckern, Wald und Wasser geraten dabei gleichermaßen in den Fokus.

ing Nowawes, and the Mühlentor (Mill Gate) (demolished after 1945) were built in 1866. In 1868 Strack converted the Matrosenhaus (Sailor's House), which dates back to a time when a factory had stood on what later became park land. It was the home of the sailor and his assistants, who maintained the royal fleet. With its stepped gables inspired by the 15th-century town hall of Stendal, the house shows forms of the North German Gothic style. This is also true of the 13th-century Gerichtslaube, a historic building Strack rebuilt on a hill in 1871/72, and which was part of a town hall demolished in 1872 in Berlin.

In the 19th century, memorials such as the Bildstöckl (wayside shrine) were erected. The Bildstöckl had been given to William in memory of his Baden campaign in 1849 by Grand Duke Leopold of Baden. Allegedly it had saved William's life during an exchange of fire when it was struck by a bullet intended for the prince. A neo-Gothic sandstone structure with Archangel Michael killing a dragon, by August Kiss (1802–1865), also memorialises the suppression of the freedom movement in Baden. Frederick William IV gave this replica of the memorial, which Kiss originally created at the cemetery of Karlsruhe for the Prussian soldiers killed in action, to his brother as a reproachful present: He compelled him to erect it on an elevation behind the palace as a constant point of focus from the tea salon and the ballroom. The wars of unification in 1864, 1866 and 1870/71 were memorialized with reproductions of medals commemorating the wars, affixed at the base of the Victory Column that has crowned the highest point of Babelsberg, the Victoriahöhe, since 1866. In 1882 the Feldherrenbank (Generals' Bench), which honoured the commanders of the war of 1870/71 with bronze busts, was added below the Siegessäule (Victory Column).

In 1872 the park was expanded by adding the Nuthewiesen wetlands in the area of present-day Kindermannsee (Kindermann Lake), and in 1875 it was enlarged for one last time, this time on the other side of the avenue leading to Glienicke, to a total of 150 hectares. In the east, by the avenue to Glienicke, an additional gatehouse was built in 1880; now that the most recently added section of the park has been separated from the rest (in 1912), the gatehouse is being used as an observatory. Until his death Babelsberg continued to be William I's favourite residence.

In 1908 workmen began to remove topsoil east of the palace for the construction of an additional wing; the wing was never built. In the period after World War II the palace was used for other purposes, more buildings were added and parts of the grounds were partitioned off: The palace became a school for (East German) people's judges, later the Akademie für Staats- und Rechtswissenschaften (Academy for Political Science and Law), and the student residence of the Filmhochschule (Film Academy). After 1963 it was used by the Museum für Ur- und Frühgeschichte (Museum for Pre- and Early History). Student residences were built on the east side of the park. The park served the paramilitary »Gesellschaft für Sport und Technik« (Society for Sport and Technology) as a training ground with a firing range, toboggan run, naval base and equestrian centre. In parts the transformation of the landscape garden into a sport and culture park was implemented by landscape architects Walter Funcke (1907–1987) and Henrik. Hans Scharoun (1893 to 1972) participated in designs for Babelsberg in 1949/50, providing site appraisals and sketches for a proposed student refectory.[118]

The restoration work begun in 1960 under garden director Harri Günther (b. 1928) had to be abandoned due to the construction of the Berlin Wall. The bank of the Havel River became a border area and a prohibited zone.[119] Since 1989, there has been ongoing restoration of the park landscape based on the ideas of Lenné and Pückler-Muskau.

Prince Hermann von Pückler-Muskau

The fact that the pump house had ensured the irrigation of the park was the essential precondition for the work of Prince Pückler-Muskau. Pückler chose long-lived linden and oak trees in order to create a texture of large trees that would frame landscape scenes and demarcate specific areas in the park.[120]

Its situation on a slope, the nearby residence city of Potsdam, Glienicke and the Havel River were the reasons Schinkel had planned Babelsberg as a belvedere. Starting with the pergola near the palace in the east, which leads from the natural landscape to the building, there are more and more potential views of the water, from the state rooms and offices of the *bel étage,* with their large windows, to the battlements of the round tower in the west and the slender flag tower.

Like the palace, the garden designs of Lenné and Pückler-Muskau were literally meant to prepare the way for selected views[121]: The layout and formation of paths opens up the landscape. It makes movement possible and is concentrated in select places that are additionally marked by benches or small structures.

From these spots there are views and counterviews, views through openings and panoramic views into the natural landscape, predestined to be the focus of sightseers because of their picturesque character. This focus is both on man-made gardens and on the surrounding landscape of villages, fields, woods and water.

For Pückler the paths are the »invisible hand, [»the silent guides of people going for a stroll«, which] lead to the finest spots, [...] and teach them to know and understand the park in its entirety«, and at the same time, being the »most advantageous line«, allow them »to discover every pleasure without being forced to«.[122] The paths, modulated down to the last nuance to fit the profile of the terrain and produce the desired vistas, are impulses that guide and teach strollers how to perceive their environment. Pückler succeeds in intentionally imparting rhythm to movement through the park.

His paths are always curved, and he clearly distinguishes footpaths from drives. For instance, the chronological sequence of landscape scenes – the Glienicke hunting lodge, the Belvedere, Glienicke Bridge, Schloß Babelsberg – on the drive from the main gate down Glienicke Avenue into the park, corresponds to the speed at which the changing scenery can be observed from a moving carriage. Meanwhile motifs along the walks designed by Pückler appear at relatively larger intervals. When Pückler has highways and footpaths running parallel along a slope, the fusion of the two sequences of landscape scenes, each adjusted to the speed at which the observer travels, resembles a canon sung in several voices. Pückler softens the abruptness of clearly defined topographical edges, such as the transition zones from meadow to water surface, by turning their curve as an abstracted line without indentations into the module of surrounding paths and road-

Für Pückler sind die Wege die »unsichtbare Hand, (»die stummen Führer des Spazierengehenden«, die) auf die schönsten Stellen hinführt, […] das Ganze kennen und verstehen lehrt«, dabei als »günstigste Linie«, »ohne Zwang jeden Genuß auffinden« läßt.[122] Ihr bis in letzte Nuancen vollständig in das Geländeprofil und die gewünschten Blicke hineinmodulierter Aufbau begreift sie als Impulse, die die Wahrnehmung der Umgegend anleiten. Pückler gelingt die zielgerichtete Rhythmisierung der Bewegung durch den Park.

Seine Wege sind stets geschwungen, klar unterscheidet er Fuß- von Fahrwegen. Die zeitliche Abfolge der Landschaftsbilder Jagdschloß Glienicke, Belvedere, Glienicker Brücke, Schloß Babelsberg, die sich etwa entlang des Fahrwegs vom Haupttor an der Glienicker Allee in den Park zeigt, entspricht der Geschwindigkeit mit der die Bildwechsel von einer fahrenden Kutsche aus wahrgenommen werden kann. In verhältnismäßig größeren Abständen erscheinen die Motive entlang der Pücklerschen Promenaden. Eine dem mehrstimmigen Kanon gemäße Durchdringung der auf die jeweilige Geschwindigkeit hin angepaßten Reihung der Bildfolgen erreicht Pückler, indem er Fahr- und Fußwege am Hang parallel verlaufen läßt. Markante Geländekanten, etwa die Übergangsstreifen von Wiese zu Wasserfläche, beruhigt Pückler, indem er ihre Kurve als abstrahierte zackenlose Linie zum Modul der umliegenden Wegführungen werden läßt. Fuß und Auge folgen ihm nahezu zwangsläufig, als gäbe es die Melodie der Landschaft vor, in die sich Vegetation, Wasser, Kunstwerke sowie Höhen und Senken im Zusammenklang einpassen. Kurve folgt auf Gegenkurve, der Erhebung antwortet die Mulde.

An der natürlichen, aufgrund ihrer Bearbeitung durch Lenné später nach ihm benannten Gewässerausbuchtung zwischen Babelsberger Enge und Glienicker Lake erbaute Pückler die Rosentreppe.

Der eiserne, mit Rosen bewachsene und mit Kielbögen überwölbte Laubengang stellt die Verbindung des etwa 9 m tiefer liegenden Fahrwegs an der Lennébucht mit dem vor dem Schloß liegenden *pleasure ground*[123] her. Repton hatte als einer der spätesten Meister der englischen Landschaftsgartenkunst bei seinen schloßnahen Anlagen, etwa in Chiswick, Dropmore, Chatsworth oder Windsor, auf formal-symmetrische Gartenbildungen zurückgegriffen und formalisierte Separatgärten in die Freinatur gebettet. In der Formulierung durch Christian Cay Lorenz Hirschfeld liest sich das so: »In England tritt man oft aus einem Palaste voll Marmor, Gemälden und Gold, auf einmal in eine wilde Gegend. Dieser Uebergang von der höchsten Pracht der Kunst zu der nachlässigen Einfalt der Natur ist zu plötzlich. Der Zwischenraum, der zwischen beyden Enden liegt, sollte durch gegenseitige Verbindungen von Stufe zu Stufe mehr zusammengezogen seyn. Es ist mehr dem Lauf unserer Ideen gemäß, wenn wir bey dem allmähligen Zurückweichen der Kunst nach und nach in die angenehme Unordnung der Natur hineinirren.«[124]

Nach seinem über Weimar vermittelten Vorbild gestaltete auch Pückler den Gartenbereich unmittelbar vor dem Schloß durch Blumenschmuck äußerst kunstvoll, als handele es sich um ein Stück Innenraum im Außen, das sich mit der Natur vermählt. In diesem Sinne wird die für einen Landschaftsgarten eher ungewöhnliche Treppen-Lauben-Architektur verständlich. Sie ist der direkte Kommunikationsweg zwischen *pleasure ground* und Landschaft, zwischen Kunst- und vermeintlichem Naturraum. Die von ihr angebotenen Ausblicke unterscheiden sie vom Laubengang oder Berceau der Renaissance- und Barockzeit.

Der durch Podeste unterbrochene Treppenlauf ist in leichter Biegung geführt, so daß Auf- und Abstieg von unterschiedlich gerichteten Ausblicken begleitet werden. Das Schloß als Höhepunkt der Sichtenschau zeigt sich gar erst beim Heraustreten auf den Panoramaweg am oberen Ende der Treppe. Dort, wo die Wegbögen sich treffen, lockt in der Entfernung zu Seiten des Schlosses der Torbogen des Küchengebäudes, der sich über den im Westen am *pleasure ground* entlang schwingenden Pfad erreichen läßt: Pücklers Wegparabeln, deren eine er als Rosengang formuliert, beinhalten auch das Gleichnis des Märchens der Gebrüder Grimm, *Dornröschen* (handschriftliche Urfassung 1810, erste Auflage 1812). Eine nach 100 Jahren in Rosen verwandelte Dornenhecke, das verwunschene Schloß sind die traumhaften Bilder des Märchens ebenso wie des Gartens. Der Gang der Dichtung endet wie der Gang durch den Park als wunderbare Synthese – der Prinz erlöst Dornröschen mitsamt dem Hofstaat aus 100jährigem Schlaf, das kunstvolle Nadelöhr der Rosentreppe lenkt den Wanderer im Park zum formvollendeten *pleasure ground* vor dem Schloß.

Der Abstieg durch die Rosentreppe präsentiert linker Hand die Sicht zum Tiefen See bis hin zum Ruinenberg, nach rechts Turm und Schloß Glienicke und die Große Neugierde; vom unteren Treppenabschnitt sind das Glienicker Horn mit dem Pfingstberg zu sehen.

Im Westen führt ein Weg in weitem Schwung vom Matrosenhaus, über die Kuppe des Generalseichenplateaus als westlichste Erhebung im Park, zum heutigen Flatowturm. Fugenlos verläuft der Übergang des in geschickter Krümmung über die Plateaukuppe gelenkten Weges in das Bodenrelief. Und doch liegt die überhöhte Wegdecke, noch bevor der Fahrweg die Kuppe erreicht, 2 m über dem höchsten Punkt des natürlichen Geländeplateaus. Die geradezu heimlich hinzugewonnene Höhe kommt der Aussicht zugute: Abschnittsweise zeigen sich bereits bei der Annäherung an die Hügelkuppe Pfingstberg-Belvedere, Marmorpalais, Flatowturm, Nikolaikirche und Kindermannsee, die die baumgerahmte Dreiviertelkreisperspektive des Generalseichenplateaus bilden.[125]

An mehreren Orten im Park konfrontiert Pückler die freie mit der idealisierten Natur: Im *pleasure ground*, in dem sich Blumenschmuck und Fontänen konzentrieren, und in den vier um das Schloß herum angelegten terrassenförmigen Schmuckgärten begegnet uns ein wahres Feuerwerk an Farben, Formen und Material.

In ihren Namen »Goldene«, »Blaue« und »Porzellan-Terrasse« klingt die märchengleiche Ausstattung an, die auch die »Voltaireterrasse« auf der Südseite des Schlosses kennzeichnete: zahlreiche Tierplastiken, Bildnisse der Hohenzollernfamilie vom Großen Kurfürsten bis hin zu Friedrich Wilhelm IV.,[126] Springbrunnen, Formbäume, vergoldete Blumenständer, Vasen, keramische oder porzellanene Gartensitze, reliefartige Blumenarrangements, fließendes Wasser nachahmendes Rankenwerk, mit Marmormosaiken gepflasterte Wege und vieles mehr.

In Anlehnung an Gärten der Renaissance in Italien umzäunte Pückler den in eine Mulde eingebetteten *pleasure ground* mit einem feinen Gitter. Kunstvolle, mit glasierten Tonformsteinen eingefaßte Beete in Füllhorn- oder Blumenkorbgestalt, der Goldene Rosengarten und die Gotische Fontäne machen auch heute wieder den Reiz dieser künstlichen Spielerei inmitten der land-

ways. Feet and eyes are almost compelled to follow this module as if it were dictating the melody of the landscape in which the vegetation, water, artworks, hills and valleys are incorporated harmoniously. A curve follows a counter-curve, and a hollow responds to a rise in the ground.

Near the natural cove between the Babelsberger Enge und Glienicke Lake, later named after Lenné because he had landscaped it, Pückler built the Rosentreppe (Rose Staircase).

The cast-iron pergola, overgrown with roses and overarched with ogee arches, connects the road along the Lennébucht (Lenné Cove), which is about 9 m lower down, with the pleasure ground[123] in front of the palace. As one of the latest masters of English landscape art, Repton had chosen to use formal, symmetrical garden designs in his parks which were situated close to palaces, such as Chiswick, Dropmore, Chatsworth or Windsor. He had embedded formalized independent gardens in uncultivated natural landscapes. Christian Cay Lorenz Hirschfeld puts it as follows: »In England you often suddenly step out of a palace full of marble, paintings and gold, into a wild environment. This transition from the greatest splendour of art to the careless simplicity of nature is too sudden. The space between the two ends should be drawn together more by establishing connections between art and nature from stage to stage. It is more in accordance with our ideas if we can gradually wander into the pleasant disorder of nature as the art gradually recedes.«[124]

In accordance with the model he had learned about through Weimar, Pückler also designed the garden space directly in front of the palace extremely elaborately through the use of floral ornamentation, as though the garden were a piece of interior transported outdoors, becoming one with nature. This is how we are to understand the architectural structure combining staircase and arbour, rather unusual for a landscape garden. It is the direct path of communication between the pleasure ground and the landscape, between a space of art and what is supposedly natural space. The vistas it offers distinguish it from the pergola or *berceau* (vaulted trellis) of the Renaissance and Baroque period.

The flight of stairs is interrupted by landings. It curves slightly, so that the views as one ascends or descends face in different directions. The castle, being the high point of the sequence of views, does not become visible until one reaches the panoramic path at the upper end of the staircase. At the point where the curves of the paths meet, the archway of the kitchen building beckons in the distance on the side of the castle. It can be reached by the path that sweeps along the pleasure ground in the west. Pückler's paths, one of which is designed as a rose walk, also reference the Grimm Brothers' fairy tale *Dornröschen* (manuscript of original version in 1810, first edition in 1812). A hedge of thorns that was transformed into roses after 100 years, and the enchanted castle, are the dreamlike images of both the fairy tale and of the garden. The story, like the walk through the park, ends as a wonderful synthesis – the prince awakens Sleeping Beauty and her courtiers from a hundred years of slumber, while the elaborate eye of the needle – the Rosentreppe – guides the wanderer in the park to the perfectly designed pleasure ground in front of the castle.

As one goes down the Rosentreppe, there is a view of Tiefer See and the more distant Ruinenberg hill on the left, and of Glienicke Tower and Castle, and Große Neugierde on the right; from the lower section of the stairs one can see the Horn of Glienicke and Pfingstberg hill.

In the west a path describes a wide curve from the Matrosenhaus, over the top of the Generalseichenplateau (Plateau of the General's Oak) as the westernmost elevation in the park, to what is now called Flatowturm. There is a seamless transition as the path elegantly curves across the top of the plateau into the terrain. And yet the surface of the road, even before the road reaches the top of the plateau, is 2 m above the highest point of the natural terrain. The additional elevation that has been gained virtually in secret benefits the view: In sections, as one approaches the top of the hill, one can already see the Pfingstberg Belvedere, Marmorpalais, Flatowturm, Nikolaikirche and Kindermannsee, which together form the tree-framed three-quarter perspective of the Generalseichenplateau.[125]

At several places in the park Pückler confronts uncultivated nature and idealized nature: In the pleasure ground, in which ornamental flowerbeds and fountains are concentrated, and in the four terrace-shaped ornamental gardens laid out around the castle we encounter a veritable explosion of colours, forms and precious material.

The names of the gardens – »Golden«, »Blue« and »Porcelain Terrace« – contain a hint of the fabulously beautiful ornamentation that was also characteristic of »Voltaire Terrace« on the palace's south side: numerous sculptures of animals, portraits of the Hohenzollern family from the Great Elector to Frederick William IV,[126] fountains, topiary trees, gilded flower stands, vases, ceramic or porcelain garden seats, relief-type flower arrangements, arabesques that imitate flowing water, paths paved with marble mosaics and much more.

Following the model of Italian Renaissance gardens, Pückler fenced in the pleasure ground, which was embedded in a hollow, with a fine lattice. Elaborate beds, bordered with glazed clay bricks in the shape of cornucopias or baskets of flowers, the Goldener Rosengarten and the Gotische Fontäne still make this playful man-made oasis surrounded by the natural landscape as charming as ever. Contrasting with the tranquillity of the well-kept lawn of the bowling green sloping gently down to the water, there is the pleasure ground's explosion of colours and forms.

The dot on the i is the geyser-like Havelfontäne, which leaps up in vibrant contrast to the velvety smooth bowling green and the colourful order of the pleasure ground in front of the vertical outline of the palace and the open landscape. At the same time it is a response to the waterworks of Frederick II in the pleasance of Park Sanssouci, which only Persius' steam engine house, built in the shape of a mosque on a bay in the Havel by Neustadt about 100 years after their installation, enabled to function.

Peter Joseph Lenné – the plan

»I have sent for you so that you will make me a plan.«
Frederick William IV to Lenné

At the very beginning of his work in Potsdam, the garden artist Lenné, who had been summoned to Potsdam in 1816, ventured to redesign Park Sanssouci (illus. 42). His blueprints did away with the geographically and icono-

schaftlichen Umgebung aus. Gegenüber der Ruhe der sich sanft zum Wasser hin neigenden, in gepflegter Manier kurz gehaltenen Rasenfläche *bowling green* steht das Feuerwerk der Farben und Formen des *pleasure ground*.

Das I-Tüpfelchen ist die geysirartige Havelfontäne, die in spannungsvollem Kontrast zum samtig-glatten *bowling green* und zur bunten Ordnung des *pleasure ground* vor der Vertikalität des Schloßumrisses und der freien Landschaft emporschießt. Zugleich ist sie eine Entgegnung auf die Wasserspiele Friedrichs II. im Lustgarten von Park Sanssouci, deren Sprudeln nun erst, rund 100 Jahre nach ihrer Einrichtung, Persius' als Moschee gestaltetes Dampfmaschinenhaus an der Neustädter Havelbucht ermöglicht hatte.

Peter Joseph Lenné – der Plan

»Ich habe Sie rufen lassen, damit Sie mir einen Plan machen.« Friedrich Wilhelm IV. an Lenné

Gleich zu Beginn seiner Tätigkeit in Potsdam wagte sich der 1816 nach Potsdam berufene Gartenkünstler Lenné an die Umgestaltung des Parks Sanssouci (Abb. 42). Am Zeichentisch machte er der geographisch und ikonographisch zentralen friderizianischen Ost–West-Achse den landschaftlichen Garaus, indem er sie als schmales Wiesenband zur nicht begehbaren Sichtachse ummodulierte. Sie faßt Lust- und Rehgarten als zusammenhängenden Naturraum auf, den locker geschwungene Wege zwischen Wiesen, dichter Gehölzpflanzung und kleinen Wasserflächen mit unregelmäßiger Uferlinie im Norden und Süden durchziehen. Nur vereinzelt durchschneiden Wege den markanten Mittelstreifen. Am Rande der großen Sicht scheinen die Bauten Friedrichs II. auf – Architekturflecken in einer weiten Landschaft. Gezielt gerichtete Wege führen nicht auf sie zu. Das Chinesische Teehaus wird zum Landschaftsprospekt. Die Geometrie der friderizianischen Wegestrahlen im Osten und das Neue Palais im Westen fassen Lennés Plan ein.

Das Wunschziel des jungen Gartengesellen auf Probezeit, den Friedrich Wilhelm IV. – Gipfel einer steilen Karriere – im Jahr 1854 zum General-Gartendirektor ernannte, zeigt sein ambitionierter Plan von 1816 in aller Deutlichkeit.[127]

Nahezu 50 Jahre lang widmete sich Lenné der Verwandlung des etwa 180 km^2 großen Gebietes der Potsdamer Kulturlandschaft in »ein harmonisches Kunstwerk«, wie der Romancier Carl Ludwig Häberlin (Belani) 1855 schreibt. Die Stadt Potsdam als der »Potsdamer Werder« im Zentrum, im Norden die Grenzlinie des Sacrow-Paretzer-Kanals – jedes Wort von Häberlins knapper Formulierung ist Lennésches Programm. Die bestehenden Anlagen der jeweiligen Monarchen und die noch wüsten Vorwerke will der Gartenkünstler derart miteinander verschmelzen, daß ganz Potsdam und Umgebung einem begehbaren Landschaftsgemälde gleich kommen.[128]

In Potsdam und Brandenburg

Was aus Lennés ambitioniertem Plan zur landschaftlichen Umgestaltung von Park Sanssouci wurde, nachdem Friedrich Wilhelm III. diesen zunächst komplett abgelehnt hatte, hielt sein Schüler und engster Mitarbeiter Johann Heinrich Gustav Meyer (1816–1877) in den von ihm gezeichneten *Koeniglichen Gaerten und Parkanlagen bei Potsdam im Jahre 1853* fest (Abb. 41). Meyers Plan zeigt das Ergebnis der teilweisen Verwirklichung von Lennés Initiationsprojekt von 1816: seine neuen Teilplanungen für die Gegend um Antiken- und Freundschaftstempel, für das Parterre am Neuen Palais und für das Blumenstück vor den Neuen Kammern seit 1820 sowie seine Parkvergrößerungen.

Als Erweiterungen des friderizianischen Parks gestaltete Lenné ab 1827 den Hopfengarten, 1825–36 Charlottenhof und 1841–42 das sich im Westen daran anschließende Gelände für die vom Tiergarten in Berlin nach Potsdam verlegte Fasanerie, 1842 den Paradiesgarten, 1846/47 den Marlygarten, 1851–60 die Anlagen an der Neuen Orangerie mit Sizilianischem und Nordischem Garten und 1859 Lindstedt. Im Norden ließ Lenné ab 1841 den Ruinenberg aus der Zeit Friedrichs II. zur Gelenkstelle zwischen Sanssouci, Bornstedt und der Feldflur von Bornstedt, Bornim und Nedlitz werden. Die Gewässer des Hopfengartens und das Wasserbecken der Fasanerie als Verbindung zu den Anlagen des Neuen Palais wurden in den 1880er Jahren zugeschüttet.

Das ehemals für die Hopfenzucht genutzte schmale Gartenstück zwischen der Straße zum Neuen Palais und der Maulbeerallee war Mittler zwischen Palais und Rehgarten sowie dem Klausberg-Belvedere, es verband den Park Sanssouci mit Lindstedt (Abb. 40). Lenné verwandelte das sumpfige Gelände in eine anmutige Wasserlandschaft mit einem See und spannungsreich bewegtem Bodenrelief. Hinter der erhöhten Südwestböschung des Sees ruhte der nach dem Original von Thorvaldsen abgegossene *Sitzende Hirtenknabe*[129] in Begleitung seines Hundes nackt auf einem Felsstück, gegen dessen rauhe Oberfläche ihn ein übergeworfenes Schafsfell schützt. Die seit 1945 verschollene Skulptur, die direkt nach der Natur komponiert zu sein vorgibt und doch die künstlerische Verarbeitung antiker Motive darstellt, gab sich der Kontemplation in Lennés Kunstnatur hin. Den Hopfengarten wählte Friedrich Wilhelm IV., um seinen Gartenkünstler Lenné in arkadischer Miniaturwelt mit der Aufstellung einer von Heinrich Berges ausgeführten Marmorkopie der von Christian Daniel Rauch 1847 in Gips geschaffenen Lennébüste zu ehren.

Die Gartenräume Römische Bäder, Meierei und Hippodrom des Charlottenhofs, zu dem einst auch der Karpfenteich jenseits des Dichterhains und das Italienische Kulturstück vor den Römischen Bädern gehörten, resultieren aus dem schöpferischen Zusammenwirken von Lenné und Schinkel.

Lennés eigenhändig gezeichneter, nicht zur konkreten Umsetzung bestimmter Charlottenhof-Plan vermittelt die Grundidee der Anlage, die ein nahezu halbkreisförmig geformter Weg mit dem Park Friedrichs II. saumlos verbindet. Sparsam sind die weich geschwungenen Wege im etwa 70 ha großen Parkraum verteilt, den dichter Bewuchs an den Außenkanten abschirmt. Die gern zu Hainen verdichtete Verteilung der Gehölzpflanzungen entlang der Wege und ihrer Knotenpunkte dient der Abwechslung und zieht den Blick in die Parkräume. Beständig bietet sich dem Auge ein optisches Ziel, ohne daß der Weg in gerader Linie darauf zuführt. Das eigens modulierte Bodenrelief im von Natur aus tischebenen Terrain trägt zum Erleben bei. Kaum merklich schwillt es an, hebt es sich und kündigt allein durch sein aufsteigendes, langsameres Gehen einforderndes Gefälle eine Sicht an. Noch ist sie durch Umpflanzung der Weg-

40. Nach Karl Blechen, Hopfengarten im Park Sanssouci, um 1835. Lithographie. (SPSG, Potsdam.)
41. Johann Heinrich Gustav Meyer, Park Sanssouci und Umgebung, Plan, 1853. Stahlstich. (SPSG, Potsdam.)
42. Peter Joseph Lenné, Park Sanssouci und Umgebung, Planentwurf, 1816. Feder, Bleistifteintragungen. (SPSG, Potsdam.)

40. After Karl Blechen, Hopfengarten in Park Sanssouci, ca. 1835. Lithograph. (SPSG, Potsdam.)
41. Johann Heinrich Gustav Meyer, Park Sanssouci and surroundings, plan, 1853. Steel engraving. (SPSG, Potsdam.)
42. Peter Joseph Lenné, Park Sanssouci and surroundings, plan draft, 1816. Pen, pencil inscriptions. (SPSG, Potsdam.)

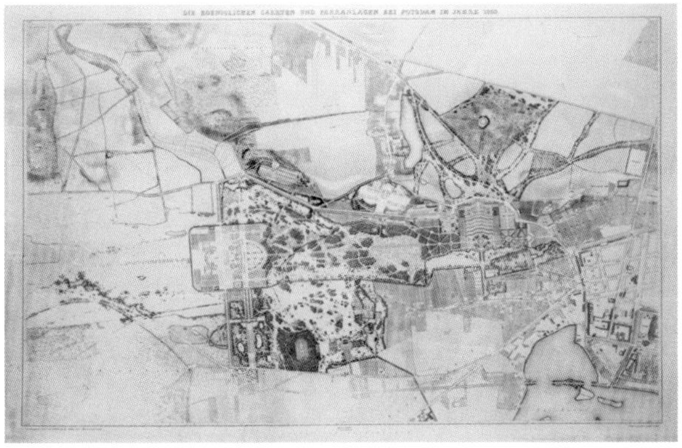

graphically central east–west axis of the landscape in the Friderician design. Lenné remodelled it as a narrow strip of meadowland, making it an inaccessible sight axis. It conceives of the pleasance and the Rehgarten as a continuum of natural space, crossed in the north and south by loosely curving paths through meadows, dense trees and shrubbery and small bodies of water with irregular shorelines. Only rarely do paths intersect with the prominent central strip. At the edge of the large vista appear the buildings of Frederick II – dots in a vast landscape. There are no paths specifically leading to them. The Chinese teahouse becomes a backdrop in the landscape. Lenné's plan is framed by the geometry of the radiating Friderician paths in the east and the Neues Palais in the west.

The ambitious plan Lenné drew up in 1816 very clearly shows the dream of the young gardener's assistant, hired on probation, whom Frederick William IV was to appoint to the position of general garden administrator in 1854 – the pinnacle of a successful career path.[127]

Lenné spent almost 50 years transforming the roughly 180 km^2 area of the Potsdam countryside into »a harmonious work of art«, as novelist Carl Ludwig Häberlin (Belani) writes in 1855. The city of Potsdam as the »Potsdamer Werder« in the centre, and the borderline of the Sacrow-Paretz Canal in the north – every word in Häberlin's brief description is Lenné's programme. The garden artist intends to fuse the existing parks and gardens of the various monarchs and the still undeveloped outlying areas in such a way that all of Potsdam and its environs come to resemble a walkable landscape painting.[128]

In Potsdam and Brandenburg

What became of Lenné's ambitious plan to redesign the landscape of Park Sanssouci after Frederick William III had initially completely rejected it? His pupil and closest collaborator Johann Heinrich Gustav Meyer (1816–1877) records developments in the park in his *Koenigliche Gaerten und Parkanlagen bei Potsdam im Jahre 1853*, which he drew himself (illus. 41). Meyer's plan shows the result of the partial implementation of Lenné's 1816 initiation project: his new partial plans for the area surrounding the Antikentempel and the Freundschaftstempel, for the *parterre* by the Neues Palais and for the flower bed in front of the Neue Kammern from 1820 onwards, and his enlargements of the park.

As expansions of the Friderician park, Lenné designed the Hopfengarten (Hop Garden) (from 1827 onwards), Charlottenhof (1825–36) and the terrain immediately adjacent to it in the west for the pheasantry, which was moved to Potsdam from the Berlin zoo (1841–42), the Paradiesgarten (1842), the Marlygarten (1846/47), the grounds near the Neue Orangerie with the Sizilianischer and the Nordischer Garten (1851–60) and Lindstedt (1859). On the north side, from 1841 onwards, Lenné made Ruinenberg, from the time of Frederick II, into a link between Sanssouci, Bornstedt and the fields of Bornstedt, Bornim and Nedlitz. In the 1880s the bodies of water in the Hopfengarten and the pond in the pheasantry, a connection to the grounds of the Neues Palais, were filled in.

The narrow piece of garden formerly used for raising hops between the road to the Neues Palais and the Maulbeerallee was the transition between the Palais and the Rehwiese as well as the belvedere on Klausberg hill, connecting Park Sanssouci with Lindstedt (illus. 40). Lenné transformed the marshy terrain into a charming water landscape with a suspenseful lively relief of the ground. Behind the elevated southwest embankment of the lake was a statue of the *Seated Shepherd Boy* cast after the original by Thorvaldsen.[129] Accompanied by his dog, the boy is seated naked on a rock against whose rough surface a sheepskin protects him. The sculpture has been missing since 1945. It purports to have been composed directly from nature, yet is an artistic treatment of classical motifs, and reflects the contemplative side of Lenné the artist. Frederick William IV paid homage to his garden artist Lenné in the Arcadian miniature world of the Hopfengarten, putting up Heinrich Berges' marble copy of an 1847 plaster bust of Lenné by Christian Daniel Rauch.

Garden features such as the Römische Bäder, the dairy and the hippodrome at Charlottenhof, which once also included the carp pond on the other side of the Dichterhain (Poets' Grove) and the Italian orchard in front of the Römische Bäder, are the result of Lenné's creative collaboration with Schinkel.

The plan of Charlottenhof, drawn by Lenné's own hand, and not intended to be actually implemented, conveys the basic idea of the park, which an almost semicircular path seamlessly connects with the park of

biegung verdeckt, bis die Erwartung eingelöst wird, ein neuer Raum sich eröffnet, ein Bauwerk heraustritt, bevor der Boden sich senken, die Spannung sich lösen kann.

Lennés Plan ist einbeschrieben, was sich noch heute etwa im Übergleiten von den Römischen Bädern zum Charlottenhof und weiter in den friderizianischen Rehgarten mit dem eindrucksvollen Baukörper des Neuen Palais in der Ferne erspüren läßt. Ein letztlich nie verwirklichter See im Nordwesten hätte das Neue Palais, die Fanfaronade Friedrichs II., in das intime Ensemble eingefügt und zwei Momente der Gartengeschichte sanft aufeinanderprallen lassen. Inmitten dieser Assemblage der Kunststile aus zwei Jahrhunderten machte das von Lenné vor dem Neuen Palais in retrobarocken Formen angelegte Parterre die Gartenkunst selbst zu ihrem Thema.

Die brilliant gezeichnete Farblithographie des Lenné-Mitarbeiters Gerhard Koeber (1809–1852) brachte Charlottenhof 1839 zur öffentlichen Anschauung (Abb. 45). In der von Ost nach West laufenden Achse vereinigen sich Garten und Architektur: Rosengarten, Terrasse, Schloß, Kastanienhain, ehemaliger Karpfenteich und Hippodrom liegen auf einer Geraden, deren strenge Geometrie seitlich gepflanzte Buschgruppen verschleiern. War mit dem Ausblick auf das alte Neue Palais und der geplanten Montage der friderizianischen Architektur in die Lenné-Moderne Geschichte gärtnerisch inszeniert worden, ist die Achse des Charlottenhof-Ensembles zugleich auch ein Gang durch die geschichtlichen Stilstufen von der Antike über das Mittelalter und die Renaissance bis hin zur Neuzeit und dem Schinkel-Klassizismus.[130]

Die Themen, die Lenné mit dem Charlottenhof-Garten bearbeitete – Pikturalisierung der Landschaft und Historie als Gartendiskurs – sind auch seinem Marlygarten eigen. Von Friedrich Wilhelm I. war der rechteckige Küchengarten mit regelmäßiger Beeteinteilung auf Friedrich Wilhelm IV. gekommen, in ironischer Namensgebung nach dem prunkvollen Marly des französischen »Sonnenkönigs« benannt. Im einstigen Nutzgarten, von dem die Mauer im Norden zeugt, reizte Lenné erneut sein Können aus, die Erdoberfläche zu skulptieren und mit Hilfe vor- und zurückgesetzter Gehölzgruppierungen das einmal kurz dem Auge dargebotene Wegziel – hier: Campanile und Atrium – eher zufällig in Umwegen erreichen zu lassen. Unterwegs lenkt die Skulptur der Flora von Albert Wolff (1814–1892, vor 1850) vor ihrem bunten Fächerbeet vom Weg ab und leitet zur Rundbank am Teeplatz. Ein anderer Weg lädt ein, die zentrale Talmulde des Gartens zu queren, um mit Blick in ein kleines landschaftliches Stück Alpental zu verweilen.

Über zwei Blickachsen erreichte Lenné die Verquickung von friderizianischem Rokoko des Parks Sanssouci mit dem in stilistischer ebenso wie religiöser Antithese benachbarten Landschaftsgarten Marly. Unmittelbar südlich des friderizianischen Obeliskportals liegt der Friedensteich, in dem sich das Ensemble der Friedenskirche spiegelt: eine geniale Paraphrase der virtuellen Erscheinung fürstlicher Architektur wie etwa die Versailles zentral vorgelagerten *pièces d'eau*. Von der auf Sanssouci zuführenden Achse erscheint der Campanile der Friedenskirche Friedrich Wilhelms IV. als fernes Ziel – gleichsam als christliches Gegenmodell zum Lustschloß des Philosophenkönigs (Abb. 43).[131]

Außerhalb des friderizianischen Parks, im Neuen Garten, wurde Lenné bereits mit einem ebenfalls 1816 gezeichneten Plan tätig, dem Planungen aus den Jahren 1828 bis 1864 folgten. Sie sahen zuletzt auch ein modernes Parterre vor dem Marmorpalais vor. Dieser Plan ist seit 1945 verschollen. Die jeweils in sich geschlossenen Eyserbeckschen Gartenräume waren um eine Vielzahl sentimentaler Staffagebauten kreiert worden, die sich an die Landschaftsgemälde Nicolas Poussins (1594–1665), Claude Lorrains (1600–1682) oder Jacob Isaacksz. van Ruisdaels (1628/29–1682) anlehnten.

Lenné verband dieses kleinteilige Staccato zu einer geordneten ästhetischen Gesamtkomposition. Sie verläßt die Zeit des frühen Landschaftsgartens mit seinen literarischen, politischen und historischen Implikationen, wie sie in den *Unconnected Thoughts on Gardening* (1764) von William Shenstone (1714–1763) zusammengetragen worden waren. Fällungen und Auslichtungen der mittlerweise zu hoch und dicht gewachsenen Bäume und Büsche aus der Zeit Friedrich Wilhelms II. schufen Durchsichten, die den engen Blickkontakt zur Umgebung, nach Glienicke und zur Pfaueninsel bewirkten. Im Neuen Garten erreichte Lenné den von ihm beschriebenen »besonders angenehmen Effekt, [...] die Gewässer in mehreren scheinbar hinter einander aufsteigenden Spiegeln darzustellen«:[132] Vom Marmorpalais aus spiegelt sich die Pfaueninsel im Heiligen See ebenso, wie sie ein zweites Mal im Spiegel der dahinter liegenden Havel erscheint.

Die neuen Gartenanlagen auf dem Pfingstberg hatten Lenné seit 1830 beschäftigt, bis sie nach seinem Plan aus dem Jahr 1862 ausgeführt wurden (Abb. 44). Mit ihnen konnte die bereits von Friedrich Wilhelm II. gewünschte Verbindung vom Neuem Garten und Pfingstberg parkartig realisiert werden. Die Verschönerung des Pfingstbergs blieb das einzige, noch nach dem Tod Friedrich Wilhelms IV. ausgearbeitete Lenné-Projekt. Aus der Regelmäßigkeit des Halbkreis- und Ringwegs entwickelte Lenné ein langgezogenes, irreguläres Wegesystem bis hin zur Großen Weinmeisterstraße. Es umgibt die üppigen, dem Belvedere vorgelagerten Schmuckanlagen und nimmt Schinkels Pomonatempel von 1800 in ihre Mitte.[133]

Nachdem Lenné das am Nordufer des Jungfernsees gelegene Sacrow schon 1833 als Landschaftsgarten zeichnerisch vorformuliert hatte, erlaubte ihm die Krönung Friedrich Wilhelms IV. 1840, die Vision in die Tat umzusetzen. Sacrow bildet den Schlußakkord der Lenné-Gärten, die sich um den Jungfernsee reihen: Neuer Garten, Pfaueninsel, Glienicke und Babelsberg.[134]

Zu einer von den vielen Gartenanlagen, die Lenné für private, nicht fürstliche Auftraggeber anlegte, zählt Caputh im Südwesten von Potsdam am Templiner See. Gut und Garten waren 1549 von Kurfürstin Katharina erworben und als Sommersitz mit umliegender Musterwirtschaft aus Weinberg, Obstgarten und Karpfenteichen genutzt worden. Kammerjunker und Generalquartiermeister Philipp de Chieze, dem der Große Kurfürst das Land 1662 geschenkt hatte, gestaltete den Garten neu, indem er ihn zur Havel ausrichtete, locker mit Obstbäumen bepflanzte und zwei symmetrische Terrassen sowie eine 240 m lange Lindenallee anlegen ließ. Caputh ging 1671 an den Großen Kurfürsten zurück. Er gab es seiner zweiten Frau Dorothea zum Geschenk, die das Schloß vergrößern ließ und über eine Freitreppe im Norden zugänglich machte. Der Garten erfuhr eine üppigere Ausstattung mit Rasen- und Blumenparketten, Skulpturenschmuck und Springbrunnen.

Der gesamte Besitz ging 1690 an Kurfürstin Sophie Charlotte, die es vier Jahre lang nutzte, um dann Lüt-

43. Julius Schlegel, Marlygarten mit Friedenskirche im Park Sanssouci, 1858. Graphit, Deckfarbe in Weiß. (SPSG, Potsdam.)
44. Johann Heinrich Gustav Meyer, Garten am Pfingstberg, Plan, nach 1862. Feder. (SPSG, Potsdam.)
45. Gerhard Koeber und Peter Joseph Lenné, Schloß Charlottenhof und Umgebung im Park Sanssouci, Plan, 1839. Lithographie. (SPSG, Potsdam.)

43. Julius Schlegel, Marlygarten with Friedenskirche in Park Sanssouci, 1858. Graphite, opaque colour in white. (SPSG, Potsdam.)
44. Johann Heinrich Gustav Meyer, garden at Pfingstberg, plan, after 1862. Pen. (SPSG, Potsdam.)
45. Gerhard Koeber and Peter Joseph Lenné, Schloß Charlottenhof and surroundings in Park Sanssouci, plan, 1839. Lithograph. (SPSG, Potsdam.)

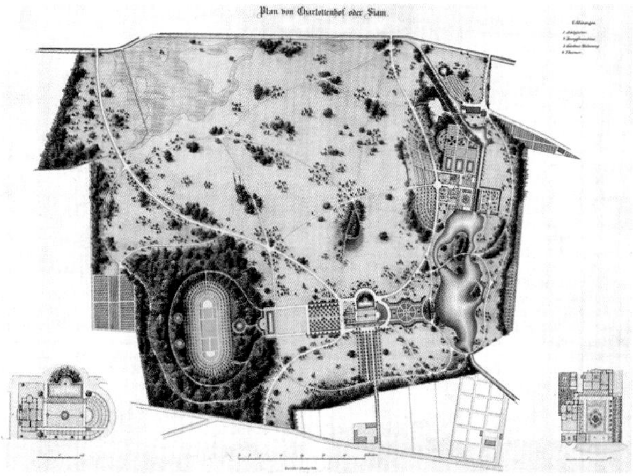

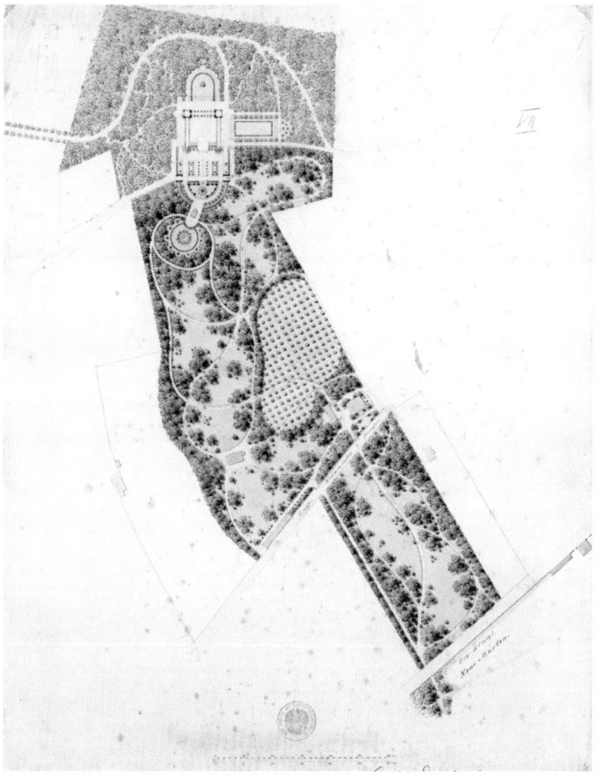

Frederick II. Gently curving paths are sparingly dispersed throughout the roughly 70 hectare area of the park, screened at its outer edges by dense vegetation. The distribution of trees and shrubbery, which tend to form dense groves along the paths and their intersections, makes for variety and draws the viewer's gaze into the various sections of the park. There is constantly a visual goal, even though the path does not lead to it in a straight line. The specially modulated relief of the soil in a terrain that is as flat as a board provides visitors with an added experience. The ground swells barely perceptibly, rises and announces a vista solely by its ascending slope, which requires slower walking. The view is still concealed by the vegetation planted at the bend of the path, until one's expectation is met, a new space opens up, a building rises to view, before the ground dips and the tension is resolved.

In Lenné's plan is inscribed something that it is still possible to recognize today, for instance, in the way the Römische Bäder blend into Charlottenhof and farther on into Frederick II's Rehgarten, with the impressive building of the Neues Palais in the distance. A lake on the northwest side that was never realized would have incorporated the Neues Palais, Frederick II's *fanfaronade*, in the intimate collection of buildings, a gentle collision between two epochs in garden history. In the midst of this assemblage of the artistic styles of two centuries, the *parterre* Lenné created in front of the Neues Palais in retro-Baroque forms focussed on garden art per se.

The brilliantly drawn colour lithograph by Lenné's colleague Gerhard Koeber (1809–1852) brought Charlottenhof into public view in 1839 (illus. 45). In the axis that runs from east to west, garden and architecture merge: The rose garden, terrace, palace, horse chestnut grove, former carp pond and hippodrome lie on a straight line whose strict geometry is veiled by groups of bushes planted on its sides. While the vista of the old Neues Palais and the planned montage of Faridician architecture into Lennés modern design was a horticultural staging of history, the axis of the Charlottenhof ensemble is at the same time also a walk through historical styles from classical antiquity to the Middle Ages and Renaissance, and on to modern times and Schinkel's classicism.[130]

The themes Lenné addressed in the garden of Charlottenhof – pictorialization of the landscape, and history as a garden discourse – are typical of his Marly garden as well. It was from Frederick William I that the rectangular kitchen garden, regularly divided into beds, had come into the possession of Frederick William IV. It was ironically named after the ostentatious Marly of the French »Sun King«. In the former kitchen garden, a fact attested to by the wall on the north side, Lenné again used all his skill as he sculpted the earth's surface and with the help of groups of trees and bushes that were set forward or back led visitors, as if by chance and by detours, to a destination they had glimpsed only briefly – in this case, the campanile and atrium. Along the way the sculpture of Flora by Albert Wolff (1814–1892, before 1850) in front of its colourful fan-shaped flowerbed invites strollers to leave the path and head for the round bench by the tearoom. Another path invites them to cross the central hollow of the garden to take a long look at a small stretch of alpine valley.

By way of two visual axes Lenné achieved the fusion of the Faridician Rococo of Park Sanssouci with the adjacent landscape garden of Marly, which was its stylistic and religious antithesis. Immediately south of the Faridician Obeliskportal is the Friedensteich (Peace Pond), in which the Friedenskirche (Peace Church) complex is reflected: an ingenious paraphrase of the virtual appearance of royal buildings – for instance, the *pièces d'eau* centrally situated in front of Versailles. From the axis that leads towards Sanssouci, the campanile of Frederick William IV's Friedenskirche appears as a distant goal – a Christian counter-model, as it were, to the philosopher king's summer residence (illus. 43).[131]

Outside the Faridician park, in the Neuer Garten, Lenné was already at work with a plan he had also drawn up in 1816, followed by plans from the period between 1828 and 1864. These also provided for a modern *parterre* in front of the Marmorpalais. This plan has been missing since 1945. The Eyserbeck gardens, each of which was self-contained, had been created around a large number of sentimental decorative buildings that were inspired by the landscape paintings of Nicolas Poussin (1594–1665), Claude Lorrain (1600–1682) or Jacob Isaackszoon van Ruisdael (1628/29–1682).

Lenné joined together this fragmented staccato configuration into an ordered aesthetic whole, thus leaving behind the period of the early landscape garden with its literary, political und historical implications, as compiled in the *Unconnected Thoughts on Gardening* (1764) of William Shenstone (1714–1763). Cutting down and clearing the trees and bushes from the time of Frederick William II, which had in the meantime grown too tall or too thick, created vistas that established close visual contact with the surrounding area, with Glienicke, and with Pfaueninsel. In the Neuer Garten Lenné achieved an effect he described as »particularly pleasant, [...] where the bodies of water acted as a number of mirrors that seemingly rose one behind the other«:[132] Looking from the Marmorpalais, Pfaueninsel is reflected both in Heiliger See and in the mirror of the Havel River, which lies behind it.

The new gardens on Pfingstberg hill had kept Lenné busy from 1830 onwards until they were completed according to his 1862 plan (illus. 44). They made it possible to create the connection, by way of the park, between the Neuer Garten and Pfingstberg, something Frederick William II had already wished for. The beautification of Pfingstberg was the only Lenné project to be planned after Frederick William IV's death. Instead of the regularity of the semicircular path and ring path Lenné developed an elongated, irregular system of paths over to Große Weinmeisterstraße. It surrounds the luxuriant decorative gardens in front of the Belvedere and has Schinkel's Pomonatempel, dated 1800, in its centre.[133]

After Lenné drew up preliminary sketches in 1833 showing Sacrow, located on the north shore of Jungfernsee, as a landscape garden, the coronation of Frederick William IV in 1840 made it possible for him to make the vision a reality. Sacrow is the successful conclusion of the Lenné gardens that encircle Jungfernsee: the Neuer Garten, Pfaueninsel, Glienicke and Babelsberg.[134]

Caputh, southwest of Potsdam near Templiner See, is one of the many gardens Lenné designed for private, non-princely patrons. The estate and garden had been purchased in 1549 by Electress Catherine and had been used as a summer residence with a surrounding model farm consisting of a vineyard, an orchard and carp ponds. Chamberlain and general quartermaster Philipp de Chieze, to whom the Great Elector had given the land in 1662, redesigned the garden by having it face the

zow/Lietzenburg, das spätere Charlottenburg, zu ihrer Sommerresidenz zu wählen. Unter Friedrich Wilhelm I., der die Regierung 1713 übernahm, diente das Schloß nurmehr zeitweiligen Jagdaufenthalten. Die 74 Statuen, Kübelpflanzen und der Nutzgartenbestand aus Obstbäumen, Weinstöcken, Wurzelgemüsen, Kohl und Salat wurden 1713 genauestens inventarisiert.

Caputh wurde dann 1815 an die Familie des Generalleutnants Hans Hermann Heinrich von Thümen übergeben und von Lenné verändert. Von seiner Hand stammt ein Verschönerungsplan aus den 1820er Jahren. Die ausgezeichnete Lage an der Havel mit ihren weiten Sichten arbeitete Lenné heraus, indem er den Garten am Ufer vergrößerte. Sein in Schleifen geführtes Wegenetz umschließt drei große Gartenräume.[135] Seit Mitte des 19. Jahrhunderts verbindet ein Uferweg Caputh mit Potsdam. Er führt an einer von Stüler 1855 gebauten Wildtränke, der sogenannten Marienquelle und dem Forsthaus Templin vorbei.

In der Provinz Brandenburg erhielt Lenné, angefangen vom Gut Neuhardenberg im Kreis Lebus, 1821, bis Neumühle im Kreis Ruppin, 1840, zahlreiche Aufträge fürstlicher Staatsdiener. Ihre schön gelegenen Gutshäuser inmitten der märkischen Landschaft mit ihrem feuchten Grasland, den sandigen Hügeln und dem reizvollen Oderbruch boten Lenné Gelegenheit, im kleinen durchzuspielen, was er mit dem großen landschaftlichen Wurf Potsdam/Berlin erarbeitete.

Mit dem zur einstigen Burg Wusterhausen gehörenden Garten im Kreis Teltow beschäftigte er sich in seinen unausgeführten Plänen des Jahres 1832. Die Burg war 1698 durch Friedrich Wilhelm I. erworben und zum Jagdschloß umfunktioniert worden. Kurfürstin Sophie Charlotte hatte auf die Anlage des Barockgartens eingewirkt. Abgesehen von den seit 1798 zweimal jährlich stattfindenden Besuchen des Prinzen Heinrich, hatte Königs Wusterhausen bis zur Zuweisung des Schlosses an Prinz August von Preußen, Neffe Friedrichs II., ungenutzt gelegen.

In Berlin

Lennés Wirken in den barock überkommenen Berliner Schloßgärten setzte mit seinem großartigen Entwurf für Charlottenburg 1819 ein, der sich wie der frühe Sanssouci-Plan mit Friedrich Wilhelms III. restaurativer und sparsamer Gesinnung nicht vereinen ließ, so daß es nur zu stückweisen landschaftsgärtnerischen Veränderungen kam. Für Friedrich Wilhelms III. zweite Gemahlin, Auguste von Harrach, Fürstin von Liegnitz (1800–1873), schuf Lenné 1830 einen kleinen separaten Garten, den ein Weg an der Ostseite des Knobelsdorffschen Schloßflügels mit dem Schinkelpavillon verband. 1865 zeichnete Meyer eine Bestandsaufnahme des Charlottenburger Schloßplatzes, der das Ende der Lennéschen Arbeit in diesem Garten markiert.

Um den Park von Schloß Schönhausen in Berlin begann Lenné sich 1827 zu kümmern. Das Schloß hatte Kurfürst Friedrich III. 1691 erworben; es wurde im 18. Jahrhundert von Königin Elisabeth Christine, Gemahlin Friedrichs II., bewohnt. Nach deren Tod, 1797, hielt sich dort Friederike von Mecklenburg-Strelitz auf, die Schwester Königin Luises von Preußen. Ihr Interesse für den Park, in dem Johann Lorenz Samuel Busch (1776? bis 1832) tätig war, veranlaßte Friedrich Wilhelm III., Lenné die Neugestaltung des barocken Parks zu übertragen. Dieser empfand die nach seinen Worten »würdige Aufschmückung« des »wenngleich veralteten, doch in Rücksicht seines Baumschmucks ausgezeichneten königlichen Gartens«,[136] den die durchfließende Panke bewässerte, als Herausforderung und zeichnete 1827 einen ersten von ihm kommentierten Plan: Vor dem Schloß sah er einen mit Blumen und Strauchwerk geschmückten Rasenplatz vor, an den eine Wasserfläche aus der teichartig verbreiterten Panke als Hauptattraktion des Parks grenzen sollte, umgeben von Baummassen.

Ein Hauptfahrweg und untergeordnete Gehwege sollten den Park, harmonisch auf den Flußlauf und die anmutigen Gartenpartien abgestimmt, großzügig erschließen. Der Fluß ermöglichte die Anlage mehrerer Wasserfälle. Die angrenzenden Bauernwiesen ergaben einen reizvollen landschaftlichen Hintergrund. Die neue Anlage konnte 1829–31 unter zahlreichen Änderungen seitens des Königs ausgeführt werden. Die Schönhauser Baumschule des Hofgärtners Busch lieferte die Gehölze.

In Glienicke (Abb. 46) wurde Lenné von Karl August Graf von Hardenberg damit beauftragt, einem *pleasure ground* an dem vor zwei Jahren erworbenen Gutshaus des Oberstallmeisters Heinrich August Graf von Lindenau Form zu geben.[137] Das geschah zeitgleich mit den Verbesserungen für Sanssouci und den Vorschlägen, den Neuen Garten landschaftlich zu öffnen.

Die Vorbedingung für die Wiederaufnahme historisch-geometrischer Gartenelemente hatte die in Frankreich Ende des 18. Jahrhunderts begonnene Diskussion über das Pittoreske geschaffen. Humphry Repton (1752 bis 1818) legte sie in seinen *Observations on the Theory and Practice of Landscape Gardening* 1803 dar, und drei Jahre später entwickelte John Claudius Loudon (1783 bis 1843) sie in *A Treatise on Forming, Improving and Managing Country Residences* [...] weiter. Den Ausgleich aller konträren Elemente erreichte schließlich Ludwig von Sckell (1750–1823) mit den *Beiträgen zur bildenden Gartenkunst* (1818, 1825). Gabriel Thouin (1747–1829) veröffentlichte 1819/20 seine berühmten *Plans raisonnés de toutes les espèces de jardin*, in denen er verschiedenste Gartentypen – für den Nutzen, die Zierde oder die Gesundheit – und die in das jeweilige Umfeld passenden Pflanzen vorstellt.

Thouin und Sckell beeinflußten Lenné maßgeblich, der bei Gabriels Bruder, dem Botaniker André am Pariser Jardin des Plantes, hospitiert hatte und in München bei der Anlage des Englischen Gartens durch Sckell zugegen gewesen war. Eine typologische Sortierung, nicht von Garten-, sondern von Architekturstilen, hatte 1800 bereits der Architekt Jean-Nicolas-Louis Durand (1760 bis 1834) in seinem Erstlingswerk *Recueil et parallèle des édifices de tout genre anciens et modernes* vorgenommen. Lenné hatte sich bei Durand, der an der Pariser École Polytechnique lehrte, in der Entwurfslehre geübt.

Bezeichnend für Lennés Wirken als Landschaftsgestalter war sein Vorschlag, Graf Hardenberg solle das am Havelwasser gelegene Land (Lehmannsche Büdnerstelle und Sandschelle) hinzukaufen, damit er »Herr der Aussichten« bliebe.[138] Folgerichtig akzentuierte Lenné den *pleasure ground* als Landschaftsprospekt mit Hilfe dreier belaubter Hügel im Dreieck um die sanft zum Wasser gleitende Wiesenfläche. Die Gestaltung des Glienicker *pleasure ground*, das erste von Lenné an der Havel verwirklichte Projekt, ist bereits Teil seiner Vision einer die einzelnen Gartengrenzen übergreifenden Aufschmückung.

46. Xaver Sandmann nach Ferdinand Marohn, Glienicker Ufer mit Casino und Brücke, um 1845. Kolorierte Lithographie. (SPSG, Potsdam.)

46. Xaver Sandmann after Ferdinand Marohn, Glienicke riverbank with Casino und bridge, ca. 1845. Coloured lithograph. (SPSG, Potsdam.)

Havel River; he planted scattered fruit trees and had two symmetrical terraces laid out and a 240-m long avenue of linden trees planted. Caputh reverted to the Great Elector in 1671. He gave it to his second wife Dorothea as a present, and she had the castle enlarged and a staircase built to make it accessible on the north side. The garden layout now became more luxuriant, with *parquets* of lawn and flowers, sculptures and fountains.

In 1690, the entire property went to Electress Sophia Charlotte, who used it for four years and then chose Lützow/Lietzenburg, the later Charlottenburg, as her summer residence. Under Frederick William I, who took the reins of power in 1713, the castle was used only for hunting excursions. An exact inventory of the 74 statues, tub plants and the stock of fruit trees, grapevines, root vegetables, cabbage and lettuce was drawn up in 1713.

Then, in 1815, Caputh was handed over to the family of Lieutenant-General Hans Hermann Heinrich von Thümen and was transformed by Lenné. There is a beautification plan drafted by him from the 1820s. By enlarging the garden on the river bank, Lenné designed the excellent location on the Havel River with its distant views. His network of looping paths encircles three large garden areas.[135] Since the middle of the 19th century a road along the riverbank has connected Caputh with Potsdam. It goes past a drinking trough for game animals built in 1855 by Friedrich August Stüler, the so-called Marienquelle (the Virgin Mary's Spring) and the Templin forester's lodge.

In the province of Brandenburg, Lenné was given a large number of commissions by the prince's public servants, starting with the Neuhardenberg estate in the district of Lebus, in 1821, and ending with Neumühle in the district of Ruppin, in 1840. Their beautifully located manor houses in the midst of the Mark Brandenburg landscape with its damp grassland, sandy hills and charming Oderbruch marshes gave Lenné the opportunity to do on a small scale what he was doing on a grand scale with the landscape of Potsdam/Berlin.

Among his unrealized plans, dated 1832, were blueprints for the garden belonging to the former Burg Wusterhausen in the district of Teltow. This castle had been acquired by Frederick William I in 1698 and had been converted into a hunting lodge. Electress Sophia Charlotte had had an impact on the layout of the Baroque garden. Except for two visits a year by Prince Henry since 1798, Königs Wusterhausen had lain idle until the castle was assigned to Prince Augustus of Prussia, the nephew of Frederick II.

In Berlin

Lenné's work in the traditional Baroque castle gardens of Berlin began with his magnificent design for Charlottenburg in 1819. Like the early plan for Sanssouci it was not consistent with Frederick William III's reactionary and frugal disposition, so that there were only peacemeal landscaping changes. For Frederick William III's second wife, Augusta von Harrach, Princess of Liegnitz (1800 to 1873), Lenné created a small separate garden in 1830, connected with the Schinkel Pavilion by a path on the east side of the Knobelsdorff wing of the castle. In 1865 Meyer drew up an inventory of the Charlottenburg Schloßplatz (castle square), which marks the end of Lenné's work in this garden.

It was in 1827 that Lenné began taking care of the park of Schloß Schönhausen in Berlin. Elector Frederick III had acquired the castle in 1691; in the 18th century Queen Elisabeth Christine, the wife of Frederick II, lived there. After her death, in 1797, it was the home of Frederica of Mecklenburg-Strelitz, the sister of Queen Louise of Prussia. Her interest in the park, in which Johann Lorenz Samuel Busch (1776?–1832) worked as gardener, was the reason Frederick William III commissioned Lenné with redesigning the Baroque park. The latter felt it would be a challenge to »embellish as it deserves« the royal garden »which, though old-fashioned, is outstanding in respect to its fine trees«[136] – landscape watered by the Panke River, which flowed through it. In 1827 Lenné drew up an initial plan with his own comments: In front of the palace he planned to have a lawn with flowers and shrubbery, adjacent to which there would be a body of water – the Panke River widened to a pond, the main attraction of the park, surrounded by masses of trees.

A main drive and secondary footpaths were intended to provide generous access to the park, harmoniously coordinated with the course of the river and the more charming parts of the garden. The river made it possible to create several waterfalls. The adjacent farm meadows provided an attractive scenic background. It was finally possible to implement the new park in 1829–31 after numerous changes by the king. The Schönhausen tree nursery of court gardener Busch supplied the trees and shrubbery.

In Glienicke (illus. 46) Lenné was commissioned by Count Karl August von Hardenberg to design a pleasure ground near the manor house of chief equerry Count Heinrich August von Lindenau, which the latter had purchased two years earlier.[137] This took place at the same time as the improvements at Sanssouci and proposals that the landscape of the Neuer Garten be opened up.

A discussion about the picturesque, begun in the late 18th century in France, had created the precondition for resuming the use of historical geometric garden features. Humphry Repton (1752–1818) expounded the idea in his *Observations on the Theory and Practice of Landscape Gardening* in 1803, and three years later John Claudius Loudon (1783–1843) further developed it in *A Treatise on Forming, Improving and Managing Country Residences* [...]. Finally, Ludwig von Sckell (1750–1823) in his *Beiträge zur bildenden Gartenkunst* (1818, 1825) suggested how all contrary elements could be brought into balance. Gabriel Thouin (1747–1829) published his famous *Plans raisonnés de toutes les espèces de jardin* (1819/1820), in which he introduces a variety of different types of gardens – kitchen gardens, ornamental or medicinal gardens – and the plants suitable for each setting.

Thouin and Sckell substantially influenced Lenné, who had attended lectures by Gabriel's brother, the botanist André Thouin at the Paris Jardin des Plantes, and had been present in Munich when the Englischer Garten was laid out by Sckell. A typological systematization, not of garden styles, but of architectural ones, had already been undertaken in 1800 by the architect Jean-Nicolas-Louis Durand (1760–1834) in his first work, *Recueil et parallèle des édifices de tout genre anciens et modernes*. Lenné had practiced design theory with Durand, who was teaching at the École Polytechnique in Paris.

Characteristic of Lenné's work as a landscape architect was his proposal that Count Hardenberg should

Mit dem Tod Hardenbergs und dem Verkauf Glienickes an Prinz Carl von Preußen 1824 wurde die begonnene Gestaltung fortgesetzt. Die Arbeit am Casino war zugleich der Beginn und einer der Höhepunkte des Zusammenspiels des Landschaftskünstlers Lenné mit dem Architekten und Maler Schinkel. Ihre Korrespondenz belegt und beleuchtet sie,[139] die ausgeführten, überkommenen Werke sind die Zeugen ihrer in die Landschaft einbeschriebenen Geistesverwandtschaft.

»Land der Phantasien« – Lenné und Schinkel

Das Casino in Glienicke am Hochufer der Havel, das Billardhaus einer vorherigen Gutsanlage, entstanden nach der Mitte des 18. Jahrhunderts, wurde durch Schinkel in den Jahren 1824–28 aufgestockt und umgebaut, während Lenné die Umgebung gestaltete. Die beiden Pergolen, die im Norden und Süden an die Schmalseiten des Casinos gefügt wurden, lassen Natur, Mensch und Architektur in Beziehung treten. In der rhythmischen Verschiebung ihrer Höhenniveaus und der ungleichen Anzahl der Pfeilerpaare schwingt das unregelmäßig Gewachsene der umliegenden Landschaft mit. Durch die Zwischenräume ihrer Pfeiler dringt die Natur, geht der Blick aufs Havelwasser. Die Pergolen selbst sind, zusammen mit dem Baukörper des Casinos, kulissenhafter Hinweis auf die Gegenwart und das Agieren des Menschen in der Natur: Sanft leitet die südliche Pergola über Stufen zum Glienicker *pleasure ground*, während die nördliche an einem erhöhten Plateau endet, späterer Baugrund für den Klosterhof Prinz Carls.

Innerhalb der aktuellen Diskussion um die Rangfolge der Kunstgattungen wertete die architektonische Staffage die Landschaft zur »Kulturlandschaft« auf. Ihr sollte, vor dem Stilleben, der reinen Landschaft sowie der Historie, das höchste Prädikat zukommen.[140] Dem Maler Schinkel war die menschliche Existenz beziehungsweise die Spur derselben in der Natur unabdingbar für eine malerisch konstruierte, ideale Landschaft, in der Natur, Mensch und Architektur eine allumfassende Einheit bilden. »Durch seine Beziehung auf den Menschen gewinnt das Landschaftsbild erst seine Vollendung«, bemerkten der Geheime Oberregierungsrat Carl G. Bethe und sein Mitautor Lenné in ihrer Schrift *Über Trift- und Feldpflanzungen*.[141] Ähnlich wie Schinkel setzt Lenné Kultursymbole wie Haus und Schloß, Weg und Beet in Szene.[142]

Das Fenster als Topos der Malerei für die Grenze zwischen Wirklichkeit und Fiktion überträgt Lenné in seine Gemälde der Landschaft. Vegetabiles Rahmenwerk aus Stämmen, Astwerk und anderes begrenzt visuelle Felder. Lenné nutzt sie, wie Schinkel seine Architekturen über bühnengleiche Ausblicke öffnet, um durch Rückbezug auf die im jeweiligen Ausschnitt dargebotene historische Epoche Aussagen zur Gegenwart treffen zu können.

In bedeutungsvoller Steigerung erscheinen Stadtmotive wie die Kuppel der Nikolaikirche, die vom Glienicker Stibadium her gesehen werden kann. Dies ist als eine Umdeutung zu verstehen, dem Blick von der Villa Medici zur Kuppel des Petersdoms in Rom vergleichbar. Überhöhung erfahren Naturzeichen wie die alten Eichenbäume auf der Pfaueninsel oder Zeugnisse der Geschichte, wie etwa das westlich im Schatten vor untergehender Sonne gelegene Neue Palais Friedrichs II. Vergleichbar mit der Kunst der Romantiker streben Schinkel und Lenné in ihren malerischen, architektonischen und landschaftlichen Œuvres eine höhere Ebene geschichtlicher und philosophischer Reflexion an.

Die ehemals vom Lauf des Wassers begleitete Ost–West-Achse von Charlottenhof stellt die Abläufe in der Natur als romantische Metapher auf den ewig sich erneuernden Kreis allgemeinen Werdens und Vergehens dar, sowohl in Natur als auch in der Geschichte. Das beginnt im Osten beim Maschinenteich und geht über den Rosengarten, die Schloßterrasse, den Dichterhain, das Maiblumenstück, die als Schlaf und Tod gedeutete Ildefonso-Gruppe bis hin zum Hippodrom im Westen und läßt sich als Zyklus von Tag und Nacht oder Auf- und Untergang lesen.[143] Gleiches hatte der Romantiker Philipp Otto Runge in seinen allegorischen Tageszeitenbildern seit 1802 formuliert.

Das romantische Motiv der Rückenfigur entlehnte Schinkel von Caspar David Friedrich (*Mönch am Meer*, 1810) direkt, wie beispielsweise in seiner *Landschaft mit Pilger* von 1813. Bei Lenné ist es als Angebot greifbar, an eigens dafür geschaffenen Plätzen den Blick in die Landschaft zu richten, um sich – mit dem Rücken zur äußeren Welt – ihrer Betrachtung hinzugeben. Schinkels Rückenfiguren und Lennés für sie reservierte Orte führen nicht nur in die Landschaft ein. Zugleich stellen sie den Zusammenhang von Mensch und Natur her. Nur in Bezug auf den Betrachter scheint die Landschaft zu existieren.

Ist die Rückenfigur das Sehnsuchtsmotiv der Romantik schlechthin, begegnet Lenné dieser Denkfigur in der Organisation seiner Wege. Wie die Friedenskirche oder Charlottenhof läßt sich auch Glienicke keinesfalls auf dem direkten Weg erreichen, den das imposante Ensemble Palmettenbeet, Löwenfontäne und Freitreppe zunächst suggerieren. »Der Ankommende fährt nicht vor ein Schloßportal, eine Freitreppe auf einer Terrasse vor, sondern steigt vor der an die Hausecke gelehnten Pergola ab, die dreimal umknickend den Blumenhof umzieht, mit ihrer Berankung die Wände mit den eingelassenen Antikenfragmenten verschattend und unauffällig und scheinbar irgendwo, in Wahrheit aber in der Achse des jenseitigen, von der [Potsdamer] Chaussee her als Schloßportal wirkenden Risalits, findet er die schlichte Eingangstür […].«[144]

Das Erahnen, das Umherschweifen, die verheißungsvollen Ausschnitte, in denen Landschaftsräume oder Architekturen kurzzeitig dargeboten werden, sind dem Lennéschen Wegelauf eigen, deren eigentliches Ziel die Ferne ist. Lenné spricht von der »bläulichen Ferne, die sich wie eine zweite Welt, wie der Ring des Saturn um seinen Kern, wie ferne Küsten und Wolkenbildungen, an den farbigen Gesichtskreis anschmiegt. Dies ist […] das Land der Phantasien, der weithin führenden Gedanken und einer unendlichen Sehnsucht.«[145]

purchase additional land by the Havel River (Lehmannsche Büdnerstelle and Sandschelle) so that he would remain »in charge of the views«.[138] Accordingly Lenné accentuated the pleasure ground as a scenic landscape by means of three wooded hills in a triangle around the meadow that gently sloped down to the water. The landscaping of the Glienicke pleasure ground, the first project Lenné implemented by the Havel River, is already part of his vision of beautification that goes beyond the boundaries of individual gardens.

After Hardenberg's death and the sale of Glienicke to Prince Charles of Prussia in 1824 the landscaping project was continued. Work on the Casino was both the beginning and one of the high points of the collaboration of the landscape artist Lenné with the architect and painter Schinkel. Their correspondence documents and sheds light on it,[139] and the work they accomplished is a testimony to their spiritual affinity, which is inscribed in the landscape.

»Land of fantasies« – Lenné and Schinkel

The Casino in Glienicke on the bluff of the Havel River, the billiard hall of a previous estate, built in the second half of the 18th century, was expanded and modified by Schinkel in 1824–28, while Lenné designed its environs. The two pergolas that were added to the narrow sides of the Casino in the north and south create a connection between nature, human beings and architecture. The rhythmical shift of their heights and the uneven number of the pairs of pillars is reminiscent of the irregular growth of the surrounding landscape. Nature comes in through the spaces between the pillars of the pergolas, and there is a view of the Havel. The pergolas themselves, together with the Casino building, are like a stage setting pointing to the present and the actions of human beings in nature: Gently, by stages, the south pergola leads to the Glienicke pleasure ground, while the north pergola ends on a raised plateau, the later site of Prince Charles' Klosterhof (Cloisters).

In discussions by Schinkel's contemporaries on how artistic genres should be ranked, the prevailing opinion was that architectonic decoration would upgrade a landscape into a »cultural landscape«. It was supposed to receive the highest rating, higher than still lifes, pure landscapes or history.[140] For the painter Schinkel, human existence, or the traces of it in nature, were indispensable in a picturesquely constructed, ideal landscape in which nature, human beings and architectural structures form an all-encompassing whole. »A landscape is only perfected by its relation to human beings«, wrote senior civil servant Carl G. Bethe and his co-author Lenné in their essay *Über Trift- und Feldpflanzungen*.[141] Like Schinkel, Lenné draws attention to cultural symbols such as house and castle, path and flowerbed.[142]

Lenné transfers to his paintings of landscapes the window as a topos of painting representing the boundary between reality and fiction. Visual fields are framed by vegetation such as tree trunks, branches etc. Lenné uses them in the same way that Schinkel opens up his architectural structures by means of stage-like vistas, in order to make statements regarding the present by referring back to the historical epoch presented in each section.

Urban motifs appear considerably intensified – for instance, the dome of the Nikolaikirche, which is visible from the *stibadium* of Glienicke. This is to be understood as a reinterpretation, comparable to the view of the dome of St. Peter's Basilica in Rome from the Villa Medici. Heightened, too, are natural symbols like the old oak trees on Pfaueninsel and objects that bear witness to history, such as the Neues Palais of Frederick II, located on the west side in the shadow against the setting sun. Like the Romantics in their art, Schinkel and Lenné in their painterly, architectonic and landscaping works strive for a higher level of historical and philosophical reflection.

The east–west axis of Charlottenhof, which formerly paralleled the stream, represents natural processes as a romantic metaphor for the forever recurring cycle of birth and death, both in nature and in history. This starts on the east side with the Maschinenteich (Engine Pond) and goes on by way of the rose garden, the castle terrace, the Dichterhain (Poets' Grove), the Maiblumenstück (Garden of the Lilies of the Valley), the Ildefonso group, interpreted as Sleep and Death, and all the way to the hippodrome in the west; it may be interpreted as the cycle of day and night, or rise and fall.[143] The Romantic artist Philipp Otto Runge had expressed similar ideas in his allegorical paintings Times of Day (from 1802 onwards).

Schinkel borrowed the Romantic motif of the rear-view figure directly from Caspar David Friedrich (*Mönch am Meer* (Monk by the Sea), 1810, for instance, in his 1813 *Landschaft mit Pilger* (Landscape with Pilgrim). In the work of Lenné the motif is palpable as an invitation to gaze at the landscape at spots specifically created for the purpose of contemplation – with one's back turned to the outside world. Schinkel's rear-view figures and the sites Lenné has reserved for them do not merely introduce people into landscape. At the same time, they create a connection between human beings and nature. The landscape seems to exist only in relation to the observer.

If the rear-view figure is the Romantics' motif of longing as such, Lenné uses this concept in the way he organizes his paths and roads. Like the Friedenskirche or Charlottenhof, Glienicke too cannot be reached directly, though the impressive ensemble of the palmette bed, Löwenfontäne and flight of stairs initially suggests this. »The visitors' vehicle does not arrive in front of the portal of a castle, a flight of stairs on a terrace; rather, visitors get off in front of the pergola that leans against the corner of the house. This pergola surrounds the Blumenhof, bending sharply three times; it is overgrown with vines shading the walls that have fragments of antiquities embedded in them. Inconspicuous and seemingly at an arbitrary point, but actually in the axis of the projection on the other side, which from the [Potsdam] highway looks like the castle gate, the visitors find the simple entrance door [...].«[144]

Typical of Lenné's roads and paths are anticipation, leisurely roaming, and promising gaps in the horizon where landscapes or buildings briefly come into view. The real destination of his pathways is distance. Lenné speaks of the »bluish distance that hugs the colourful horizon like a second world, like the ring of Saturn around its core, like distant coastlines and cloud formations. This is [...] the land of fantasies, of thoughts that lead one far away, and of an infinite longing.«[145]

Anmerkungen

[1] Clemens Alexander Wimmer, unter Mitarbeit von Martin Schaefer, »Die Bedeutung Simon Godeaus für die deutsche Gartenkunst«, in: AKat. 1999 a, S. 130–140.
[2] Grundlegend: Kühn 1955; Wimmer 1987.
[3] Adelheid Schendel, »Der Große Kurfürst und seine Residenzen«, in: AKat. 1988, S. 100–115.
[4] Clemens Alexander Wimmer, *Sichtachsen des Barock in Berlin und Umgebung* (*Berliner Hefte*, Nr. 2), Berlin 1985; Leonardo Benevolo, *Fixierte Unendlichkeit. Die Erfindung der Perspektive in der Architektur*, Frankfurt am Main und New York 1993, S. 101–104.
[5] Martin Sperlich, »Perspektivische Architektur im Schloß Charlottenburg«, in: Burkhard Bergius (Hrsg.), *Architektur, Stadt und Politik. Julius Posener zum 75. Geburtstag*, Gießen 1979, S. 71–76.
[6] Grundlegend: AKat. 1999 a.
[7] Hellmut Lorenz (Hrsg.), *Berliner Baukunst der Barockzeit. Die Zeichnungen und Notizen aus dem Reisetagebuch des Architekten Christoph Pitzler (1657–1707)*, Berlin 1998, Abb. 59, S. 193; Wimmer 1987, S. 25 bis 27.
[8] Bernard Jeannel, *André Le Nôtre*, Basel, Boston und Berlin 1988.
[9] Clemens Alexander Wimmer u.a., »Die Charlottenburger Gärten«, in: AKat. 1997, S. 285–292.
[10] Eva Börsch-Supan, *Karl Friedrich Schinkel. Arbeiten für König Friedrich Wilhelm III. von Preußen und Kronprinz Friedrich Wilhelm (IV.)*, Berlin und München 2011, S. 247–254.
[11] Zit. nach Kühn 1955, S. 122.
[12] Clemens Alexander Wimmer, *Der Skulpturenschmuck im Charlottenburger Schloßpark*, Berlin 1992.
[13] Tilo Eggeling, Regina Hanemann und Jürgen Julier, *Ein Schloß in Trümmern – Charlottenburg im November 1943*, Berlin 1993.
[14] Zit. nach Clemens Alexander Wimmer, »Nachschöpfung, Rekonstruktion, Pasticcio – Die Rezeption der französischen Neobarockparterres in Deutschland«, in: Rohde 2007, S. 272–277, hier S. 276.
[15] Karg 1981; Wendland 1987; Clemens Alexander Wimmer, »Zur Geschichte der Rheinsberger Schloßinsel«, in: AKat. 1996, S. 89–94; Michael Seiler, »Gartendenkmalpflegerische Wiederherstellung der Schloßinsel«, in: AKat. 1996, S. 95–102.
[16] Hansmann 1992.
[17] Paul Seidel, »Friedrich der Große als Kronprinz in Rheinsberg und die bildenden Künste«, in: *Jahrbuch der Königlich Preußischen Kunstsammlungen*, 9, 1888, S. 108–128.
[18] Hans-Joachim Giersberg, »Der Bacchustempel im Rheinsberger Garten«, in: AKat. 1999 b, S. 143–149.
[19] Zit. nach Kunisch 2012, S. 97.
[20] *Histoire Romaine depuis la fondation de Rome jusqu'à la Bataille d'Actium*, Amsterdam 1738–41.
[21] *Considérations sur les causes de la grandeur des Romains et de leur décadence*, Amsterdam 1734.
[22] »[…] des progrès de l'esprit humain dans les arts et dans les sciences«, Kapitelüberschrift der *Mémoires pour servir à l'histoire de la Maison de Brandebourg*, dt.: *Denkwürdigkeiten zur Geschichte des Hauses Brandenburg*, Berlin 1746.
[23] Zit. nach Ullrich Sachse, »Kultur für den Staat und den Nachruhm. Friedrichs des Großen Reflexionen über Künste und Wissenschaften«, in: *Friedrich300 – Colloquien*, 4, 2010, URL: http://www.perspectivia.net/content/publikationen/friedrich300-colloquien/friedrich-kulturtransfer/sachse_kultur (16.10.2012).
[24] Zit. nach Sibylle Badstübner-Gröger, »Knobelsdorff und die märkische Landschaft«, in: AKat. 1999 b, S. 72 bis 76, hier S. 75.
[25] Hansmann 1992, S. 52.
[26] Götterstatuen 1786 durch antikische Vasen in Urnenform ersetzt. Putten auf der Billardbrücke 1765 durch antikische Vasen in Urnenform und Nachbildungen des Borghese-Kraters ersetzt.
[27] Zit. nach Kurth 1962, S. 186.
[28] Zit. nach Inge Baumert und Karin Niemann, *Das stille Schloß am Boberow-Walde. Rheinsberg in Literatur und Kunst*, Rheinsberg 1984, S. 32.
[29] Michael Seiler, »Das Rheinsberger Gartenreich des Prinzen Heinrich«, in: AKat. 2002, S. 325–358.
[30] Saskia Hüneke, »Neun Marmorskulpturen von Giovanni Antonio Cybei im Park Rheinsberg«, in: AKat. 2002, S. 434–454.
[31] Zit. nach AKat. 2002, S. 327.
[32] Zit. ebd., S. 158.
[33] Detlef Fuchs, »›Aliis inserviendo consumor‹ – im Dienste für andere verzehre ich mich. Carl Wilhelm Hennert, Bauintendant des Prinzen Heinrich«, in: AKat. 2002, S. 285–302.
[34] Zit. nach AKat. 2002, S. 286.
[35] Carl Wilhelm Hennert, *Beschreibung des Lustschlosses und Gartens Sr. Königl. Hoheit des Prinzen Heinrich […]*, Berlin 1778.
[36] Willem Frijhoff, »Prinz Heinrich in den Niederlanden 1768«, in: AKat. 2002, S. 153–160; Magnus Olausson, »Die Schwedenreise Prinz Heinrichs von Preußen im Sommer 1770«, in: AKat. 2002, S. 161–176.
[37] Samuel Wittwer, »Prinz Heinrich und das Porzellan«, in: AKat. 2002, S. 467–483, hier S. 469.
[38] Ludwig Dehio zit. nach Kunisch 2012, S. 190.
[39] Andreas Pečar, »Ein Prinz von Geblüt auf dem Abstellgleis. Prinz Heinrich als Politiker«, in: *Jahrbuch SPSG*, 4, 2001/02, S. 113–124; Karoline Zielosko, »Prinz Heinrich als Hofhaltender Nachgeborener. Selbstdarstellung und Funktionalisierung«, in: *Jahrbuch SPSG*, 4, 2001/02, S. 51–75.
[40] Zit. nach Karoline Zielosko, »Eine Frage der Ehre«, in: *Friedrich300 – Studien und Vorträge*, URL: http://www.perspectivia.net/content/publikationen/friedrich300-studien/zielosko_ehre (20.10.2012), ‹33›.
[41] Zit. nach AKat. 2002, S. 84.
[42] Jürgen Luh, Michael Kaiser und Daniel Hohrath im Kapitel III »Der Feldherr« in: AKat. 2002, S. 81–119.
[43] Claudia Sommer, »Das Grab in der Pyramide«, in: AKat. 2002, S. 524–535; Dorgerloh 2012, S. 297 f.
[44] Grundlegend: Kehn 1985; Harri Günther, »Sanssouci – ein Beispiel friderizianischer Gartenkunst«, in: AKat. 1986 a, S. 180–191; Jörg Wacker, »Der friderizianische Lustgarten in Sanssouci«, in: AKat. 2001 a, S. 43; Saskia Hüneke, »Flora und Pomona im Paradies – Garten und Bildhauerkunst in Potsdam«, in: AKat. 2001 a, S. 330 bis 338; Dorgerloh 2005; ders. 2010; Buttlar, Köhler 2012; Michael Rohde, »Friedrich II. und die Gartenkunst in Sanssouci«, in: AKat. 2012, S. 46–55; Jörg Wacker, »Die Einbindung des Parks Sanssouci in die Potsdamer Landschaft durch Friedrich II.«, in: AKat. 2012, S. 62–71.
[45] Hüneke 2004. – Grundlegend für alle Ausführungen zu den Skulpturen: dies. 2002; zum denkmalpflegerischen Umgang mit Gartenfiguren: Hans Huth, »Pflege und Erhaltung der Bildwerke und der baulichen Ausstattungselemente«, in: Hennebo 1985, S. 330–345.
[46] 1773/86 wurde die Terrassenanlage vollständig verglast, der »gläserne Berg« dann 1982/83 in seinen Originalzustand zurückgeführt.
[47] Anne-Grit Reichelt, »Die gartendenkmalpflegerische Unterhaltung des Parterre von Schloß Sanssouci und der Wechselflor der Plates-bandes de Fleurs«, in: *Jahrbuch SPSG*, 6, 2004, S. 117–130; Karg 1980, S. 13. – Zum Parterre im allgemeinen: Wilfried Hansmann, »Parterres: Entwicklung, Typen, Elemente«, in: Hennebo 1985, S. 141–204.
[48] Monika Deißler, »Der Ruinenberg«, in: AKat. 2001 a, S. 133–139.
[49] *Das Chinesische Haus im Park von Sanssouci*, hrsg. von der SSG, Berlin 1993.
[50] Sibylle Badstübner-Gröger, *Das Neue Palais in Potsdam*, Berlin 1991; Klaus Dorst, »Das Neue Palais von Sanssouci«, in: AKat. 2012, S. 280–285.
[51] Jörg Wacker, »Die Gartenanlagen vor dem Neuen Palais«, in: AKat. 1993, S. 268–279.
[52] Astrid Dostert, »Friedrich der Große als Sammler antiker Skulptur«, in: *Friedrich300 – Colloquien*, 1, 2007, URL: http://www.perspectivia.net/content/publikationen/friedrich300-colloquien/friedrich-bestandsaufnahme/Doster_Sammler (20.10.2012).
[53] Hans-Joachim Giersberg, *Friedrich als Bauherr. Studien zur Architektur des 18. Jahrhunderts in Berlin und Potsdam*, Berlin 1986.
[54] Für Watteaus Grotesken von Tilo Eggeling geprägter Begriff. – AKat. 1999 b, S. 262.
[55] Zit. nach Kehn 1985, S. 148.
[56] Zit. nach Gustav Berthold Volz, *Antimachiavell und Testamente* (*Die Werke Friedrichs des Großen*, Bd. 7), Berlin 1913, S. 287; Andreas Pečar, »Friedrich der Große als Roi Philosophe«, in: *Friedrich300 – Colloquien*, 4, 2010, URL: http://www.perspectivia.net/content/publikationen/friedrich300-colloquien/friedrich-kulturtransfer/pecar_roi-philosophe (16.10.2012).
[57] Saskia Hüneke, »Kostbare Altertümer im Park Sanssouci und die Suche nach vergleichbaren Ausstattungen«, in: Rohde 2007, S. 146–149; Annette Dorgerloh und Michael Niedermeier, »Helden, Hirten und gefälschte Götter. Anciennitätskonzepte in herrschaftlichen Gärten des 18. und frühen 19. Jahrhunderts«, in: Rohde 2007, S. 162–165.
[58] Zit. nach Clemens Alexander Wimmer, »Der Garten – ein Bild. Knobelsdorff und die Gartenkunst«, in: AKat. 1999 b, S. 77–98, hier S. 77.
[59] Zit. nach Mielke 1998, S. 65.
[60] Zit. nach Kunisch 2012, S. 263.
[61] Übersetzung zit. nach Max Theuer, *Leon Baptista Alberti, Zehn Bücher über die Baukunst*, Wien und Leipzig 1912, S. 263.
[62] Wimmer 1989, S. 134.
[63] Wilfried Hansmann, »Sanssouci und der Terrassengarten der Zisterzienserabtei Kamp«, in: Rohde 2007, S. 142–145.
[64] Mielke 1998, S. 60.
[65] Saskia Hüneke, »Die Säulen- und Kolonnadenarchitektur Knobelsdorffs«, in: AKat. 1999 b, S. 119–126.
[66] Zit. nach AKat. 1999 b, S. 134; Barbara Rietzsch, *Künstliche Grotten des 16. und 17. Jahrhunderts*, München 1987.
[67] AKat. 1999 b, S. 134.
[68] Ingrid Weibezahn, *Geschichte und Funktion des Monopteros*, Hildesheim und New York 1975; Helmut-Eberhard Paulus, »Monopteros und Antikentempel. Ein Thema der europäischen Gartenkunst zwischen Allegorie,

Notes

[1] Clemens Alexander Wimmer, in collaboration with Martin Schaefer, »Die Bedeutung Simon Godeaus für die deutsche Gartenkunst«, in: AKat. 1999 a, pp. 130–140.
[2] Seminal works: Kühn 1955; Wimmer 1987.
[3] Adelheid Schendel, »Der Große Kurfürst und seine Residenzen«, in: AKat. 1988, pp. 100–115.
[4] Clemens Alexander Wimmer, *Sichtachsen des Barock in Berlin und Umgebung* (*Berliner Hefte*, no. 2), Berlin, 1985; Leonardo Benevolo, *Fixierte Unendlichkeit. Die Erfindung der Perspektive in der Architektur*, Frankfurt am Main and New York, 1993, pp. 101–104.
[5] Martin Sperlich, »Perspektivische Architektur im Schloß Charlottenburg«, in: Burkhard Bergius (ed.), *Architektur, Stadt und Politik. Julius Posener zum 75. Geburtstag*, Gießen, 1979, pp. 71–76.
[6] Seminal work: AKat. 1999 a.
[7] Hellmut Lorenz (ed.), *Berliner Baukunst der Barockzeit. Die Zeichnungen und Notizen aus dem Reisetagebuch des Architekten Christoph Pitzler (1657–1707)*, Berlin, 1998, illus. 59, p. 193; Wimmer 1987, pp. 25 to 27.
[8] Bernard Jeannel, *André Le Nôtre*, Basel, Boston, and Berlin, 1988.
[9] Clemens Alexander Wimmer et al., »Die Charlottenburger Gärten«, in: AKat. 1997, pp. 285–292.
[10] Eva Börsch-Supan, *Karl Friedrich Schinkel. Arbeiten für König Friedrich Wilhelm III. von Preußen und Kronprinz Friedrich Wilhelm (IV.)*, Berlin and Munich, 2011, pp. 247–254.
[11] Quoted after Kühn 1955, p. 122.
[12] Clemens Alexander Wimmer, *Der Skulpturenschmuck im Charlottenburger Schloßpark*, Berlin, 1992.
[13] Tilo Eggeling, Regina Hanemann und Jürgen Julier, *Ein Schloß in Trümmern – Charlottenburg im November 1943*, Berlin, 1993.
[14] Quoted after Clemens Alexander Wimmer, »Nachschöpfung, Rekonstruktion, Pasticcio – Die Rezeption der französischen Neobarockparterres in Deutschland«, in: Rohde 2007, pp. 272–277, here p. 276.
[15] Karg 1981; Wendland 1987; Clemens Alexander Wimmer, »Zur Geschichte der Rheinsberger Schloßinsel«, in: AKat. 1996, pp. 89–94; Michael Seiler, »Gartendenkmalpflegerische Wiederherstellung der Schloßinsel«, in: AKat. 1996, pp. 95–102.
[16] Hansmann 1992.
[17] Paul Seidel, »Friedrich der Große als Kronprinz in Rheinsberg und die bildenden Künste«, in: *Jahrbuch der Königlich Preußischen Kunstsammlungen*, 9, 1888, pp. 108–128.
[18] Hans-Joachim Giersberg, »Der Bacchustempel im Rheinsberger Garten«, in: AKat. 1999 b, pp. 143–149.
[19] Quoted after Kunisch 2012, p. 97.
[20] *Histoire Romaine depuis la fondation de Rome jusqu'à la Bataille d'Actium*, Amsterdam, 1738–41.
[21] *Considérations sur les causes de la grandeur des Romains et de leur décadence*, Amsterdam, 1734.
[22] »[…] des progrès de l'esprit humain dans les arts et dans les sciences«, chapter heading of *Mémoires pour servir à l'histoire de la Maison de Brandebourg*, German: *Denkwürdigkeiten zur Geschichte des Hauses Brandenburg*, Berlin, 1746.
[23] Quoted after Ullrich Sachse, »Kultur für den Staat und den Nachruhm. Friedrichs des Großen Reflexionen über Künste und Wissenschaften«, in: *Friedrich300 – Colloquien*, 4, 2010, URL: http://www.perspectivia.net/content/publikationen/friedrich300-colloquien/friedrich-kulturtransfer/sachse_kultur (16.10.2012).
[24] Quoted after Sibylle Badstübner-Gröger, »Knobelsdorff und die märkische Landschaft«, in: AKat. 1999 b, pp. 72–76, here p. 75.
[25] Hansmann 1992, p. 52.
[26] The statues of the gods were replaced in 1786 by vases in the ancient style in the shape of urns. Putti on the Billardbrücke were replaced in 1765 by vases in the ancient style in the shape of urns and reproductions of the Borghese Crater.
[27] Quoted after Kurth 1962, p. 186.
[28] Quoted after Inge Baumert und Karin Niemann, *Das stille Schloß am Boberow-Walde. Rheinsberg in Literatur und Kunst*, Rheinsberg, 1984, p. 32.
[29] Michael Seiler, »Das Rheinsberger Gartenreich des Prinzen Heinrich«, in: AKat. 2002, pp. 325–358.
[30] Saskia Hüneke, »Neun Marmorskulpturen von Giovanni Antonio Cybei im Park Rheinsberg«, in: AKat. 2002, pp. 434–454.
[31] Quoted after AKat. 2002, p. 327.
[32] Ibid., p. 158.
[33] Detlef Fuchs, »›Aliis inserviendo consumor‹ – im Dienste für andere verzehre ich mich. Carl Wilhelm Hennert, Bauintendant des Prinzen Heinrich«, in: AKat. 2002, pp. 285–302.
[34] Quoted after AKat. 2002, p. 286.
[35] Carl Wilhelm Hennert, *Beschreibung des Lustschlosses und Gartens Sr. Königl. Hoheit des Prinzen Heinrich […]*, Berlin, 1778.
[36] Willem Frijhoff, »Prinz Heinrich in den Niederlanden 1768«, in: AKat. 2002, pp. 153–160; Magnus Olausson, »Die Schwedenreise Prinz Heinrichs von Preußen im Sommer 1770«, in: AKat. 2002, pp. 161–176.
[37] Samuel Wittwer, »Prinz Heinrich und das Porzellan«, in: AKat. 2002, pp. 467–483, here p. 469.
[38] Ludwig Dehio quoted after Kunisch 2012, p. 190.
[39] Andreas Pečar, »Ein Prinz von Geblüt auf dem Abstellgleis. Prinz Heinrich als Politiker«, in: *Jahrbuch SPSG*, 4, 2001/02, pp. 113–124; Karoline Zielosko, »Prinz Heinrich als Hofhaltender Nachgeborener. Selbstdarstellung und Funktionalisierung«, in: *Jahrbuch SPSG*, 4, 2001/02, pp. 51–75.
[40] Quoted after Karoline Zielosko, »Eine Frage der Ehre«, in: *Friedrich300 – Studien und Vorträge*, URL: http://www.perspectivia.net/content/publikationen/friedrich300-studien/zielosko_ehre (20.10.2012), ‹33›.
[41] Quoted after AKat. 2002, pp. 84.
[42] Jürgen Luh, Michael Kaiser and Daniel Hohrath im Kapitel III »Der Feldherr« in: AKat. 2002, pp. 81–119.
[43] Claudia Sommer, »Das Grab in der Pyramide«, in: AKat. 2002, pp. 524–535; Dorgerloh 2012, pp. 297 ff.
[44] Seminal works: Kehn 1985; Harri Günther, »Sanssouci – ein Beispiel friderizianischer Gartenkunst«, in: AKat. 1986 a, pp. 180–191; Jörg Wacker, »Der friderizianische Lustgarten in Sanssouci«, in: AKat. 2001 a, p. 43; Saskia Hüneke, »Flora und Pomona im Paradies – Garten und Bildhauerkunst in Potsdam«, in: AKat. 2001 a, pp. 330 to 338; Dorgerloh 2005; id. 2010; Buttlar, Köhler 2012; Michael Rohde, »Friedrich II. und die Gartenkunst in Sanssouci«, in: AKat. 2012, pp. 46–55; Jörg Wacker, »Die Einbindung des Parks Sanssouci in die Potsdamer Landschaft durch Friedrich II.«, in: AKat. 2012, pp. 62–71.
[45] Hüneke 2004. – Seminal for all comments on the sculptures: id. 2002; on the monument preservation of garden figures: Hans Huth, »Pflege und Erhaltung der Bildwerke und der baulichen Ausstattungselemente«, in: Hennebo 1985, pp. 330–345.
[46] In 1773/86 the terrace complex was completely glassed in, the »glass hill« was returned to its original state in 1982/83.
[47] Anne-Grit Reichelt, »Die gartendenkmalpflegerische Unterhaltung des Parterre von Schloß Sanssouci und der Wechselflor der Plates-bandes de Fleurs«, in: *Jahrbuch SPSG*, 6, 2004, pp. 117–130; Karg 1980, p. 13. – On the *parterre* in general: Wilfried Hansmann, »Parterres: Entwicklung, Typen, Elemente«, in: Hennebo 1985, pp. 141–204.
[48] Monika Deißler, »Der Ruinenberg«, in: AKat. 2001 a, pp. 133–139.
[49] *Das Chinesische Haus im Park von Sanssouci*, ed. by the SSG, Berlin, 1993.
[50] Sibylle Badstübner-Gröger, *Das Neue Palais in Potsdam*, Berlin, 1991; Klaus Dorst, »Das Neue Palais von Sanssouci«, in: AKat. 2012, pp. 280–285.
[51] Jörg Wacker, »Die Gartenanlagen vor dem Neuen Palais«, in: AKat. 1993, pp. 268–279.
[52] Astrid Dostert, »Friedrich der Große als Sammler antiker Skulptur«, in: *Friedrich300 – Colloquien*, 1, 2007, URL: http://www.perspectivia.net/content/publikationen/friedrich300-colloquien/friedrich-bestandsaufnahme/Doster_Sammler (20.10.2012).
[53] Hans-Joachim Giersberg, *Friedrich als Bauherr. Studien zur Architektur des 18. Jahrhunderts in Berlin und Potsdam*, Berlin, 1986.
[54] A term coined by Tilo Eggeling for Watteau's grotesques. – AKat. 1999 b, p. 262.
[55] Quoted after Kehn 1985, p. 148.
[55] Quoted after Gustav Berthold Volz, *Antimachiavell und Testamente* (*Die Werke Friedrichs des Großen*, vol. 7), Berlin, 1913, p. 287; Andreas Pečar, »Friedrich der Große als Roi Philosophe«, in: *Friedrich300 – Colloquien*, 4, 2010, URL: http://www.perspectivia.net/content/publikationen/friedrich300-colloquien/friedrich-kulturtransfer/pecar_roi-philosophe (16.10.2012).
[57] Saskia Hüneke, »Kostbare Altertümer im Park Sanssouci und die Suche nach vergleichbaren Ausstattungen«, in: Rohde 2007, pp. 146–149; Annette Dorgerloh and Michael Niedermeier, »Helden, Hirten und gefälschte Götter. Anciennitätskonzepte in herrschaftlichen Gärten des 18. und frühen 19. Jahrhunderts«, in: Rohde 2007, pp. 162–165.
[58] Zit. nach Clemens Alexander Wimmer, »Der Garten – ein Bild. Knobelsdorff und die Gartenkunst«, in: AKat. 1999 b, pp. 77–98, here p. 77.
[59] Quoted after Mielke 1998, p. 65.
[60] Quoted after Kunisch 2012, p. 263.
[61] Translation quoted after Max Theuer, *Leon Baptista Alberti, Zehn Bücher über die Baukunst*, Vienna and Leipzig, 1912, p. 263.
[62] Wimmer 1989, p. 134.
[63] Wilfried Hansmann, »Sanssouci und der Terrassengarten der Zisterzienserabtei Kamp«, in: Rohde 2007, pp. 142–145.
[64] Mielke 1998, p. 60.
[65] Saskia Hüneke, »Die Säulen- und Kolonnadenarchitektur Knobelsdorffs«, in: AKat. 1999 b, pp. 119–126.
[66] Quoted after AKat. 1999 b, p. 134; Barbara Rietzsch, *Künstliche Grotten des 16. und 17. Jahrhunderts*, Munich, 1987.
[67] AKat. 1999 b, p. 134.
[68] Ingrid Weibezahn, *Geschichte und Funktion des Monopteros*, Hildesheim and New York, 1975; Helmut-Eber-

Antikensehnsucht und Palladianismus«, in: Rohde 2007, S. 16–19.
[69] Zit. nach Dorgerloh 2010, ‹11›.
[70] Marc-Antoine Laugier, *Essai sur l'architecture*, Paris 1753, zit. nach der dt. Übersetzung Frankfurt am Main und Leipzig 1758, S. 10 (erste dt. Übersetzung 1756).
[71] Hans Huth, »Chambers and Potsdam«, in: *Essays presented to Rudolf Wittkower on his sixty-fifth birthday*, New York 1967, S. 214–216; John Harris, *Sir William Chambers. Knight of the Polar Star*, London 1970; Thomas Weiss, *Sir William Chambers und der Englisch-chinesische Garten in Europa*, Ostfildern-Ruit 1997.
[72] Eva-Maria Engel, »Come à Rheinsberg oder come à Rome? Der Obelisk am Parkeingang von Sanssouci«, in: Rohde 2007, S. 150–153; Buttlar, Köhler 2012, S. 79– 83.
[73] Wimmer 1989, S. 468.
[74] »Welch ein schrecklicher Mann war mein Vater, aber zugleich wie gerecht, wie klug, wie geschäftskundig!« Friedrich II. an seinen Vorleser und Sekretär Heinrich von Catt, 1758, zit. nach Kunisch 2012, S. 133.
[75] Friedrich II. an seine Mutter Sophie Dorothea am 25.8.1743. – Kurth 1962, S. 15.
[76] Grundlegend zum Landschaftsgarten: Buttlar 1989; zum Neuen Garten: AKat. 1997, S. 418–447; Hans Heinrich Gerlitz, »Der Neue Garten«, in: AKat. 2001 a, S. 72 bis 75.
[77] Reinhard Zimmermann, *Künstliche Ruinen. Studien zu ihrer Bedeutung und Form*, Wiesbaden 1989.
[78] Zit. nach *Des Abts Laugier neue Anmerkungen über die Baukunst*, Leipzig 1786, S. 83 f. nach Marc-Antoine Laugier, *Observations sur l'architecture*, Paris 1765, S. 116 ff.
[79] *Die Gotische Bibliothek Friedrich Wilhelms II. im Neuen Garten zu Potsdam*, hrsg. von der SPSG, Potsdam 1998.
[80] Stefan Gehlen, »Ein- und Ausfahrt mit Osiris. Zur Portalhalle der Orangerie im Neuen Garten«, in: AKat. 2001 b, S. 48–53.
[81] Clemens Alexander Wimmer, »Die Geheimnisse des Neuen Gartens«, in: AKat. 1993, S. 164–171.
[82] Günther, Schönemann 1988.
[83] Zit. nach Michael Seiler, »Die Gestaltung des Neuen Gartens und der Pfaueninsel unter Friedrich Wilhelm II. – gartenkünstlerische Einheit und Verschiedenheit«, in: AKat. 1997, S. 451–458, hier S. 456.
[84] AKat. 1997, S. 448–450; Michael Seiler, »Die Pfaueninsel – Inszenierung des Exotischen«, in: AKat. 2001 a, S. 78–90; ders., »Die Pfaueninsel. Anmerkungen zur Ideen- und Rezeptionsgeschichte«, in: AKat. 2007, S. 50–53.
[85] Zit. nach AKat. 1997, S. 456.
[86] Seiler, Koppelkamm 1993; Seiler 2000; ders., »Lennés Wirken auf der Pfaueninsel«, in: AKat. 1989, S. 171–189.
[87] Michael Seiler, *Das Palmenhaus auf der Pfaueninsel. Geschichte seiner baulichen und gärtnerischen Gestaltung*, Berlin 1989; Börsch-Supan 2011, S. 261–283.
[88] Michael Seiler, »Der Pfaueninsel-Rosengarten«, in: AKat. 1989, S. 125–137.
[89] Grundlegend: AKat. 1995; Ludwig Dehio, *Friedrich Wilhelm IV. von Preußen. Ein Baukünstler der Romantik*, Berlin 2001, S. 23–56; Johannsen 2007.
[90] Jörg Wacker, »Das Triumphstraßenprojekt in Sanssouci«, in: AKat. 2001 a, S. 148–166.
[91] Zit. nach Carl Ludwig Haeberlein [Häberlin], *Sanssouci, Potsdam und Umgebung. Mit bes. Berücksichtigung der Regierungszeit Friedrich Wilhelms IV., König von Preußen*, Berlin und Potsdam 1855, S. IX.
[92] Zit. nach Mielke 1998, S. 153.
[93] Schönemann 1981; ders., »Charlottenhof – Schinkel, Lenné und der Kronprinz«, in: AKat. 1993, S. 173–181; ders., *Karl Friedrich Schinkel. Charlottenhof, Potsdam-Sanssouci*, Stuttgart und London 1997; ders., »Der Park Charlottenhof«, in: AKat. 2001 a, S. 91–103; ders., »Schinkels Traum«, in: Hillert Ibbeken und Elke Blauert (Hrsg.), *Karl Friedrich Schinkel. Das architektonische Werk heute*, Stuttgart und London 2001, S. 8 f.
[94] Gabriele Horn, »Das Kunstdorf Bornstedt«, in: AKat. 2001 a, S. 167–175.
[95] Matthias Noell, »Altnormännischer Charakter oder normannischer Baustil? Anmerkungen zur Architekturterminologie im 19. und 20. Jahrhundert«, in: *Jahrbuch SPSG*, 5, 2003, S. 203–220.
[96] Seiler, Wacker 1991, S. 34.
[97] Friedrich Wilhelm 1845 an Bischof Rulemann Friedrich Eylert. – Zit. nach Mielke 1998, S. 149.
[98] *Gedanken über die Nachahmung der Griechischen Werke in der Malerei und Bildhauerkunst*, Dresden 1755 (2. Aufl. Dresden und Leipzig 1756); *Gedanken über die Nachahmung der griechischen Werke in der Malerei und Bildhauerkunst und Geschichte der Kunst des Altertums. Geschichte der Kunst des Alterthums*, Dresden 1764.
[99] Michael Seiler, »Die Entstehungsgeschichte des Landschaftsgartens Klein-Glienicke«, in: AKat. 1987, S. 109 bis 158; ders., »Glienicke und die Potsdamer Parklandschaft«, in: AKat. 1987, S. 167–184.
[100] Sepp-Gustav Gröschel, »Glienicke und die Antike«, in: AKat. 1987, S. 243–267, hier S. 248 ff.
[101] Zit. nach Wimmer 1989, S. 6.
[102] Zit. nach Hinz 1989, S. 88.
[103] Hinz 1989, S. 88; Stefan Gehlen (AKat. 1993, S. 182 bis 189) verweist auf die vermutlich unhistorische Begebenheit, die jedoch noch im AKat. 2001 a zitiert wird.
[104] Horst-Johs Tümmers, *Rheinromantik. Romantik und Reisen am Rhein*, Köln 1968; Ursula Rathke, *Preußische Burgenromantik am Rhein. Studien zum Wiederaufbau von Rheinstein, Stolzenfels und Sooneck (1823–1860)*, München 1979; Klaus Honnef, Klaus Weschenfelder und Irene Haberland (Hrsg.), *Vom Zauber des Rheins ergriffen ... Zur Entdeckung der Rheinlandschaft vom 17. bis 19. Jahrhundert*, AKat. Bonn und Koblenz, München 1992.
[105] Zit. nach Carl Gustav Carus, *Reisen und Briefe*, ausgewählt von Eckhardt von Sydow, 2. Teil, Leipzig [1926], S. 7.
[106] Zit. nach John Claudius Loudon (Hrsg.), *The Landscape Gardening and Landscape Architecture of the Late Humphry Repton […]*, London 1840, Abb. 165, S. 427.
[107] Edmund Burke, *A Philosophical Enquiry into the Origin of our Ideas of the Sublime and Beautiful*, London 1757.
[108] Batty Langley, *Gothic Architecture. Improved by Rules and Proportions*, London 1747.
[109] Alfred P. Hagemann, »Das Nauener Tor«, in: *Friedrich300 – Colloquien*, 4, 2010, URL: http://www.perspectivia.net/content/publikationen/friedrich300-colloquien/friedrich-kulturtransfer/hagemann_tor (16.12.2012).
[110] Stefan Gehlen, »Frühe Gartengotik an der Havel«, in: *Die Gotische Bibliothek Friedrich Wilhelms II. im Neuen Garten zu Potsdam*, hrsg. von der SPSG, Potsdam 1998, S. 13–25. – Zur »Hinwendung zu byzantinischen Vorbildern […] als preußische Variante [des] ›Gothic Revival‹«: Gerd-H. Zuchold, *Byzanz in Berlin. Der Klosterhof im Schloßpark Glienicke*, Berlin 1984.
[111] Stefan Gehlen, »Neugotik in Babelsberg«, in: AKat. 1993, S. 182–188.
[112] Rolf Bothe, *Das Weimarer Residenzschloß vom Mittelalter bis zum Anfang des 19. Jahrhunderts*, Ostfildern-Ruit 2000, S. 64, Abb. 106.
[113] Humphrey Repton, *Fragments on the Theory and Practice of Landscape Gardening including some Remarks on Grecian and Gothic Architecture*, London 1816; John B. Papworth, *Rural Residences. Consisting of a Series of Designs to Cottages*, London 1818, ^{2}1832; Robert Lugar, *Architectural Sketches for Cottages, Rural Dwellings and Villas in the Grecian, Gothic and Fancy Styles*, London 1815; James Thomson, *Retreats. A Series of Designs, consisting of Plans and Elevations for Cottages, Villas and Ornamental Buildings*, London 1827.
[114] Abgedruckt bei Helmut Rippl, »Pücklers Parkanlagen in Muskau, Babelsberg und Branitz«, in: Fait, Karg 1989, S. 41–176, hier S. 123–132.
[115] Karg 1992.
[116] Stefan Gehlen, Katalogeintrag »Dampfmaschinenhaus«, in: AKat. 2001 a, S. 125.
[117] Hüneke 2010, S. 98 f.
[118] Gehlen 2004.
[119] Heinrich Hamann, »Daten zum Park und zu den Bauten in Babelsberg«, in: Fait, Karg 1989, S. 261–266; ders., »Hofgärtner im Park Babelsberg«, in: Fait, Karg 1989, S. 267–272; ders. 1989.
[120] Karl Eisbein, »Der Park Babelsberg«, in: AKat. 2001 a, S. 116–125; Eisbein, Wacker 2004; Eisbein 2006.
[121] Michael Seiler, »Potsdam – Schlösser, Gärten, Stadt und Parklandschaft. Durchsichten, Aussichten, Einblicke und Gesichtslinien«, in: AKat. 1993, S. 157–163.
[122] Zit. nach Günter J. Vaupel (Hrsg.), *Hermann Fürst von Pückler-Muskau, Andeutungen über Landschaftsgärtnerei*, Frankfurt am Main 1988, S. 106 f.
[123] Klaus von Krosigk, »Anmerkungen zum Pleasureground«, in: *Gartendenkmalpflege. Berlin 1978–1985*, ^{2}1985, S. 10–17; Anne Schäfer, »Zur Ausstattung von Landschaftsgärten im 19. Jahrhundert mit Kleinarchitekturen, mobilen Gartenausstattungen und Pflanzungen unter besonderer Berücksichtigung von Park Branitz«, in: Fait, Karg 1989, S. 177–201, hier S. 177, 180–182.
[124] Zit. nach Christian Cay Lorenz Hirschfeld, *Theorie der Gartenkunst*, Bd. 3, 1779–85, S. 13 (Reprint mit einem Vorwort von Hans Foramitti, Hildesheim, Zürich und New York 1985).
[125] Eisbein, Wacker 2004.
[126] Hüneke 2010.
[127] Günther, Harksen 1993, mit allen hier erwähnten Gartenplänen von Lenné; Michael Seiler, »Auswertung historischer Pläne der Landschaftsgärten«, in: Hennebo 1985, S. 120–140.
[128] Adrian von Buttlar, »Vom Landschaftsgarten zur Gartenlandschaft. Peter Joseph Lenné und seine Parkschöpfungen in Berlin und Potsdam«, in: AKat. 1985, S. 137–147; Hinz 1989; Buttlar 1989; Harri Günther, »›Daß uns die Zeit wieder zu tagen beginnt, welche den Musen und Grazien vertraut‹. Lennés Kunstlandschaft der Insel Potsdam«, in: AKat. 2001 a, S. 223–234; Karg 2005.
[129] Jørgen Birkedal Hartmann, Antike Motive bei Thorvaldsen. Studien zur Antikenrezeption des Klassizismus, Tübingen 1979, S. 60, Tafel 16.
[130] Vgl. auch die Ausführungen von Heinz Schönemann seit 1981.
[131] Michael Seiler, »Der Marly-Garten«, in: AKat. 2001 a, S. 140–147; Günther 1972.
[132] Zit. nach Seiler, Hamm 1999, S. 24.

hard Paulus, »Monopteros und Antikentempel. Ein Thema der europäischen Gartenkunst zwischen Allegorie, Antikensehnsucht und Palladianismus«, in: Rohde 2007, pp. 16–19.

69 Quoted after Dorgerloh 2010, ‹11›.

70 Marc-Antoine Laugier, *Essai sur l'architecture*, Paris 1753, quoted from the German translation Frankfurt am Main and Leipzig, 1758, p. 10 (first German translation 1756).

71 Hans Huth, »Chambers and Potsdam«, in: *Essays presented to Rudolf Wittkower on his sixty-fifth birthday*, New York, 1967, pp. 214–216; John Harris, *Sir William Chambers. Knight of the Polar Star*, London 1970; Thomas Weiss, *Sir William Chambers und der Englisch-chinesische Garten in Europa*, Ostfildern-Ruit, 1997.

72 Eva-Maria Engel, »Come à Rheinsberg oder come à Rome? Der Obelisk am Parkeingang von Sanssouci«, in: Rohde 2007, pp. 150–153; Buttlar, Köhler 2012, pp. 79–83.

73 Wimmer 1989, p. 468.

74 »What a terrible man my father was, but at the same time how just, how intelligent, how experienced in business affairs!« Frederick II to his reader and secretary Heinrich von Catt, 1758, quoted after Kunisch 2012, p. 133.

75 Frederick II. to his mother Sophia Dorothea on 25.8. 1743. – Kurth 1962, p. 15.

76 Seminal work on the landscape garden: Buttlar 1989; on the Neuer Garten: AKat. 1997, pp. 418–447; Hans Heinrich Gerlitz, »Der Neue Garten«, in: AKat. 2001 a, pp. 72–75.

77 Reinhard Zimmermann, *Künstliche Ruinen. Studien zu ihrer Bedeutung und Form*, Wiesbaden, 1989.

78 Quoted after *Des Abts Laugier neue Anmerkungen über die Baukunst*, Leipzig, 1786, pp. 83 f. after Marc-Antoine Laugier, *Observations sur l'architecture*, Paris, 1765, pp. 116 ff.

79 *Die Gotische Bibliothek Friedrich Wilhelms II. im Neuen Garten zu Potsdam*, ed. by the SPSG, Potsdam, 1998.

80 Stefan Gehlen, »Ein- und Ausfahrt mit Osiris. Zur Portalhalle der Orangerie im Neuen Garten«, in: AKat. 2001 b, pp. 48–53.

81 Clemens Alexander Wimmer, »Die Geheimnisse des Neuen Gartens«, in: AKat. 1993, pp. 164–171.

82 Günther, Schönemann 1988.

83 Quoted after Michael Seiler, »Die Gestaltung des Neuen Gartens und der Pfaueninsel unter Friedrich Wilhelm II. – gartenkünstlerische Einheit und Verschiedenheit«, in: AKat. 1997, pp. 451–458, here p. 456.

84 AKat. 1997, pp. 448–450; Michael Seiler, »Die Pfaueninsel – Inszenierung des Exotischen«, in: AKat. 2001 a, pp. 78–90; id., »Die Pfaueninsel. Anmerkungen zur Ideen- und Rezeptionsgeschichte«, in: AKat. 2007, pp. 50–53.

85 Quoted after AKat. 1997, p. 456.

86 Seiler, Koppelkamm 1993; Seiler 2000; id., »Lennés Wirken auf der Pfaueninsel«, in: AKat. 1989, pp. 171–189.

87 Michael Seiler, *Das Palmenhaus auf der Pfaueninsel. Geschichte seiner baulichen und gärtnerischen Gestaltung*, Berlin, 1989; Börsch-Supan 2011, pp. 261–283.

88 Michael Seiler, »Der Pfaueninsel-Rosengarten«, in: AKat. 1989, pp. 125–137.

89 Seminal works: AKat. 1995; Ludwig Dehio, *Friedrich Wilhelm IV. von Preußen. Ein Baukünstler der Romantik*, Berlin, 2001, pp. 23–56; Johannsen 2007.

90 Jörg Wacker, »Das Triumphstraßenprojekt in Sanssouci«, in: AKat. 2001 a, pp. 148–166.

91 Quoted after Carl Ludwig Haeberlein [Häberlin], *Sanssouci, Potsdam und Umgebung. Mit bes. Berücksichtigung der Regierungszeit Friedrich Wilhelms IV., König von Preußen*, Berlin and Potsdam, 1855, p. IX.

92 Quoted after Mielke 1998, p. 153.

93 Schönemann 1981; id., »Charlottenhof – Schinkel, Lenné und der Kronprinz«, in: AKat. 1993, pp. 173 to 181; id., *Karl Friedrich Schinkel. Charlottenhof, Potsdam-Sanssouci*, Stuttgart and London, 1997; id., »Der Park Charlottenhof«, in: AKat. 2001 a, pp. 91–103; id., »Schinkels Traum«, in: Hillert Ibbeken and Elke Blauert (eds.), *Karl Friedrich Schinkel. Das architektonische Werk heute*, Stuttgart and London, 2001, pp. 8 f.

94 Gabriele Horn, »Das Kunstdorf Bornstedt«, in: AKat. 2001 a, pp. 167–175.

95 Matthias Noell, »Altnormännischer Charakter oder normannischer Baustil? Anmerkungen zur Architekturterminologie im 19. und 20. Jahrhundert«, in: *Jahrbuch SPSG*, 5, 2003, pp. 203–220.

96 Seiler, Wacker 1991, p. 34.

97 Friedrich Wilhelm in 1845 to Bishop Rulemann Friedrich Eylert. – Quoted after Mielke 1998, p. 149.

98 *Gedanken über die Nachahmung der Griechischen Werke in der Malerei und Bildhauerkunst*, Dresden, 1755 (2nd ed. Dresden and Leipzig, 1756); *Gedanken über die Nachahmung der griechischen Werke in der Malerei und Bildhauerkunst und Geschichte der Kunst des Altertums. Geschichte der Kunst des Alterthums*, Dresden, 1764.

99 Michael Seiler, »Die Entstehungsgeschichte des Landschaftsgartens Klein-Glienicke«, in: AKat. 1987, pp. 109 to 158; id., »Glienicke und die Potsdamer Parklandschaft«, in: AKat. 1987, pp. 167–184.

100 Sepp-Gustav Gröschel, »Glienicke und die Antike«, in: AKat. 1987, pp. 243–267, here pp. 248 ff.

101 Quoted after Wimmer 1989, p. 6.

102 Quoted after Hinz 1989, p. 88.

103 Hinz 1989, p. 88; Stefan Gehlen (AKat. 1993, pp. 182–189) refers to the allegedly unhistorical event, which, however, is still cited in AKat. 2001 a.

104 Horst-Johs Tümmers, *Rheinromantik. Romantik und Reisen am Rhein*, Cologne, 1968; Ursula Rathke, *Preußische Burgenromantik am Rhein. Studien zum Wiederaufbau von Rheinstein, Stolzenfels und Sooneck (1823 to 1860)*, Munich, 1979; Klaus Honnef, Klaus Weschenfelder und Irene Haberland (eds.), *Vom Zauber des Rheins ergriffen ... Zur Entdeckung der Rheinlandschaft vom 17. bis 19. Jahrhundert*, AKat. Bonn and Koblenz, Munich, 1992.

105 Quoted after Carl Gustav Carus, *Reisen und Briefe*, selected by Eckhardt von Sydow, 2nd part, Leipzig, [1926], p. 7.

106 Quoted after John Claudius Loudon (ed.), *The Landscape Gardening and Landscape Architecture of the Late Humphry Repton […]*, London, 1840, illus. 165, p. 427.

107 Edmund Burke, *A Philosophical Enquiry into the Origin of our Ideas of the Sublime and Beautiful*, London, 1757.

108 Batty Langley, *Gothic Architecture. Improved by Rules and Proportions*, London, 1747.

109 Alfred P. Hagemann, »Das Nauener Tor«, in: *Friedrich300 – Colloquien*, 4, 2010, URL: http://www.perspectivia.net/content/publikationen/friedrich300-colloquien/friedrich-kulturtransfer/hagemann_tor (16.12.2012).

110 Stefan Gehlen, »Frühe Gartengotik an der Havel«, in: *Die Gotische Bibliothek Friedrich Wilhelms II. im Neuen Garten zu Potsdam*, ed. by the SPSG, Potsdam, 1998, pp. 13–25. – On »the adoption of Byzantine models [...] as a Prussian variant [of] ›Gothic Revival‹«: Gerd-H. Zuchold, *Byzanz in Berlin. Der Klosterhof im Schloßpark Glienicke*, Berlin, 1984.

111 Stefan Gehlen, »Neugotik in Babelsberg«, in: AKat. 1993, pp. 182–188.

112 Rolf Bothe, *Das Weimarer Residenzschloß vom Mittelalter bis zum Anfang des 19. Jahrhunderts*, Ostfildern-Ruit, 2000, p. 64, illus. 106.

113 Humphrey Repton, *Fragments on the Theory and Practice of Landscape Gardening including some Remarks on Grecian and Gothic Architecture*, London, 1816; John B. Papworth, *Rural Residences. Consisting of a Series of Designs to Cottages*, London, 1818, ^{2}1832; Robert Lugar, *Architectural Sketches for Cottages, Rural Dwellings and Villas in the Grecian, Gothic and Fancy Styles*, London, 1815; James Thomson, *Retreats. A Series of Designs, consisting of Plans and Elevations for Cottages, Villas and Ornamental Buildings*, London, 1827.

114 Reprinted in Helmut Rippl, »Pücklers Parkanlagen in Muskau, Babelsberg und Branitz«, in: Fait, Karg 1989, pp. 41–176, here pp. 123–132.

115 Karg 1992.

116 Stefan Gehlen, catalogue entry »Dampfmaschinenhaus«, in: AKat. 2001 a, p. 125.

117 Hüneke 2010, pp. 98 f.

118 Gehlen 2004.

119 Heinrich Hamann, »Daten zum Park und zu den Bauten in Babelsberg«, in: Fait, Karg 1989, pp. 261–266; id., »Hofgärtner im Park Babelsberg«, in: Fait, Karg 1989, pp. 267–272; id. 1989.

120 Karl Eisbein, »Der Park Babelsberg«, in: AKat. 2001 a, pp. 116–125; Eisbein, Wacker 2004; Eisbein 2006.

121 Michael Seiler, »Potsdam – Schlösser, Gärten, Stadt und Parklandschaft. Durchsichten, Aussichten, Einblicke und Gesichtslinien«, in: AKat. 1993, pp. 157–163.

122 Quoted after Günter J. Vaupel (ed.), *Hermann Fürst von Pückler-Muskau, Andeutungen über Landschaftsgärtnerei*, Frankfurt am Main, 1988, pp. 106 f.

123 Klaus von Krosigk, »Anmerkungen zum Pleasureground«, in: *Gartendenkmalpflege. Berlin 1978–1985*, ^{2}1985, pp. 10–17; Anne Schäfer, »Zur Ausstattung von Landschaftsgärten im 19. Jahrhundert mit Kleinarchitekturen, mobilen Gartenausstattungen und Pflanzungen unter besonderer Berücksichtigung von Park Branitz«, in: Fait, Karg 1989, pp. 177–201, here pp. 177, 180–182.

124 Quoted after Christian Cay Lorenz Hirschfeld, *Theorie der Gartenkunst*, vol. 3, 1779–85, p. 13 (reprint with a foreword by Hans Foramitti, Hildesheim, Zurich, and New York, 1985).

125 Eisbein, Wacker 2004.

126 Hüneke 2010.

127 Günther, Harksen 1993, with all garden plans by Lenné mentioned here; Michael Seiler, »Auswertung historischer Pläne der Landschaftsgärten«, in: Hennebo 1985, pp. 120–140.

128 Adrian von Buttlar, »Vom Landschaftsgarten zur Gartenlandschaft. Peter Joseph Lenné und seine Parkschöpfungen in Berlin und Potsdam«, in: AKat. 1985, pp. 137–147; Hinz 1989; Buttlar 1989; Harri Günther, »›Daß uns die Zeit wieder zu tagen beginnt, welche den Musen und Grazien vertraut‹. Lennés Kunstlandschaft der Insel Potsdam«, in: AKat. 2001 a, pp. 223–234; Karg 2005.

129 Jørgen Birkedal Hartmann, Antike Motive bei Thorvaldsen. Studien zur Antikenrezeption des Klassizismus, Tübingen 1979, p. 60, plate 16.

133 Gerd Schurig, »Der Pfingstberg«, in: AKat. 2001a, S. 178–184.
134 Gerd Schurig, »Der Park von Sacrow«, in: AKat. 2001 a, S. 126–132; Seiler, Hamm 1999.
135 Gerd Schurig, »Der Park des Schlosses Caputh«, in: AKat. 2001a, S. 24–29.
136 Zit. nach Hinz 1989, S. 131.
137 AKat. 1987; Klaus von Krosigk und Heinz Wiegand, *Glienicke*, Berlin 1984; Michael Seiler, »Glienicke«, in: AKat. 2001a, S. 30–42.
138 August Kopisch, 1854, zit. nach Michael Seiler, »Entstehungsgeschichte des Landschaftsgartens Klein-Glienicke«, in: AKat. 1987, S. 109–156, hier S. 115.
139 Jürgen Julier, »Parkgebäude nach Entwürfen Schinkels«, in: AKat. 1987, S. 33–43, hier S. 33f.
140 Michael Gamper, *Die Natur ist republikanisch. Zu den ästhetischen, anthropologischen und politischen Konzepten der deutschen Gartenliteratur im 18. Jahrhundert*, Würzburg 1998, S. 32, 176; Stefan Groß, *Die Weimarer Klassik und die Gartenkunst*, Frankfurt am Main, 2009, S. 12.
141 Zit. nach Bethe, Lenné 1826, S. 337. – Zur Koautorenschaft Bethe, Lenné: Seiler, Hamm 1999, S. 9, 14; Clemens Alexander Wimmer, »Äußerungen Lennés zur Gartentheorie«, in: AKat. 1989, S. 60–69.
142 Seiler, Hamm 1999, S. 8.
143 Schönemann 1981; ders. 1993.
144 Zit. nach Martin Sperlich, »Nicht Schloß, sondern Villa«, in: AKat. 1987, S. 27–31, hier S. 28; ders., »Vorgefundener und gestalteter Raum. Der Weg bei Lenné«, in: Zobel 1992, S. 47–53.
145 Zit. nach Bethe, Lenné 1826, S. 340.

AKat.: Ausstellungskatalog

Literatur

Anders, Friedhild-Andrea, *Schlösser in der Stunde Null. Die Berliner und Potsdamer Schlösser während der Kriegs- und Nachkriegszeit*, Potsdam 1999.

Bethe, Carl G., und Peter Joseph Lenné, »Über Trift- und Feldpflanzungen«, in: *Verhandlungen des Vereins zur Beförderung des Gartenbaues in den königlich preußischen Staaten*, 2, 1826, S. 270–349.

Bewahrt – Wiederhergestellt – Erneuert. Restaurierungsführer durch die preußischen Schlösser, hrsg. von der SPSG, Potsdam 2006.

Bisky, Jens, *Poesie der Baukunst. Architekturästhetik von Winckelmann bis Boisserée*, Weimar 2000.

Blanning, Thimothy C. W., *The Culture of Power and the Power of Culture. Old Regime Europe 1660–1789*, Oxford 2002.

Buttlar, Adrian von, »Englische Gärten in Deutschland. Bemerkungen zu Modifikationen ihrer Ikonologie«, in: *›Sind Briten hier‹. Relations between British and Continental Art 1680–1880*, hrsg. vom Zentralinstitut für Kunstgeschichte in München, München 1981.

Buttlar, Adrian von, *Der englische Landsitz 1715–1760. Symbol eines liberalen Weltentwurfs*, Mittenwald 1982.

Buttlar, Adrian von, *Der Landschaftsgarten. Gartenkunst des Klassizismus und der Romantik*, Köln 1989.

Buttlar, Adrian von, »Sanssouci und der ›ewige Osten‹. Freimaurerische Aspekte im Garten Friedrichs des Großen«, in: *Gartenkunst*, 6, 1994, S. 219–226.

Buttlar, Adrian von, »Das Grab im Garten. Zur naturreligiösen Deutung eines arkadischen Gartenmotivs«, in: Heike Wunderlich (Hrsg.), *Landschaft und Landschaften im achtzehnten Jahrhundert*, Heidelberg 1995, S. 79–119.

Buttlar, Adrian von, und Marcus Köhler, *Tod, Glück und Ruhm in Sanssouci. Ein Führer durch die Gartenwelt Friedrichs des Großen*, Ostfildern 2012.

Dehio, Ludwig, *Friedrich Wilhelm von Preußen – ein Baukünstler der Romantik*, München 1961.

Dennerlein, Ingrid, *Die Gartenkunst der Régence und des Rokoko in Frankreich*, Worms 1981.

Dohna, Ursula Gräfin zu, *Die Gärten Friedrichs des Großen und seiner Geschwister*, Berlin 2000.

Dorgerloh, Annette, »Friedrich II. als Gartengestalter – Repräsentation und historische Verortung«, in: Brunhilde Wehinger (Hrsg.), *Geist und Macht. Friedrich der Große im Kontext der europäischen Kulturgeschichte*, Berlin 2005, S. 225–243.

Dorgerloh, Annette, »Friedrich II. und seine Gärten«, in: *Friedrich300 – Colloquien*, 4, 2010, URL: http://www.perspectivia.net/content/publikationen/friedrich300-colloquien/friedrich-kulturtransfer/dorgerloh_gaerten (16.10.2012).

Dorgerloh, Annette, *Strategien des Überdauerns. Das Grab- und Erinnerungsmal im frühen deutschen Landschaftsgarten*, Düsseldorf 2012.

Eisbein, Karl, und Jörg Wacker, »Drei Maßnahmen der Gartendenkmalpflege im Park Babelsberg«, in: *Jahrbuch SPSG*, 6, 2004, S. 149–172.

Eisbein, Karl, »Der Park Babelsberg«, in: *Fürst Pückler. Parkomanie in Muskau und Branitz. Ein Führer durch seine Anlagen in Sachsen, Brandenburg und Thüringen*, hrsg. von der Stiftung Fürst-Pückler-Park Bad Muskau, Berlin 2006, S. 220–233.

Fait, Joachim, und Detlef Karg, *Hermann Ludwig Heinrich von Pückler-Muskau. Gartenkunst und Denkmalpflege*, Weimar 1989.

Frühsorge, Gotthardt, *Die Kunst des Landlebens. Vom Landschloß zum Campingplatz. Eine Kulturgeschichte*, München und Berlin 1993.

Gehlen, Stefan, »Scharoun neben Schinkel? Zur real existierenden Moderne im Babelsberger Park«, in: *Jahrbuch SPSG*, 6, 2004, S. 173–184.

Geiss, Axel (Hrsg.), *Potsdam und sein Weltkulturerbe*, Stahnsdorf o.J.

Gerndt, Siegmar, *Idealisierte Natur. Die literarische Kontroverse um den Landschaftsgarten des 18. und 19. Jahrhunderts in Deutschland*, Stuttgart 1981.

Giersberg, Hans-Joachim, und Adelheid Schendel, *Potsdamer Veduten*, Potsdam 1984.

Giersberg, Hans-Joachim, und Jürgen Julier (Hrsg.), *Preußische Königsschlösser in Berlin und Potsdam*, Leipzig 1992.

Giersberg, Hans-Joachim, und Hillert Ibbeken, *Schloß Sanssouci. Die Sommerresidenz Friedrichs des Großen*, Berlin 2005.

Gothein, Marie Luise, *Geschichte der Gartenkunst*, 2 Bde., Hildesheim und New York 1977.

Günther, Harri, »Zur Wiederherstellung des Marlygartens in Sanssouci«, in: *Landschaftsarchitektur*, 1, 1972, S. 39–41.

Günther, Harri, *Peter Joseph Lenné. Gärten, Parke, Landschaften*, Stuttgart 1985.

Günther, Harri, und Heinz Schönemann, *Cecilienhof und der Neue Garten*, Potsdam 1988.

Günther, Harri, und Sibylle Harksen, *Peter Joseph Lenné. Katalog der Zeichnungen,* Tübingen und Berlin 1993.

Hamann, Heinrich, *Der Park Babelsberg*, Potsdam 1989.

Hansmann, Wilfried, »Friderizianisches Rokoko«, in: *Baukunst in Brandenburg*, hrsg. von der Landesregierung Brandenburg, Köln 1992, S. 46–110.

Harten, Ulrike, überarbeitet von Helmut Börsch Supan und Gottfried Riemann, *Die Bühnenentwürfe* (*Karl Friedrich Schinkel. Lebenswerk*, Bd. 17), Berlin 2000.

Hartmann, Günter, *Die Ruine im Landschaftsgarten*, Köln 1989.

Hasselhorst, Christa, und Hans Bach, *Park Sanssouci*, Berlin 2012.

Heilmeyer, Marina, und Hans Bach, *Die Gärten der Könige*, München 2009.

Hennebo, Dieter, und Alfred Hoffmann, *Geschichte der Gartenkunst*, 3 Bde., Hamburg 1962–65.

Hennebo, Dieter (Hrsg.), *Gartendenkmalpflege. Grundlagen der Erhaltung historischer Gärten und Grünanlagen*, Stuttgart 1985.

Hinz, Gerhard, *Peter Joseph Lenné. Das Gesamtwerk des Gartenarchitekten und Städteplaners*, 2 Teile, Hildesheim, Zürich und New York 1989.

Hobhouse, Penelope, *Plants in Garden History*, London 1992.

Hübinger, Petra, »Oranienburg. Die Restaurierung des Schloßparks zur Landesgartenschau 2009 – eine Bilanz«, in: *Brandenburgische Denkmalpflege*, 20, 2011, Heft. 2, S. 23–30.

Hüneke, Saskia, *Bauten und Bildwerke im Park Sanssouci* (amtlicher Führer SPSG), Potsdam ^{2}2002.

Hüneke, Saskia, »Aus dem Garten gelesen … Ikonographische Strukturen im Park Sanssouci«, in: *Jahrbuch SPSG*, 6, 2004, S. 205–226.

130 Cf. also the statements by Heinz Schönemann since 1981.
131 Michael Seiler, »Der Marly-Garten«, in: AKat. 2001 a, pp. 140–147; Günther 1972.
132 Quoted after Seiler, Hamm 1999, p. 24.
133 Gerd Schurig, »Der Pfingstberg«, in: AKat. 2001 a, pp. 178–184.
134 Gerd Schurig, »Der Park von Sacrow«, in: AKat. 2001 a, pp. 126–132; Seiler, Hamm 1999.
135 Gerd Schurig, »Der Park des Schlosses Caputh«, in: AKat. 2001 a, pp. 24–29.
136 Quoted after Hinz 1989, p. 131.
137 AKat. 1987; Klaus von Krosigk and Heinz Wiegand, *Glienicke*, Berlin, 1984; Michael Seiler, »Glienicke«, in: AKat. 2001 a, pp. 30–42.
138 August Kopisch, 1854, quoted after Michael Seiler, »Entstehungsgeschichte des Landschaftsgartens Klein-Glienicke«, in: AKat. 1987, pp. 109–156, here p. 115.
139 Jürgen Julier, »Parkgebäude nach Entwürfen Schinkels«, in: AKat. 1987, pp. 33–43, here pp. 33 f.
140 Michael Gamper, *Die Natur ist republikanisch. Zu den ästhetischen, anthropologischen und politischen Konzepten der deutschen Gartenliteratur im 18. Jahrhundert*, Würzburg, 1998, pp. 32, 176; Stefan Groß, *Die Weimarer Klassik und die Gartenkunst*, Frankfurt am Main, 2009, p. 12.
141 Quoted after Bethe, Lenné 1826, p. 337. – On the co-authorship of Bethe and Lenné: Seiler, Hamm 1999, pp. 9, 14; Clemens Alexander Wimmer, »Äußerungen Lennés zur Gartentheorie«, in: AKat. 1989, pp. 60–69.
142 Seiler, Hamm 1999, p. 8.
143 Schönemann 1981; id. 1993.
144 Quoted after Martin Sperlich, »Nicht Schloß, sondern Villa«, in: AKat. 1987, pp. 27–31, here p. 28; id., »Vorgefundener und gestalteter Raum. Der Weg bei Lenné«, in: Zobel 1992, pp. 47–53.
145 Quoted after Bethe, Lenné 1826, p. 340.

AKat.: exhibition catalogue

Bibliography

Anders, Friedhild-Andrea, *Schlösser in der Stunde Null. Die Berliner und Potsdamer Schlösser während der Kriegs- und Nachkriegszeit*, Potsdam, 1999.

Bethe, Carl G., and Peter Joseph Lenné, »Über Trift- und Feldpflanzungen«, in: *Verhandlungen des Vereins zur Beförderung des Gartenbaues in den königlich preußischen Staaten*, 2, 1826, pp. 270–349.

Bewahrt – Wiederhergestellt – Erneuert. Restaurierungsführer durch die preußischen Schlösser, ed. by the SPSG, Potsdam, 2006.

Bisky, Jens, *Poesie der Baukunst. Architekturästhetik von Winckelmann bis Boisserée*, Weimar, 2000.

Blanning, Thimothy C. W., *The Culture of Power and the Power of Culture. Old Regime Europe 1660–1789*, Oxford, 2002.

Buttlar, Adrian von, »Englische Gärten in Deutschland. Bemerkungen zu Modifikationen ihrer Ikonologie«, in: *›Sind Briten hier‹. Relations between British and Continental Art 1680–1880*, ed. by the Zentralinstitut für Kunstgeschichte in Munich, Munich, 1981.

Buttlar, Adrian von, *Der englische Landsitz 1715–1760. Symbol eines liberalen Weltentwurfs*, Mittenwald, 1982.

Buttlar, Adrian von, *Der Landschaftsgarten. Gartenkunst des Klassizismus und der Romantik*, Cologne, 1989.

Buttlar, Adrian von, »Sanssouci und der ›ewige Osten‹. Freimaurerische Aspekte im Garten Friedrichs des Großen«, in: *Gartenkunst*, 6, 1994, pp. 219–226.

Buttlar, Adrian von, »Das Grab im Garten. Zur naturreligiösen Deutung eines arkadischen Gartenmotivs«, in: Heike Wunderlich (ed.), *Landschaft und Landschaften im achtzehnten Jahrhundert*, Heidelberg, 1995, pp. 79–119.

Buttlar, Adrian von, and Marcus Köhler, *Tod, Glück und Ruhm in Sanssouci. Ein Führer durch die Gartenwelt Friedrichs des Großen*, Ostfildern, 2012.

Dehio, Ludwig, *Friedrich Wilhelm von Preußen – ein Baukünstler der Romantik*, Munich, 1961.

Dennerlein, Ingrid, *Die Gartenkunst der Régence und des Rokoko in Frankreich*, Worms, 1981.

Dohna, Ursula Gräfin zu, *Die Gärten Friedrichs des Großen und seiner Geschwister*, Berlin, 2000.

Dorgerloh, Annette, »Friedrich II. als Gartengestalter – Repräsentation und historische Verortung«, in: Brunhilde Wehinger (ed.), *Geist und Macht. Friedrich der Große im Kontext der europäischen Kulturgeschichte*, Berlin, 2005, pp. 225–243.

Dorgerloh, Annette, »Friedrich II. und seine Gärten«, in: *Friedrich300 – Colloquien*, 4, 2010, URL: http://www.perspectivia.net/content/publikationen/friedrich300-colloquien/friedrich-kulturtransfer/dorgerloh_gaerten (16.10.2012).

Dorgerloh, Annette, *Strategien des Überdauerns. Das Grab- und Erinnerungsmal im frühen deutschen Landschaftsgarten*, Düsseldorf, 2012.

Eisbein, Karl, and Jörg Wacker, »Drei Maßnahmen der Gartendenkmalpflege im Park Babelsberg«, in: *Jahrbuch SPSG*, 6, 2004, pp. 149–172.

Eisbein, Karl, »Der Park Babelsberg«, in: *Fürst Pückler. Parkomanie in Muskau und Branitz. Ein Führer durch seine Anlagen in Sachsen, Brandenburg und Thüringen*, ed. by the Stiftung Fürst-Pückler-Park Bad Muskau, Berlin, 2006, pp. 220–233.

Fait, Joachim, and Detlef Karg, *Hermann Ludwig Heinrich von Pückler-Muskau. Gartenkunst und Denkmalpflege*, Weimar, 1989.

Frühsorge, Gotthardt, *Die Kunst des Landlebens. Vom Landschloß zum Campingplatz. Eine Kulturgeschichte*, Munich and Berlin, 1993.

Gehlen, Stefan, »Scharoun neben Schinkel? Zur real existierenden Moderne im Babelsberger Park«, in: *Jahrbuch SPSG*, 6, 2004, pp. 173–184.

Geiss, Axel (ed.), *Potsdam und sein Weltkulturerbe*, Stahnsdorf, no year.

Gerndt, Siegmar, *Idealisierte Natur. Die literarische Kontroverse um den Landschaftsgarten des 18. und 19. Jahrhunderts in Deutschland*, Stuttgart, 1981.

Giersberg, Hans-Joachim, and Adelheid Schendel, *Potsdamer Veduten*, Potsdam, 1984.

Giersberg, Hans-Joachim, and Jürgen Julier (eds.), *Preußische Königsschlösser in Berlin und Potsdam*, Leipzig, 1992.

Giersberg, Hans-Joachim, and Hillert Ibbeken, *Schloß Sanssouci. Die Sommerresidenz Friedrichs des Großen*, Berlin, 2005.

Gothein, Marie Luise, *Geschichte der Gartenkunst*, 2 vols., Hildesheim and New York, 1977.

Günther, Harri, »Zur Wiederherstellung des Marlygartens in Sanssouci«, in: *Landschaftsarchitektur*, 1, 1972, pp. 39–41.

Günther, Harri, *Peter Joseph Lenné. Gärten, Parke, Landschaften*. Stuttgart, 1985.

Günther, Harri, and Heinz Schönemann, *Cecilienhof und der Neue Garten*, Potsdam, 1988.

Günther, Harri, and Sibylle Harksen, *Peter Joseph Lenné. Katalog der Zeichnungen,* Tübingen und Berlin, 1993.

Hamann, Heinrich, *Der Park Babelsberg*, Potsdam, 1989.

Hansmann, Wilfried, »Friderizianisches Rokoko«, in: *Baukunst in Brandenburg*, ed. by the Landesregierung Brandenburg, Cologne, 1992, pp. 46–110.

Harten, Ulrike, revised by Helmut Börsch Supan und Gottfried Riemann, *Die Bühnenentwürfe* (*Karl Friedrich Schinkel. Lebenswerk*, vol. 17), Berlin, 2000.

Hartmann, Günter, *Die Ruine im Landschaftsgarten*, Cologne, 1989.

Hasselhorst, Christa, and Hans Bach, *Park Sanssouci*, Berlin, 2012.

Heilmeyer, Marina, and Hans Bach, *Die Gärten der Könige*, Munich, 2009.

Hennebo, Dieter, and Alfred Hoffmann, *Geschichte der Gartenkunst*, 3 vols., Hamburg, 1962–65.

Hennebo, Dieter (ed.), *Gartendenkmalpflege. Grundlagen der Erhaltung historischer Gärten und Grünanlagen*, Stuttgart, 1985.

Hinz, Gerhard, *Peter Joseph Lenné. Das Gesamtwerk des Gartenarchitekten und Städteplaners*, 2 parts, Hildesheim, Zurich, and New York, 1989.

Hobhouse, Penelope, *Plants in Garden History*, London, 1992.

Hübinger, Petra, »Oranienburg. Die Restaurierung des Schloßparks zur Landesgartenschau 2009 – eine Bilanz«, in: *Brandenburgische Denkmalpflege*, 20, 2011, no. 2, pp. 23–30.

Hüneke, Saskia, *Bauten und Bildwerke im Park Sanssouci* (official guide SPSG), Potsdam, ^{2}2002.

Hüneke, Saskia, »Aus dem Garten gelesen … Ikonographische Strukturen im Park Sanssouci«, in: *Jahrbuch SPSG*, 6, 2004, pp. 205–226.

Hüneke, Saskia, »Die Bildwerke des Babelsberger Parkes«, in: *Der Bär von Berlin. Jahrbuch des Vereins für die Geschichte Berlins*, 59, 2010, S. 89–116.
Hunt, John Dixon, und Peter Willis (Hrsg.), *The Genius of the Place. The English Landscape Garden 1620 to 1820*. London 1975.
Johannsen, Rolf H., »Belriguardo – ein Schloß für den Kronprinzen von Preußen 1814–1823«, in: Annette Dorgerloh, Michael Niedermeier und Horst Bredekamp (Hrsg.), *Klassizismus – Gotik. Karl Friedrich Schinkel und die patriotische Baukunst*, München 2007, S. 123–133.
Johannsen, Rolf H., *Friedrich Wilhelm IV. von Preußen. Von Borneo nach Rom. Sanssouci und die Residenzprojekte 1814 bis 1848*, Kiel 2007.
Johannsen, Rolf H., »Der Traum vom Bauen, Bilden und Schauen. Die späten Utopien«, in: *Karl Friedrich Schinkel. Geschichte und Poesie*, AKat. Berlin und München, München 2012, S. 257–260.
Karg, Detlev, *Die Entwicklungsgeschichte der Terrassenanlage und des Parterres vor dem Schloß Sanssouci*, Potsdam 1980.
Karg, Detlef, *Der Schloßpark von Rheinsberg. Ein Führer durch den Schloßpark und seine Geschichte*, Rheinsberg 1981.
Karg, Detlef, »Gartenkunst in der Mark Brandenburg – Landschaftsgärten – Zur Tätigkeit von Hermann von Pückler und Peter Joseph Lenné«, in: *Baukunst in Brandenburg*, hrsg. von der Landesregierung Brandenburg, Köln 1992, S. 135–161.
Karg, Detlef, *Peter Joseph Lenné. Parks und Gärten im Land Brandenburg*, Worms 2005.
Kehn, Wolfgang, »Sanssouci als Garten des aufgeklärten Absolutismus«, in: Jürgen Ziechmann (Hrsg.), *Panorama der Friderícianischen Zeit. Friedrich der Große und seine Epoche*, Bremen 1985, S. 146–151.
Kopisch, August, *Geschichte der Königlichen Schlösser und Gärten zu Potsdam. Von der Zeit ihrer Gründung bis zum Jahre MDCCCLII […]*, Berlin 1854.
Kruft, Hanno-Walter, *Geschichte der Architekturtheorie. Von der Antike bis zur Gegenwart*, München 1991.
Kühn, Margarete, *Schloß Charlottenburg*, Berlin 1955.
Kubitz, Gisela, und Ernst-Hermann Kubitz, *Peter Lenné hinter dem grünen Gitter!*, Berlin 1989.
Kunisch, Johannes, *Friedrich der Große. Der König und seine Zeit*, München ^{3}2012.
Kurth, Willy, *Sanssouci. Ein Beitrag zur Kunst des deutschen Rokoko*, Berlin 1962.
Maisak, Petra, *Arkadien. Genese und Typologie einer idyllischen Wunschwelt*, Frankfurt am Main und Bern 1981.
Mielke, Friedrich, *Potsdamer Baukunst. Das klassische Potsdam*, Berlin ^{3}1998.
Mowl, Thimothy, *Gentlemen Gardeners. The Men who created the English Landscape Garden*, Stroud ^{3}2010.
Peter Joseph Lenné. Gartenkunst im 19. Jahrhundert. Beiträge zur Lenné-Forschung, hrsg. vom Brandenburgischen Landesamt für Denkmalpflege, Berlin und München 1992.
Pevsner, Nikolaus, *The Picturesque Garden and its Influence outside the British Isles*, Washington, D.C. 1974.
Piltz, Georg, *Schlösser und Gärten in der Mark Brandenburg*, Leipzig ^{3}1991.
Poensgen, Georg, *Schloß Babelsberg*, Berlin 1929.
Rohde, Michael (Hrsg.), *Preußische Gärten in Europa. 300 Jahre Gartengeschichte*, Leipzig 2007.
Schepers, Wolfgang, *Hirschfelds Theorie der Gartenkunst 1779–1785*, Worms 1980.
Schönemann, Heinz, »Schloß Charlottenhof und die Römischen Bäder – ein utopisches Gesellschaftsmodell«, in: *Das Werk Schinkels und seine Bedeutung für die DDR*, Berlin 1981, S. 122–127.
Schönemann, Heinz, »Der Hippodrom in Charlottenhof«, in: *Mitteilungen der Pückler Gesellschaft*, N.F. 9, 1993, S. 99–116.
Sckell, Friedrich Ludwig von, *Beiträge zur bildenden Gartenkunst*, Worms 1982 (Reprint).
Seiler, Michael, und Jörg Wacker (Hrsg.), *Insel Potsdam. Ein kulturhistorischer Begleiter durch die Potsdamer Parklandschaft*, Berlin 1991.
Seiler, Michael, und Stefan Koppelkamm, *Pfaueninsel, Berlin*, Tübingen und Berlin 1993.
Seiler, Michael, und Manfred Hamm, *Inszenierte Landschaften. Blicke ins Preussische Arkadien*, Berlin 1999.
Seiler, Michael, *Pfaueninsel* (amtlicher Führer SPSG), Potsdam 2000.
Streidt, Gert, und Klaus Frahm, *Potsdam. Die Schlösser und Gärten der Hohenzollern*, Köln 1996.
Streidt, Gert, und Peter Feierabend (Hrsg.), *Preußen. Kunst und Architektur*, Köln 1999.
Trotha, Hans von, *GartenKunst. Auf der Suche nach dem verlorenen Paradies*, Köln 2012.
Volkmann, Torsten, »Oranienburg. Gartendenkmalpflege im Schloßpark«, in: *Brandenburgische Denkmalpflege*, 5, 1996, Heft. 2, S. 22–30.
Wendland, Folkwin, *Berlins Gärten und Parke. Von der Gründung der Stadt bis zum ausgehenden neunzehnten Jahrhundert*, Frankfurt am Main, Berlin und Wien 11979.
Wendland, Folkwin, »Garten und Park Rheinsberg«, in: *Jahrbuch für brandenburgische Landesgeschichte*, 38, 1987, S. 102–141.
Wimmer, Clemens Alexander, *Die Gärten des Charlottenburger Schlosses* (*Gartendenkmalpflege*, 2), Berlin ^{3}1987.
Wimmer, Clemens Alexander, *Geschichte der Gartentheorie*, Darmstadt 1989.
Wimmer, Clemens Alexander, *Der Potsdamer Lustgarten*, Berlin 2004.
Zehn Jahre Unesco-Welterbe der Potsdam-Berliner-Kulturlandschaft, hrsg. von der SPSG, Potsdam/Großbeeren 2000.
Zobel, Hans-Jürgen (Hrsg.), *Peter Joseph Lenné und die europäische Landschafts- und Gartenkunst im 19. Jahrhundert. 6. Greifswalder Romantikkonferenz*, Greifswald 1992.

Ausstellungskataloge

Berlin durch die Blume oder Kraut und Rüben. Gartenkunst in Berlin-Brandenburg, hrsg. von Marie-Louise Plessen, AKat. Berlin, Berlin 1985.
Friedrich II. und die Kunst, hrsg. von der SSG, AKat. Potsdam, Potsdam 1986.
Friedrich der Große, von Friedrich Benninghoven, Helmut Börsch-Supan und Iselin Gundermann, AKat. Berlin, Berlin 1986.
Schloß Glienicke. Bewohner. Künstler. Parklandschaft, hrsg. von der SSG, AKat. Berlin, Berlin 1987.
Der Große Kurfürst. Sammler, Bauherr, Mäzen, 1620 bis 1688, hrsg. von der SSG, AKat. Potsdam, Potsdam 1988.
Peter Joseph Lenné. Volkspark und Arkadien, hrsg. von Florian von Buttlar, AKat. Berlin, Berlin 1989.
Potsdamer Schlösser und Gärten. Bau- und Gartenkunst vom 17. bis 20. Jahrhundert, hrsg. von der SSG, AKat. Potsdam, Potsdam 1993.
Friedrich Wilhelm IV. Künstler und König, hrsg. von der SPSG, AKat. Potsdam, Frankfurt am Main 1995.
Rheinsberg. Wiederherstellung von Schloß und Park, hrsg. von der SPSG, AKat. Rheinsberg, Berlin 1996.
Friedrich Wilhelm II. und die Künste. Preußens Weg zum Klassizismus, hrsg. von der SPSG, AKat. Potsdam, Potsdam 1997.
Sophie Charlotte und ihr Schloß. Ein Musenhof des Barock in Brandenburg-Preußen, hrsg. von der SPSG, AKat. Berlin, München, London und New York 1999.*»Zum Maler und zum großen Architekten geboren«. Georg Wenzeslaus von Knobelsdorff. 1699–1753*, hrsg. von der SPSG, AKat. Berlin, Berlin ^{2}1999.
Nichts gedeiht ohne Pflege. Die Potsdamer Parklandschaft und ihre Gärtner, hrsg. von der SPSG, AKat. Potsdam, Potsdam 2001.
Wo die Zitronen blühen, Orangerien – historische Arbeitsgeräte, Kunst und Kunsthandwerk, hrsg. von der SPSG, AKat. Potsdam, Potsdam ^{2}2001.
Gärten und Höfe der Rubenszeit, hrsg. von Ursula Härting, AKat. Hamm und Mainz, München 2001.
Prinz Heinrich von Preußen. Ein Europäer in Rheinsberg, hrsg. von der SPSG, AKat. Rheinsberg, München und Berlin 2002.
Preußisch Grün. Hofgärtner in Brandenburg-Preußen, hrsg. von der SPSG, AKat. Berlin, Berlin 2004.
Schön und nützlich. Aus Brandenburgs Kloster-, Schloss- und Küchengärten, hrsg. vom Haus der Brandenburgisch-Preußischen Geschichte, AKat. Potsdam, Leipzig 2004.
Friederisiko. Friedrich der Große, hrsg. von der SPSG, AKat. Potsdam, München 2012.

Hüneke, Saskia, »Die Bildwerke des Babelsberger Parkes«, in: *Der Bär von Berlin. Jahrbuch des Vereins für die Geschichte Berlins*, 59, 2010, pp. 89–116.
Hunt, John Dixon, and Peter Willis (eds.), *The Genius of the Place. The English Landscape Garden 1620 to 1820*. London, 1975.
Johannsen, Rolf H., »Belriguardo – ein Schloß für den Kronprinzen von Preußen 1814–1823«, in: Annette Dorgerloh, Michael Niedermeier, and Horst Bredekamp (eds.), *Klassizismus – Gotik. Karl Friedrich Schinkel und die patriotische Baukunst*, Munich, 2007, pp. 123–133.
Johannsen, Rolf H., *Friedrich Wilhelm IV. von Preußen. Von Borneo nach Rom. Sanssouci und die Residenzprojekte 1814 bis 1848*, Kiel, 2007.
Johannsen, Rolf H., »Der Traum vom Bauen, Bilden und Schauen. Die späten Utopien«, in: *Karl Friedrich Schinkel. Geschichte und Poesie*, AKat. Berlin and Munich, Munich, 2012, pp. 257–260.
Karg, Detlev, *Die Entwicklungsgeschichte der Terrassenanlage und des Parterres vor dem Schloß Sanssouci*, Potsdam, 1980.
Karg, Detlef, *Der Schloßpark von Rheinsberg. Ein Führer durch den Schloßpark und seine Geschichte*, Rheinsberg, 1981.
Karg, Detlef, »Gartenkunst in der Mark Brandenburg – Landschaftsgärten – Zur Tätigkeit von Hermann von Pückler und Peter Joseph Lenné«, in: *Baukunst in Brandenburg*, ed. by the Landesregierung Brandenburg, Cologne, 1992, pp. 135–161.
Karg, Detlef, *Peter Joseph Lenné. Parks und Gärten im Land Brandenburg*, Worms, 2005.
Kehn, Wolfgang, »Sanssouci als Garten des aufgeklärten Absolutismus«, in: Jürgen Ziechmann (ed.), *Panorama der Fridericianischen Zeit. Friedrich der Große und seine Epoche*, Bremen, 1985, pp. 146–151.
Kopisch, August, *Geschichte der Königlichen Schlösser und Gärten zu Potsdam. Von der Zeit ihrer Gründung bis zum Jahre MDCCCLII […]*, Berlin, 1854.
Kruft, Hanno-Walter, *Geschichte der Architekturtheorie. Von der Antike bis zur Gegenwart*, Munich, 1991.
Kubitz, Gisela, and Ernst-Hermann Kubitz, *Peter Lenné hinter dem grünen Gitter!*, Berlin, 1989.
Kühn, Margarete, *Schloß Charlottenburg*, Berlin, 1955.
Kunisch, Johannes, *Friedrich der Große. Der König und seine Zeit*, Munich, ^{3}2012.
Kurth, Willy, *Sanssouci. Ein Beitrag zur Kunst des deutschen Rokoko*, Berlin, 1962.
Maisak, Petra, *Arkadien. Genese und Typologie einer idyllischen Wunschwelt*, Frankfurt am Main and Bern, 1981.
Mielke, Friedrich, *Potsdamer Baukunst. Das klassische Potsdam*, Berlin, ^{3}1998.
Mowl, Thimothy, *Gentlemen Gardeners. The Men who created the English Landscape Garden*, Stroud, ^{3}2010.
Peter Joseph Lenné. Gartenkunst im 19. Jahrhundert. Beiträge zur Lenné-Forschung, ed. by the Brandenburgisches Landesamt für Denkmalpflege, Berlin and Munich, 1992.
Pevsner, Nikolaus, *The Picturesque Garden and its Influence outside the British Isles*, Washington, D.C., 1974.
Piltz, Georg, *Schlösser und Gärten in der Mark Brandenburg*, Leipzig, ^{3}1991.
Poensgen, Georg, *Schloß Babelsberg*, Berlin, 1929.
Rohde, Michael (ed.), *Preußische Gärten in Europa. 300 Jahre Gartengeschichte*, Leipzig, 2007.
Schepers, Wolfgang, *Hirschfelds Theorie der Gartenkunst 1779–1785*, Worms, 1980.
Schönemann, Heinz, »Schloß Charlottenhof und die Römischen Bäder – ein utopisches Gesellschaftsmodell«, in: *Das Werk Schinkels und seine Bedeutung für die DDR*, Berlin, 1981, pp. 122–127.
Schönemann, Heinz, »Der Hippodrom in Charlottenhof«, in: *Mitteilungen der Pückler Gesellschaft*, N.F. 9, 1993, pp. 99–116.
Sckell, Friedrich Ludwig von, *Beiträge zur bildenden Gartenkunst*, Worms, 1982 (reprint).
Seiler, Michael, and Jörg Wacker (eds.), *Insel Potsdam. Ein kulturhistorischer Begleiter durch die Potsdamer Parklandschaft*, Berlin, 1991.
Seiler, Michael, and Stefan Koppelkamm, *Pfaueninsel, Berlin*, Tübingen and Berlin, 1993.
Seiler, Michael, and Manfred Hamm, *Inszenierte Landschaften. Blicke ins Preussische Arkadien*, Berlin, 1999.
Seiler, Michael, *Pfaueninsel* (official guide SPSG), Potsdam, 2000.
Streidt, Gert, and Klaus Frahm, *Potsdam. Die Schlösser und Gärten der Hohenzollern*, Cologne, 1996.
Streidt, Gert, and Peter Feierabend (eds.), *Preußen. Kunst und Architektur*, Cologne, 1999.
Trotha, Hans von, *GartenKunst. Auf der Suche nach dem verlorenen Paradies*, Cologne, 2012.
Volkmann, Torsten, »Oranienburg. Gartendenkmalpflege im Schloßpark«, in: *Brandenburgische Denkmalpflege*, 5, 1996, no. 2, pp. 22–30.
Wendland, Folkwin, *Berlins Gärten und Parke. Von der Gründung der Stadt bis zum ausgehenden neunzehnten Jahrhundert*, Frankfurt am Main, Berlin, and Vienna, 1979.
Wendland, Folkwin, »Garten und Park Rheinsberg«, in: *Jahrbuch für brandenburgische Landesgeschichte*, 38, 1987, pp. 102–141.
Wimmer, Clemens Alexander, *Die Gärten des Charlottenburger Schlosses* (*Gartendenkmalpflege*, 2), Berlin, ^{3}1987.
Wimmer, Clemens Alexander, *Geschichte der Gartentheorie*, Darmstadt, 1989.
Wimmer, Clemens Alexander, *Der Potsdamer Lustgarten*, Berlin, 2004.
Zehn Jahre Unesco-Welterbe der Potsdam-Berliner-Kulturlandschaft, ed. by the SPSG, Potsdam/Großbeeren, 2000.
Zobel, Hans-Jürgen (Hrsg.), *Peter Joseph Lenné und die europäische Landschafts- und Gartenkunst im 19. Jahrhundert. 6. Greifswalder Romantikkonferenz*, Greifswald, 1992.

Exhibition catalogues

Berlin durch die Blume oder Kraut und Rüben. Gartenkunst in Berlin-Brandenburg, ed. by Marie-Louise Plessen, AKat. Berlin, Berlin, 1985.
Friedrich II. und die Kunst, ed. by the SSG, AKat. Potsdam, Potsdam, 1986.
Friedrich der Große, by Friedrich Benninghoven, Helmut Börsch-Supan and Iselin Gundermann, AKat. Berlin, Berlin, 1986.
Schloß Glienicke. Bewohner. Künstler. Parklandschaft, ed. by the SSG, AKat. Berlin, Berlin, 1987.
Der Große Kurfürst. Sammler, Bauherr, Mäzen, 1620 bis 1688, ed. by the SSG, AKat. Potsdam, Potsdam, 1988.
Peter Joseph Lenné. Volkspark und Arkadien, ed. by Florian von Buttlar, AKat. Berlin, Berlin, 1989.
Potsdamer Schlösser und Gärten. Bau- und Gartenkunst vom 17. bis 20. Jahrhundert, ed. by the SSG, AKat. Potsdam, Potsdam, 1993.
Friedrich Wilhelm IV. Künstler und König, ed. by the SPSG, AKat. Potsdam, Frankfurt am Main, 1995.
Rheinsberg. Wiederherstellung von Schloß und Park, ed. by the SPSG, AKat. Rheinsberg, Berlin, 1996.
Friedrich Wilhelm II. und die Künste. Preußens Weg zum Klassizismus, ed. by the SPSG, AKat. Potsdam, Potsdam, 1997.
Sophie Charlotte und ihr Schloß. Ein Musenhof des Barock in Brandenburg-Preußen, ed. by the SPSG, AKat. Berlin, Munich, London, and New York, 1999.
»Zum Maler und zum großen Architekten geboren«. Georg Wenzeslaus von Knobelsdorff. 1699–1753, ed. by the SPSG, AKat. Berlin, Berlin, ^{2}1999.
Nichts gedeiht ohne Pflege. Die Potsdamer Parklandschaft und ihre Gärtner, ed. by the SPSG, AKat. Potsdam, Potsdam, 2001.
Wo die Zitronen blühen, Orangerien – historische Arbeitsgeräte, Kunst und Kunsthandwerk, ed. by the SPSG, AKat. Potsdam, Potsdam, ^{2}2001.
Gärten und Höfe der Rubenszeit, ed. by Ursula Härting, AKat. Hamm und Mainz, Munich, 2001.
Prinz Heinrich von Preußen. Ein Europäer in Rheinsberg, ed. by the SPSG, AKat. Rheinsberg, Munich and Berlin, 2002.
Preußisch Grün. Hofgärtner in Brandenburg-Preußen, ed. by the SPSG, AKat. Berlin, Berlin, 2004.
Schön und nützlich. Aus Brandenburgs Kloster-, Schloss- und Küchengärten, ed. by the Haus der Brandenburgisch-Preußischen Geschichte, AKat. Potsdam, Leipzig, 2004.
Friederisiko. Friedrich der Große, ed. by the SPSG, AKat. Potsdam, Munich, 2012.

Hillert Ibbeken

Gedanken des Gartenphotographen

Jedes Bild ist eine Entscheidung, der ein Urteil vorausgeht. Im Studio ist der Photograph frei, seine Objekte zu beurteilen, zu arrangieren, zu inszenieren und seine Entscheidungen zu treffen. Verläßt er aber sein Studio, um draußen zu arbeiten, muß er sich einen großen Schritt zurücknehmen, weil die wichtigsten Entscheidungen für sein Bild bereits von anderen getroffen wurden: von der Natur, wenn er Naturlandschaften abbilden will, von der Land- und Forstwirtschaft, wenn er Kulturlandschaften photographiert, oder von einem Gartenkünstler, wenn es um einen Park oder Garten geht, eben eine Kunstlandschaft. Diese drei Bildthemen aus Natur-, Kultur- und Kunstlandschaft sind der Schönheit verpflichtet. Was die Naturlandschaft anbelangt, so können auch die Naturwissenschaften wichtig werden, etwa Geologie und Geomorphologie, aber auch die Botanik. Bei der Kulturlandschaft sind es Land- und Forstwirtschaft, aber nur bei den Bildern der Kunstlandschaft geht es fast ausschließlich um Schönheit, allein weil die Kunstlandschaft *a priori* um ihrer Schönheit willen vom Gartenkünstler geschaffen wurde. In jedem der drei Fälle muß der Landschaftsphotograph mit dem Vorhandenen, mit dem Gegebenen arbeiten, seine Gestaltungsmöglichkeiten sind eingeschränkt.

Reine Naturlandschaften gibt es nicht mehr sehr häufig in der Welt, der Mensch hat sich die Erde wirklich weitgehend untertan gemacht. Ich hatte das Glück, als Naturwissenschaftler, als Geologe einige dieser Landschaften besuchen und photographieren zu können: in Australien und auf Hawai, im Iran und in Chile, in Kalifornien und Alaska. Dabei stand der wissenschaftliche Aspekt im Vordergrund, zum Beispiel die Frage nach der Genese einer gegebenen Struktur, ob etwa die Verebnungsfläche in einem Gebirge etwas über seine Heraushebung aussagt? Das galt es zu photographieren, wissenschaftlich deutlich und aussagekräftig, aber auch bildmäßig möglichst gut gestaltet. Der des wissenschaftlichen Gehalts unkundige Landschaftsphotograph dagegen trachtet nur nach der möglichen Schönheit desselben Objekts. Die Verebnungsfläche würde ihn nur interessieren, weil darauf eine Herde von Wildpferden grast und weil dahinter das Hochgebirge einer Cordillere aufragt. Er würde diese Szene vielleicht nicht nur als schön, sondern sogar als erhaben betrachten.

Ganz anders begegnet der Photograph der Kulturlandschaft. Vom Menschen geprägt, kann sie ihre Verknüpfung mit der Naturlandschaft, aus der sie hervorging, zwar nicht leugnen, aber die Verhüllung, die Verdrängung der Naturlandschaft durch die menschliche Kultur geht, zumindest in unseren Breiten, doch sehr weit. Berg und Tal, Fluß und Küste sind in ihren Grundzügen erhalten geblieben, aber der wissenschaftliche Blick auf ihre Entstehung ist doch sehr verstellt. So sind die Ebenen Norddeutschlands fast alle eiszeitlich geprägt, heute aber von Wiesen, Äckern und Wäldern zugedeckt, die allesamt einem ökonomischen Interesse dienen, keinem wissenschaftlichen. Die Kulturlandschaften sind ein reiches Feld für die Landschaftsphotographie und eine ästhetische Betrachtung, man denke sich nur den Blick von einem erhöhten Standpunkt über den Teppich der landschaftsprägenden, gelb blühenden Rapsfelder im Mai, die wunderbar aussehen können.

Das bisher über die Natur- und Kulturlandschaften Gesagte soll klarmachen, daß diese Landschaften zwar einen ästhetischen Reiz besitzen können, niemals aber wegen dieses Reizes geschaffen wurden. Das ist der Kunstlandschaft vorbehalten, die zwar auf Elemente der Natur- und Kulturlandschaft zurückgreift, das ist sogar unverzichtbar, sie aber in ästhetische Kategorien wie in eine neue Sprache übersetzt. Diese Sprache zu verstehen, das ist das Problem des Photographen. Natürlich schärft eine wissenschaftlich geschulte Betrachtung ganz allgemein den Blick auf Strukturen, gleichgültig welcher Entstehung, aber der Photograph ist kein Gartenhistoriker. Deshalb also muß er sich kundig machen, er muß Fragen stellen und sich belehren lassen. Er hört von Wasser und Wegen, Alleen, Sichtachsen und Sichten, Terrassen und Bodenbewegungen, Rondellen und Bosketten, Architekturen und Skulpturen, architektonischen und Landschaftsgärten und, natürlich, von Bäumen und Blumen, von Rosengärten.

Ein wesentliches Element von Gärten ist das Wasser. Die wasserreiche Umgebung von Berlin und Potsdam macht es dem Photographen leicht, diesem Gartenthema nachzugehen. Da reine Wasserflächen photographisch unergiebig sind, läßt sich Wasser am besten über Uferlinien definieren, die meist locker von Bäumen bestanden sind, wie die Ufer des Neuen Gartens, der Karpfenteich in Charlottenburg, der Grienericksee in Rheinsberg oder die Glienicker Lake bei Babelsberg. Auch kleinere Gewässer sind reizvoll wie der Friedensteich im östlichen Marlygarten oder die Kanäle in Königs Wusterhausen mit ihren Spiegelungen, aber auch ganz winzige Gewässer wie der Gartenteich der Villa Illaire im Marlygarten oder der Tümpel der Egeriagrotte in Rheinsberg. Ein wesentlicher Effekt von Wasserflächen ist die von Lenné besonders betonte scheinbare Stapelung, wenn hintereinanderliegende, durch einen schmalen Landstrich getrennte Wässer wie übereinandergelegt erscheinen, etwa wie beim Blick vom Grünen Haus über den Heiligen See und den Jungfernsee/die Havel zum Turm des Gärtner- und Maschinenhauses von Schloß Glienicke. Neben diesen ruhenden Wasserflächen sind Fontänen das zweite bestimmende Wasserelement der Gärten, photographisch eigentlich immer interessant. Die bedeutendste Fontäne ist hier, Wasser im Wasser, der maximal 42 m hohe Geysir an der Lennébucht in der Glienicker Lake in Babelsberg. Die meisten Fontänen finden sich im Park Sanssouci, sie bilden den Mittelpunkt vieler Rondelle und bieten sich zur Gliederung eines Bildes an. Das geringe Relief der ganzen Gegend verhindert schneller fließende Gewässer wie Bäche, eine künstlich geschaffene Ausnahme ist die Marmorkaskade im Paradiesgarten, deren Stufen von Wasser überflossen werden und einen Sturzbach vortäuschen. Mit einem Wort, das Wasser in den Gärten ist kein photographisches Problem, die ästhetische Intention ist leicht zu erkennen, das Wasser als Metapher für eine lebenspendende, ja, paradiesische Kraft zu diskutieren ist des Photographen Sache nicht.

Wege sind dagegen ein großes photographisches Problem. Die sich beim Beschreiten eines Weges ablösenden Perspektiven sind nicht abbildbar. Oft ist eine deutliche Zielführung nicht zu erkennen und offensichtlich auch nicht intendiert. Trotzdem führen die Wege zu den markanten Punkten eines Gartens oder nahe an ihnen vorbei, jedenfalls ist es nie nötig, einen Weg zu verlassen, um einen erhofften »besseren« Standpunkt zu erreichen, die Wege bieten bereits alles an. Die meisten Wege sind unsichtbar, bis auf den Abschnitt, den man gerade unter den Füßen hat. Der berühmte Pücklerweg in Babelsberg, der von der Rosentreppe aus nach Osten »geht«, schmiegt sich der Krümmung des tiefer liegenden Ufers und damit der Gartengrenze an, hebt sich optisch ein wenig in die Tiefe des Blicks hinein und verschmilzt dort mit der zurückspringenden Uferlinie. So etwas läßt sich ausnahmsweise photographieren.

Alleen, Sichtachsen und Sichten sind ein Paradethema der Gartenphotographie, ihre Darstellung ist zumindest dann kein Problem, wenn man sie als Strukturen sieht. Hier läßt sich fast verallgemeinernd sagen, daß die baumbegleitete Allee oder Sichtachse zu einem Fluchtpunkt das dramatische Hochformat verlangt, während die zumeist mehr raumgreifende Sicht das epischere Querformat benötigt. Alleen und schmale Sichtachsen haben einen hinführenden Charakter, der Fluchtpunkt, gleichgültig ob Belvedere oder Mausoleum, soll aufgesucht werden. In der Weite einer Sicht kann man gut verweilen, das sollte im Bild deutlich werden.

Terrassen sind schwierig, Bodenbewegungen kaum zu photographieren. In unserer reliefarmen Gegend sind Gartenterrassen selten, die bekanntesten sind die sechs Terrassen des Weinbergs, auf dem Schloß Sanssouci steht, und die Erdterrassen von Rheinsberg. Die Terrassen können nur in einer Richtung, nämlich von unten aufgenommen werden. Beim Schloß Sanssouci kommt noch der mißliche Umstand hinzu, daß es auf der obersten Terrasse weit zurückgelegt ist, weshalb es von unten, etwa von der Großen Fontäne her gesehen, halb versunken erscheint, ein Anblick, über den sich schon Voltaire amüsiert haben soll. Im Gegensatz zu den steilen Terrassenfolgen etwa der mediterranen Gebirge sind unsere hiesigen, flachen Terrassen eigentlich ziemlich langweilig. Das gilt nicht für die sogenannten Bodenbewegungen, künstliche morphologische Strukturen, längliche wohlgerundete Hügel, wie sie im *pleasure ground* von Glienicke angelegt wurden oder an der Kanonenberg-Serpentine in Babelsberg. Sie bereichern das Raumgefühl ungemein, sind aber nur dann gut zu photographieren, wenn man die abgeleiteten Schatten der umstehenden Bäume mit erfassen kann.

Das Photographieren von Rondellen ist einfach, solange sie klein sind, aber schwierig bis unmöglich, wenn sie sehr groß angelegt wurden. Das kleine Athena-Rondell im Charlottenburger Garten ist kein photographisches Problem, das große Halbrondell von Paretz dagegen ist kaum zu erfassen, die Weitwinkelaufnahme umgreift zwar praktisch alles, läßt aber das Halbrondell als solches kaum erkennen, hier würde nur ein Luftbild helfen. Das Halbrondell von Königs Wusterhausen wird sowohl auf der Karte als auch beim Begehen deutlich, kann aber nicht aussagekräftig aufgenommen werden, weil es mit den fast unmittelbar dahinter stehenden Bäumen optisch verschmilzt. Boskette, das Rahmenwerk der Wege, sind überhaupt kein photographisches Problem, man denke nur an die Hainbuchenboskette der Hauptallee und der Querachsen von Sanssouci, den Dichterhain von Charlottenhof oder die Boskette von Rheinsberg, die in den Kulissen des Heckentheaters vielleicht ihren schönsten Ausdruck finden.

Architekturen wie ein Belvedere, Orangerien, Stibadien oder Tempel und Skulpturen wie die Figuren in Charlottenhofs Dichterhain, die Krönungsvasen in Charlottenburg oder die Cybei-Skulpturen im Salon von Rheinsberg, sie alle sind notwendiges Beiwerk der Gärten und setzen Akzente, sollten photographisch aber nie für sich allein aufgenommen werden, sondern nur im Zusammenhang mit einem Gartenelement, alles andere

Hillert Ibbeken

Reflections of the garden photographer

Every picture is a decision preceded by a judgment. In the studio the photographer is free to judge, to arrange, to stage and to make his decisions. But once he leaves his studio to work outside, he must take a big step back, because the most important decisions for his picture have already been made by others: by nature when he depicts natural landscapes, by agriculture and forestry when he photographs cultivated and developed land, or by a garden designer if he is photographing a park or a garden, that is, a landscape designed by an artist. All three themes – depictions of natural, cultivated and artist-designed landscapes – are dedicated to the idea of beauty. In a natural landscape, other important factors may be the natural sciences, such as geology, geomorphology or botany. In the depiction of a cultivated landscape, agriculture and forestry play an important part, but it is only in images of an art landscape that the focus is almost exclusively on beauty, simply because that landscape was created by the garden designer a priori for the sake of its beauty. In each of these three cases the landscape photographer must work with what is there, with the given: his options are limited.

Pure natural landscapes hardly exist in the world anymore. To a large extent, human beings have indeed brought the Earth under their dominion. As a natural scientist, a geologist, I had the good fortune to visit some of these landscapes: in Australia and Hawaii, in Iran and Chile, in California and Alaska. During these visits, my primary interest was in the landscapes' scientific aspect, for instance, the genesis of a given structure: does the planation surface in a mountain range convey information about its uplift? My job was to take pictures, scientifically clear and meaningful, but also pictorially as well designed as possible. On the other hand, a landscape photographer who has no knowledge of the scientific content seeks only to record the potential beauty of the same object. The planation surface would interest him only because there is a herd of wild horses grazing on it and because the high mountains of the Cordilleras loom behind it. He might regard this scene not only as beautiful but even as sublime.

A photographer's approach to a cultivated landscape is entirely different. Shaped by human agency, such a landscape can hardly deny its connection to the natural landscape from which it originally developed, but the extent to which human culture has disguised and replaced the natural landscape is quite considerable, at least in our part of the world. While the basic features of mountains and valleys, rivers and coastlines have been preserved, the scientist's view of how they developed has been seriously obstructed. Thus, for instance, the plains of North Germany are almost all glacial in origin, but are today concealed by meadows, fields and woods that serve economic, not scientific, interests. Cultivated landscapes are a rich field for landscape photography and aesthetic contemplation – you have only to think of the wonderful view from an elevated vantage point, in May, of the carpet of golden fields of rape in bloom.

What I have said so far about natural and cultivated landscapes is meant to explain that while these landscapes may have aesthetic appeal, they were never created because of this appeal. That is reserved to the art landscape: While falling back on elements of the natural and cultivated landscape, which is even essential, it translates them into aesthetic categories, into a new language, as it were. Understanding this language is the problem of the photographer. Naturally, if a photographer has been scientifically trained to observe the landscape, he will quite generally have a sharpened awareness of structures, regardless of how they developed, but he is not a garden historian. That is why he has to inform himself, ask questions and let others teach him. He will hear about water and paths, avenues, visual axes and vistas, architectural structures and sculptures, architectonic gardens and landscape gardens and, of course, about trees and flowers, and rose gardens.

An essential element of gardens is water. The surrounding area of Berlin and Potsdam has many bodies of water, and makes it easy for a photographer to pursue this feature of gardens. Since water surfaces alone are photographically unproductive, water is best defined by its banks or shorelines, which are usually loosely covered with trees, like the shorelines of the Neuer Garten, the carp pond in Charlottenburg, Grienericksee in Rheinsberg or Glienicker Lake near Babelsberg. Smaller bodies of water are appealing, too – for instance, the Friedensteich in the eastern part of the Marly Garden or the canals in Königs Wusterhausen with their reflections, but even quite tiny ponds, like the one by Villa Illaire in the Marly Garden or the one near the Grotto of Egeria in Rheinsberg. An important effect of water surfaces is the illusion especially emphasized by Lenné, when bodies of water lying one behind the other and separated by a narrow strip of land appear to be stacked above each other, for instance when one is looking from the Green House across Heiliger See and Jungfernsee / the Havel River towards the tower of the gardener's house and engine house of Schloß Glienicke. In addition to these still water surfaces, fountains are the second determining water element of the garden, really always photographically interesting. Here the most significant fountain – water in water – is the geyser near the Lennébucht in Glienicker Lake in Babelsberg, which reaches a maximum height of 42 m. The largest number of fountains are found in Park Sanssouci; they are the centre of many rondels and are the obvious feature that gives structure to a picture. Because the topography of the entire region is so level, there are no fast-flowing waters such as brooks, an artificially created exception being the marble cascade in the Paradiesgarten, over whose steps water rushes continuously, giving the illusion of a torrent. In a word, the water in the gardens is not a photographic problem, the aesthetic intention is easily recognisable, and it is not the photographer's responsibility to question the use of water as a metaphor for a life-giving, indeed a paradisiacal force.

Paths, on the other hand, are a big photographic problem. It is not possible to record photographically the perspectives that unfold when one takes a certain path. Often a clear destination cannot be discerned, nor is one obviously intended. Even so, the paths lead to the distinctive features of a garden or closely past them; at any rate it is never necessary to leave a path in order to reach a hoped-for »better« vantage point – the paths already offer all the vantage points. Most of the paths cannot be seen, except for the section on which one happens to be walking. The famous Pückler path in Babelsberg, which »goes« from the Rosentreppe in an easterly direction, hugs the bend of the lower-lying shore and thus of the garden's boundary, visually rises a little into the depth of the view, where it merges with the receding shoreline. This is something that can only rarely be captured photographically.

Avenues, visual axes and vistas are a favourite theme of garden photography, or at least depicting them is not a problem if one sees them as structures. Here one might almost generalize that a tree-lined avenue or visual axis moving towards a vanishing point demands the dramatic upright format, while the usually more expansive view needs the more epic horizontal format. Avenues and narrow visual axes lead somewhere, and it is necessary to locate the vanishing point, whether it is a belvedere or a mausoleum. It is pleasant to dwell on a wide view, and that should become clear in the picture.

Terraces are hard, and earthworks are almost impossible to photograph. In our region, which is without topography, garden terraces are rare, the best known being the six terraces of the vineyard hill on which Schloß Sanssouci is located, and the earth terraces of Rheinsberg. The terraces can be photographed only in one direction, i.e., from below. In the case of Schloß Sanssouci there is the added regrettable circumstance that the palace is built far to the rear of the uppermost terrace, and therefore appears to be half sunken when seen from below, for instance, from the Große Fontäne, a sight that is said to have amused Voltaire. In contrast to the steep series of terraces, like those in the Mediterranean mountains, the shallow terraces of our region are actually rather boring. This is not true of the so-called earthworks, man-made morphological structures, elongated rounded hills of a type created in the pleasure ground of Glienicke or along the serpentine road of Kanonenberg in Babelsberg. They enhance one's sense of space immensely, but can be effectively photographed only if it is possible to include the shadows of the surrounding trees.

The photographing of rondels is simple as long as they are small, but difficult to impossible if they were laid out on a large scale. The little Athena-Rondell in the Charlottenburg garden is not a photographic problem, while the large semi-rondel of Paretz, on the other hand, can scarcely be captured; while a wide-angle shot encompasses practically everything, it barely makes it possible to recognize the semi-rondel as such – only an aerial shot would work here. The semi-rondel of Königs Wusterhausen becomes clear both on the map and when one enters it, but cannot be photographed in a meaningful way because it blends visually with the trees that stand almost directly behind it. *Bosquets*, the framework of the paths, are definitely not a photographic problem – just think of the hornbeam *bosquets* of the main avenue and the transverse axes of Sanssouci, the Dichterhain (Poets' Grove) of Charlottenhof or the *bosquets* of Rheinsberg, which probably find their loveliest expression in the backdrops of the hedge theatre.

Architectural structures such as a belvedere, orangeries, stibadia or temples, and sculptures such as the figures in the Dichterhain of Charlottenhof, the coronation vases in Charlottenburg or the Cybei sculptures in the salon of Rheinsberg are all necessary accessories of the gardens and emphasize their features, but should never be photographed separately, only in connection with a garden element, as anything else would not do justice to their subordinate role in the garden. This is also partly true of the palaces that belong to all the gardens. The palaces, though, are the focal points of the gardens; the gardens are always oriented towards the palaces, and

würde ihrer beigeordneten Rolle im Garten nicht gerecht. Das gilt bedingt auch für die Schlösser, die zu allen Gärten gehören. Die Schlösser sind allerdings die Schwerpunkte der Gärten, die immer zu den Schlössern hin ausgerichtet sind; diese Orientierung muß photographisch erkennbar werden, sowohl vom Schloß her als zum Schloß hin gesehen. Das Schloß selbst, als Architektur, spielt in diesem Zusammenhang photographisch keine Rolle.

Ein architektonischer Garten wie das barocke Parterre von Charlottenburg ist nur schwer oder fast gar nicht zu photographieren. Es fehlt der erhöhte Standpunkt, hier würden eigentlich nur Luftbilder weiterhelfen, um die Broderien, die geometrischen Muster abzubilden. Künstlich erhöhte Standpunkte, wie etwa von Leitern aus, widersprechen mit Sicherheit der Konzeption des Gartenkünstlers. Beim Sizilianischen Garten gelingt, von der Maulbeerallee herab gesehen, die Photographie.

Das eigentliche Feld der Gartenphotographie sind die Landschaftsgärten. Das Vokabular der Natur- und Kulturlandschaften ist bekannt: Baum und Wald, Wiese, Gebüsch, Wasser, Ufer, Bach, Wasserfall und so fort. Das Wunder des künstlerischen Landschaftsgartens ist, daß diese Vokabeln zu einer neuen Sprache zusammengesetzt, komponiert, inszeniert werden, wie Michael Seiler sagt, zu einer Gartensprache mit, um beim Thema zu bleiben, einer neuen Grammatik. Die wichtigsten Elemente eines Gartens, schreibt Hans von Trotha, sind das Wasser und die Begrenzung des Gartens. Zum Wasser wurde oben schon einiges gesagt, eine erste, dankbar zu photographierende Begrenzung ist die Uferlinie, man denke nur an Rheinsberg, Babelsberg, Sacrow, Glienicke und, herausragend, die Pfaueninsel. Oft zitiertes Beispiel für eine Gartenbegrenzung ist die ehemalige Küchenmauer am Rande des Marlygartens, wenngleich zugewachsen und kaum photographierbar. Die Landschaftsgärten von Charlottenburg, Babelsberg oder der Pfaueninsel sind keine Natur- oder Kulturlandschaften, sondern Kunstlandschaften. Dagegen sind die malerischen Baumgruppen der »drunken forests« in Alaska zufällig aus dem Zusammenspiel der sie formenden Naturkräfte zustande gekommen, und wenn der Förster hierzulande eine Schneise durch den Wald schlagen läßt, dann ist das eben nur eine Schneise und keine Sichtachse. Beide, Baumgruppe und Schneise, können schön sein, aber nur der Garten ist um seiner Schönheit willen zustande gekommen, als Ausdruck der Schönheitsvorstellungen seiner Zeit.

Bäume und Blumen schließlich sind das Herzstück eines Gartens. Einheimische oder exotische Bäume stehen einzeln, in lockeren Gruppen oder dichter bis hin zu einem Wald wie auf der Pfaueninsel. Bäume sind, photographisch gesehen, ein schwieriges Feld. Von Ausnahmen abgesehen, bringen Solitäre keine guten Bilder, auch Wälder, genauer ihre Ränder, ergeben meist gar nichts, kaum auflösbare, oft zu dunkle Massen und nur selten befriedigende Bilder. Gruppen oder Reihen sind viel interessanter: etwa die Baumgruppen im Rehgarten von Sanssouci oder dem Potentestück und in Caputh, die eleganten Doppelreihen von Linden in Charlottenburg oder die tief gestaffelte Knobelsdorff-Allee in Rheinsberg. Blumen mit ihren vielfältigen Farben und Strukturen sind ebenfalls ein dankbares Bildobjekt. Leider gilt auch hier das bereits zu den Parterres Gesagte, daß meist der erforderliche erhöhte Standpunkt fehlt. Bei den hochstämmigen Rosen im Rosengarten der Pfaueninsel ist das kein Problem, schon gar nicht beim Rosengarten von Charlottenhof, der unterhalb des östlichen Endes der Pergola des Schlosses liegt. Das wunderbare Blumenmeer vor der Orangerie des Neuen Gartens ist derart reich und tief gegliedert, daß es aus Augenhöhe photographiert werden kann. Das wohl schönste Blumenensemble der Gärten ist das von Lenné geschaffene Rondell der Gotischen Fontäne im *pleasure ground* von Babelsberg. Die Umgebung bietet erhöhte Standpunkte, die Weinfestons heben das Ganze aus der Ebene heraus, besonders überzeugend in den Farben des Herbstes.

Zum Schluß noch ein Wort zur Praxis und zu einem spezifischen Problem der Photographie. Von der Großformatphotographie herkommend, die ohne Stativ nicht machbar ist, habe ich auch bei der digitalen Kleinbildphotographie stets ein Stativ benutzt, also fast genau wie der »Open-air-Maler« mit seiner Staffelei. Ein Stativ zwingt zur Ruhe, es bringt Ruhe ins Bild, nur am Stativ läßt sich der Bildausschnitt sorgfältig tarieren. Bei der eigentlichen Aufnahme denke ich mir jedes Bild horizontal und vertikal dreigeteilt, so daß es in jeder der beiden Richtungen einen zentralen und zwei randliche Bereiche gibt. In dieses Schema verteile ich die Bildgewichte und Strukturen, wobei die Trennungslinien zwischen den Bereichen so etwas wie die Kraftlinien des Bildes darstellen können. Dazu gehört auch die Berücksichtigung der Schnittlinien planarer oder der Schnittpunkte linearer Bildelemente. Neben diesen formalen Gesichtspunkten geht es mir inhaltlich immer um eine sachliche Photographie. Blutrote Sonnenuntergänge und wallende Morgennebel haben hier keinen Platz, womit nichts gegen ihre mögliche Schönheit gesagt sein soll. Ein spezifisches Problem der Photographie schließlich sehe ich darin, daß sich die körperliche Raumerfahrung der Wirklichkeit letzten Endes nicht einfangen läßt. Das beschreitende Erleben eines Weges mit seinen sich im Gehen verändernden Perspektiven ist, wie bereits gesagt, nicht abbildbar, aber eine wie immer geartete Objektivität oder Wiedergabe der Wirklichkeit ist auch gar nicht das Ziel der Photographie. Sie bringt und übersetzt die räumliche Vorstellung des Gartenkünstlers auf die photographische Bildebene. Photographie ist Interpretation und schafft damit eine eigene Realität.

this orientation must become evident photographically, both as viewed from the palace and towards the palace. The palace itself, as a building, plays no photographic role in this context.

An architectonic garden such as the Baroque *parterre* of Charlottenburg can be photographed only with difficulty or almost not at all. There is no raised vantage point; here only aerial shots would actually help to depict the *broderies*, the geometrical patterns. Artificially elevated vantage points, for instance, from ladders, definitely go against the garden artist's concept. In the case of the Sizilianischer Garten the photograph succeeds, viewed looking down from the Maulbeerallee.

The actual field of garden photography is landscape gardens. The vocabulary of natural and cultivated landscapes is well known: Tree and forest, meadow, shrubbery, water, shore, brook, waterfall and so on. The amazing thing about the artistic landscape garden is that this vocabulary is reassembled into a new language, composed, staged, as Michael Seiler says, to become a garden language with a new grammar, to continue the metaphor. The most important elements of a garden, writes Hans von Trotha, are water and the boundary of the garden. Water was discussed above to some extent; an initial boundary, worthwhile to photograph, is the shoreline or riverbank – just think of Rheinsberg, Babelsberg, Sacrow, Glienicke and especially Pfaueninsel. A frequently quoted example for a garden boundary is the former kitchen wall at the edge of the Marlygarten, although it has become overgrown and is hardly photographable. The landscape gardens of Charlottenburg, Babelsberg or Pfaueninsel are neither natural nor cultivated landscapes, but art landscapes. On the other hand, the picturesque clusters of trees of the »drunken forests« in Alaska came about by chance through the interaction of the natural forces that formed them, and if the local forester has a firebreak cut through the forest, that is simply a firebreak and not a visual axis. Both – the group of trees and the firebreak – may be beautiful, but only the garden was created for its beauty, as an expression of the concepts of beauty of its time.

Ultimately, trees and flowers are at the very heart of a garden. Native or exotic trees stand alone, in loose clusters or in denser woods, as they do on Pfaueninsel. From a photographer's point of view trees are a difficult area. With a few exceptions, solitaire trees do not make for good pictures; forests too, or, to be more precise, their edges, generally do not amount to anything, coming out as barely resolvable masses, often too dark – pictures that are rarely satisfactory. Groups or rows are much more interesting: for instance, the clusters of trees in the Rehgarten of Sanssouci or the Potente garden and in Caputh, the elegant double rows of linden trees in Charlottenburg or the deeply staggered Knobelsdorff-Allee in Rheinsberg. Flowers with their diverse colours and structures are also a rewarding photographic subject. Unfortunately the same arguments apply here as those above about the *parterres*: for the most part the required elevated vantage point is not there. This is not a problem when it comes to the tall-stemmed roses in the Pfaueninsel rose garden, and certainly not in the case of the rose garden of Charlottenhof situated below the eastern end of the castle's pergola. The wonderful sea of flowers in front of the orangery of Neuer Garten is so abundant and perfectly structured that it can be photographed from eye level. Probably the most beautiful flowerbed design in the gardens is the rondel of the Gotische Fontäne created by Lenné in the pleasure ground of Babelsberg. There are elevated vantage points in the area, and the festoons of vines make the entire design stand out against the level ground, an effect that is particularly convincing in the colours of autumn.

Finally, a few words on the practice and on a specific problem of photography. Coming from large-format photography, which is not feasible without a tripod, I have always used a tripod for digital small-format photography as well, in other words, almost exactly like the »open-air painter« with his easel. A tripod forces one to be still, it brings calm into the picture; only at the tripod is it possible to tare the detail of a photograph carefully. When I actually take a picture, I imagine every picture divided into three horizontally and vertically, so that in each of the two directions there are one central and two peripheral areas. I distribute the weight of image and structure in this scheme, and here the dividing lines between the areas can represent something like the lines of force of the picture. This also includes taking into consideration the lines of intersection of planar, or the points of intersection of linear, picture elements. In addition to these formal aspects what I am always after in terms of content is matter-of-fact photography. There is no room here for blood-red sunsets and swirling morning mists, by which I don't mean to imply that they may not be beautiful. Finally, I see one specific problem of photography in the fact that ultimately the real, physical experience of space cannot be captured. As I said above, it is impossible to depict the experience of a path one takes, where the perspectives change as one walks on it, but at the same time objectivity of whatever kind, or representation of reality, is not the goal of photography. It brings and translates the spatial conception of the garden artist into a photographic image. Photography is interpretation and thus creates a reality of its own.

Berliner Vorstadt
Babelsberg Nord
Tiefer See
Havel
Glienicker Lake
Lenné - Bucht
Theater
Schiffbauerg.
Glienicker Brücke
Schloss-garten
Königstr.
Park Glienicke
Jagdschloss Glienicke
Mövenstr.
Bildstöckl
Geysir
Liegewiese
Drive
Kleines Schloss
Rosen-treppe
Marstall
Erinnerungs-vasen-anhöhe
Gotische Fontäne
Bowlinggreen
Pleasure-ground
Schloss Babelsberg
Wilhelm-Wasserfall
Goldene Rosenlaube
Adler-brunnen
Moos-beet
Voltaire-terrasse
Michaels-denkmal
Maschinen-haus
Schloss-küche
Strandbad
Matrosen-haus
Schwarz-Weißer Weg
Gerichts-laube
Generals-eichen
Havelhaus
Bismarck-brücke
Flatowturm
Ehemaliger Chinesischer Blumengarten
Fürstenhöhe
Kindermannsee
Kutscherhaus
Nuthestr.
Sicht Jagdschloss Stern
Augustablick
Schwarzes Meer
Universität Potsdam
Park-brücke
Waldmüllerstr.
Lankestr.
Ehemalige Hofgärtnerei
Friedrich-Wilhelm-Höhe
Mühlenberg
Feldherrenbank Siegessäule
Achterbecken (Hochbehälter)
Ehemalige Schanze
Pförtnerhaus I
Victoriahöhe
Liege-wiese
Lange Sicht
Großer See
Luisenhöhe
Grüner Weg
Ehemaliges Pförtnerhaus III Mühlentor
Allee nach Glienicke
Karl-Marx-Str.
Wasserstr.
Fontänenplateau
Mühlenstr.
Wollestr.
Grenzstr.
Jutestr.
Östliches Aussichts-plateau
Pförtnerhaus II
Neue Str.
Alt Nowawes
Spindelstr.
Karl-Liebknecht-Str.
Hoher Weg
Donarstr.
An der Sternwarte
H. Maaß-S
-List-Str.
N
0 50 100 200m

Park Babelsberg

1. Ein Durchblick zum westlichen Erweiterungsteil des Schlosses mit dem schlanken Fahnenturm, nach dem Tode von Karl Friedrich Schinkel und Ludwig Persius von Johann Heinrich Strack und Martin Gottgetreu errichtet. Das Schloß wurde in den Jahren 1834–49 für den Prinzen Wilhelm gebaut, den späteren Kaiser Wilhelm I. Im Vordergrund der *pleasure ground* mit dem Blumenbeetweg.

Park Babelsberg

1. Vista of the western expanded section of the palace with the slender flag tower, erected after the death of Karl Friedrich Schinkel and Ludwig Persius by Johann Heinrich Strack and Martin Gottgetreu. The palace was built in 1834–49 for Prince William, later Emperor William I. In the foreground, the pleasure ground with flowerbed path.

Park Babelsberg

2. Ein Durchblick vom Blumenbeetweg zum Schloß Babelsberg, zum Oktogon. Links eine Scheinzypresse, rechts Eichen.
3. Ein Durchblick zum Schloß Babelsberg, zum westlichen Erweiterungsteil, Eichen und Fichten.

Park Babelsberg

2. Schloß Babelsberg, the octagon, seen from flowerbed path. A Lawson false cypress on the left, oaks on the right.
3. Vista of Schloß Babelsberg, of the western expanded section, oaks and spruces.

Park Babelsberg

4. Das Rund der Gotischen Fontäne im *pleasure ground* mit den Festons für Wilden Wein. Rechts zwischen Rund und Weg das sogenannte Füllhornbeet. Im Hintergrund Eichen.
5. Der Garten im Rund der Gotischen Fontäne. Die Beete in Lilien- und Kreisform wurden von Peter Joseph Lenné konzipiert.

Park Babelsberg

4. The circle of the Gotische Fontäne in the pleasure ground with festoons for wild vines. On the right, between the circle and path, the so-called Cornucopia Bed. Oaks in the background.
5. The garden in the circle of the Gotische Fontäne. The beds shaped like lilies and circles were designed by Peter Joseph Lenné.

Park Babelsberg

6. Der Goldene Rosengarten mit einer dreistämmigen Eiche. Über dem *pleasure ground* in der Ferne Turm und Schloß von Glienicke.
7. Ein Durchblick zum Schloß, links das Gestell des Goldenen Rosengartens, dem Herzstück des *pleasure ground*.

Park Babelsberg

6. The Goldene Rosengarten and an oak with three trunks. Above the pleasure ground in the distance, the tower and palace of Glienicke.
7. Vista of the castle, on the left the trellis of the Goldene Rosengarten, the centerpiece of the pleasure ground.

Park Babelsberg

8. Ein Durchblick zur Küche von Schloß Babelsberg. Rechts, etwas verdeckt, die Dornröschenpforte. Die Küche wurde 1859/60 von Martin Gottgetreu gebaut, sie ist mit dem Schloß durch einen unterirdischen Gang verbunden.
9. Das Rund der Gotischen Fontäne mit den Weinfestons im *pleasure ground*, rechts das Schloß.

Park Babelsberg

8. Vista of the kitchen of Schloß Babelsberg. On the right, somewhat obscured, the Dornröschenpforte (Sleeping-Beauty Gate). The kitchen was built in 1859/1860 by Martin Gottgetreu and is connected with the palace by a subterranean passage.
9. The circle of the Gotische Fontäne with wild-vine festoons in the pleasure ground, with the palace on the right.

Park Babelsberg

10. Die Blutbuche im *bowling green*, links dahinter die Glienicker Lake und die Glienicker Brücke sowie rechts der Turm von Schloß Glienicke.
11. Links die Blutbuche im *bowling green*, rechts die nachgepflanzte Pückler-Pappel, vom Schloß aus gesehen. Im Hintergrund die Glienicker Lake und die Glienicker Brücke. Rechts die eingerüstete Große Neugierde von Schloß Glienicke. Dahinter, oberhalb der Brücke, der Jungfernsee und der Schloßpark Sacrow.

Park Babelsberg

10. The copper beech in the bowling green, on the left behind it Glienicker Lake and Glienicker Brücke, on the right, the tower of Schloß Glienicke.
11. On the left, the copper beech in the bowling green, on the right the replanted Pückler Poplar, seen from the palace. In the background, Glienicker Lake and Glienicker Brücke. On the right, surrounded by scaffolding, the Große Neugierde (Great Curiosity) of Schloß Glienicke. Behind it, above the bridge, Jungfernsee and Schloßpark Sacrow.

Park Babelsberg

12. Die Bodenbewegung an der Kanonenberg-Serpentine oberhalb des Uferwegs, die Schatten zeichnen das Bodenrelief nach. Diese durch die ehemaligen Grenzbefestigungen zerstörte Bodenmodellierung konnte rekonstruiert werden. Dahinter die Babelsberger Enge der Havel und die Häuser am Glienicker Horn.
13. Das Bildstöckl unter drei Linden, eine Betsäule, 1849 von Martin Gottgetreu errichtet, Geschenk des Großherzogs Leopold von Baden an den Prinzen Wilhelm als Erinnerung an dessen Sieg im Badischen Aufstand. Dahinter die Havel und das Potsdamer Ufer.

Park Babelsberg

12. The ground movement at the Kanonenberg-Serpentine above the riverside path, the shadows trace the topography. It was possible to reconstruct the modelling of the terrain that had been destroyed by former border fortifications. Behind it, the Babelsberger Enge (Babelsberg Narrows) of the Havel River and houses by the Glienicker Horn.
13. The Bildstöckl, a wayside shrine under three linden trees, erected in 1849 by Martin Gottgetreu, a gift of Grand Duke Leopold of Baden to Prince William in memory of the latter's victory in the Rebellion of Baden. Behind it, the Havel River and the Potsdam riverbank.

Park Babelsberg

14. Der maximal 42 m hohe Geysir an der Lennébucht und die Glienicker Lake. Links am gegenüberliegenden Ufer oben der Schloßpark Glienicke und unten der Park des Jagdschlosses Glienicke. Die Stämme rechts sind Spitzahorne.
15. Der von Hermann von Pückler angelegte gekrümmte Weg. Links hinter der Glienicker Lake die Glienicker Brücke, rechts die Große Neugierde und Schloß Glienicke. Der gekrümmte Weg schmiegt sich an die Uferlinie der Glienicker Lake an und kommt ganz im Hintergrund mit der Uferlinie zur Deckung.

Park Babelsberg

14. The geyser, with a maximum height of 42 m, near Lennébucht and Glienicker Lake. On the left, on the opposite bank above, Schloßpark Glienicke and below, the park of the Jagdschloß Glienicke (Glienicke Hunting Lodge). The trunks on the right are Norway maples.
15. The curving path laid out by Hermann von Pückler. On the left, behind Glienicker Lake is the Glienicker Brücke, while on the right is the Große Neugierde (Great Curiosity) and Schloß Glienicke. The curving path hugs the shoreline of Glienicker Lake and, all the way in the background, is flush with the shoreline.

Park Babelsberg

16. Ein Blick von der Fürstenhöhe zum *pleasure ground* hinab, der Adlerbrunnen ist eingehaust. Über der von den Bäumen weitgehend verdeckten Glienicker Brücke der Jungfernsee, darunter die Glienicker Lake.
17. Das Rund der Gotischen Fontäne im *pleasure ground* mit den Weinfestons, dahinter Eichenwald, vorn der verschneite »Fruchtkorb«.

Park Babelsberg

16. A view from Fürstenhöhe down to the pleasure ground, the Adlerbrunnen (Eagle Fountain) has been covered over. Jungfernsee is visible above the Glienicker Brücke, which is largely concealed by the trees, below it is Glienicker Lake.
17. The circle of the Gotische Fontäne in the pleasure ground with the festoons of Virginia creeper, behind them the oak forest, in front, the snow-covered »Fruchtkorb« (Fruit Basket).

Park Babelsberg

18. Die an die Siege der preußischen Kriege 1863/64, 1865, 1866 und 1871 erinnernde Siegessäule. Die Granitsäule wurde von Johann Heinrich Strack entworfen, sie stammt von dem Markgrafenstein in den Rauener Bergen. Die Siegesgöttin und das Kapitell wurden von Christian Daniel Rauch modelliert. Die Säule steht auf der höchsten Erhebung des Parks, auf der Victoriahöhe (77,4 m) am Lennéschen Umfahrweg.
19. Die Sicht vom Flatowturm zum Jagdschloß Stern in umgekehrter, westlicher Richtung zum Turm hin gesehen. Der Flatowturm wurde 1853–56 nach Plänen von Johann Heinrich Strack gebaut, er wurde aus Mitteln des westpreußischen Kronguts Flatow finanziert.

Park Babelsberg

18. The Victory Column, memorializing the victories of the Prussian wars in 1863/64, 1865, 1866 and 1871. The granite column was designed by Johann Heinrich Strack, and comes from Markgrafenstein in the Rauen Mountains. The Goddess of Victory and the capital were sculpted by Christian Daniel Rauch. The column stands at the highest point of the park, on Victoriahöhe (77,4 m) by the Lenné drive.
19. Vista from Flatowturm to Jagdschloß Stern (Stern Hunting Lodge) seen in the reverse, western direction facing the tower. The Flatowturm was built 1853–56 according to plans by Johann Heinrich Strack, and was financed by funds received from the West Prussian crown estate of Flatow.

Park Babelsberg

20. Die Lange Sicht im Südosten des Parks, in Richtung Südwesten gesehen.
21. Die Lange Sicht in Richtung Nordosten gesehen.

Park Babelsberg

20. The Lange Sicht (Long Perspective) in the southeast part of the park, seen facing southwest.
21. The Lange Sicht, seen facing northeast.

Templiner See
Schiffsanlegestelle
Schloss Caputh
Kavalierhaus
Logierhaus
ehem. Wirtschaftshof
Lindenstr.
Potsdam
Str. der Einheit
Ortszentrum
Seestr.
Kirche
Michendorfer Chaussee

Schloßgarten Caputh

1. Ein Durchblick zur Gartenseite des Schlosses mit der doppelten Freitreppe. Das Schloß wurde 1662 im Auftrag des Großen Kurfürsten Friedrich Wilhelm gebaut, er schenkte es 1671 seiner zweiten Gemahlin Dorothea von Brandenburg.

Schloßgarten Caputh

1. Vista of garden façade of the palace with its double flight of stairs. The palace was built in 1662, commissioned by the Great Elector Frederick William, in 1671, he presented it to his second wife Dorothea of Brandenburg.

Schloßgarten Caputh

2. Die Sicht vom Templiner See nach Süden zur Gartenseite des Schlosses. Rechts stehen Eichen, links Platanen.
3. Der nördliche Garten und der Templiner See mit dem gegenüberliegenden Ufer der Pirschheide, ganz im Vordergrund der Schatten des Schlosses. Der beherrschende Baum ist eine Platane.

Schloßgarten Caputh

2. Vista from Templiner See looking south toward the garden façade of the palace. On the right are oaks, with plane trees on the left.
3. North part of garden and Templiner See with Pirschheide on the opposite bank, in the immediate foreground, the shadow of the palace. The dominant tree is a plane tree.

Schloßgarten Caputh

4. Das westliche Waldstück mit Spitzahorn, von der Freitreppe des Schlosses aus aufgenommen.
5. Der östliche Park mit Platanen am Kavalierhaus, um 1820 unter General August von Thümen erbaut, dem damaligen Gutsherrn.

Schloßgarten Caputh

4. Western woodland with Norway maple, photographed from the stairs in front of the palace.
5. East part of the park with plane trees by the Kavalierhaus, built ca. 1820 under General August von Thümen, the lord of the manor at the time.

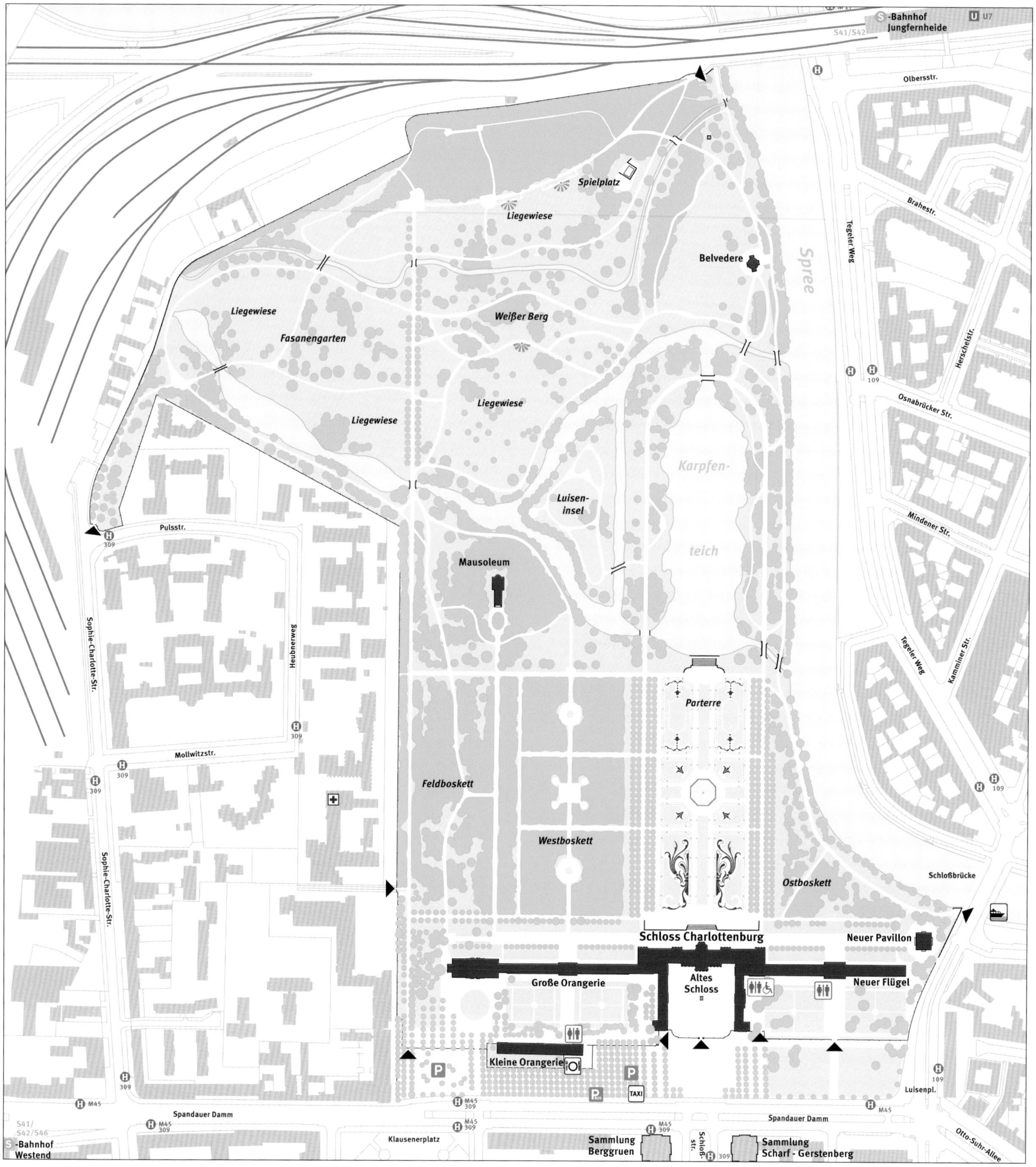
S-Bahnhof Jungfernheide
U7
S41/S42
Olbersstr.
Brahestr.
Tegeler Weg
Spree
Herschelstr.
Osnabrücker Str.
Mindener Str.
Tegeler Weg
Kamminer Str.
Spielplatz
Liegewiese
Belvedere
Liegewiese
Fasanengarten
Weißer Berg
Liegewiese
Liegewiese
Karpfen-teich
Luisen-insel
Mausoleum
Pulsstr.
Sophie-Charlotte-Str.
Heubnerweg
Mollwitzstr.
Parterre
Feldboskett
Westboskett
Ostboskett
Schloßbrücke
Schloss Charlottenburg
Neuer Pavillon
Große Orangerie
Altes Schloss
Neuer Flügel
Kleine Orangerie
TAXI
Luisenpl.
Spandauer Damm
Spandauer Damm
S41/S42/S46
S-Bahnhof Westend
Klausenerplatz
Sammlung Berggruen
Schloßstr.
Sammlung Scharf - Gerstenberg
Otto-Suhr-Allee
309
109
M45

Schloßgarten Charlottenburg

1. Das Broderieparterre und das Schloß. Das Beet wird von den schmalen Streifen einer Busbaumhecke gesäumt, die dunklen Kegel sind Eiben. Im Hintergrund links die östliche Doppelallee mit Linden. Mit dem Bau des Schlosses wurde 1696 begonnen, Auftraggeberin war Sophie Charlotte von Hannover, Königin in Preußen, die Gemahlin Friedrichs III. (I.).

Schloßgarten Charlottenburg

1. The *parterre de broderie* and the palace. The bed is bordered by narrow strips of a box hedge, the dark cones are yews. In the background left, the eastern double avenue with linden trees. Construction of the palace was begun in 1696, and was commissioned by Sophia Charlotte of Hanover, queen in Prussia, the wife of Frederick III (I).

Schloßgarten Charlottenburg

2. Die westliche Hauptachse nach Süden zur Großen Orangerie hin gesehen. Im Hintergrund das Athena-Rondell, seitlich Hainbuchenboskette. Der Betonweg im Vordergrund ist ein erster Betonguß zu Beginn des 19. Jahrhunderts.
3. Im Rondell der westlichen Hauptachse mit den Hainbuchenbosketten steht *Athena* (*Minerva*), eine 1991 hergestellte Aluminium-Kopie der Statue aus dem Oranienburger Schloß, einer Arbeit von Bartholomeus Eggers (1682).

Schloßgarten Charlottenburg

2. The western main axis seen as one faces south toward the Große Orangerie. In the background, the Athena-Rondell, with hornbeam *bosquets* on the sides. The concrete path in the foreground is one of the first concrete paths poured at the beginning of the 19th century.
3. *Athena* (*Minerva*), an aluminium copy of the statue from the Oranienburg palace made in 1991 after a work by Bartholomeus Eggers (1682). It stands in the circular flowerbed of the western main axis near the hornbeam bosquets.

Schloßgarten Charlottenburg

4. Der große nördliche Querweg. Blick nach Norden auf den Uferwald der Luiseninsel mit Erlen, in der Bildmitte Pappeln.
5. Ein Blick vom großen nördlichen Querweg nach Süden in die westliche Zeile der westlichen doppelten Lindenallee. Rechts und links Hainbuchenboskette.

Schloßgarten Charlottenburg

4. The large north diagonal path. View looking north at the woods on the shoreline of Luiseninsel with alder trees. Poplars in centre of photograph.
5. View from the large north diagonal path looking south into the western row of the western double linden avenue. Hornbeam *bosquets* on the right and left.

Schloßgarten Charlottenburg

6. Karpfenteich und Belvedere. Die Bögen der roten, eisernen Brücke berühren sich in der Mitte. Die beiden an Porzellan erinnernden Putti von 1984 sind aus Aluminium, sie gehen auf Modelle der Porzellanfabrik Wedely zurück, 1751 gegründet, dem Vorläufer der Königlichen Porzellanmanufaktur Berlin.
7. Das Belvedere im nördlichen Landschaftsgarten englischen Stils, 1788 von Carl Gotthard Langhans für Friedrich Wilhelm II. erbaut.

Schloßgarten Charlottenburg

6. Carp pond and Belvedere. The arches of the red iron bridge touch in the middle. The two putti, made in 1984, reminiscent of porcelain, are actually made of aluminium, they go back to models by the Wedely porcelain factory, founded in 1751, the precursor of the Königliche Porzellanmanufaktur Berlin.
7. Belvedere in the north part of the English-style landscape garden, built in 1788 by Carl Gotthard Langhans for Frederick William II.

Schloßgarten Charlottenburg

8. Die eiserne Balustrade markiert die Grenze zwischen dem südlichen Broderieparterre und dem nördlichen Landschaftsgarten mit dem Karpfenteich. Die Krönungsvase wurde erst nach dem 2. Weltkrieg aufgestellt, sie bezieht sich auf die Krönung des Kurfürsten Friedrich III. zum König Friedrich I. in Preußen, 1701 in Königsberg.
9. Die Balustrade aus Gußeisen soll die Trennung markieren zwischen dem französischen Broderiegarten im Süden und dem englischen Landschaftsgarten im Norden. Die Szene wird beherrscht von einer großen doppelten Platane.

Schloßgarten Charlottenburg

8. The iron balustrade marks the boundary between the south part of the *parterre de broderie* and the north part of the landscape garden with the carp pond. The Coronation Vase was not installed until after World War II, and refers to the coronation of Elector Frederick III as Frederick I King in Prussia, which took place in 1701 in Königsberg.
9. The cast-iron balustrade is intended to mark the separation between the French *broderie* garden in the south and the English landscape garden in the north. Dominating the scene is a tall double plane tree.

Schloßgarten Charlottenburg

10. Der von Wald umgebene Karpfenteich im nördlichen Landschaftsgarten.
11. Das Parterre des französischen architektonischen Gartens mit seinen abgezirkelten Beeten, rechts und links von doppelten Lindenalleen begleitet. Die Sommerbepflanzung steht in voller Blüte. Der Kegel links ist eine Eibe, rechts davon eine hohe Passionsblume. Die Beete werden von Buchs gesäumt.

Schloßgarten Charlottenburg

10. The carp pond, surrounded by woods, in the north part of the landscape garden.
11. The *parterre* of the French architectonic garden with its sharply delineated beds, double linden avenues on the right and left. The summer planting is in full bloom. The cone on the left is a yew, while to the right of it is a tall passionflower. The beds are bordered by boxwood.

Schloßgarten Charlottenburg

12, 13. Das Broderieparterre wird im Westen und Osten von einer doppelten Lindenallee begleitet. Dies ist die östliche Zeile der westlichen Doppelallee, nach Norden gesehen. Die Linden sind im so genannten Herzschnitt geschnitten und sollen umgekehrten Herzen entsprechen, unten gerundet und oben spitz.

Schloßgarten Charlottenburg

12, 13. The *parterre de broderie* is bordered in the west and east by a double linden avenue. This is the eastern row of the western double avenue, viewed facing north. The linden trees have been trimmed in the shape of an upside-down heart, rounded below and pointed on top.

Schloßgarten Charlottenburg

14. Die Beete des Broderieparterres, dahinter die begleitende Lindenallee mit dem Herzschnitt. Die Krönungsvase erinnert an die Krönung des ersten preußischen Königs, Friedrich, 1701 in Königsberg. Im Beet Wechsel von Eiben, den Kegeln, und Passionsblumen.
15. Die nach Osten zum Neuen Pavillon führende südliche Querachse. Die hohen Bäume sind Linden, darunter Hainbuchen, die Kugelbäume der vorderen Reihe in den eckigen Kübeln sind Lorbeerbäume, im Wechsel mit Schmucklilien und Pelargonien in den runden Kübeln.

Schloßgarten Charlottenburg

14. The beds of the *parterre de broderie*, and behind them the avenue of linden trees trimmed in the shape of a heart. The Coronation Vase is in memory of the coronation of the first Prussian king, Frederick, in 1701 in Königsberg. In the bed, cone-shaped yews alternate with passionflowers.
15. The southern transverse axis leading east to the Neuer Pavillon. The tall trees are lindens, interspersed with hornbeams, the globe-shaped trees in the front row in rectangular tubs are laurel trees, alternating with African lilies and geraniums in the round tubs.

Schloßgarten Charlottenburg

16. Die Fichtenallee im Westen des Schloßgartens zum Mausoleum der Königin Luise von Preußen hin gesehen.
17. Das Rundbeet mit Rosen »Madame Boll« und der viersäulige Portikus des Mausoleums für Königin Luise von Preußen, 1810, von Heinrich Gentz und Karl Friedrich Schinkel. Der Vorläufer aus Sandstein wurde 1828 auf die Pfaueninsel versetzt.

Schloßgarten Charlottenburg

16. The spruce avenue in the west of the palace garden seen facing the mausoleum of Queen Louisa of Prussia.
17. The round bed with »Madame Boll« roses, and the four-column portico of the mausoleum for Queen Louisa of Prussia, 1810, by Heinrich Gentz and Karl Friedrich Schinkel. Its sandstone predecessor was moved to the Pfaueninsel in 1828.

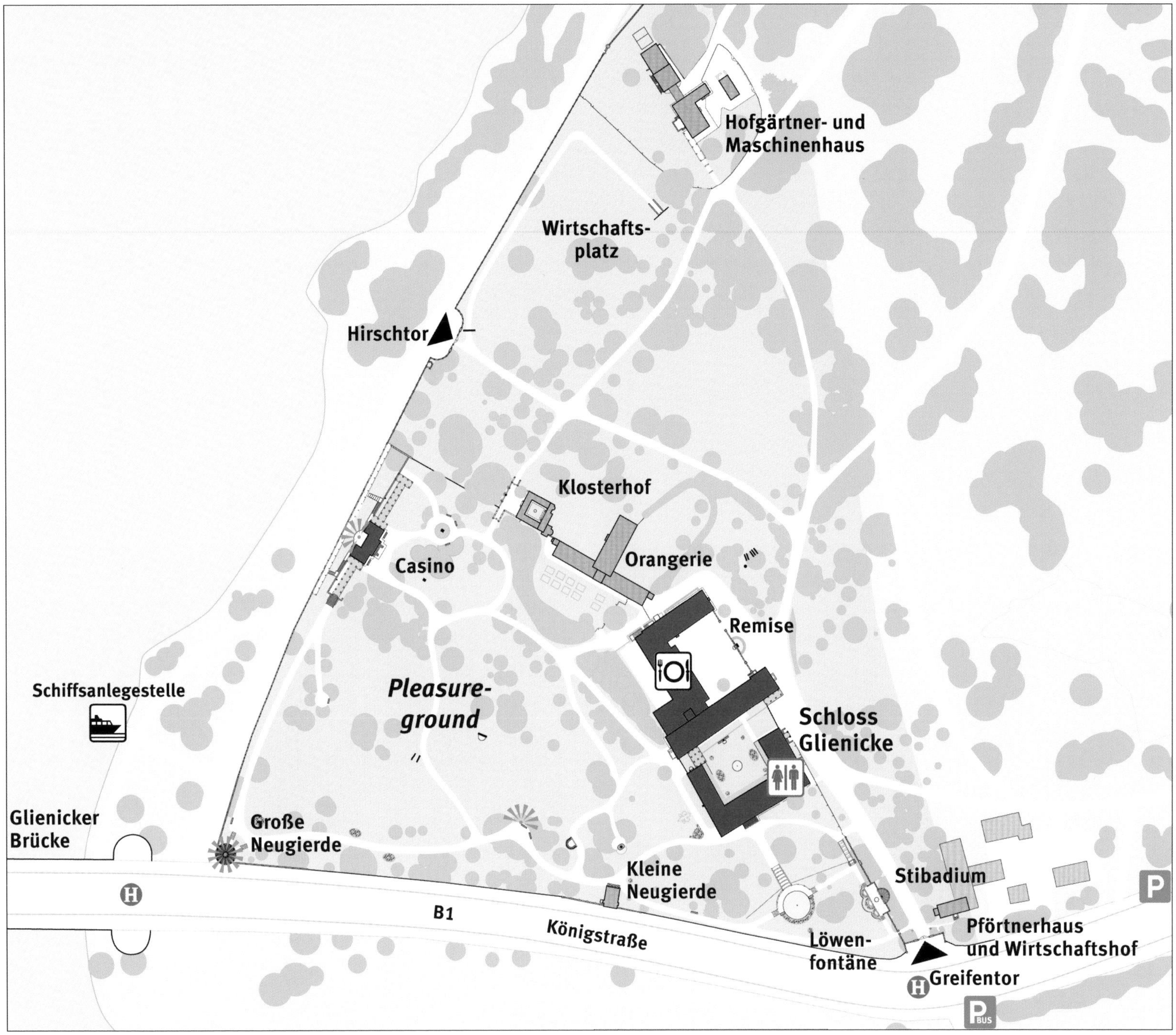
Hofgärtner- und Maschinenhaus
Wirtschafts-platz
Hirschtor
Klosterhof
Casino
Orangerie
Remise
Schiffsanlegestelle
Pleasure-ground
Schloss Glienicke
Glienicker Brücke
Große Neugierde
Kleine Neugierde
Stibadium
B1
Königstraße
Löwen-fontäne
Pförtnerhaus und Wirtschaftshof
Greifentor

Park Glienicke

1. Die Löwenfontäne, ein gemeinschaftliches Werk von Karl Friedrich Schinkel, Ludwig Persius und Peter Joseph Lenné, dahinter das Schloß. Das Schloß wurde von 1825 an von Schinkel für den Prinzen Carl von Preußen umgebaut. Als dieses Photo im Januar 2009 aufgenommen wurde, befand sich der zweite Löwe, durch einen umgestürzten Baum beschädigt, in der Werkstatt.

Park Glienicke

1. The Löwenfontäne, the joint work of Karl Friedrich Schinkel, Ludwig Persius and Peter Joseph Lenné, behind it, the palace. The palace was remodelled by Schinkel beginning in 1825 for Prince Charles of Prussia. When this photo was taken in January 2009, the second lion, which had been damaged by a falling tree, was in the workshop for repairs.

Park Glienicke

2. Das von Ludwig Persius 1840 entworfene Stibadium, eine halbrunde, überdachte Ruhebank nach antikem Vorbild. Von hier aus sollte man einen schönen Blick auf Potsdam haben, was heute wegen der Vegetation nur noch eingeschränkt möglich ist.
3. Der Weg über den Lennéhügel und der Blick auf das Casino und die südwestliche Pergola. Das Casino wurde 1824/25 von Karl Friedrich Schinkel aus einem Vorgängerbau umgebaut.

Park Glienicke

2. The stibadium, designed by Ludwig Persius in 1840, a semicircular, roofed-over seat based on a classical model. There was supposed to be a lovely view of Potsdam from here, something that is possible only to a limited degree today because of the vegetation.
3. Path over the Lennéhügel and view of the Casino and the southwest pergola. The Casino was remodelled in 1824/25 by Karl Friedrich Schinkel from a previous building.

Park Glienicke

4. Ein Blick vom Lennéhügel über den *pleasure ground* zur südwestlichen Pergola des Casinos und die Havel. Im Vordergrund Gartenbänke von Karl Friedrich Schinkel, links die große Platane, rechts eine Gruppe von Linden.
5. Der *pleasure ground*, rechts im Mittelgrund der Froschbrunnen von Friedrich August Stüler, links hinten Spolien des Poseidontempels auf Kap Sunion, Griechenland. Im Hintergrund die Havel.

Park Glienicke

4. View of the southwest pergola of the Casino and the Havel River across the pleasure ground from Lennéhügel. In the foreground, garden benches by Karl Friedrich Schinkel, on the left, the large plane tree, with a group of linden trees on the right.
5. The pleasure ground, on the right in the middle distance the Froschbrunnen (Frog Fountain) by Friedrich August Stüler, to the left in the back, spolia of the Poseidon Temple on Cape Sounion, Greece. In the background, the Havel River.

Park Glienicke

6. Ein Blick über den *pleasure ground* zur Pergola des Casinos und der Havel. Vorne der Lennéhügel mit dem Glockenbrunnen, rechts hinter der Wiese der Froschbrunnen von Friedrich August Stüler.
7. Die Spolien des Poseidontempels auf Kap Sunion. Dahinter die südwestliche Pergola des Casinos von Karl Friedrich Schinkel und die Havel.

Park Glienicke

6. View across the pleasure ground of the pergola of the Casino and the Havel River. In the foreground, Lennéhügel with the Glockenbrunnen (Bell Fountain), to the right in back of the meadow, the Frog Fountain by Friedrich August Stüler.
7. The spolia of the Poseidon Temple on Cape Sounion. Behind them the southwest pergola of the Casino by Karl Friedrich Schinkel and the Havel River.

Park Glienicke

8. Ein Blick durch den *pleasure ground* zur Havel. Rechts der Laitièrenbrunnen, mit der bronzenen Milchmädchenfigur von Pawel Petrovitch Sokolow. Das Original stammt von 1816, diese Kopie von 1989. Links ein Zierbeet mit Palmettenterrakotten.
9. Der Klosterhof, 1850 aus den Bauteilen eines abgerissenen Klosters bei Venedig von Ferdinand von Arnim errichtet. Auftraggeber war Prinz Carl von Preußen. Der Klosterhof diente im wesentlichen als Museum, besonders für venezianische Kunst.

Park Glienicke

8. View of the Havel River through the pleasure ground. On the right, the Laitièrenbrunnen (Laitièren Fountain), with the bronze figure of a milkmaid by Pavel Petrovich Sokolov. The original dates back to 1816, this copy is dated 1989. On the left, an ornamental bed with palmette terracottas.
9. The Klosterhof (Cloisters), rebuilt in 1850 by Ferdinand von Arnim from the building parts of a demolished monastery near Venice. It was commissioned by Prince Charles of Prussia. The Klosterhof was basically used as a museum, especially for Venetian art.

Park Glienicke

10. Das Lindenoktogon aus der barocken Gartenanlage vor der gärtnerischen Umgestaltung durch Peter Joseph Lenné.
11. Der *Betende Knabe*, ein Bronzenachguß der von Friedrich II. erworbenen Skulptur, die vor der Bibliothek des Schlosses Sanssouci aufgestellt ist. Im Hintergrund die Große Neugierde, eine 1835 von Karl Friedrich Schinkel errichtete Rotunde.

Park Glienicke

10. The Lindenoktogon (Linden Tree Octagon) from the Baroque garden before they were redesigned by Peter Joseph Lenné.
11. The *Betende Knabe* (*Praying Boy*), a bronze casting of the sculpture purchased by Frederick II that stands in front of the library of Schloß Sanssouci. In the background, the Große Neugierde, a rotunda built by Karl Friedrich Schinkel in 1835.

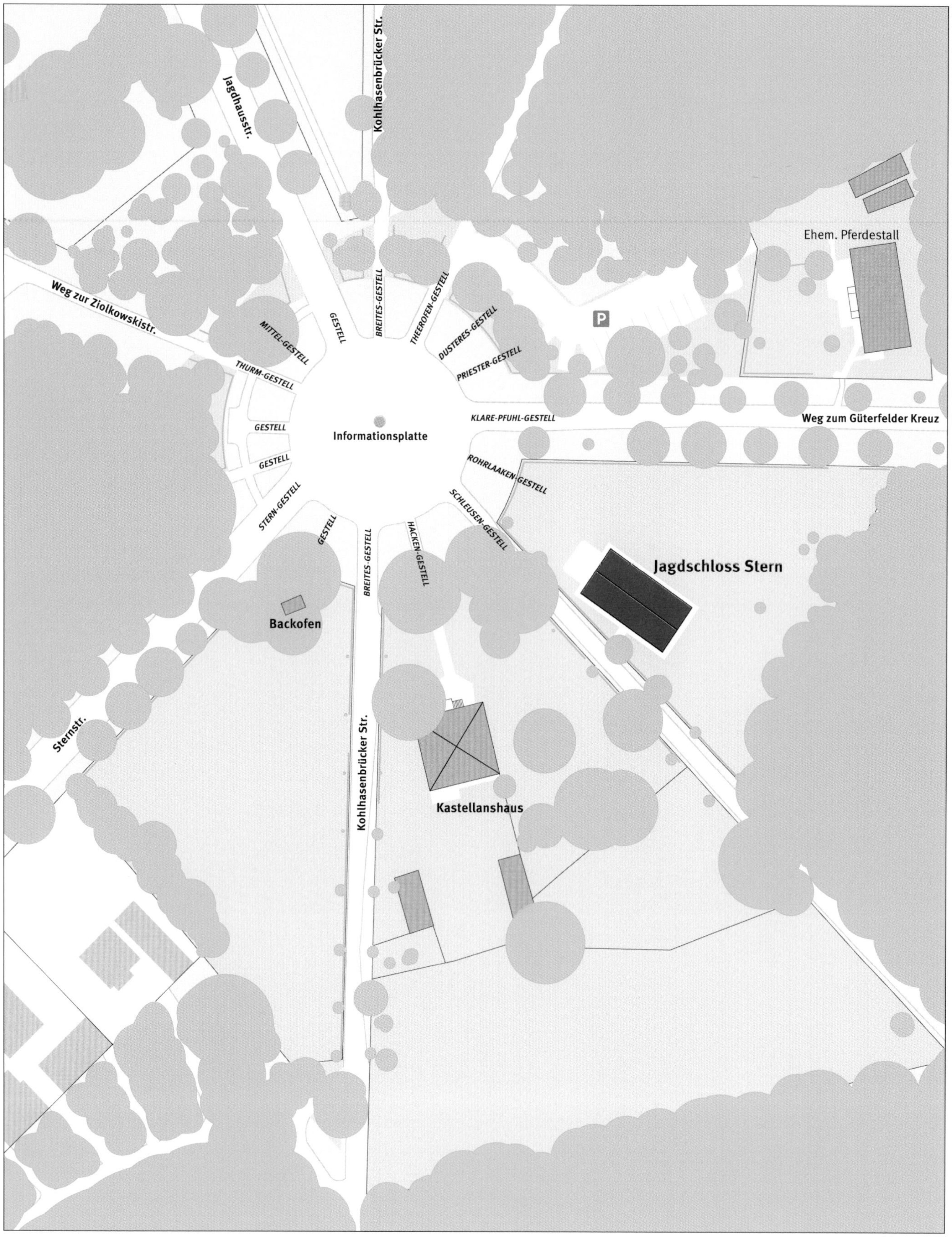

Jagdhausstr.
Kohlhasenbrücker Str.
Ehem. Pferdestall
Weg zur Ziolkowskistr.
MITTEL-GESTELL
GESTELL
BREITES-GESTELL
THEEROFEN-GESTELL
DUSTERES-GESTELL
PRIESTER-GESTELL
THURM-GESTELL
P
GESTELL
Informationsplatte
KLARE-PFUHL-GESTELL
Weg zum Güterfelder Kreuz
GESTELL
ROHRLAAKEN-GESTELL
STERN-GESTELL
SCHLEUSEN-GESTELL
GESTELL
BREITES-GESTELL
HACKEN-GESTELL
Jagdschloss Stern
Backofen
Sternstr.
Kohlhasenbrücker Str.
Kastellanshaus

Jagdschloß Stern

1. Das Jagdschloß liegt fast unmittelbar neben dem Autobahnanschluß Potsdam-Babelsberg. Die Schneise rechts ist das sogenannte Schleusengestell.

Jagdschloß Stern

1. The hunting lodge is situated almost directly next to the Potsdam-Babelsberg interchange. The lane on the right is the so-called Schleusengestell.

Jagdschloß Stern

2. Das Schloß wurde 1730–32 unter Friedrich Wilhelm I. im Stil eines holländischen Bürgerhauses gebaut, es liegt am Schnittpunkt von 16 Schneisen, den sogenannten Gestellen, die zur Parforcejagd benutzt wurden, zur Hetzjagd. Links vom Schloß das Klare-Pfuhl-Gestell, rechts das Schleusengestell.
3. Diese radialstrahlige Platte ist in der Mitte des zentralen Platzes eingelassen, im Schnittpunkt der 16 Schneisen, den Gestellen, und gibt die Namen von 13 Gestellen wieder.

Jagdschloß Stern

2. The lodge was built in 1730–32 under Frederick William I in the style of a Dutch town house, and is located at the point of intersection of 16 lanes, the so-called *Gestelle*, which were used for coursing, a type of hunt. On the left of the lodge is the Klare-Pfuhl-Gestell, on the right the Schleusengestell.
3. This plaque, showing radiating rays, is embedded in the middle of the central square, at the point of intersection of the 16 lanes – the *Gestelle* – and lists the names of 13 of them.

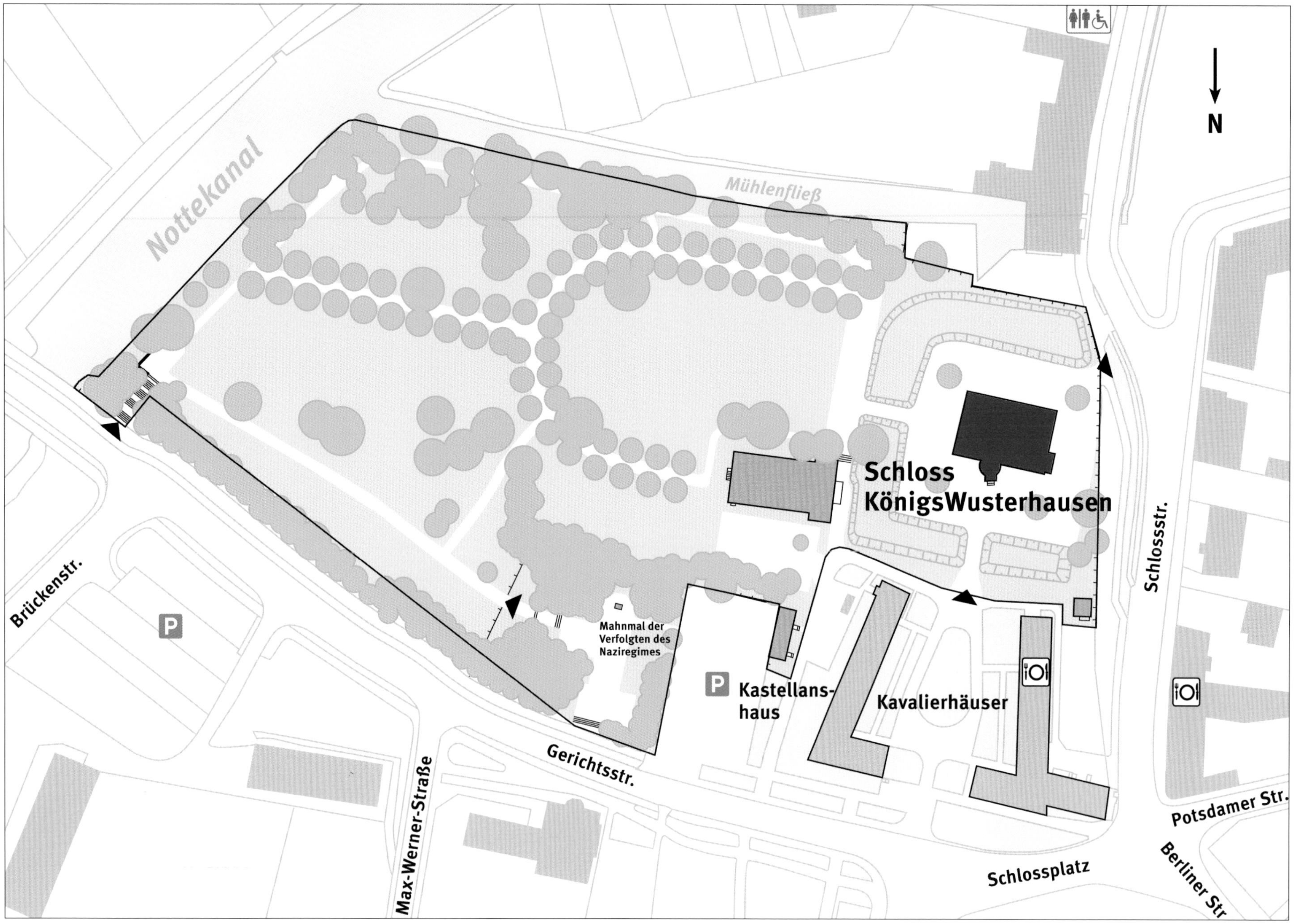
N
Nottekanal
Mühlenfließ
Schloss
KönigsWusterhausen
Schlossstr.
Brückenstr.
Mahnmal der
Verfolgten des
Naziregimes
P
Kastellans-
haus
Kavalierhäuser
Gerichtsstr.
Max-Werner-Straße
Potsdamer Str.
Berliner Str
Schlossplatz

Schloßgarten Königs Wusterhausen

1. Ein Blick vom Rondell nach Westen auf das Schloß und die Eichen. Der Große Kurfürst erwarb das Schloß 1682 für seinen Sohn Friedrich I., der es bereits 1698 dem damals zehnjährigen Friedrich Wilhelm (I.) schenkte, dem späteren Soldatenkönig.

Schloßgarten Königs Wusterhausen

1. View of the palace and the oaks from the rondel facing west. The Great Elector acquired the palace in 1682 for his son Frederick I, who gave it, as early as 1698, to the then 10-year-old Frederick William (I), later known as the Soldier-King.

Schloßgarten Königs Wusterhausen

2. Ein Blick von der Ostseite des Schlosses nach Osten in das Halbrondell.
3. Die Birken am Mühlenfließ, dem südlichen Rand des kleinen Gartens.

Schloßgarten Königs Wusterhausen

2. View from the east side of the palace looking east into the semi-rondel.
3. Birches by the Mühlenfließ, the south edge of the little garden.

Jungfernsee
Meierei
Eremitage
Borkenküche
Grotte
Schloss Cecilienhof
Liege-
wiese
Grünes Haus
Pfingstberg
Belvedere
Villa
Henckel
Gärtner-
haus
Pomona-
tempel
Villa
Lepsius
Villa
Quandt
Jüdischer
Friedhof
Kapellen-
berg
Kapelle
Alexander Newski
Ehem.
Landhaus
Gedenkstätte
KGB-Gefängnis
Pfingstkirche
Graues
Haus
Rotes
Haus
Schwanen-
brücke
Ehem. Maurischer
Tempel
Themistokles
Pyramide
Schindel-
haus
Marmorpalais
Gärtnerei
Orangerie
Küche
Weißes
Haus
Chin.
Parasol
Holländisches
Etablissement
Heiliger See
Russische
Kolonie
Alexandrowka
Braunes Haus
Treffpunkt
Freizeit
Gotische
Bibliothek
Palais
Lichtenau
Nauener Vorstadt
Berliner Vorstadt
Tiefer See
Am Pfingstberg
Höhenstr.
Große Weinmeisterstr.
Am Neuen Garten
Langhansstr.
Leistikowstr.
Esplanade
Nedlitzer Str.
Glumestr.
Persiusstr.
Beyerstr.
Am Schragen
Puschkinallee
Alleestr.
Jägerallee
Eisenhardtstr.
Hebbelstr.
Friedrich-Ebert-Str.
Helene- Lange- Str.
B.- Suttner- Str.
Behlertstr.
Tizianstr.
Böcklinstr.
Seestr.
Ludwig- Richter- Str.
Rubensstr.
Mangerstr.
Helmholtzstr.
Berliner Str.
Otto- Nagel- Str.

Neuer Garten

1. Das Marmorpalais vom Garten aus gesehen. Das Schloß wurde 1787–91 unter Friedrich Wilhelm II. von den Architekten Carl von Gontard und Carl Gotthard Langhans erbaut.

Neuer Garten

1. The Marmorpalais seen from the garden. The palace was built in 1787–91 under Frederick William II by the architects Carl von Gontard and Carl Gotthard Langhans.

Neuer Garten

2. Die Gotische Bibliothek, 1792–94 von Carl Gotthard Langhans erbaut, das Marmorpalais und das Grüne Haus, alle drei am westlichen Ufer der Heiligen Sees gelegen, nach Norden gesehen.
3. Ein Uferstück am Heiligen See, nach Süden gesehen, links die Kuppel der Nikolaikirche in Potsdam, von Karl Friedrich Schinkel, Ludwig Persius und Friedrich August Stüler, 1850 eingeweiht.

Neuer Garten

2. The Gotische Bibliothek (Gothic Library), built in 1792 to 1794 by Carl Gotthard Langhans, the Marmorpalais and the Green House, all three of them located on the western shore of Heiliger See, looking north.
3. A piece of the shore of Heiliger See, looking south, on the left, the dome of the Nikolaikirche in Potsdam, by Karl Friedrich Schinkel, Ludwig Persius and Friedrich August Stüler, consecrated in 1850.

Neuer Garten

4. Drei Platanen am Heiligen See auf der Höhe des Holländischen Etablissements, nach Süden gesehen.
5. Der Heilige See nördlich des Marmorpalais, dahinter der Jungfernsee. Die hintereinandergestaffelten, scheinbar übereinanderliegenden Wasserflächen waren ein gern betontes Element der damaligen Gartenkunst.

Neuer Garten

4. Three plane trees by Heiliger See on the level with the Holländisches Etablissement (a series of buildings in the Dutch style), looking south.
5. Heiliger See north of the Marmorpalais, behind it, Jungfernsee. Bodies of water that are layered one behind the other, seemingly stacked on top of each other, were a favourite element of garden art at the time.

Neuer Garten

6. Die Allee am Holländischen Etablissement mit Pyramideneichen, vorn der Marstall, links dahinter die Reithalle.
7. Das Blumenrondell an der Orangerie. Die Brunnenfigur von 1976 schuf der Hallenser Bildhauer Gerhard Lichtenfeld.

Neuer Garten

6. The avenue by the Holländisches Etablissement with pyramid-shaped oaks, in the foreground, the royal stables, to the left behind them, the riding arena.
7. The flower rondel by the orangery. The fountain figure, dated 1976, was created by the sculptor Gerhard Lichtenfeld of Halle.

Neuer Garten

8. Die künstliche Tempelruine der Schloßküche südlich vor dem Marmorpalais, 1788–90 von Carl von Gontard geschaffen.
9. Die Marmorexedra vor dem Marmorpalais. Sie stand früher im Rondell des Schlosses und wurde im 19. Jahrhundert aus verschiedenen Fragmenten wieder restauriert. Die umgebenden Büsche sind Myrten.

Neuer Garten

8. The artificial temple ruin of the palace kitchen in the south in front of the Marmorpalais, created in 1788–90 by Carl von Gontard.
9. The marble exedra in front of the Marmorpalais. It used to stand in the rondel of the palace and was restored again in the 19th century from various fragments. The surrounding bushes are myrtles.

Neuer Garten

10. Eine Gedächtnisurne nördlich des Marmorpalais für den 1787 verstorbenen, damals nur achtjährigen Grafen Alexander von der Mark, den unehelichen Sohn von Friedrich Wilhelm II. und seiner Geliebten Wilhelmine, Gräfin von Lichtenau.
11. Die berühmteste Sichtachse des Neuen Gartens: der Blick unmittelbar von der nordwestlichen Ecke des Marmorpalais über den Heiligen See und den Jungfernsee/die Havel hinweg zum Schloß auf der Pfaueninsel, 4 km entfernt.

Neuer Garten

10. A memorial urn north of the Marmorpalais for Count Alexander von der Mark, who died in 1787 at the early age of eight, the illegitimate son of Frederick William II and his mistress Wilhelmina, Countess of Lichtenau.

11. The most famous visual axis of Neuer Garten: direct view of the palace on Pfaueninsel, 4 km away, from the northwest corner of Marmorpalais across Heiliger See and Jungfernsee/the Havel River.

Neuer Garten

12. Ein Blick vom Rondell des Marmorpalais zum Schindelhaus, einer um 1790 von Andreas Ludwig Krüger gebauten Adjudantenwohnung.
13. Ein Blick nach Norden, links die 1791/92 von Carl Gotthard Langhans und Andreas Ludwig Krüger errichtete Pyramide. Sie steht über dem 5 m tiefen Eiskeller, wo die im Winter aus dem Heiligen See gesägten Eisplatten zur Kühlung der Speisen in der warmen Jahreszeit gelagert wurden. Am Sockel eine ägyptisierende Zeile mit Hieroglyphen.

Neuer Garten

12. View of the Schindelhaus, the home of an adjutant built ca. 1790 by Andreas Ludwig Krüger, from the rondel of the Marmorpalais.
13. View facing north, on the left, the pyramid erected in 1791/92 by Carl Gotthard Langhans and Andreas Ludwig Krüger. It stands above the 5-m-deep cold cellar where blocks of ice sawed in winter from Heiliger See and used to keep food cold during the warmer months of the year were stored. On its base there is a faux-Egyptian line of hieroglyphs.

Neuer Garten

14. Das Grüne Haus, ein bereits vor der Anlage des eigentlichen Gartens errichtetes Gebäude am nördlichen Ende des Heiligen Sees.
15. Die Sichtachse vom Grünen Haus über das nördliche Ende des Heiligen Sees und den Jungfernsee/die Havel zum Wasserturm des Maschinen- und Gärtnerhauses im Schloßgarten Glienicke, 1,7 km entfernt. Auf derartige Sichten legte die damalige Gartenkunst großen Wert. Der Wasserspiegel der Havel liegt scheinbar über dem des Heiligen Sees.

Neuer Garten

14. The Grünes Haus, built before the actual garden was laid out at the north end of Heiliger See.
15. The visual axis from the Grünes Haus across the north end of Heiliger See and Jungfernsee/the Havel River to the water tower of the engine- and gardener's house in Schloßgarten Glienicke, 1.7 km away. During this period, garden art attached great importance to this type of vistas. The water level of the Havel River appears to be higher than that of Heiliger See.

Neuer Garten

16. Die Meierei ganz im Norden des Gartens am Jungfernsee, 1791 von Carl Gotthard Langhans und Andreas Ludwig Krüger als Ökonomiegebäude für die Milchwirtschaft begonnen, 1843/44 mit Obergeschoß und Turm von Ludwig Persius fortgeführt. Der Schornstein stammt von 1861. Links davor die Crystall- und Muschelgrotte, 1791/92 von Andreas Ludwig Krüger erbaut, davor eine Gruppe von Eichen.
17. Das Schloß Cecilienhof ganz im Norden des Gartens, 1913–17 für Kronprinz Wilhelm und seine Gemahlin Cecilie von Paul Schultze-Naumburg erbaut. Das Haus war Tagungsort der Potsdamer Konferenz von 1945, heute dient ein Teil als Hotel.

Neuer Garten

16. The dairy in the northernmost part of the garden by Jungfernsee, begun in 1791 by Carl Gotthard Langhans and Andreas Ludwig Krüger as a building for dairy farming, and continued in 1843/44 with an upper storey and tower by Ludwig Persius. The chimney dates back to 1861. On the left, in front of it, the Crystall- und Muschelgrotte (Crystal and Seashell Grotto), built in 1791/92 by Andreas Ludwig Krüger, with a cluster of oaks in front of it.
17. Schloß Cecilienhof in the northernmost part of the garden, built in 1913–17 for Crown Prince William and his wife Cecilie by Paul Schultze-Naumburg. The house was the site of the 1945 Potsdam Conference, and today part of it is being used as a hotel.

Neuer Garten

18. Ein Uferstück am Jungfernsee im Norden des Neuen Gartens. Im Hintergrund der Quapphorn-Vorsprung, auf dem ehemals eine Einsiedelei stand.
19. Der Pfingstberg liegt westlich hoch über dem Neuen Garten, berühmt durch das von Friedrich Wilhelm IV. angeregte Belvedere. Hier steht auch der Pomonatempel, das Erstlingswerk von Karl Friedrich Schinkel, 1800/1801, errichtet.

Neuer Garten

18. Part of the shoreline of Jungfernsee in the north part of Neuer Garten. In the background, the Quapphorn promontory, on which a hermitage used to stand.
19. Pfingstberg is located in the west high above Neuer Garten, and is famous because of the Belvedere first proposed by Frederick William IV. Also located here is the Pomonatempel, the first project of Karl Friedrich Schinkel, built in 1800/01.

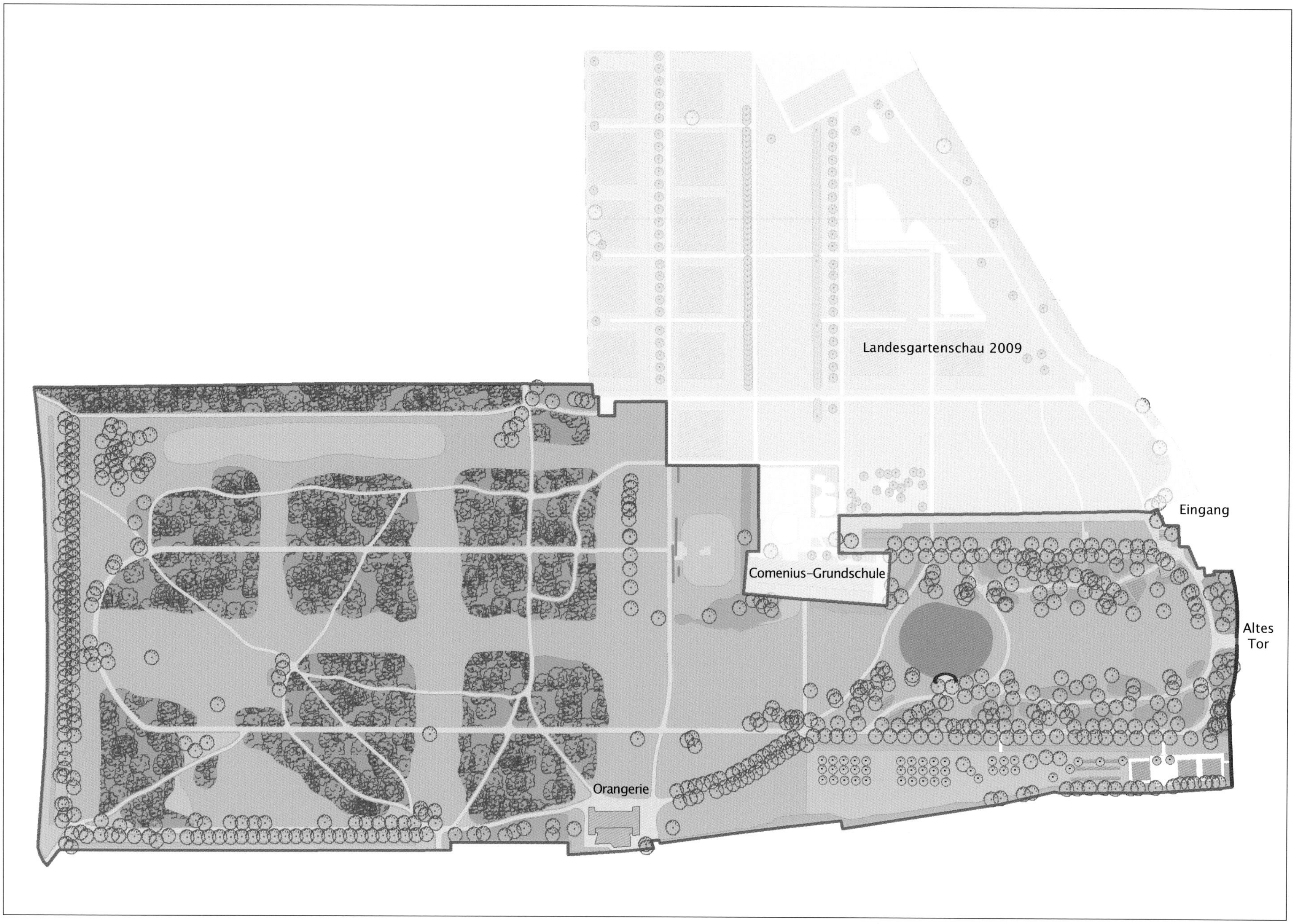
Landesgartenschau 2009
Eingang
Comenius-Grundschule
Altes
Tor
Orangerie

Schloßpark Oranienburg

1. Die Fontäne am südöstlichen Beginn des Parks, links das 1690 von Johann Arnold Nering geschaffene Eingangsportal.

Schloßpark Oranienburg

1. The fountain at the southeast end of the park, on the left, the entrance gateway created in 1690 by Johann Arnold Nering.

Schloßpark Oranienburg

2. Ein Blick die zentrale Schneise entlang zum südöstlichen Beginn des Parks. Die beiden quer laufenden Lichtstreifen markieren die quer laufenden breiten Schneisen zwischen den Waldbosketten von Eichen und Linden. Die sechs großen Boskette spiegeln andeutungsweise noch die Struktur des Parks der Entstehungszeit aus der Mitte des 17. Jahrhunderts wider.
3. Ein Blick von dem Eichensolitär am westlichen Ende des Parks auf die zentrale Achse und die beiden südlichen Waldboskette. Ganz im Hintergrund die Fontäne.

Schloßpark Oranienburg

2. View of the southeast end of the park along the central lane. The two transverse strips of light mark the wide transverse lanes between the forest *bosquets* of oaks and linden trees. The six large *bosquets* still faintly reflect the structure of the park during the period when it was created in the the middle of the 17th century.
3. View of the central axis and the two forest *bosquets* in the south from the solitaire oak at the west end of the park. The fountain is visible all the way in the background.

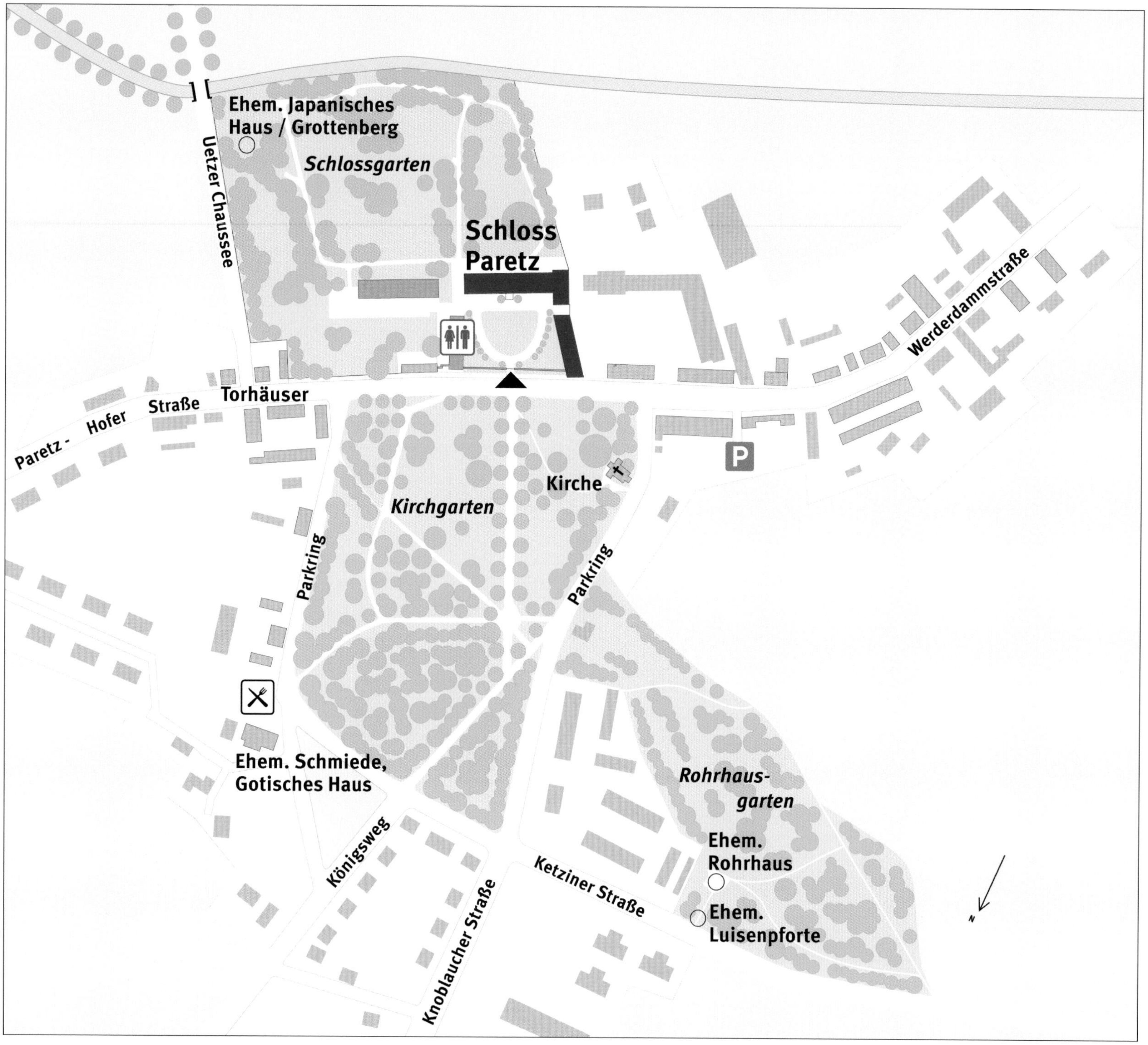
Ehem. Japanisches Haus / Grottenberg
Schlossgarten
Uetzer Chaussee
Schloss Paretz
Torhäuser
Paretz - Hofer Straße
Werderdammstraße
Kirche
Kirchgarten
Parkring
Parkring
Ehem. Schmiede, Gotisches Haus
Rohrhaus-garten
Ehem. Rohrhaus
Ehem. Luisenpforte
Königsweg
Knoblaucher Straße
Ketziner Straße
P
N

Schloßgarten Paretz

1. Das Rondell vor dem Schloß mit den Säulenpappeln. Das Schloß wurde 1797–1804 von David Gilly für den Kronprinzen Friedrich Wilhelm, den späteren König Friedrich Wilhelm III. von Preußen, und seine Gemahlin Luise als Sommersitz erbaut.

Schloßgarten Paretz

1. The rondel in front of the palace with its Lombardy poplars. The palace was built in 1797–1804 by David Gilly as a summer residence for Crown Prince Frederick William, later to become King Frederick William III of Prussia, and his wife Louise.

Schloßgarten Paretz

2. Die Lindenallee im nördlich des Schlosses gelegenen Kirchgarten führt zentral zum Schloßeingang mit dem Thermenfenster von Gilly.
3. Die südöstliche Gartenfassade des Schlosses, die große Hängeweide und der kleine Schloßgarten.

Schloßgarten Paretz

2. The linden avenue in the churchyard north of the palace leads centrally to the palace entrance with the thermal window by Gilly.
3. The southeast garden façade of the palace, the big weeping willow and the little Schloß garden.

Schloßgarten Paretz

4. Ein Blick vom Gartensaal in den Garten mit drei großen Rotbuchen.
5. Ein besonderer Reiz des Schloßgartens Paretz liegt in dem fast unmerklichen Übergang des Gartens in die weite Weidelandschaft mit grasenden Pferden und Rindern.

Schloßgarten Paretz

4. View from the garden room of the garden, with three tall beeches.
5. One thing that is especially appealing about Schloßgarten Paretz is that there is an almost imperceptible transition from the garden into the open pastureland, where horses and cattle graze.

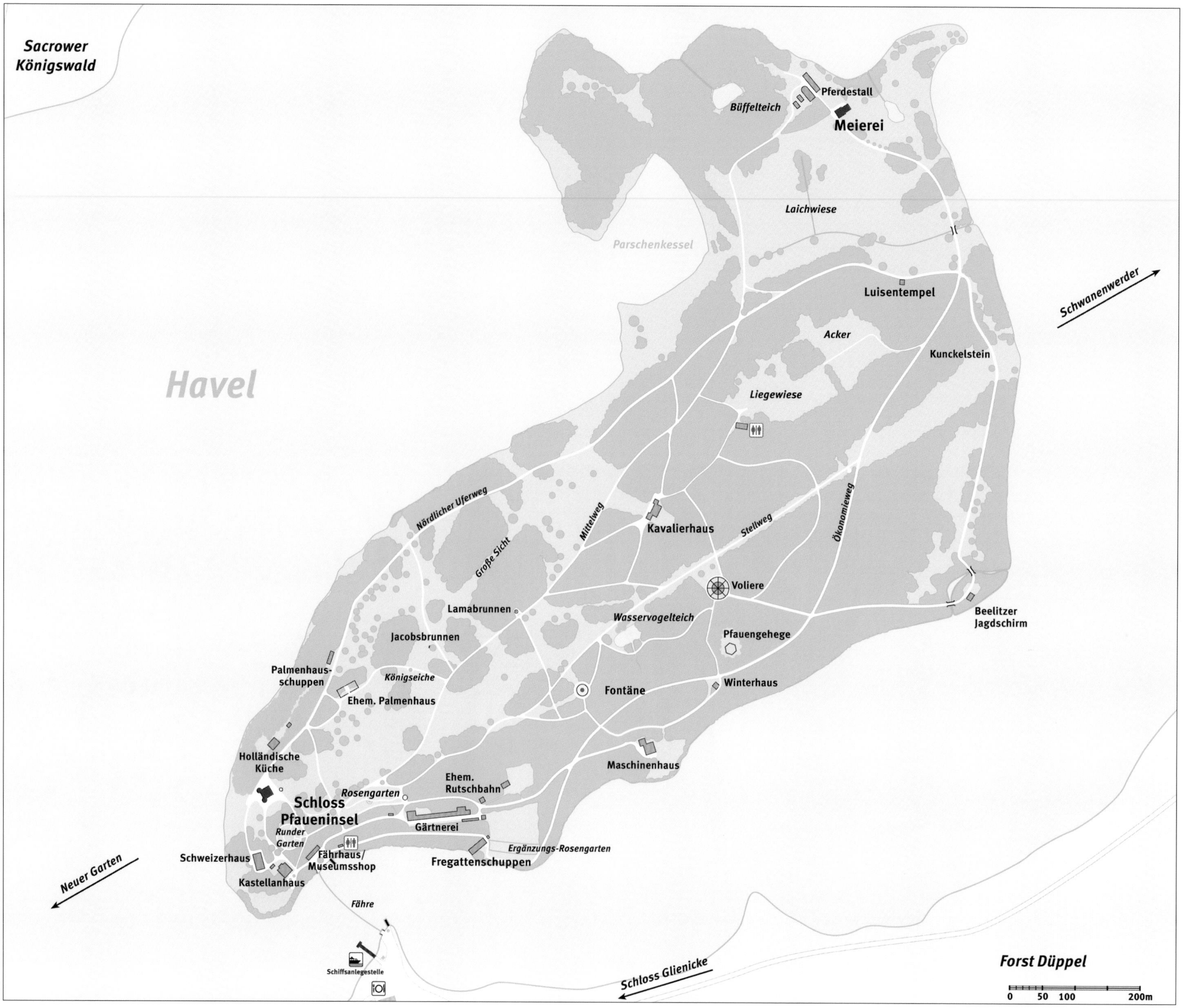

Sacrower Königswald
Havel
Parschenkessel
Büffelteich
Pferdestall
Meierei
Laichwiese
Luisentempel
Schwanenwerder
Acker
Kunckelstein
Liegewiese
Nördlicher Uferweg
Mittelweg
Große Sicht
Kavalierhaus
Stellweg
Ökonomieweg
Voliere
Beelitzer Jagdschirm
Lamabrunnen
Wasservogelteich
Jacobsbrunnen
Pfauengehege
Palmenhaus-schuppen
Königseiche
Ehem. Palmenhaus
Fontäne
Winterhaus
Holländische Küche
Maschinenhaus
Ehem. Rutschbahn
Rosengarten
Schloss Pfaueninsel
Gärtnerei
Runder Garten
Schweizerhaus
Fährhaus/ Museumsshop
Ergänzungs-Rosengarten
Fregattenschuppen
Kastellanhaus
Neuer Garten
Fähre
Schiffsanlegestelle
Schloss Glienicke
Forst Düppel
0 50 100 200m

Pfaueninsel

1. Ein Blick zwischen den Eichen zum Schloß mit der Schloßwiese. Das Schloß wurde 1794 von Johann Gottlieb Brendel im Auftrag von Friedrich Wilhelm II. erbaut.

Pfaueninsel

1. View of the palace and the palace meadow through the oaks. The palace was built for Frederick William II by Johann Gottlieb Brendel in 1794.

Pfaueninsel

2. Die gewundene Wegeführung an der Schloßwiese vor dem Schloß.
3. Die Sichtachse von den Platanen am Schloß, am Schaukelweg, durch die gesamte Länge der Insel bis zur 1,2 km entfernten Meierei.

Pfaueninsel

2. Winding path by the palace meadow in front of the palace.
3. Visual axis from the plane trees by the palace, near Schaukelweg, through the entire length of the island to the dairy 1.2 km away.

Pfaueninsel

4. Der Rosengarten ganz in der Nähe des Schlosses wurde 1821 von Peter Joseph Lenné angelegt und 1989 wieder hergestellt. Es gibt noch viele der Namen gebenden Pfauen auf der Insel.
5. Der Rosengarten geht in den herbstlichen Inselwald über.

Pfaueninsel

4. The Rosengarten directly by the palace was designed in 1821 by Peter Joseph Lenné and restored in 1989. There are still many of the eponymous peacocks on the island.
5. The Rosengarten merges with the island's autumnal forest.

Pfaueninsel

6. Der Rosengarten in winterlicher Verhüllung und das Schloß.
7. Ein Blick durch den Eichenwald zur Fontäne fast in der Bildmitte, links der große Eichensolitär.

Pfaueninsel

6. The Rosengarten, wrapped up for the winter, and the palace.
7. View through the oak forest of the fountain almost in the centre of the picture, the big solitaire oak is on the left.

Pfaueninsel

8. Eine Weggabelung vor der Fontäne.
9. Die 1824 geschaffene gußeiserne Fontäne von Martin Friedrich Rabe und ein Durchblick zum Schloß.

Pfaueninsel

8. Fork in the path in front of the fountain.
9. The cast-iron fountain created by Martin Friedrich Rabe in 1824, and a glimpse of the palace.

Pfaueninsel

10. Eine Weggabelung am Rosengarten, links der Rand der Schloßwiese.
11. In der Mitte der Insel südöstlich vom Kavalierhaus eine große Eiche und die Voliere von 1825. Das in seiner Art sehr seltene Gebäude wurde 2009–11 aufwendig restauriert.

Pfaueninsel

10. Fork in the path by the Rosengarten, the edge of the palace meadow is on the left.
11. Large oak in the middle of the island southeast of the Kavalierhaus, and the aviary of 1825. The building, of a type that is very rare, underwent an expensive restoration in 2009–11.

Pfaueninsel

12. Der Jacobsbrunnen, um 1795 von Johann Gottlieb Brendel als künstliche Ruine konzipiert. Im Hintergrund Kladow jenseits der Havel.
13. Das Kavalierhaus im Zentrum der Insel, 1803/04 von Friedrich Karl Krüger errichtet, 1824–26 von Karl Friedrich Schinkel umgebaut, dabei wurde die abgebrochene Fassade eines Danziger Patrizierhauses vorgeschaltet.

Pfaueninsel

12. The Jacobsbrunnen (Jacob's Fountain), conceived as a faux ruin ca. 1795 by Johann Gottlieb Brendel. In the background is Kladow on the other side of the Havel River.
13. The Kavalierhaus in the centre of the island, built in 1803/04 by Friedrich Karl Krüger, and converted by Karl Friedrich Schinkel in 1824–26, when the dismantled façade of a Danzig patrician house was superposed on it.

Pfaueninsel

14. Eine alte Eiche und ein Waldstück mit Buschwerk in der Mitte der Insel.
15. Ein Blick vom Pferdestall neben der Meierei auf das Kladower Ufer der Havel, links eine Buche, rechts eine Erle.

Pfaueninsel

14. An old oak tree and a piece of woodlands with bushes in the centre of the island.
15. View from the horse stable next to the dairy of the Kladow bank of the Havel River, a beech is on the left, and an alder on the right.

Pfaueninsel

16. Die Meierei, um 1794 von Johann Gottlieb Brendel als künstliche Ruine erbaut, rechts eine große Platane.
17. Herbstfarben an der Laichwiese und dem Hechtgraben ganz im Norden der Insel, neben der Meierei. Der Baum rechts ist eine Sumpfzypresse.

Pfaueninsel

16. The dairy, built ca. 1794 by Johann Gottlieb Brendel as an artificial ruin, on the right is a tall plane tree.
17. Autumn colours on the Laichwiese (a meadow) and on the Hechtgraben (a trench) in the northernmost part of the island, next to the dairy. The tree on the right is a deciduous cypress.

Pfaueninsel

18. Der Luisentempel am Rande der Laichwiese. Der Sandsteinportikus war 1810 von Heinrich Gentz entworfen und im Schloßpark von Charlottenburg an das Luisenmausoleum angefügt worden, 1828 wurde er auf die Insel versetzt.
19. Die Laichwiese und die Meierei im Norden der Insel.

Pfaueninsel

18. Luisentempel at the edge of the Laichwiese. The sandstone portico had been designed in 1810 by Heinrich Gentz and added to the Luisenmausoleum in the park of Charlottenburg, in 1828 it was moved to the island.
19. The Laichwiese and the dairy farm in the north of the island.

Pfaueninsel

20. Das Reetufer am Parschenkessel, einer Bucht im Nordosten der Insel, rechts eine Erle.
21. Das Reetufer nahe der sogenannten Erdzunge mit der kleinen Insel Kälberwerder in der zugefrorenen Havel, links von der Birke.

Pfaueninsel

20. Reedy bank near Parschenkessel, a bay in the northeast part of the island, an alder is on the right.
21. Reedy bank near the so-called Erdzunge (cape) with the small island of Kälberwerder in the frozen Havel River, to the left of the birch tree.

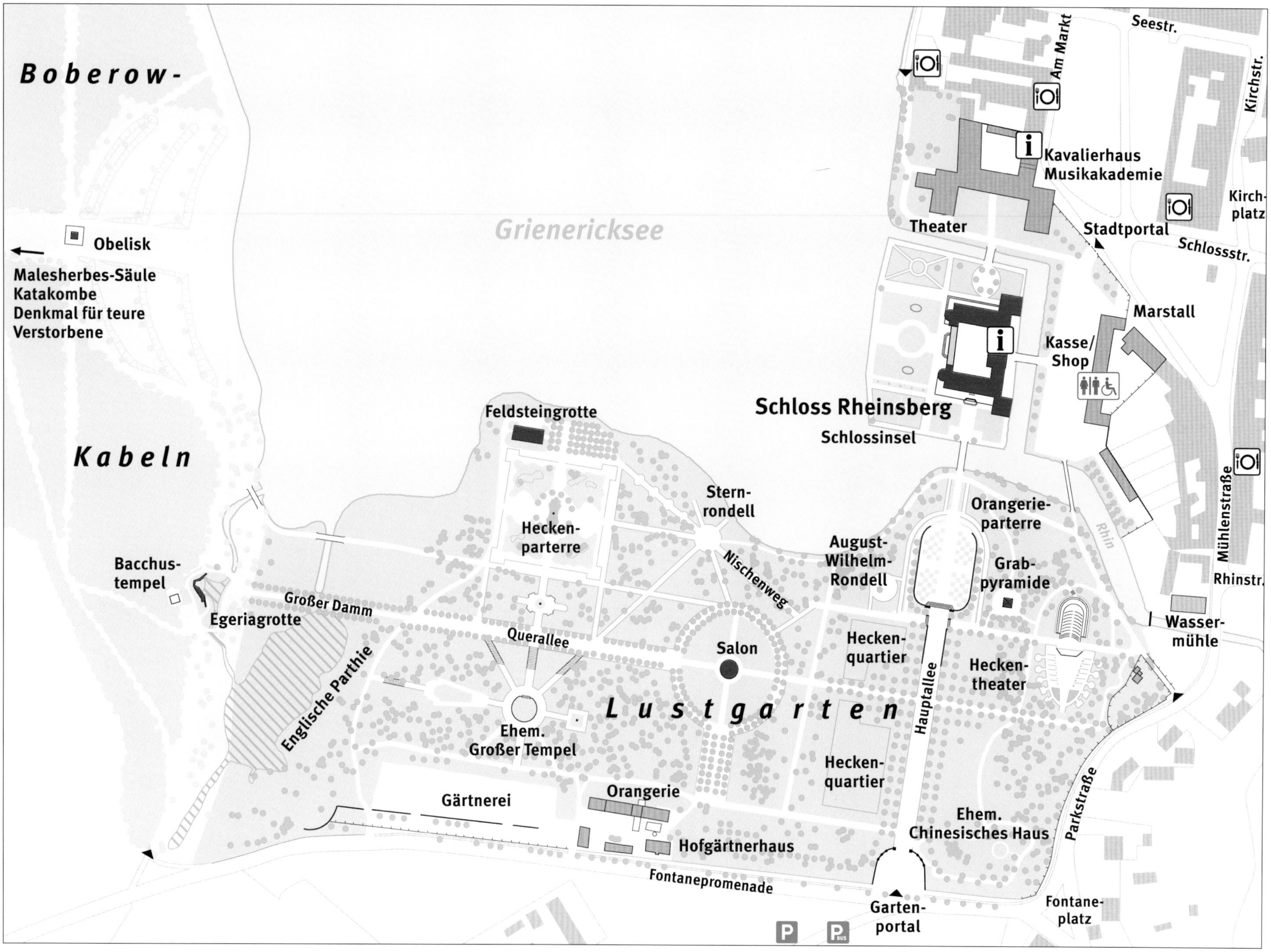
Boberow-
Kabeln
Obelisk
Malesherbes-Säule
Katakombe
Denkmal für teure
Verstorbene
Grienericksee
Seestr.
Am Markt
Kirchstr.
Kavalierhaus
Musikakademie
Kirch-
platz
Theater
Stadtportal
Schlossstr.
Marstall
Kasse/
Shop
Schloss Rheinsberg
Schlossinsel
Feldsteingrotte
Stern-
rondell
Orangerie-
parterre
Hecken-
parterre
August-
Wilhelm-
Rondell
Grab-
pyramide
Rhin
Mühlenstraße
Rhinstr.
Bacchus-
tempel
Egeriagrotte
Großer Damm
Nischenweg
Querallee
Salon
Hecken-
quartier
Hecken-
theater
Wasser-
mühle
Englische Parthie
Lustgarten
Hauptallee
Ehem.
Großer Tempel
Hecken-
quartier
Gärtnerei
Orangerie
Hofgärtnerhaus
Ehem.
Chinesisches Haus
Parkstraße
Fontanepromenade
Garten-
portal
Fontane-
platz

Schloßpark Rheinsberg

1. Ein Blick von den Boberow-Kabeln und der obersten Erdterrasse mit dem Obelisken über das Reetufer zum Grienericksee und dem Schloß. Rechts im Mittelgrund der Schloßgarten mit der Feldsteingrotte und dem Heckenparterre. Friedrich Wilhelm I. schenkte das Schloß, ein Renaissancebau, seinem Sohn Friedrich (II.). Mit dem Ausbau der Anlage wurde 1734 begonnen.

Schloßpark Rheinsberg

1. View, across the reedy bank, of Grienericksee and the palace from the Boberow-Kabeln and the uppermost earth terrace with the obelisk. On the right in the middle distance is the park with the rocky grotto and the hedge *parterre*. Frederick William gave the palace, a Renaissance building, to his son Frederick (II). The development of the park began in 1734.

Schloßpark Rheinsberg

2. Das Gartenportal am südlichen Beginn der Hauptallee wurde 1741 von Georg Wenzeslaus von Knobelsdorff und Friedrich Christian Glume geschaffen, flankiert von Flora und Pomona, den Göttinnen der Blumen und der Baumfrüchte. Das Portal diente als Vorbild für das östliche Hauptportal im Park Sanssouci.
3. Der zentrale Teil der Hauptallee in nordöstlicher Richtung gesehen. Die Allee, von Georg Wenzeslaus von Knobelsdorff angelegt, zeigt eine vierzeilige Wechselbepflanzung von Linden und Fichten.

Schloßpark Rheinsberg

2. The garden entrance gate at the south end of the main avenue was created in 1741 by Georg Wenzeslaus von Knobelsdorff and Friedrich Christian Glume, and is flanked by Flora and Pomona, the goddesses of flowers and fruit. The gate served as a model for the main east gate in Park Sanssouci.
3. The central part of the main avenue viewed facing northeast. The avenue, laid out by Georg Wenzeslaus von Knobelsdorff, has four rows of alternating lindens and spruces.

Schloßpark Rheinsberg

4. Der vermutlich 1802 angelegte Dunkle Weg zu der abgebrochenen Pyramide, dem Grabmal des Prinzen Heinrich von Preußen, zwischen Heckentheater und Orangerieparterre. Er wurde dort am 5. August 1802 beigesetzt.
5. Das 1753/54 angelegte Heckentheater, eine Wechselbepflanzung von Hainbuchenbosketten und Eibenpyramiden. Das Naturtheater bietet fast 1000 Zuschauern Platz, es wird häufig bespielt. Im Vordergrund hinter der Hainbuchenhecke der Orchestergraben.

Schloßpark Rheinsberg

4. Dunkler Weg (Dark Path), presumably laid out in 1802, to the truncated pyramid, the monument of Prince Henry of Prussia, between the hedge theatre and the orangery *parterre*. He was interred there on 5 August 1802.
5. The hedge theatre, created in 1753/54, hornbeam *bosquets* alternating with pyramid-shaped yews. The outdoor theatre has seating for almost 1 000 spectators, and is a frequently used venue. In the foreground, behind the hornbeam hedge, is the orchestra pit.

Schloßpark Rheinsberg

6. Der südwestliche Teil der vierzeiligen Hauptallee nach Süden gesehen. Die Wechselbepflanzung mit Linden und Fichten wurde von Georg Wenzeslaus von Knobelsdorff angelegt.
7. Das Orangerieparterre am nördlichen Ende der Hauptallee vor dem Schloß wurde unter dem Kronprinzen Friedrich von Georg Wenzeslaus von Knobelsdorff angelegt. Das Schachbrettmuster stammt von 1760. Hier werden im Sommer Zitrusbäume aufgestellt, die Pomeranzen. Dahinter Fichten und der Laubengang.

Schloßpark Rheinsberg

6. The southwest section of the four-row avenue viewed facing south. Alternately planted with lindens and spruces, the avenue was laid out by Georg Wenzeslaus von Knobelsdorff.
7. The orangery *parterre* at the north end of the main avenue in front of the palace was laid out under Crown Prince Frederick by Georg Wenzeslaus von Knobelsdorff. The checkerboard pattern dates back to 1760. This is where citrus trees – Seville orange trees – are set out in summer. Behind them are spruce trees and the pergola.

Schloßpark Rheinsberg

8. Die Hauptsichtachse durch die Kolonnaden über das Schloßparterre mit der Statue des Apoll von Giovanni Antonio Cybei, 1766, zum Grienericksee und den 1762 angelegten Erdterrassen mit dem Obelisken von 1791 sowie der dahinter fortlaufenden Perspektivallee in den Boberow-Kabeln.
9. Ein Blick aus der Bibliothek des Kronprinzen Friedrich über Parterre und See zu den Erdterrassen mit dem Obelisken. Das Szenario jenseits des Sees gab es zu jener Zeit allerdings noch nicht.

Schloßpark Rheinsberg

8. The main view axis through the colonnades across the palace *parterre* with the statue of Apollo by Giovanni Antonio Cybei, 1766, leading to Grienericksee and the earth terraces laid out in 1762, with the 1791 obelisk and the Perspektivallee in the Boberow-Kabeln that continues behind the obelisk.
9. View of the earth terraces and the obelisk from the library of Crown Prince Frederick across the parterre and lake. Of course, the scenario on the other side of the lake did not exist yet at the time.

Schloßpark Rheinsberg

10. Die Marmorskulptur des Apoll von Giovanni Antonio Cybei, 1766, auf dem Rondell der Schloßinsel. Dahinter der Grienericksee und die drei Erdterrassen mit dem Obelisken am östlichen Ausgang der Perspektivallee in den Boberow-Kabeln.
11. Ein Blumenkorb mit Frühlingsbepflanzung und die Marmorskulpturen auf dem Schloßparterre, links *Die Luft* und rechts *Das Feuer* von Giovanni Antonio Cybei.

Schloßpark Rheinsberg

10. The marble sculpture of Apollo by Giovanni Antonio Cybei, 1766, on the rondel of the palace island. Behind it, Grienericksee and the three earth terraces with the obelisk at the east end of the Perspektivallee in the Boberow-Kabeln.
11. A flower basket with spring flowers, and the marble sculptures on the palace's *parterre*, on the left is *Air* and on the right is *Fire,* both by Giovanni Antonio Cybei.

Schloßpark Rheinsberg

12. Der Salon, Mittelteil der von Georg Wenzeslaus Knobelsdorff geplanten Orangerie, umgeben von vier, 1765 geschaffenen Marmorskulpturen von Giovanni Antonio Cybei, die die vier Jahreszeiten darstellen. Die große Ost–West-Achse führt zur Egeria Grotte von 1790 im Hintergrund. Das Rondell wird von Linden umstanden.
13. Das Rondell des Salons im Lustgarten. Marmorskulptur *Der Winter*, geschaffen 1765 von Giovanni Antonio Cybei. Hinter der Hainbuchenhecke der Grienericksee.

Schloßpark Rheinsberg

12. The salon, the central part of the orangery planned by Georg Wenzeslaus Knobelsdorff, surrounded by four marble sculptures representing the four seasons, created in 1765 by Giovanni Antonio Cybei. The large east-west axis leads to the Grotto of Egeria, dated 1790, in the background. The rondel is encircled by linden trees.
13. The rondel of the salon in the pleasure ground. The marble sculpture *Winter* was created in 1765 by Giovanni Antonio Cybei. Visible behind the hornbeam hedge is Grienericksee.

Schloßpark Rheinsberg

14. Der kleine Tümpel der Egeriagrotte ganz im Westen der Querallee und des Großen Damms. Egeria ist eine der Nymphen, Egeriagrotten gibt es in vielen Parks. Die Spiegelung im Teich ist ein beliebter gartentechnischer Kunstgriff jener Zeit.
15. Birnenförmige Schmuckvasen und Hainbuchenboskette im Heckenparterre, dahinter der Grienericksee.

Schloßpark Rheinsberg

14. The small pond of the Egeriagrotte to the far west of the transverse avenue and the Large Dam. Egeria is one of the nymphs, and there are Egeria grottoes in many parks. The reflection in the pond is a favourite device used by period landscape designers.
15. Pear-shaped ornamental vases and hornbeam *bosquets* in the hedge *parterre*, visible behind them is Grienericksee.

Schloßpark Rheinsberg

16. Ein Blick durch die 1772 angelegte Meiereiallee in den Boberow-Kabeln zum Schloß. Als das Alleensystem in den Boberow-Kabeln angelegt wurde, gab es hier noch keinen Wald, sondern freies Land mit Bürgeräckern. Der Wald mit Winterlinden entstand erst im 19. Jahrhundert. Nach der Wiedervereinigung wurden die Schneisen der Alleen wieder freigelegt.
17. Der Böbereckensee bildet die Grenze zwischen den Boberow-Kabeln im Osten und dem Boberow-Park weiter im Westen. Das Alleensystem war mehrfach radialstrahlig angelegt, wenige Schritte hinter dem Standpunkt dieser Aufnahme liegt der Sechs-Alleen-Platz von 1753 mit einer Hinweisplakette.

Schloßpark Rheinsberg

16. View of the castle through Meiereiallee, laid out in 1772 in the Boberow-Kabeln. When the system of avenues in the Boberow-Kabeln was laid out, there was no forest here yet, only open country with the fields of the townspeople. The basswood forest did not appear until the 19th century. After German reunification, the lanes of the avenues were cleared once more.
17. Böbereckensee is the boundary between the Boberow-Kabeln in the east and Boberow-Park farther west. Often the system of avenues radiated from a central point. A few steps behind the point from which this photo was taken is the Sechs-Alleen-Platz (Square of Six Avenues), dated 1753, with an information plaque.

Schloßpark Rheinsberg

18. Die Katakombe von 1790 an der Allee zur Katakombe in den Boberow-Kabeln westlich des Obelisken – eine sentimentale Erinnerungsarchitektur. Ein Marmorblock mit einer Inschrift von Prinz Heinrich von Preußen wird von einer fiktiven Grabkammer aus Feldsteinen umschlossen.
19. Die Malesherbessäule von 1794 an der großen Perspektiv-Allee westlich des Obelisken in den Borberow-Kabeln. Der französische Minister war wegen seiner Treue zu Ludwig XVI. hingerichtet worden. Aus der Sicht von Prinz Heinrich war diese Treue ein großer Freundschaftsdienst, den es zu würdigen galt.

Schloßpark Rheinsberg

18. The Catacomb, dated 1790, along the Allee zur Katakombe in the Boberow-Kabeln west of the obelisk – a sentimental memorial structure. A block of marble with an inscription by Prince Henry of Prussia is enclosed in a fictitious burial chamber constructed with boulders.
19. The Malesherbessäule, dated 1794, by the large Perspektiv-Allee west of the obelisk in the Borberow-Kabeln. The French minister had been executed because of his loyalty to Louis XVI. From Prince Henry's perspective this loyalty was a great service of friendship that must be honoured.

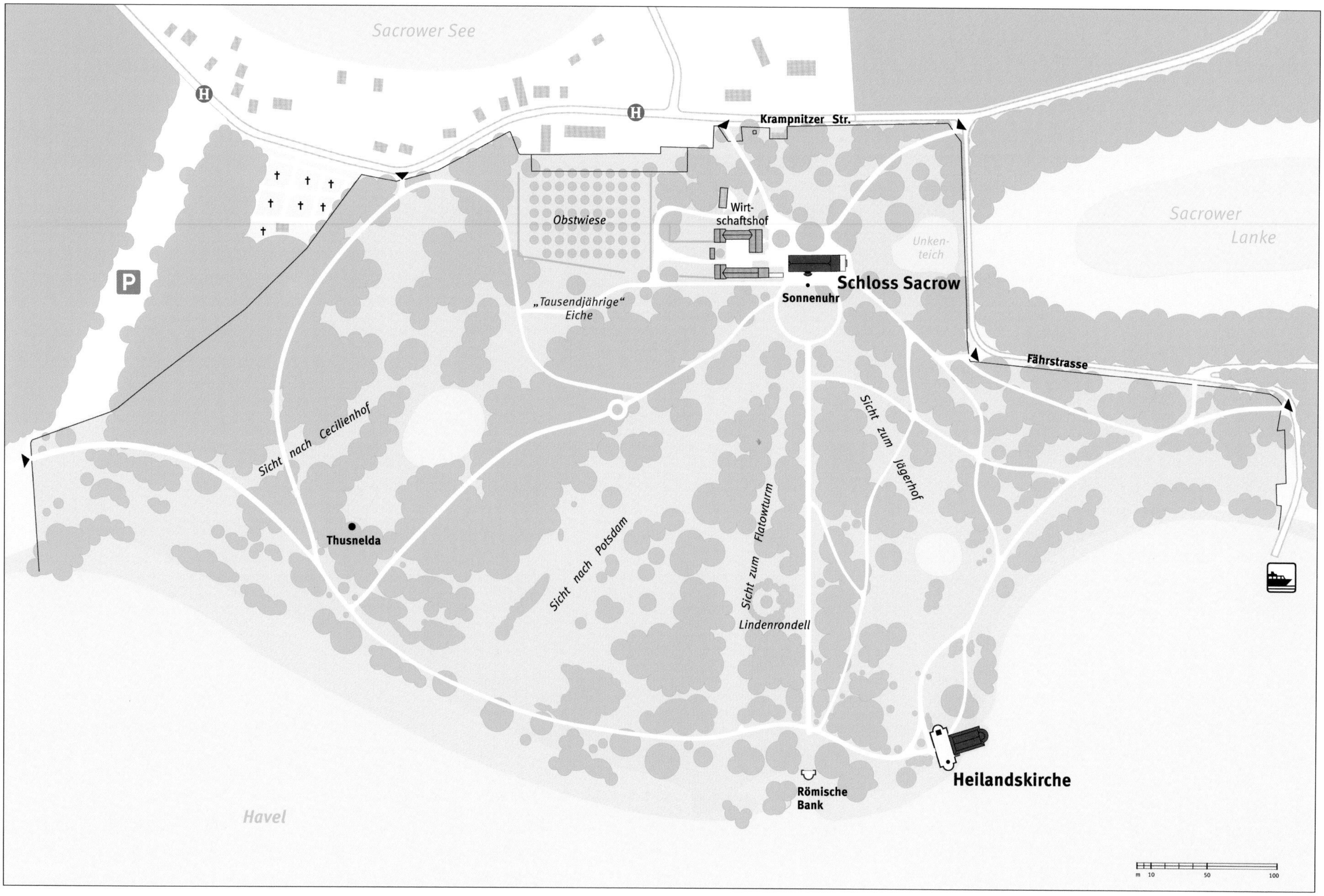
Sacrower See
Krampnitzer Str.
Obstwiese
Wirt-
schaftshof
Unken-
teich
Sacrower
Lanke
Schloss Sacrow
Sonnenuhr
„Tausendjährige"
Eiche
Fährstrasse
Sicht nach Cecilienhof
Sicht zum Jägerhof
Sicht zum Flatowturm
Sicht nach Potsdam
Thusnelda
Lindenrondell
Heilandskirche
Römische
Bank
Havel
m 10 50 100

Garten Sacrow

1. Ein Blick von Süden aus der »Sicht nach Potsdam« auf das Gut und das Schloß von 1773. 1840 wurde der Besitz von Friedrich Wilhelm IV. von Preußen erworben.

Garten Sacrow

1. View of the estate and the palace, 1773, from the south looking from the »Sicht nach Potsdam«. In 1840 the property was acquired by Frederick William IV of Prussia.

Garten Sacrow

2. Die unter Naturschutz stehende tausendjährige Eiche im Westen des Parks und die Wirtschaftsgebäude des Schlosses.
3. Die Marmorkopie der Skulptur der Thusnelda, der Frau von Hermann dem Cherusker, wurde 1858/59 von Albert Wolff geschaffen, die Anregung dazu geht auf Königin Elisabeth von Preußen zurück, die Gemahlin von Friedrich Wilhelm IV., beide hatten das Original auf ihrer Italienreise in Florenz gesehen. Die Skulptur steht seit 1904 im Sacrower Park.

Garten Sacrow

2. The thousand-year oak, which is now protected, in the west part of the park, and the palace's farm buildings.
3. This marble copy of the sculpture of Thusnelda, the wife of Herman the Cheruscan, was created in 1858/59 by Albert Wolff, who got the idea for it from Queen Elisabeth of Prussia, the wife of Frederick William IV, the two had seen the original on their tour of Italy, in Florence. The sculpture has been in Sacrow Park since 1904.

Garten Sacrow

4. Die Römische Bank, die Havel, das Glienicker Ufer, die Glienicker Brücke und der Flatowturm, nach Süden gesehen. Die Bank wurde 1843 von Ludwig Persius errichtet, Vorbild ist die antike Grabbank der römischen Priesterin Mamia an der Gräberstraße in Pompeji.
5. Das Schloß aus der »Sicht zum Flatowturm«, allerdings in umgekehrter Richtung. Von den drei vom Schloß ausgehenden Sichten ist neben dieser nur die Potsdamer Sicht erhalten, die zum Jägerhof in Glienicke ist zugewachsen.

Garten Sacrow

4. The Römische Bank, the Havel River, the Glienicke bank, Glienicker Brücke and Flatowturm, viewed facing south. The bench was erected in 1843 by Ludwig Persius, modelled on the classical Roman tomb bench of the Roman priestess Mamia on the Road of Tombs in Pompeii.
5. The palace seen from the »Sicht zum Flatowturm«, though facing in the reverse direction. Of the three views that begin at the palace, only this view and that of Potsdam still exist, the view towards the Jägerhof (hunting lodge) in Glienicke has become overgrown.

Garten Sacrow

6. Die Eichengruppe am Ufer der Havel mit der Römischen Bank und dem Turm der Heilandskirche.
7. Die Heilandskirche von der Römischen Bank aus durch die Eichengruppe gesehen. Die Kirche ist wohl das berühmteste Gebäude von Ludwig Persius, 1843/1844 erbaut, unter intensiver Mitwirkung von Friedrich Wilhelm IV. Rechts die Havel und das Glienicker Ufer.

Garten Sacrow

6. The cluster of oaks on the bank of the Havel River with the Roman bench and the tower of the Heilandskirche (Church of Our Savior).
7. The Heilandskirche as seen from the Römische Bank through the cluster of oaks. The church is probably Ludwig Persius' most famous building, built in 1843/44, with the close collaboration of Frederick William IV.

Garten Sacrow

8. Ein Blick durch den lockeren Eichenwald über den südöstlichen Parkteich hinweg zur Havel und dem Glienicker Ufer. Der Weg führt rechts zur Heilandskirche.
9. Ein Blick von der Römischen Bank über das Reetufer und den Jungfernsee zum Ufer des Neuen Gartens, überwölbt vom Pfingstberg mit den Doppeltürmen des Belvedere. Rechts am Ufer die Meierei.

Garten Sacrow

8. View of the Havel River and the Glienicke riverbank through the scattered oak forest across the park pond in the southeast. Followed towards the right, the path leads to the Heilandskirche.
9. The Neuer Garten shore viewed from the Roman bench across the reedy lakefront and Jungfernsee, in the background is Pfingstberg with the double towers of the Belvedere. On the right along the lakeshore is the dairy.

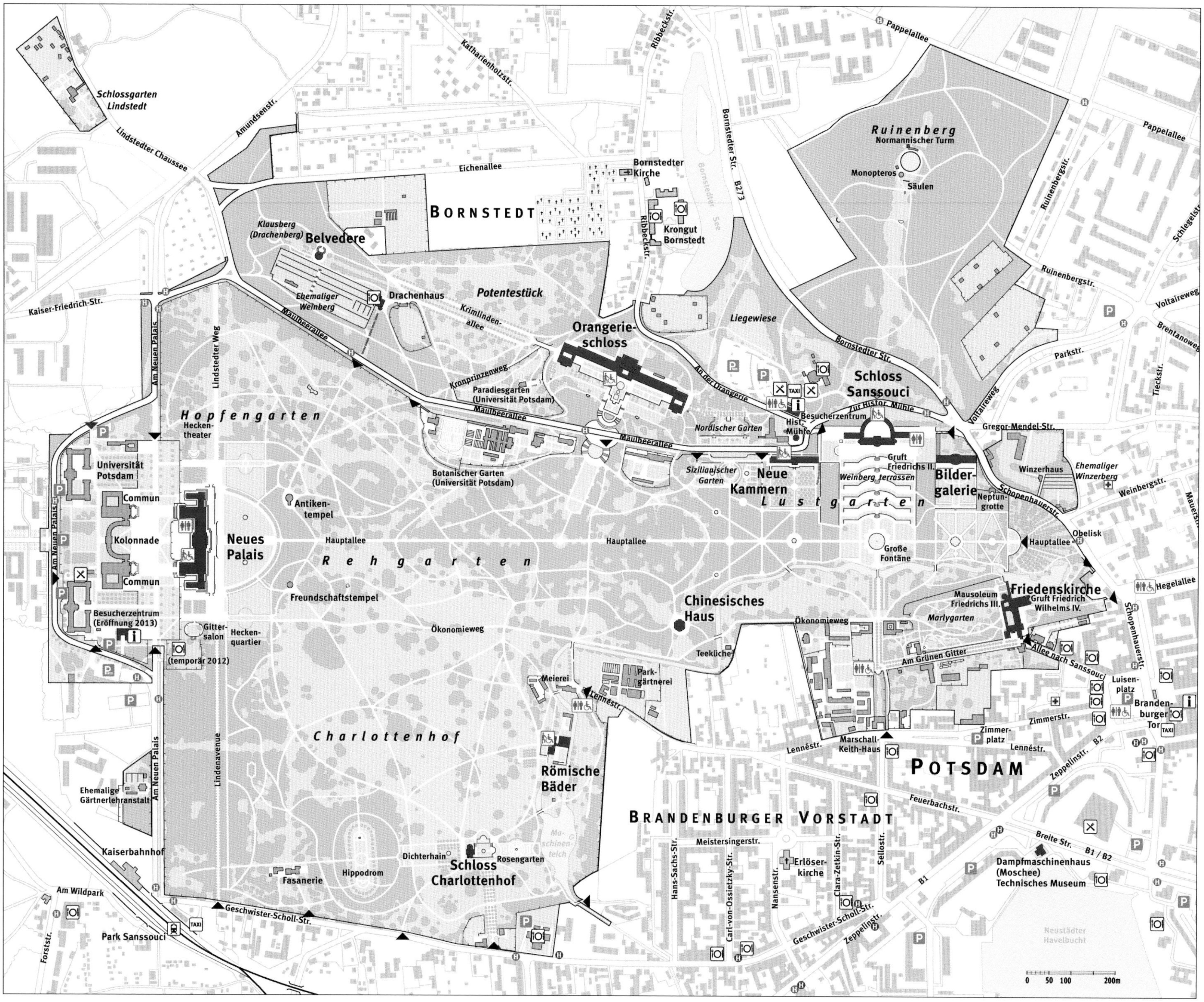
Schlossgarten Lindstedt
Lindstedter Chaussee
Amundsenstr.
Katharinenholzstr.
Ribbeckstr.
Pappelallee
Eichenallee
Bornstedter Kirche
Bornstedter Str.
B273
Ruinenberg
Normannischer Turm
Monopteros
Säulen
Ruinenbergstr.
Schlegelstr.
BORNSTEDT
Krongut Bornstedt
Klausberg (Drachenberg)
Belvedere
Kaiser-Friedrich-Str.
Ehemaliger Weinberg
Drachenhaus
Potentestück
Krimlinden-allee
Maulbeerallee
Liegewiese
Voltaireweg
Brentanoweg
Parkstr.
Tieckstr.
Orangerie-schloss
Kronprinzenweg
An der Orangerie
Bornstedter Str.
Schloss Sanssouci
Zur Histor. Mühle
Paradiesgarten (Universität Potsdam)
Hist. Mühle
Besucherzentrum
Gregor-Mendel-Str.
Am Neuen Palais
Lindstedter Weg
Hopfengarten
Hecken-theater
Nordischer Garten
Universität Potsdam
Botanischer Garten (Universität Potsdam)
Sizilianischer Garten
Neue Kammern
Gruft Friedrichs II.
Weinberg terrassen
Bildergalerie
Winzerhaus
Ehemaliger Winzerberg
Weinbergstr.
Commun
Antiken-tempel
Lustgarten
Neptun-grotte
Schopenhauerstr.
Mauerstr.
Kolonnade
Neues Palais
Hauptallee
Hauptallee
Große Fontäne
Hauptallee
Obelisk
Rehgarten
Commun
Friedenskirche
Hegelallee
Freundschaftstempel
Chinesisches Haus
Mausoleum Friedrichs III.
Gruft Friedrich Wilhelms IV.
Marlygarten
Besucherzentrum (Eröffnung 2013)
Gitter-salon
Hecken-quartier
Ökonomieweg
Ökonomieweg
Teeküche
Am Grünen Gitter
Allee nach Sanssouci
Schopenhauerstr.
(temporär 2012)
Meierei
Park-gärtnerei
Lennéstr.
Luisen-platz
Branden-burger Tor
Lindenavenue
Charlottenhof
Zimmerstr.
Zimmer-platz
Lennéstr.
Marschall-Keith-Haus
Lennéstr.
Römische Bäder
POTSDAM
Zeppelinstr.
B2
Ehemalige Gärtnerlehranstalt
Feuerbachstr.
BRANDENBURGER VORSTADT
Ma-schinen-teich
Meistersingerstr.
Breite Str.
B1 / B2
Kaiserbahnhof
Dichterhain
Schloss Charlottenhof
Rosengarten
Erlöser-kirche
Dampfmaschinenhaus (Moschee) Technisches Museum
Hippodrom
Fasanerie
Am Wildpark
Hans-Sachs-Str.
Carl-von-Ossietzky-Str.
Nansenstr.
Clara-Zetkin-Str.
Sellostr.
Geschwister-Scholl-Str.
Geschwister-Scholl-Str.
Zeppelinstr.
B1
Park Sanssouci
Forststr.
Neustädter Havelbucht
0 50 100 200m

Park Sanssouci

1. Das *parterre* und die sechs Terrassen des Weinberg-Schlosses. Die beiden großen Bäume sind Stieleichen, der Großbusch ist ein Katsura- oder Kuchenbaum, aus Japan stammend. Im Herbst, wenn die Blätter fallen, verbreiten sie einen betörenden Geruch nach Kuchen.

Park Sanssouci

1. The *parterre* and the six terraces of the palace on the vineyard hill. The two tall trees are English oaks, while the large bush is a katsura tree, or Japanese Judas tree. In autumn, as the leaves start to fall, they give off the delicious smell of cakes.

Park Sanssouci, zentraler Bereich

2. Das Obeliskportal am östlichen Beginn des Parks und die große Hauptallee nach Westen, zum Neuen Palais hin gesehen. Das Portal wurde 1747 von Georg Wenzeslaus von Knobelsdorff entworfen. Vorbild ist das von Knobelsdorff errichtete Eingangsportal vom Park Rheinsberg von 1741. Hier, am Obeliskportal, beginnt der zentrale, der friderizianische Sanssouci-Park, der sich die Hauptallee entlang mit vielen Querachsen und Rondellen bis zum Neuen Palais hinzieht.
3. Das nördliche Halbrondell am östlichen Obeliskportal mit der Sichtachse zum Winzerhaus an dem ehemaligen Winzerberg. Links die Baldachinfontäne mit Terracottaarbeiten von Ernst March von 1844. Auf der Mauer Schmuckvasen und links als Abschluß der Mauer eine Nymphe.

Park Sanssouci, central area

2. The Obeliskportal at the east end of the park und the large main avenue leading west, viewed facing the Neues Palais. The portal was designed in 1747 by Georg Wenzeslaus von Knobelsdorff. It was modelled on the entrance portal of Park Rheinsberg, which Knobelsdorff built in 1741. Here, at the Obeliskportal, begins the central, Friderician, Sanssouci Park, which extends along the main avenue with many transverse axes and rondels all the way to the Neues Palais.
3. The north semi-rondel at the east Obeliskportal, the visual axis is towards the vintner's house near the former vineyard. On the left, the Baldachinfontäne with terracotta work by Ernst March, dated 1844. On the wall are ornamental vases and on the left is a nymph, the termination point of the wall.

Park Sanssouci, zentraler Bereich

4. Figur im Mohrenrondell südlich der Neptungrotte, eine Kopie von 1992–97, nach Vorbildern von einem unbekannten Bildhauer des 17. Jahrhunderts.
5. Am Oranierrondell an der Kleinen Fontäne, im Hintergrund die Bildergalerie jenseits des Holländischen Gartens. Die Skulpturen stellen Angehörige des Hauses Oranien dar, sie stammen von François Dieussart, geschaffen um 1647, die heutigen Kopien in Marmor sind von 1992–98. Im Bild Philipp Wilhelm von Oranien (1554 bis 1618), mit einer interessanten Vita wohl der einzige Katholik der Oranier.

Park Sanssouci, central area

4. Figure in the Mohrenrondell south of the Neptungrotte, a 1992–97 copy modelled on work by an anonymous 17th-century sculptor.
5. By the Oranierrondell (Rondel of the House of Orange) near the Kleine Fontäne, in the background is the Bildergalerie on the other side of the Holländischer Garten. The sculptures represent members of the House of Orange and were created ca. 1647 by François Dieussart, the modern, marble, copies date back to 1992–98. Shown here is Philip William of Orange (1554–1618), a man with an interesting history, probably the only Catholic member of the House of Orange.

Park Sanssouci, zentraler Bereich

6. Ein Blick über den Parkgraben zur Kleinen Fontäne ganz im Hintergrund. Davor eine Figur der Caritas von Jean de Cock, geschaffen 1727. Die Bäume sind von links nach rechts eine Esche, eine Hängerotbuche, eine Linde und eine Kastanie.
7. Ein Blick vom *Gefesselten Satyr* südlich der Kleinen Fontäne nach Süden über den Parkgraben zum Marlygarten hin.

Park Sanssouci, central area

6. View across the park canal of the Kleine Fontäne in the far background. In front of the fountain is a statue of Caritas by Jean de Cock, made in 1727. From left to right, the trees are an ash tree, a weeping copper beech, a linden and a horse chestnut tree.
7. View in the direction of the Marlygarten from the *Gefesselten Satyr* (*Fettered Satyr*) south of the Kleine Fontäne facing south, overlooking the park canal.

Park Sanssouci, zentraler Bereich

8. Das Schloß Sanssouci, die Weinbergterrassen und das vorgelagerte Parterre. Auf der Säule eine Skulptur des Apollino von 1843, eine Kopie nach antikem Vorbild. Das auf der obersten Terrasse weit zurückgelegte Schloß wirkt wie eingesunken.
9. Die Sphinx mit zwei kleinen Knaben, der eine verschleiert, an der Kreuzung des Ökonomiewegs mit der nordsüdlichen Querachse bei der Gartendirektion, von Georg Franz Ebenhech, geschaffen um 1755. Auf der gegenüberliegenden Seite der Querachse befindet sich eine weitere Sphinx von Ebenhech, so daß der Weg von zwei Sphingen gefaßt wird.

Park Sanssouci, central area

8. Schloß Sanssouci, the vineyard terraces and the *parterre* in front of them. On the column is a sculpture of Apollino dated 1843, a copy modelled on a classical statue. The palace, situated far back on the uppermost terrace, appears to have subsided in the ground.
9. Sphinx with two little boys, one of them veiled, at the point where the Ökonomieweg (a road) intersects with the north-south transverse axis near the garden administration building, by Georg Franz Ebenhech, created ca. 1755. On the opposite side of the transverse axis there is an additional sphinx by Ebenhech, so that the road is framed by two sphinxes.

Park Sanssouci, zentraler Bereich

10. Ein Blick von der obersten Weinbergterrasse die nord–südliche Querachse des Parks entlang über die Große Fontäne, die beiden Nebengräben des Parkgrabens und die vierzeilige Lindenallee an der Gartendirektion bis hin zum Marschall-Keith-Haus. Lordmarschall von Keith war ein enger Vertrauter von Friedrich II.
11. Die nord–südliche Querachse von der Einmündung der Allee Am Grünen Gitter aus nach Norden gesehen. Die Querachse wird bis zur Gartendirektion von rotblühenden Kastanien begleitet, dann folgt die Große Fontäne, darauf kommen die Terrassentreppen und schließlich das Zentrum des Schlosses mit der großen Kuppel. Jenseits des Schlosses setzt sich die Achse bis hin zum Ruinenberg fort.

Park Sanssouci, central area

10. View of the Marshal-Keith-Haus from the uppermost vineyard terrace along the north–south transverse axis of the park across the Große Fontäne, the two side branches of the park canal and the four-row linden avenue by the garden administration building. Lord Marshal von Keith was a close confidant of Frederick II.
11. The north-south transverse axis viewed looking north from its confluence with the avenue Am Grünen Gitter. All the way to the garden administration building the transverse axis is lined with red-blooming chestnut trees, then comes the Big Fountain, followed by the terrace staircases and finally the centre of the palace with its large dome. On the other side of the palace the axis continues as far as Ruinenberg.

Park Sanssouci, zentraler Bereich

12. Die Brücke über den Parkgraben südlich der Glockenfontäne, im Hintergrund das Chinesische Teehaus, 1754–57 von Johann Gottfried Büring erbaut.
13. Blutbuche und Chinesisches Teehaus. Die große Wiese erstreckt sich zwischen dem Parkgraben und dem Ökonomieweg.

Park Sanssouci, central area

12. The bridge over the park canal south of the Glockenfontäne (Bell Fountain), the Chinese teahouse in the background was built in 1754–57 by Johann Gottfried Büring.
13. Copper beech and Chinese teahouse. The large meadow stretches between the park canal and the Ökonomieweg.

Park Sanssouci, zentraler Bereich

14. Ein Blick von der Glockenfontäne südlich der Neuen Kammern die Hauptallee mit Rotbuchen entlang Richtung Westen bis zum Neuen Palais, von Hainbuchenbosketten eingerahmt.
15. Die Hauptallee nach Westen zum Neuen Palais hin gesehen. Im Vordergrund das Entführungsrondell südlich des Sizilianischen Gartens.

Park Sanssouci, central area

14. View of the Neues Palais, framed by hornbeam *bosquets*, from the Glockenfontäne south of Neue Kammern along the beech-lined main avenue going west.
15. Main avenue viewed facing west towards the Neues Palais. In the foreground, the Entführungsrondell (rondel with statuary portraying the rape of a Sabine woman) south of the Sizilianischer Garten.

Park Sanssouci, zentraler Bereich

16. Die kleine Querachse und Treppenallee, vom Musenrondell, vorn, zum Felsentor hin gesehen, zwischen den Neuen Kammern und dem Sizilianischen Garten hindurch und über die Maulbeerallee hinweg. Links Terpsichore, die Muse des Tanzes, rechts Euterpe, die Muse der Lyrik und des Flötenspiels, Marmorstatuen von Friedrich Christian Glume, entstanden vor 1752.
17. Die Treppenallee zum Felsentor, rechts schimmert die Historische Mühle durch die Bäume.

Park Sanssouci, central area

16. Small transverse axis and staircase avenue, seen from the Musenrondell, in front, facing the Felsentor (Rock Gate), between Neue Kammern and the Sizilianischer Garten and across the Maulbeerallee. On the left is Terpsichore, the Muse of dance, on the right is Euterpe, the Muse of lyric poetry and of flute playing, marble statues by Friedrich Christian Glume, created before 1752.
17. The staircase avenue to the Felsentor, on the right the Historische Mühle shimmers through the trees.

Park Sanssouci, zentraler Bereich

18. Ein Blick vom Musenrondell die Hauptallee mit den Hainbuchenbosketten entlang zum Neuen Palais. Von links nach rechts: Erato, die Muse der Liebesdichtung, Thalia, die Muse der Komödie, Melpomene, die Muse der Tragödie und Terpsichore, die Muse des Tanzes, Marmorstatuen von Friedrich Christian Glume, entstanden vor 1752.
19. Das Musenrondell an der Hauptallee mit den Hainbuchenbosketten. Hier tanzt Terpsichore, die Muse des Tanzes.

S. 252, 253
20. Ein Blick vom Entführungsrondell durch die Hainbuchenboskette nach Norden zum Sizilianischen Garten, darüber der Nordische Garten.
21. Das Entführungsrondell an der Hauptallee. Hier wird der Raub der Sabinerin dargestellt, eine Marmorarbeit von 1747, direkt aus Carrara; der Bildhauer ist nicht bekannt.

Park Sanssouci, central area

18. View of the Neues Palais from the Musenrondell along the main avenue lined by hornbeam *bosquets*. From left to right: Erato, the Muse of love poetry, Thalia, the Muse of comedy, Melpomene, the Muse of tragedy and Terpsichore, the Muse of dance, marble statues by Friedrich Christian Glume, created before 1752.
19. The Musenrondell by the main avenue and its hornbeam *bosquets*. Seen dancing here is Terpsichore, the Muse of dance.

pp. 252, 253
20. View facing north of Sizilianischer Garten from the Entführungsrondell through hornbeam *bosquets*, above them is the Nordischer Garten.
21. The Entführungsrondell on the main avenue. It represents the rape of a Sabine woman, a marble statue dated 1747, directly from Carrara, by an unknown sculptor.

Park Sanssouci, zentraler Bereich

22. Der Freundschaftstempel ganz im Westen des Parks, des Rehgartens, nahe dem Neuen Palais. Der kleine Tempel wurde von Friedrich II. als Gedächtnisstätte für seine Schwester Wilhelmine entworfen, die 1758 gestorben war. Die Ausführung von 1768–70 als offener Rundtempel stammt von Carl von Gontard. Ganz links im Hintergrund die Kuppel des Neuen Palais.
23. Der Freundschaftstempel bildet exakt das Nordende einer langen Sichtachse, die im Süden an der Fasanerie von Ludwig Persius beginnt.

Park Sanssouci, central area

22. The Freundschaftstempel (Friendship Temple) in the westernmost part of the park, the Rehgarten, near the Neues Palais. The small temple was designed by Frederick II as a memorial site for his sister Wilhelmina, who had died in 1758. The 1768–70 building – an open round temple – is by Carl von Gontard. In the far left background is the dome of the Neues Palais.
23. The Freundschaftstempel is situated precisely at the north end of a long visual axis, which begins in the south by the Fasanerie (Pheasant House) designed by Ludwig Persius.

Park Sanssouci, zentraler Bereich

24. Baumgruppe mit Eichen und Linden an der Sonnenlaube oder dem Treillagesalon von 1770 ganz in der Nähe des Freundschaftstempels, im westlichen Rehgarten.
25. Im Eichenwald, Blick von Südosten auf das Neue Palais, über den rechts nach Charlottenhof führenden Theaterweg hinweg.

Park Sanssouci, central area

24. Cluster of oaks and linden trees by the Sonnenlaube (Sun Summerhouse) or the Treillagesalon, dated 1770, immediately next to the Freundschaftstempel, in the west part of the Rehgarten.
25. In the oak forest, view of the Neues Palais from the southeast, across Theaterweg, a path leading to Charlottenhof on the right.

Park Sanssouci, zentraler Bereich

26. Eine Gruppe von Eichen und das Neue Palais am westlichen Ende der Hauptallee, vom Rehgarten her gesehen.
27. Das Neue Palais hinter den Hainbuchenbosketten, vom Ende des Theaterwegs her gesehen. Mit dem Neuen Palais hier im Westen endet sozusagen das gegenüber, am Obeliskportal im Osten beginnende Areal des friderizianischen, des zentralen Sanssouci.

Park Sanssouci, central aera

26. A clump of oaks and the Neues Palais at the west end of the main avenue, seen from the Rehgarten.
27. The Neues Palais behind hornbeam *bosquets*, viewed from the end of Theaterweg. The Neues Palais here on the west side marks the end, in a manner of speaking, of the area of the Friderician, central Sanssouci that starts opposite, at the Obeliskportal in the east.

Park Sanssouci, südlicher Bereich

28. Der Marlygarten liegt im Südosten des Parks, die südliche Begrenzung ist die Allee am Grünen Gitter, mit Roßkastanien bepflanzt, hier Richtung Westen gesehen. Links hinter der Mauer liegt das Ananashaus.
29. Die nördliche Grenze des Marlygartens zum Park, zum Lustgarten hin, bildet die sogenannte Küchenmauer, im Gebüsch hinter der grünen Bank verborgen. Friedrich Wilhelm I. nutzte das Areal als Küchengarten des Stadtschlosses und zu sommerlichen Ausflügen, wobei Kronprinz Friedrich die Gegend um den Weinberg kennengelernt haben dürfte. Der Blick geht durch die Baumgruppen zur Bildergalerie jenseits der Holländischen Gartens, links und rechts stehen Platanen.

Park Sanssouci, south area

28. The Marlygarten is located in the southeast part of the park, and the south boundary is the avenue Am Grünen Gitter, lined with horse chestnut trees, seen here facing west. On the left, behind the wall, is the Ananashaus (Pine-apple House).
29. The north boundary of the Marlygarten with the park, the pleasance ground, is the so-called *kitchen wall*, concealed in the shrubbery behind the green bench. Frederick William I used the area as the kitchen garden of the Stadtschloß, the Prussian royal palace, and for summer excursions, which is when Crown Prince Frederick probably got to know the region around the vineyard. The view is through the clusters of trees towards the picture gallery on the other side of the Holländischer Garten, to the left and right are plane trees.

Park Sanssouci, südlicher Bereich

30. Der Marlygarten beherbergt zwei Gebäude von Ludwig Persius. Die Villa Illaire wurde 1843–46 für den Kabinettsrat Ernst Emil Illaire gebaut, davor plätschert die Mosaikfontäne von 1846/47. Der Gartenteich wurde von Peter Joseph Lenné angelegt, sozusagen der Prototyp aller Gartenteiche.

31. Ein Blick vom Fächerbeet zur Friedenskirche, dem Mausoleum und den großen Platanen. Persius baute die Friedenskirche mit dem vorgelagerten Atrium 1844–48, nach seinem frühen Tode wurde die Kirche von Ludwig Ferdinand Hesse, Ferdinand von Arnim und August Stüler vollendet. Das von einer Kuppel überspannte Mausoleum wurde 1888/90 von Julius Carl Raschdorff für Kaiser Friedrich III. erbaut.

Park Sanssouci, south area

30. The Marlygarten is the site of two buildings by Ludwig Persius. Villa Illaire was built in 1843–46 for Kabinettsrat Ernst Emil Illaire, in front of it splashes the Mosaikfontäne, dated 1846/47. The garden pond was laid out by Peter Joseph Lenné, the prototype of all garden ponds, so to speak.

31. View from the fan-shaped bed, of the Friedenskirche, the Mausoleum and the big plane trees. Persius built the Friedenskirche and the atrium in front of it in 1844–48, after his premature death the church was completed by Ludwig Ferdinand Hesse, Ferdinand von Arnim and August Stüler. The Mausoleum, which is spanned by a dome, was built for Emperor Frederick III in 1888/90 by Julius Carl Raschdorff.

Park Sanssouci, südlicher Bereich

32. Die sogenannte Weißblaue Glassäule von Heinrich Berges, entstanden 1847, ein Hinweis auf die bayerische Herkunft der Königin Elisabeth. Die Säule wird bekrönt von einer Mädchenfigur mit Papagei. Der große Baum rechts ist eine Rüster, der Busch links ein Taxus.
33. Das Fächerbeet von Peter Joseph Lenné mit einer Figur der Flora von Albert Wolff, entstanden vor 1850. Das Fächerbeet ist im wesentlichen mit Begonien bepflanzt, auch Semperflorens oder Eisblume genannt.

Park Sanssouci, south area

32. The so-called Weißblaue Glassäule (White-Blue Glass Column) by Heinrich Berges, dated 1847, is a reference to the fact that Queen Elisabeth came from Bavaria. The column is crowned by the figure of a girl with a parrot. The large tree on the right is an elm, and the bush on the left is a yew.
33. Fan-shaped bed by Peter Joseph Lenné with a figure of Flora by Albert Wolff, created before 1850. The fan-shaped bed is primarily planted with begonias, also known as semperflorens.

Park Sanssouci, südlicher Bereich

34. Ganz am Westrand des Marlygartens liegt das mit Glyzinien bewachsene ehemalige Gärtnerhaus, in dem auch Peter Joseph Lenné zeitweilig wohnte. Die Statue von Friedrich II. wurde 1899 von Joseph Uphues geschaffen.
35. Hängeweiden am Friedensteich im Friedensgarten, dem ehemaligen Hopfengarten, unmittelbar östlich der Friedenskirche, deren Wände im Wasser des Teiches gründen.

Park Sanssouci, south area

34. The former gardener's house, overgrown with wisteria vines, is on the west periphery of the Marlygarten. Peter Joseph Lenné, too, temporarily lived here. The statue of Frederick II was created in 1899 by Joseph Uphues.
35. Weeping willows by the Friedensteich (Peace Pond) in the Friedensgarten (Peace Garden), the former hop garden, directly east of the Friedenskirche, the bases of the church walls are in the water of the pond.

Park Sanssouci, südlicher Bereich

36. Ein Blick vom östlichen Ende der Pergola von Schloß Charlottenhof in den Rosengarten. Links die Figur des Apoll mit einem Köcher voller Pfeile, eine verkleinerte Wiederholung der Marmorstatue in Florenz aus dem 1. Jahrhundert, rechts die Figur von Klio, der Muse der Geschichtsschreibung, Bronzenachguß von 1837 nach antikem Vorbild. Im Hintergrund der Wald jenseits des Maschinenteichs.

37. Ein Blick von der Pergola von Schloß Charlottenhof über die Terrasse. Ganz links die Säule mit der Büste der Kronprinzessin Elisabeth von Christian Friedrich Tieck, geschaffen 1835, dann die Brunnenschale und rechts im Anschnitt die halbrunde Sitzbank, die Exedra. Rechts von der Platane öffnet sich der Blick zum Turm des Hofgärtnerhauses bei den Römischen Bädern.

Park Sanssouci, south area

36. View from the east end of the pergola of Schloß Charlottenhof into the Rosengarten. On the left, the figure of Apollo with a quiver full of arrows, a scaled-down repetition of the 1st-century marble statue in Florence, on the right, the figure of Clio, the Muse of history writing, a bronze sculpture dated 1837 based on a classical model. In the background is the forest on the other side of the engine pond.

37. View from the pergola of Schloß Charlottenhof across the terrace. On the far left is the column with the bust of Crown Princess Elisabeth by Christian Friedrich Tieck, created in 1835, then the basin of the fountain and on the right a section of the semicircular bench, the exedra. To the right of the plane tree there is a view of the tower of the court gardener's house near the Römische Bäder (Roman Baths).

Park Sanssouci, südlicher Bereich

38. Die Gazelle von Wilhelm Wolff, entstanden 1846, am westlichen Eingang von Schloß Charlottenhof, ein Bronzeguß. Darunter das Fragment eines Greifen.
39. Fette Henne im Pliniusbeet der großen Laube bei den Römischen Bädern. Im Hintergrund die Rückseite des Kentaurensarkophags, darüber eine Muschel und der Butt-Brunnen. Butt ist der Neckname des Kronprinzen, des späteren Friedrich Wilhelm IV. Der 1833 entstandene Butt stammt von Christian Daniel Rauch.

Park Sanssouci, south area

38. The Gazelle by Wilhelm Wolff, created in 1846, at the west entrance of Schloß Charlottenhof, a bronze sculpture. Below it is the fragment of a griffin.
39. Sempervivum in the Pliny Bed of the large summerhouse near the Römische Bäder. In the background is the rear of the Centaur Sarcophagus, and above it is a seashell and the Butt Fountain. Butt is the nickname of the crown prince, who later became Frederick William IV. The Butt, which dates back to 1833, is by Christian Daniel Rauch.

Park Sanssouci, südlicher Bereich

40. Ein Blick vom Pfeilerportikus des Teepavillons der Römischen Bäder zum Schloß Charlottenhof. Der Pavillon wurde 1830 von Karl Friedrich Schinkel und Ludwig Persius erbaut.
41. Die in der Literatur gerühmte Sicht vom Dach der Römischen Bäder zum Schloß Charlottenhof, heute von der Platane in der Mitte des Bildes fast vollständig verdeckt. Das Turmmotiv des Hofgärtnerhauses, rechts, kehrt bei vielen Potsdamer Stadtvillen von Ludwig Persius wieder.

Park Sanssouci, south area

40. View of Schloß Charlottenhof from the pillar portico of the tea pavilion of the Römische Bäder. The pavilion was built in 1830 by Karl Friedrich Schinkel and Ludwig Persius.
41. Much praised in literature, the view of Schloß Charlottenhof from the roof of the Römische Bäder, today this view is almost completely blocked by the plane tree in the centre of the picture. The tower motif of the court gardener's house, on the right, recurs in many of Ludwig Persius' urban villas.

Park Sanssouci, südlicher Bereich

42. Der Blick vom Teesalon der Römischen Bäder auf die Insel im Maschinenteich mit der großen Blumenschale und der Blutbuche. Die Schale aus Granit stammt von Christian Daniel Rauch, entstanden 1826. Auf dem Pfeiler steht eine Statue des Germanicus, römischer Feldherr unter Kaiser Tiberius.
43. Der Blick vom Schloß Charlottenhof nach Norden auf ein kleines Waldstück mit einem nordamerikanischen Zürgelbaum unmittelbar links am Weg. Rechts der römische Grabaltar der Veja Acme.

Park Sanssouci, south area

42. The island in the engine pond with the great flower basin and the copper beech, viewed from the tea salon of the Römische Bäder. The granite basin is by Christian Daniel Rauch, and was made in 1826. On the pillar stands a statue of Germanicus, a Roman commander under Emperor Tiberius.
43. A small patch of woods with a North American hackberry tree to the left of the path, viewed facing north from Schloß Charlottenhof. On the right is the Roman funerary altar of Veia Acme.

Park Sanssouci, südlicher Bereich

44. Der Dichterhain unmittelbar westlich des Schlosses Charlottenhof. Rotblühende Kastanien sind in sechs Reihen gepflanzt, von Hainbuchenbosketten umgeben. In der Mitte der Neptunschalenbrunnen, im Hintergrund, ganz im Westen, eine Ildefonsogruppe.
45. Dante Alighieri im Dichterhain von Schloß Charlottenhof, Büste von 1851 aus Carrara Marmor von Gustav Bläser.

Park Sanssouci, south area

44. The Dichterhain (Poets' Grove) directly west of Schloß Charlottenhof. Red-blooming chestnut trees have been planted in six rows, surrounded by hornbeam *bosquets*. In the centre is the Neptunschalenbrunnen (Neptune Basin Fountain), while in the background, in the west part of the park, is an Ildefonso group.
45. Dante Alighieri in the Dichterhain of Schloß Charlottenhof, a bust dated 1851 of Carrara marble by Gustav Bläser.

Park Sanssouci, südlicher Bereich

46. Der von Peter Joseph Lenné 1836 angelegte Hippodrom westlich von Schloß Charlottenhof, mit Hopfengestänge. Links ein Ruheplatz, von Säulen umgeben, das von Karl Friedrich Schinkel 1836–39 entworfene Stibadium, 1842–44 von Ludwig Persius ausgeführt.
47. Die Fasanerie wurde 1842–44 von Ludwig Persius erbaut. Sie liegt westlich von Charlottenhof und Hippodrom und markiert so das südwestliche Ende des Parks Sanssouci. Die Sichtachse reicht von der Fasanerie bis zum Freundschaftstempel im Norden.

Park Sanssouci, south area

46. The hippodrome laid out by Peter Joseph Lenné in 1836 west of Schloß Charlottenhof, with hop poles. On the left, a seat surrounded by columns, the stibadium designed by Karl Friedrich Schinkel in 1836–39 and implemented by Ludwig Persius in 1842–44.
47. The Fasanerie was built in 1842–44 by Ludwig Persius. It is located to the west of Charlottenhof and the hippodrome, and thus marks the southwest end of Park Sanssouci. The visual axis extends from the Fasanerie to the Freundschaftstempel in the north.

Park Sanssouci, nördlicher Bereich

48. Ein Blick von der Maulbeerallee auf den westlichen Teil des Sizilianischen Gartens, den einzigen architektonischen Garten des Parks, von Peter Joseph Lenné und Gustav Meyer in den fünfziger Jahren des 19. Jahrhunderts entworfen und angelegt, Teil der Planungen von Friedrich Wilhelm IV. für die große Höhen- oder Triumphstraße. Rechts, erhöht, die Vase Medici, eine Marmorkopie des Bildhauers Bonnani aus der Mitte des 19. Jahrhunderts.
49. Das Halbrund des westlichen Laubengangs und der zentrale Teil des Sizilianischen Gartens.

Park Sanssouci, north area

48. View of the west section of the Sizilianischer Garten from the Maulbeerallee; this is the only architectonic garden in the park, designed and laid out by Peter Joseph Lenné and Gustav Meyer in the 1850s, part of Frederick William IV's plans for the great triumphal road. On the right, elevated, is the Medici Vase, a mid-19th century marble copy by the sculptor Bonnani.
49. The semicircle of the western pergola and the central part of the Sizilianischer Garten.

Park Sanssouci, nördlicher Bereich

50. Ein Blick aus dem Laubengang des Sizilianischen Gartens zur Historischen Mühle und den Neuen Kammern. Rechts die Vase Borghese, eine Marmorkopie des Bildhauers Bonnani aus der Mitte des 19. Jahrhunderts.
51. Die Historische Mühle vom Weg zum Orangerieschloß aus gesehen, über den fast gänzlich zugewachsenen Nordischen Garten hinweg, rechts ein männlicher Ginkgo biloba L., links Bergkiefern und Wacholder.

Park Sanssouci, north area

50. View of the Historische Mühle and the Neue Kammern from the pergola of the Sizilianischer Garten. On the right is the Borghese Vase, a mid-19th century marble copy by the sculptor Bonnani.
51. The Historische Mühle viewed from the road to the Orangerieschloß, across the almost completely overgrown Nordischer Garten, on the right is a male Ginkgo biloba L., on the left are mountain pines and junipers.

Park Sanssouci, nördlicher Bereich

52. Die Maulbeerallee, nach Nordwesten gesehen. Inzwischen mit Rotbuchen bepflanzt, besitzt die Allee heute nur noch zwei Maulbeerbäume, links im Bild mit hellerem Grün.
53. Die Marmorkaskade beim Stibadium im Paradiesgarten, zwischen Maulbeerallee und Krimlindenallee, von Ludwig Ferdinand Hesse, 1846. Vorne links der Hermenkopf einer Bacchantin mit Blumenschale, rechts der eines Bacchanten, beide aus Zink. Die Treppe ist wegen eines Rohrbruchs leider ohne Wasser.

Park Sanssouci, north area

52. Maulbeerallee, seen facing northwest. Only two mul-berry trees still survive – seen in the left of the photo in a lighter green colour – and the avenue has now been planted with copper beeches.
53. The Marmorkaskade (Marble Cascade) near the stibadium in the Paradiesgarten, between Maulbeerallee and Krimlindenallee (Crimean Linden Avenue), by Ludwig Ferdinand Hesse, 1846. In front on the left is the herm head of a bacchante with a basin of flowers, on the right that of a male follower of Bacchus, both made of zinc. Because of a broken pipe, there is unfortunately no water on the staircase.

Park Sanssouci, nördlicher Bereich

54. Vor dem Orangerieschloß. Die Blickachse entlang des von Friedrich Wilhelm IV. geplanten Höhenstraßenprojekts, auch Via Triumphalis genannt, durch die westlichen Doppelbögen des Schlosses hindurch bis zum Belvedere auf dem Klausberg. Die Reliefvase im Vordergrund ist die östliche von vier Marmorvasen, entstanden um 1900 und 1905 aufgestellt. In den Kübeln steht Lorbeer.
55. Krimlindenallee und Belvedere auf dem Klausberg, vom Orangerieschloß her gesehen. Vorn die Prinzenbrücke, 1905/06, über dem Kronprinzenweg. Die Allee wurde von Gustav II. Adolph Fintelmann konzipiert und 1906 von Georg Potente realisiert. Die Kastanie rechts ist die früheste im Park blühende Kastanie.

Park Sanssouci, north area

54. In front of the Orangerieschloß. Visual axis along the Höhenstraße project, also called Via Triumphalis, planned by Frederick William IV, through the western double arches of the palace to the Belvedere on Klausberg. The relief vase in the foreground is the easternmost of four marble vases, created ca. 1900 and placed here in 1905. In the tubs are laurel bushes.
55. Krimlindenallee and Belvedere on Klausberg, viewed from the Orangerieschloß. In front is the Prinzenbrücke, 1905/06, above Kronprinzenweg. The avenue was conceived by Gustav II Adolph Fintelmann and was realised in 1906 by Georg Potente. The chestnut tree on the right is the first chestnut tree to bloom in the park.

Park Sanssouci, nördlicher Bereich

56. Der Klaus- oder Drachenberg, ein ehemaliger Weinberg. Links das Drachenhaus, 1770 von Carl von Gontard als Winzerhaus erbaut, heute ein Café. Das Belvedere rechts wurde von Georg Christian Unger 1770–72 als Aussichtspunkt errichtet. Das Belvedere bildet das westliche Ende der geplanten Via Triumphalis.
57. Ein Blick zurück vom Belvedere durch die Krimlindenallee herab zum westlichen Doppelportal des Orangerieschlosses.

Park Sanssouci, north area

56. Klausberg or Drachenberg, a former vineyard. On the left, the Drachenhaus (Dragon House), built in 1770 by Carl von Gontard as a vintner's house, now a café. The Belvedere on the right was built by Georg Christian Unger in 1770–72 as a lookout point. The belvedere is the west end of the planned Via Triumphalis.
57. A look back from the belvedere through the Krimlindenallee down to the western double portal of the Orangery Palace.

Park Sanssouci, nördlicher Bereich

58. Links Rotbuchen in dem sogenannten Potentestück, dem nördlichsten Teil des Parks zum Krongut Bornstedt hin, 1904–08 unter Wilhelm II. als nordischer Landschaftsgarten von Gustav II. Adolph Fintelmann entworfen und von Georg Potente angelegt.
59. Rotbuchen im Potentestück.

Park Sanssouci, north area

58. On the left, copper beeches in the so-called Potente section, the northernmost part of the park adjacent to the Krongut Bornstedt (Bornstedt Crown Estate), designed in 1904–08 under William II as a Nordic landscape garden by Gustav II Adolph Fintelmann, and laid out by Georg Potente.
59. Copper beeches in the Potente section.

Park Sanssouci, nördlicher Bereich

60. Schloß Lindstedt liegt nordöstlich jenseits des eigentlichen Parks. Friedrich Wilhelm III. hatte das Grundstück 1828 dem Kronprinzen geschenkt. Erst 1858–60 wurde der Garten von Joseph Peter Lenné angelegt. Die Laubengänge im nordwestlichen Schloßgarten umgeben eine Stele mit der Kopie einer Jupiterbüste.
61. Auch das Krongut Bornstedt liegt jenseits des eigentlichen Parks nördlich des Orangerieschlosses. Der Gutsgarten wurde 1849/50 von Peter Joseph Lenné geschaffen. Der Blick geht über den Garten und den Bornstedter See nach Osten zum Ruinenberg.

Park Sanssouci, north area

60. Schloß Lindstedt is located to the northeast, on the other side of the actual park. Frederick William III had given the land to the crown prince as a gift in 1828. The garden was not laid out until 1858–60 and was designed by Joseph Peter Lenné. The pergolas in the northwest part of the palace garden surround a stele with the copy of a bust of Jupiter.
61. The Krongut Bornstedt, too, is located on the other side of the actual park north of the Orangerieschloß. The estate was created in 1849/50 by Peter Joseph Lenné. The view faces east in the direction of Ruinenberg across the garden and Bornstedter See.

Park Sanssouci, nördlicher Bereich

62. Der Ruinenberg (73,8 m hoch) von den Schloßkolonnaden aus gesehen. Friedrich II. ließ dort 1748 ein großes rundes Wasserreservoir für die Springbrunnen im Park anlegen sowie Ruinen nach antiken Vorbildern. Höchstes Bauwerk ist der Normannische Turm, ein Aussichtsturm, 1846 von Ferdinand von Arnim nach Plänen von Ludwig Persius errichtet.
63. Die Rundbank liegt am Westhang des Ruinenbergs gegenüber dem Krongut Bornstedt. Die halbrunde Bank mit Greifenfüßen als Armlehnen ist von der Bank vor dem Grab der Priesterin Mamia an der Gräberstraße in Pompeji abgeleitet; sie wurde von Ludwig Persius 1843/44 im Auftrag von Friedrich Wilhelm IV. errichtet. Die Photographie versucht, ein Aquarell von Carl Graeb nachzustellen. Im Hintergrund die Basilika von Bornstedt.

Park Sanssouci, north area

62. Ruinenberg (73.8 m high) seen from the colonnades of the palace. In 1748 Frederick II had a large round water reservoir for the park fountains laid out there, as well as ruins modelled on classical originals. The highest structure is the Normannischer Turm, a lookout tower, built in 1846 by Ferdinand von Arnim according to plans drawn up by Ludwig Persius.
63. The round bench is located on the western slope of Ruinenberg opposite the Krongut Bornstedt. The semicircular bench, which has griffon feet as armrests, is modelled on the bench in front of the tomb of the priestess Mamia on the Street of Tombs in Pompeii; it was erected by Ludwig Persius in 1843/44 for Frederick William IV. The photograph tries to recreate a watercolour by Carl Graeb. In the background is the basilica of Bornstedt.

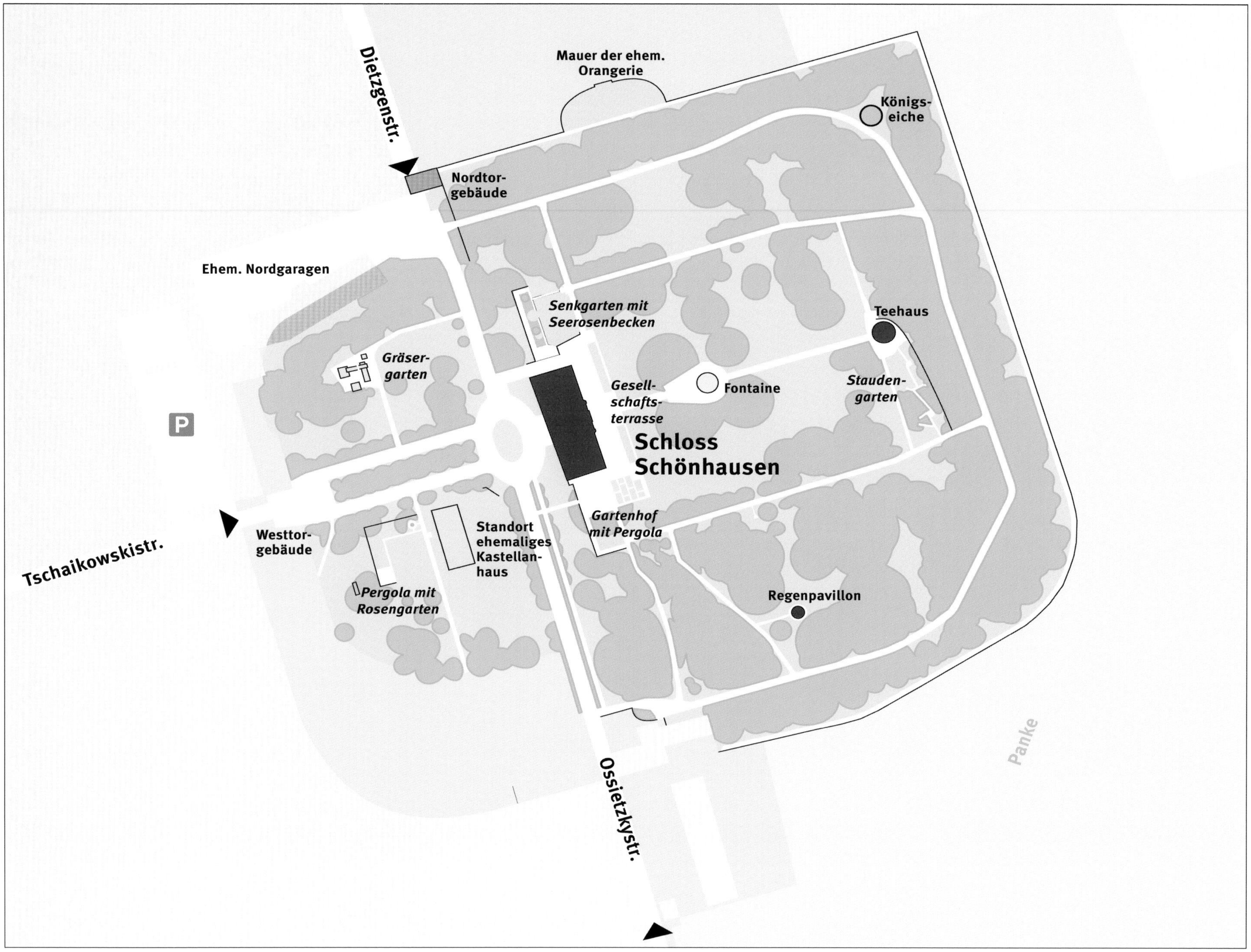
Mauer der ehem.
Orangerie
Dietzgenstr.
Königs-
eiche
Nordtor-
gebäude
Ehem. Nordgaragen
Senkgarten mit
Seerosenbecken
Teehaus
Gräser-
garten
Gesell-
schafts-
terrasse
Fontaine
Stauden-
garten
Schloss
Schönhausen
Gartenhof
mit Pergola
Westtor-
gebäude
Standort
ehemaliges
Kastellan-
haus
Tschaikowskistr.
Pergola mit
Rosengarten
Regenpavillon
Panke
Ossietzkystr.

Schloßpark Schönhausen

1. Schloß Schönhausen und die vier großen Platanen. Friedrich II. schenkte das Schloß 1740 seiner Gemahlin, Elisabeth Christine von Braunschweig-Wolfenbüttel-Bevern, die dort bis zu ihrem Tode 1797 wohnte.

Schloßpark Schönhausen

1. Schloß Schönhausen and the four large plane trees. Frederick II gave the palace to his wife, Elisabeth Christine of Brunswick-Wolfenbüttel-Bevern in 1740, and she lived there until her death in 1797.

Schloßpark Schönhausen

2. Die Pergola im Süden des Schlosses um die große Platane herum wurde um 1829 von Peter Joseph Lenné angelegt, als er den Park im Auftrag von Friederike von Mecklenburg-Strelitz in einen Landschaftspark umwandelte.
3. Im Vordergrund das mit Buchs gefaßte Pelargonienbeet auf der Gesellschaftsterrasse. Im Hintergrund die vier Platanen.

Schloßpark Schönhausen

2. The pergola on the south side of the palace around the big plane tree was laid out ca. 1829 by Peter Joseph Lenné when he transformed the park into a landscape park for Frederica of Mecklenburg-Strelitz.
3. In the foreground, the boxwood-lined geranium bed on the public terrace. In the background are the four plane trees.

Nachwort und Dank

Die hier vorgelegten Photographien der preußischen Gärten und Parks von Berlin, Potsdam und anderen Orten in Brandenburg versuchen, den künstlerischen Intentionen der Gartenschöpfer gerecht zu werden. Dabei galt es, der naheliegenden Versuchung zu widerstehen, die Stimmungen zu betonen, die die verschiedenen Tages- und Jahreszeiten wie eine Folie über die jeweilige Szene legen können. Dennoch bleibt die Arbeit des Photographen eine Interpretation der Idee des Gärtners, das Bild spricht deshalb auch immer die Sprache des Photographen.

In den Jahren von 2006 bis 2011 wurden bei 49 Gartenbesuchen über 670 Aufnahmen gemacht. 202 davon sind hier versammelt, hinzu kommen farbige Karten aller 14 Gärten. Im Gegensatz zum Textteil werden die Gärten alphabetisch aufgeführt, um das Nachschlagen zu erleichtern.

Das Projekt hätte sich ohne Hilfe aus dem Hause der Stiftung Preußische Schlösser und Gärten Berlin-Brandenburg kaum realisieren lassen. Vielfacher Rat und wertvolle Hinweise kamen sowohl von heutigen als auch von ehemaligen Mitarbeitern und Mitarbeiterinnen aus verschiedenen Abteilungen der Stiftung, besonders natürlich der Gartendirektion: Karen Andreas, Jürgen Becher, Monika Theresa Deissler, Karl Eisbein, Susanne Fontaine, Harri Günther, Saskia Hüneke, Michael Rohde, Heinz Schönemann, Gerd Schurig, Michael Seiler und Jörg Wacker.

Beate Laus von der Stiftung stellte die Karten der Parks bereit, die Kolleginnen der Fotothek besorgten die Abbildungen zum Text von Katja Schoene. Kerstin und Christian Munier von Geomaps GIS + Remote Sensing schufen die noch fehlende Karte vom Schloßpark Oranienburg, der nicht zur Stiftung gehört, aber trotzdem aufgenommen wurde. Claudia Ibbeken hat das ganze Projekt mit wichtigen Anregungen begleitet. Das Ganze schließlich wurde von den Verlegern Dorothea Duwe und Axel Menges hervorragend umsorgt und von Ilze Klavina mit großer Sorgfalt ins Englische übersetzt.

Ihnen allen gilt mein herzlicher Dank!

Hillert Ibbeken

Afterword and thanks

The photographs of the Prussian gardens and parks of Berlin, Potsdam and other localities in Brandenburg published here try to do justice to the artistic intentions of the gardens' creators. At the same time it was necessary to resist the obvious temptation to emphasize the moods that different times of day and seasons may cast like a film over a particular scene. Nevertheless the work of the photographer remains an interpretation of the gardener's idea, and therefore the image always speaks the language of the photographer as well.

Over the years from 2006 to 2011, more than 670 photographs were taken during 49 visits to the gardens. Assembled here are 202 of them, and also included are coloured maps of all 14 gardens. In contrast to the text part, the gardens are listed alphabetically in order to make it easier to look up information.

It would hardly have been possible to carry out the project without the help of the staff of the Stiftung Preußische Schlösser und Gärten Berlin-Brandenburg. A great deal of advice and valuable suggestions were received from present and former staff members of various departments of the foundation, particularly the garden administration, of course: Karen Andreas, Jürgen Becher, Monika Theresa Deissler, Karl Eisbein, Susanne Fontaine, Harri Günther, Saskia Hüneke, Michael Rohde, Heinz Schönemann, Gerd Schurig, Michael Seiler and Jörg Wacker.

Beate Laus, of the foundation, provided maps of the parks, and her colleagues at the photograph collection supplied the illustrations that go with Katja Schoene's text. Kerstin and Christian Munier of GIS + Remote Sensing drew up the one missing map of Schloßpark Oranienburg, which is not part of the foundation but was included in the project nonetheless. Claudia Ibbeken assisted the project with important suggestions. Finally, the entire project was superbly shepherded by publishers Dorothea Duwe and Axel Menges and painstakingly translated into English by Ilze Klavina.

My warmest thanks to all of them!

Hillert Ibbeken